# Aldo Rossi and the Spirit of Architecture

# Aldo Rossi and the Spirit of Architecture

Diane Y. F. Ghirardo

Yale University Press   New Haven and London

Published with assistance from the Graham Foundation for Advanced Studies in the Fine Arts.

**Graham Foundation**

Copyright © 2019 by Diane Y. F. Ghirardo.

All rights reserved.

This book may not be reproduced, in whole or in part, including illustrations, in any form (beyond that copying permitted by Sections 107 and 108 of the U.S. Copyright Law and except by reviewers for the public press), without written permission from the publishers.

yalebooks.com/art

Designed by Leslie Fitch

Set in Crimson type by Chris Crochetière, BW&A Books, Inc.

Printed in China by Regent Publishing Services Limited

Library of Congress Control Number: 2018956498

ISBN 978-0-300-27673-2 (pbk.)

A catalogue record for this book is available from the British Library.

This paper meets the requirements of ANSI/NISO Z39.48-1992 (Permanence of Paper).

10 9 8 7 6 5 4 3 2 1

Cover illustrations: (front) Aldo Rossi, Il Gioco dell'Oca; figure 6.10; (back) Aldo Rossi, Monte Amiato Housing, Gallaratese, Milan; figure 1.6

Frontispiece: Aldo Rossi, Scholastic Building, New York; detail, figure 2.3

Page vi: Aldo Rossi, San Cataldo Cemetery, Modena, Italy. Ossuary, interior. Author photo

*For Rachel and for the
memory of Christopher*

# CONTENTS

Preface  ix

Acknowledgments  xii

1  A Brief Biography  1

2  Architecture and the City  39

3  Memory and Monument  73

4  Building for Culture  103

5  Rossi and the Theater  137

6  Cemeteries for Modena and Rozzano  167

7  Aldo Rossi and the Spirit of Architecture  197

Notes  219

Chronology of Work by Rossi  243

Bibliography  253

Illustration Credits  256

Index  257

PREFACE

At the first meeting of a studio that Aldo Rossi taught at ETH Zürich in the early 1970s, he opened the class with a slide of a pale yellow sandstone façade, with a dark shadow curving over part of it. The second slide showed the same façade several minutes later, with the shadow having retreated a bit. Rossi's presentation continued with a sequence of slides taken at different intervals, until the shadow disappeared entirely and a small molding bathed in bright sunlight appeared, and then disappeared. Rossi did not illustrate the façade's ornament itself, but its appearance in different light conditions. Mark Jarzombek, then a student in that class, marveled at what he saw because, until that point, the only thing he had learned about the sun in his resolutely modern movement architecture classes was that sunlight was bad and needed to be countered with brise-soleils and other shading devices. Rossi's lesson opened up a way of thinking about architecture radically different from what was standard in those decades, remote from the dogmas of the then prevalent modern movement. This brief moment in a single class illustrated key features of Rossi's approach to architecture: his attention to space and to time, to shadows, to details, to thinking and questioning, and to not allowing his thinking to be dominated by contemporary fashion. Rossi often told his students that whatever they did it should be profound. He did not charge them, even implicitly, to mimic his designs; rather he encouraged them to undertake a personal journey of discovery and struggle just as he had, one in which he hoped they would wrestle with core beliefs, and not only about architecture. The arduous path he bade them take engaged neither style nor fashion but was instead an odyssey whose contours might never become clear.

    Rossi's life as a man and an architect was many things, but that intimate journey left traces at every point, surfacing in his drawings, his writings, his designs, and his buildings. Struggles, setbacks, and successes marked the life of a man whose unflagging optimism and delight in life merged with a character at once shy and fragile, a generous and genuinely humble man whose magnetism drew people to him. Gifted with a restless and supple intellect, he roamed the fields of theology, philosophy, literature, poetry, and the sciences with equal vigor and curiosity, reading not as a pursuit with a definite end in mind, but rather as an opportunity to grapple with ideas and reflections different from his own. In such readings he celebrated beauty of thought and of expression, content

Detail, figure 6.1

and form—just as he did in architecture—both of which enriched and deepened his own reflections, his own architecture. In his formative years, through the mid-1970s, his chosen texts included works about architecture, but over time the latter diminished, giving way to readings, and often rereadings, of the classics, of philosophy, of literature, and of poetry. Rossi often referred to himself as a pilgrim, both literally and figuratively, in that he regularly traveled to different cities and countries, he read across cultures and across disciplines, and also insistently mused on the ideas he encountered along with those he had explored in the past. In effect, he abandoned the comfort of conformity in favor of the life of a pilgrim, in life as in architecture, ever moving with curiosity and a vibrant wonder at the world and everything in it. Many have written about Rossi and his architecture in the decades since his death in 1997, often offering little in the way of a guide to comprehending his product design, drawing, writing, and architecture. This study explores Rossi's pilgrimage as it unfolded—especially, but not only, in his architecture—an enterprise assisted by the large body of writings he produced over his lifetime, some for publication and some in personal notebooks.

A recent surge of interest in Rossi two decades after his death suggests that his architecture, his designs, and his theories have once again captured the imagination of students from around the globe. Photographers still seek out his buildings to photograph, institutions mount exhibitions, and publishers issue new editions of his writings. Even if the buildings do not always appeal to everyone at first glance, grasping what he intended to accomplish will help inform assessments of his work, and for this, his writings are essential.

I was fortunate to have translated a number of his writings, to have been a regular guest in Milan, to have hosted him in turn in Los Angeles, and to consider him a friend. Those who knew him best knew him as a man who never ceased to marvel at the world, at our presence in it, at the presence of the divine at every turn. But they also knew him as a man of many joys, a playful and observant man whose delight enveloped all around him. He called my massive 1977 Buick Century Limited "Christine" after the 1983 film of the same name ("Will I be safe in this?"), and he regaled his friends with repeated showings of his favorite movies. This joyful embrace of life he also translated into his architecture. Rossi deeply believed in the personal aspects of architecture. My approach in this study departs from and relies upon Rossi's words, written and spoken, and close readings of his architecture. To understand what inspired him entailed reading the books and essays he read, visiting many of the places and buildings to which he referred repeatedly in his writings, reflecting on what he found of interest in them, and how this emerged in his architecture. Therefore, for the most part I have avoided the comments and criticisms of others, believing Rossi himself to be the best guide to his work. Even if Emil Kaufmann interpreted Boullée as having argued for architects to investigate "form for form's sake," for example, Rossi found quite different insights in Boullée that invigorated and stimulated his own thinking about architecture; form for form's sake was not one of them (see Seixas Lopes, *Melancholy and Architecture*, 182).

He loved the beautiful photographs of Luigi Ghirri and Gabriele Basilico, in part because they convey that sense of life where he imagined his architecture situated—life in all its beauty and unpredictability. For this reason, where possible I have chosen photographs that include people and the bustle of daily life, as well as photographs I took of some projects when they were barely complete, because they show the buildings in their early lives. Even though Rossi always anticipated how his buildings would change as life and time took hold of them, I also like to remember how they appeared when new and raw. Where citations from Rossi's writings have not been published in English, I have included the Italian original in the notes.

ACKNOWLEDGMENTS

This book would not have been possible without the support and friendship of some very special people, starting with Aldo's children, with whom I discussed their father and his work over several decades. My special thanks go to Vera and Fausto, and to his granddaughter Teresa, a *dantista* of whom her grandfather would have been enormously proud. I also want to thank Katherine Boller of Yale University Press for encouraging me to write this book and for nursing it along at awkward moments. Two anonymous readers of the proposal provided deeply welcome assessments, and I am equally grateful to two anonymous readers of the completed manuscript who understood my objectives in writing this book. The staffs at the MAXXI Museo nazionale delle arti del XXI secolo, Collezione Architettura, in Rome; the Getty Research Institute, Los Angeles; and the Fondazione Aldo Rossi in Milan all generously aided my research.

Once again, the Graham Foundation for Advanced Studies in the Fine Arts provided a publication grant that enabled me to bring the project to completion. I am grateful for the support of this important organization nearly twenty years after my first grant for a quite different project. Research funds from the University of Southern California were essential in enabling me to complete the research for this book, and special mention must be made of Raquel Yarber and Liz Romero, who supported me with unflagging patience.

On a more personal front, above all I acknowledge Rachel Van Cleave as an inspiration, colleague, and beloved daughter, who accompanied me on some of the trips that were fundamental to this book, and my late, patient, and dearly beloved mother, who was eager to see the finished book. My sisters Jo Ann and Sue are rocks, as are Carl Balke and Larry Galetti—in more ways than they can imagine. I wrote much of this book in the comfort of my small apartment made beautiful through the artistry, know-how, and friendship of Giacomo, Dafne, Filippo, and Federico Calò Carducci, my guardian angels in Rome. In Ferrara, Marino Bortolotti and Luca Greselin, who accompanied me on some Rossi-inspired expeditions, are superb guardian angels and collaborators. Two special mentions go to Sergio Stoisman for more than thirty years of friendship and to Gianni Piccolella, a more recent addition, both in Rome. My intellectual debt to Giuseppe Mazzotta is immense, greater than he might imagine, but his friendship has been a special one. I cannot thank enough Morris Adjmi, Vittoria Di Palma, Mark Jarzombek, Carlos Jiménez, and James Steele for having the patience to read and comment on earlier versions of this manuscript.

Others instrumental in shaping this project, including but not limited to sharing material, photographs, thoughts, and friendship over the years: Vanna Agostini, Alessandro Baracco, Renata Bignozzi, Amanda Bonagurio, Anna Bracci, Michelangelo and Vincenzo Caberletti, Marco and Francesco Cavalieri, Francesco da Mosto, Valentina De Amicis, Vittoria Di Palma, Alain Fievre, Kenneth Frampton, Serena Franceschi, Sonia Gessner, Maddalena Grasso, Victor Jones, Adelmo Lazzari, Marta Lalicata, Lisa Mahar, Antonella Meriggi, Goffredo Nardo, Maurizio Oddo, Ester Prosdocimi, Stefania Rossi, Fedora Sasso, Michael Sorkin, Dante, Marcella and Riccardo Spinotti, Ferruccio Trabalzi, and Chiara Visentin.

# 1  A Brief Biography

> I wish you knew all that I think about Genius and the Heart.
> —JOHN KEATS

At the time of Aldo Rossi's birth in 1931, the Great Depression engulfed much of the industrialized world, but Mussolini's Fascist government crowned its remarkable propaganda success the following year with a brilliant exhibition of the first ten years of Fascist government, even as European countries haltingly recovered from the devastation of The Great War, World War I.[1] In 1929 Pope Pius XI (1922–39) signed an agreement with the Italian government, known as the Lateran Accord, ending nearly fifty years of a bitter dispute largely due to the massive confiscation of church property in the wake of the unification of Italy in 1870. To the degree that the Italian economy flourished, it did so in the Milan-Turin-Genoa triangle, powered by the fervent embrace of industrialization on the part of the bourgeoisie. Culture belonged to the upper middle class or bourgeoisie, and aristocrats, who filled the universities, art, and music academies. Most Italians instead eked out a living on the land, often working as sharecroppers or day laborers. The safety valve of emigration to the United States for an increasingly impoverished population closed definitively in 1924 with the passage of the Johnson-Reed Act specifically targeting Italians, Greeks, and Eastern Europeans. Emigration shifted to Latin America, which, while not always offering equally rosy opportunities, at least kept the gates open. A few days before Rossi's birth, Milan's population reached one million, and three days after he was born, the city approved a new master plan.

In this time of economic uncertainty and nationalist bombast, the Rossi family enjoyed relative prosperity, with his paternal grandfather and father operating a small factory that produced bicycle parts in Somasca, a town in the province of Lecco, overlooking Lake Como. Rossi and his brother grew up in Milan until the dangers of the war persuaded the family to send the boys to middle school as boarders at the Alessandro Volta College operated by the Somasco fathers in Lecco, not far from the family factory.[2]

Rossi began to draw and paint as a high school student, something he commented on when he later described how his habit of drawing coffeepots and kitchen implements

Detail, figure 1.11

began in childhood as he sat in his grandmother's country kitchen amid the coffeepots, cups, bottles, and other artifacts of daily life. These subjects, with the addition of some of his architectural designs, remained constant throughout his life (fig. 1.1). More importantly, the drawings evince a lifelong habit of close, persistent observation that took hold early on. As an adult, he joined those practices with ideas and visual references drawn from many sources to be brought into play in his design process, to enhance his ability always to think architecture in unique ways. He frequently drew intimate domestic scenes, often sketching casually while sitting and chatting in a kitchen—as he did throughout his life—but he also photographed images of such down-to-earth, homey environments with his trusty Polaroid camera, with which he had a long-standing romance. He famously and repeatedly photographed the fireplace mantle in his kitchen and the Torre Velasca from a window of his apartment on Via Rugabella, with the common thread for him being the fixity of the scenes represented, the insistent presence of some items, and the repeated return to similar images in depictions produced over his lifetime.[3]

Rossi also lifted his eyes from comfortable domestic spaces to consider the city as a whole, with his attention early on directed toward Milan's industrial periphery, a landscape of factories and warehouses traversed by the trains, buses, or cars that ushered Rossi and his family to visits to his grandparents or to boarding school. In later years, he reminisced about the influence of Mario Sironi's paintings of those same areas in Milan and on Sironi's appreciation of the life of the city beyond its buildings and monuments, which for him as for Rossi served as the backdrops and built context in which the life of a community unfolds.[4] While the work of many artists interested Rossi, Sironi's hauntingly beautiful, densely industrial environments exerted a particularly powerful appeal.

Rossi enrolled in the school of architecture at the Politecnico di Milano, the Polytechnic University of Milan, in 1950. One of his first and most important teachers, Ernesto Nathan Rogers, soon recognized Rossi's unusual talent and employed him to write for one of Italy's premier architectural publications of the time, the magazine *Casabella-continuità*, which then led to invitations from other publications. Alone and with others, in the pages of *Casabella-continuità* Rossi explored the architecture of Alessandro Antonelli, architect of the Mole Antonelliana in Turin; the concept of tradition; Milanese architecture; Art Nouveau; contemporary German

FIGURE 1.1
Aldo Rossi, Untitled on antique French paper, detail with coffeepot and San Carlone, lithograph, 1989 (Private collection/ Marino Bortolotti © Aldo Rossi Heirs)

architecture; and many other topics.[5] He spent time as a course assistant for Rogers and for architect Ludovico Quaroni, one of the major protagonists at the time in both pre– and post–World War II Italian architecture. Later, he fulfilled the same role for Carlo Aymonino. The years of researching and writing outside of the school delayed his graduation until March 1959, four years later than normally expected for the five-year program, but the work opened up areas of study that he continued to explore in subsequent decades and also brought him into contact with some of the young architects destined to be among the leading figures in Italian architecture in the second half of the twentieth century, such as Gae Aulenti, Aymonino, Guido Canella, Giancarlo de Carlo, Manfredo Tafuri, and Vittorio Gregotti. The *Casabella-continuità* of those years became a forum for debate, for ongoing and provocative challenges to the status quo that continued nearly unabated into the early 1990s.

Ernesto Rogers, a member of the talented and celebrated team BBPR (Banfi Belgioioso Peresutti and Rogers) enjoyed wide recognition for his work as an architect and teacher prior to the war, but his editorship of *Casabella-continuità* in the postwar years from 1954 to 1965 extended his influence well beyond the walls of the university. Although embracing modern architecture, Rogers took the then unusual step of emphasizing that architects needed to pay attention to context, history, and traditions in their design thinking, in this directly challenging International Style leaders such as Walter Gropius, head of the architectural school at Harvard, who disdained the study of history. Rossi urged them not to accept dogmatic formalism in architecture or in teaching. As Rogers wrote in 1957, "The architectural phenomenon cannot be considered to be isolated, because it is influenced by and subject to other fields which in their turn have undergone the vicissitudes of time."[6] Rogers's influence became apparent in Rossi's first book, *The Architecture of the City,* where he advanced arguments about typology, history, and the need for architects to understand the fundamental roles of communities and of time when operating in the city. He spelled out these ideas in the opening paragraphs, where he wrote, "By architecture I mean not only the visible image of the city and the sum of its architectures, but architecture as construction, the construction of the city over time."[7] By his reference to time Rossi signaled history as essential for the architect to address. For Rogers as for Rossi, only an architecture that simultaneously excelled in form and in content merited consideration.

What did they mean? Vexed by the legacy of the rationalist movement and its affinity with the Fascist regime, the condition of architecture in postwar Italy presented a series of dilemmas for young architects.[8] When BBPR's Torre Velasca appeared in Milan in 1954, it promptly became a lightning rod for dissent (fig. 1.2).[9]

FIGURE 1.2
BBPR (Banfi Belgioioso Peressutti and Rogers), Torre Velasca, Milan, 1958

Rather than a laconic glazed skyscraper of the sort being erected by Ludwig Mies van der Rohe, BBPR proposed a tower with a medievalizing profile, the upper floors projecting out from the body of the building via a series of struts. Set pugnaciously against mainstream modernism, the tower quickly drew the wrath of partisan and dogmatic modernists in the architectural press inside and outside Italy. Opponents of buildings such as the Torre Velasca claimed a moral high ground, advancing arguments about the "morality" of modern architecture and the consequent immorality of any departure from its tenets and, above all, any foray into history. Later Rossi described his own rejection of modernism in part as a rejection of "moralizing in architecture, a moralizing that rages like this in no other artistic discipline. . . . A supposedly democratic Europe regards an architectural style as democratic (and it is more hideous) simply because it made use of glass and . . . flat roofs." He asserted instead that, "I make use of what is good, wherever I can find it."[10] In a nutshell, the Torre Velasca debate evidenced the struggle underway in Italy in architecture circles, a battle also joined across the Atlantic.[11] The style and principles of Italian modernism, deeply imbricated with Fascism, for the postwar generation could not become the model for a non-Fascist architecture; however, no ready replacement presented itself.

Many young architects, including Rossi, found themselves intrigued by the architecture of Soviet Russia and even the ideals and principles of Communism. As his former employee Arduino Cantàfora put it, "Like many young men of his generation, he was raised between his mother, the parish church where he was an altar boy, and a Roman Catholic education. Almost everyone in his generation had the same history of Catholicism pushed to extreme consequences and then, fatally [they] joined the Communist party."[12] On one of Rossi's first trips outside Italy, he visited Russia in 1954 with an organized group, and he and his friends admired the accomplishments of Communist architects in housing and monuments. Ever the dreamer and optimist, the young Rossi believed that his exposure to the architecture and urbanism he found in Russia helped banish any vestige of petit-bourgeois modern architecture by offering what he saw as "emotion mixing with a desire to construct a new world."[13] Rejecting Fascism, Rossi and his friends not only rejected trans-alpine modernism, and particularly the notion that "form follows function," they also questioned the possibility of a purely historicist architecture. Like many of his friends, Rossi found the Communist ideals of equality and justice in a classless society quite consistent with Catholic teachings, at least for a brief few years, but he too found himself dismayed by the thinness of the belief in principles of equality and justice among Italy's Communists, often known as "Gucci Communists."[14] By the 1970s, unable to vote for any Italian political party, he found himself regularly submitting blank ballots.[15]

No easy solutions presented themselves to the many problems posed to postwar architects, so in many respects the time spent researching and writing permitted Rossi to reflect on and absorb multiple influences, to work through them much as any young scholar would, exploring ideas and approaches so as to discard anything irrelevant, and to mold his own. In his most ambitious goal, he sought to discover what the aesthetic and social roles of art and architecture could be in a deeply compromised postwar world. He explored architecture's engagement with reality, a reality he understood as a combination of manifestations and artifacts typical of individual historical periods, which in the best of circumstances the architect experienced, absorbed, and then translated into an artifact or building.[16] The enigma of how this transpired, how the architect could collapse the distance among technical accomplishment, experience, and imaginative expression remained a focus of Rossi's attention throughout his life. In his early notes he pondered the conundrum of translating ephemeral experience into luminous, palpable reality even while recognizing that it would never be resolved because, far from a haphazard occurrence, this lyrical flight of imagination remained mysterious and intriguing, only tenuously tethered to something also evoked through words. Perhaps more importantly, he also believed that the architect failed when the task became an indulgence in vague self-expression, when instead it was essential to identify the common beliefs and thoughts of the community, and then to embody them in architectural projects.

In his first major book, *The Architecture of the City*, originally intended to be co-authored with a colleague, Paolo Ceccarelli, Rossi wanted to propose as a first step not a style, but an analytical approach to building in the city.[17] Cities, he argued, are complex objects designed across time, but they are also urban artifacts—streets, districts, buildings, which together summarize a history in constant evolution. He set out first to describe and classify various types of buildings, establishing a typology, starting with the forms of cities. Despite the scientific rigor of the opening, he moved quickly to considerations of quality and the uniqueness of individual structures. He turned to the rich and varied histories of buildings such as palaces, town halls, and churches, and to the way they could be understood as works of art. Like the Palazzo della Ragione (Palace of Justice) in Padua, such buildings have undergone major changes in function independent of their forms—but we today continue to experience and live the form despite the changes in function; we simply live them in different ways (fig. 1.3). A structure such as the Palazzo della Ragione also constituted an example of an architectural type, and by type he indicated "the very idea of architecture, that which is closest to its essence." Building types consist of elements that cannot be further reduced, such as centrally planned buildings, Rossi concluded, but no type can be associated with a single form, and every type interacts dialectically with technique, function, and style.[18] Analyzing type for Rossi consisted not of a mechanical activity but rather a thoughtful effort to grasp the essence of a complex entity in which feeling and reason figured at the individual as well as the collective level.

Structures such as the former Roman amphitheaters at Nimes and Lucca harbored a range of memories and design features that conveyed their uniqueness, something

FIGURE 1.3
Palazzo della Ragione, Padua

fully apparent perhaps only to those who see them firsthand. To clarify his point, Rossi emphasized the individual experience of buildings, streets, and cities as a basis for constructing a theoretical framework, which for him was also profoundly bound up with the collective experience of the city. As evidence of social life, a work of architecture or an urban artifact for Rossi emerged in unconscious life, both collective and individual, an ideal combination of what French theorist Maurice Halbwachs described as "imagination and collective memory [as] the typical characteristics of urban artifacts."[19]

The structures that constitute cities—from street networks to churches and blocks—can also be assessed as *permanences* and monuments. Rossi drew the theory of permanences, or persistences, from the work of Marcel Poète and Pierre Lavedan, who identified monuments and the streets and layout of cities as those features that resisted the damage of time to emerge as characteristics fundamental to individual cities. Rossi defined these permanences as either pathological or propelling, the latter consisting of elements still vital such as the Palazzo della Ragione, and the pathological leaving the structure isolated and bereft of important functions, such as the Alhambra in Granada, Spain. Such characterizations led Rossi to reflect on how to define study areas, to dedicate one chapter to housing, another to reflections on the role of monuments, others to architecture and issues of context. The last chapter focused on the role of time in the history of the city and the way it and its architecture evolved. Whatever aspect of

FIGURE 1.4
Aldo Rossi, Untitled on antique French paper, lithograph, 1989 (Private collection/Alexander Severin © Aldo Rossi Heirs)

architecture and building in the city he explored, Rossi continually returned to the individual and to the collective, always bearing in mind their roles in the construction and modification of buildings over time. Despite his evident desire to produce a "scientific" study, his perspective never strayed far from reflections on human activity, on values, on the collective, and on the individual—a focus often overlooked by historians but one that he elaborated in his later, more explicit writings on architectural poetics.[20] Clearly, his inclusion of figures in so many of his drawings, standing at windows, looking in or being looked at, emerging from within buildings, climbing or standing in front of some of his architectures reminded the viewer—and the architect—that every analytical passage, every constructed element found its meaning and relevance not in a resolutely rationalist and abstract theory, but in human activity in all of its crazy complexity (fig. 1.4).

### INFLUENCES AND FIRST PROJECTS

The work and writings of three architects in particular captured Rossi's interest: those of Étienne-Louis Boullée, Adolf Loos, and Karl Friedrich Schinkel. Schinkel, who figures in more detail in subsequent chapters herein, appealed more for his architecture than for his writings,[21] while Boullée and Loos appealed in both. Rossi translated and arranged for the publication of Boullée's 1788 essay *Architecture: Essai sur l'art* as *Architettura: Saggio sull'arte,* for which he also wrote an introduction in 1967, the year after the first Italian edition of *The Architecture of the City* appeared.[22] Rossi found reading Boullée invigorating, for the French architect opened up to him new ways of thinking about architecture, specifically enabling him to escape the trap of empty formalism in his own work. Boullée's essay had only become available in an English edition in 1953, and over a decade later in French; it opened with the question "What is architecture?" Boullée promptly dismissed the answer offered by Vitruvius—"the art of building"—as a notion that confused the effect with the cause. "What little attention has been paid in the past to the poetry of architecture!" Boullée lamented.[23] Reflecting on these startling insights, together with the ideas he had explored in *The Architecture of the City,* Rossi began to develop a concept he described as "exalted rationalism." By this he meant a strategy of isolating "scientific reason" in architecture and in so doing, proposing something at once far more rigorous and far more elusive, because he recognized the inability of scientific reason to embrace both rational and sentimental components, in other words to fashion a world that satisfies anything other than logical and intellectual needs. This exalted rationalism sprang from the core of rationalism, he insisted, but simultaneously projected forward to the unanticipated and the spontaneous.[24] In short, in Boullée Rossi encountered openings for thinking about architecture and poetry—that is, the imaginative content of architecture—without diminishing the importance of rigor in structure, materials, and technique and all of the essential tools of the discipline. To do so also enabled Rossi to transcend mundane functional matters within the framework of a richer, more profound theory.

With Loos, on the other hand, apart from the appeal of his architectural designs and his entertaining text on ornament and crime, Rossi especially gravitated toward the Austrian's moral and ethical considerations, not to mention his unabashed fascination with classical architecture, despite the negative judgments of modern movement architects and theorists.[25] Loos despised moralism, Rossi commented, but he adopted a moral and ethical position in his writings, especially in his recognition of the problems of the alienation of labor and his social democratic vision of a future world.[26] The moralism Rossi—along with Loos—opposed was the so-called moralism of modernist architects who through their buildings presumed to tell people how they should live.[27] For Rossi, Loos's analysis of working class housing echoed that of Friedrich Engels in his *The Condition of the Working Class in England in 1844* (1845) but stood far from the moralizing pretensions of rationalist architects of the interwar period.[28]

Loos also deliberately chose the perspective of time as a point of departure in his studies—that is, a personal and historical time not unrelated to Boullée's architecture of shadows—but also particular to Loos was what Rossi described as an eclectic way of observing things.[29] That the architect of buildings exhibiting a "formalist terrorism" (such as in the Tristan Tzara house of 1925–26) could at once wax enthusiastic about Beaux Arts skyscrapers in New York and about Louis Sullivan's designs for Chicago captured Rossi's imagination, for he shared the Austrian modernist's breadth of interests and openness to many kinds of architecture. Rossi also agreed with Loos's skepticism about the Secession movement, as well as his view of architecture as fundamentally rooted in antiquity. Rossi appreciated the "literary" Loos, the richness of his thought as presented through his writings, because, as Rossi noted, "the means of expression or communication is a vehicle that finds its perfection in its very content."[30] Rossi's first complete building, a residential duplex named Villa ai Ronchi, testifies to Loos's influence on the young Rossi. The house sits within a thick pine grove in Versilia, just

FIGURE 1.5
Aldo Rossi and Leonardo Ferrari, Villa ai Ronchi, Versilia, 1960 (Martin Feiersinger)

south of the Mediterranean coastal town La Spezia (fig. 1.5). White walls, cubic massing, and roof terraces certainly drew in part on local traditions of white houses near the sea, but even more, along with the high narrow windows they echoed Loos's Villa Müller in Prague (1930), which Rossi had visited, and his concept of the *Raumplan*, meaning designing through spatial planning rather than producing plans, sections, and elevations. Rossi followed Loos's lead in Villa ai Ronchi's scheme of tying together with exterior and interior stairs a group of shifted and interlocking cubes deployed on multiple levels. At a certain point, Rossi observed that he had so absorbed lessons from Loos as to obscure the border between the two, "as in a love that has been consumed."[31]

While Rossi worked through the enigmas of poetry in architecture, he designed his earliest projects, mostly unbuilt, from the monument at Cuneo to the town halls of Scandicci and Muggio, the theater at Parma, and urban plans for Milan and Turin. The questions raised by Boullée did not surface in *The Architecture of the City*, but many others did. Rossi's growing disillusion with Communism in the early 1960s kept pace with an equally strong disillusion with the banal modern movement architecture of much postwar building. Thus in many respects *The Architecture of the City* was a clarion cry to dismiss the formalist dogmas of the first half of the twentieth century, a demand rooted in his years working with Rogers as teacher and mentor. Rogers lamented the failures of those architects "who have understood [the modern movement] in a formalistic way [and] have fallen into the error of following its . . . 'style.'" Instead, Rogers challenged them not to declare reactionary the embrace of tradition and continuity, but rather to grasp "the more profound significance of this investigation into the past [and] perceive its fundamental logical coherence and its cultural enrichment."[32] Rossi's book and projects emphatically rejected the modern movement formulas that Rogers had defined as hollow and myopic. As major building enterprises such as the San Cataldo cemetery at Modena evidence, Rossi plunged deeply into and opened up internal dimensions quite at odds with such stylistic formulas—but not only those of the modern movement. For Rossi, the notion of formulas itself constituted the greatest problem: he invited reflection rather than conformity to fashion. Even had he not begun to develop a theoretical framework within which to explore Boullée's plea for poetry, in his lyrical drawings and buildings Rossi extracted an expressive richness from apparently impoverished forms remote from the modern movement's stifling dictates as it was then practiced.

When Carlo Aymonino offered Rossi a job to design one of the apartment blocks for the Monte Amiata public housing estate on the western periphery of Milan, Rossi seized the opportunity to realize his ideas in built form and, best of all, on a large scale. Though responsible for only one of the five units in the complex, known informally as Gallaratese (1969–70), his project immediately attracted international attention, largely sidelining the other four by Aymonino (fig. 1.6). The fascination endures even a half century later precisely because of the startlingly elegant simplicity of the forms, a radical departure from the busy, crowded blocks typified by Aymonino's design. Set on sloping terrain, the Gallaratese adapts to the shift in level by a simple staircase and by four massive concrete columns, each nearly 1.8 meters (6 feet) in diameter. On either side of the columns, slender slabs, or pilasters (most of which were unnecessary structurally but compelling aesthetically), of different heights proceed at a rhythmic distance also of 1.8 meters. Rossi adopted a traditional Lombard housing type, the single-loaded gallery with units opening on the corridor, and each apartment enjoyed one or two balconies. Unusually for a low-cost project in Italy, Rossi recessed the balconies, rendering them invisible from the exterior and rupturing the typology and some of the stigma associated with subsidized housing (fig. 1.7). For him, these early choices contributed to the project's success, in large part because of their clarity. The haunting imagery of Rossi's building captured attention because of its disarming aloofness from dry modern movement designs, but also in its distance from typically over-designed, over-complicated, and out-of-scale complexes tyrannically indifferent to those who would have to live in them, such as Mario Fiorentino's Corviale housing in Rome (1972–82), among many others. Then and later, visitors commented on the appealing character of the Gallaratese's classicism. In the absence of typical features such as capitals or entablatures, the classicism springs rather from the rhythmic sequences, the grand columns, and the majestic pilasters. In

FIGURES 1.6 AND 1.7
Aldo Rossi, Monte Amiato Housing, Gallaratese, Milan, completed ca. 1972

effect, Rossi opened a world of possibilities for architects tired of arid modernist buildings, an opening he enhanced in the projects that immediately followed: the schools at Fagnano Olona and Broni, the cemetery at Modena, and the project for student housing in Chieti.

### THE TENDENZA

As Rossi continued to explore ways to theorize an architecture for the contemporary world, a group of young practitioners gravitated toward him and formed a loose coalition that came to be known as *Tendenza* (trend, or tendency). Active roughly between 1972 and 1985, Tendenza amounted to another broad and open challenge to the hegemony of twentieth-century modernist architecture, with Rossi's *The Architecture of the City* an early opening salvo in the battle. Tendenza's origins date to a 1946 essay by Rogers in which he identified three elements of a program for a new architecture: coherence, tendency, and style. The artist identifies actions to pursue with coherence in harmony with a moral world; tendency is the intellectual path in which such actions are realized; and style results from the previous two actions.[33] In the 1970s version, Daniele Vitale, Massimo Scolari, Rosaldo Bonicalzi, and others flanked Rossi, and many of them also participated in the 1973 XV Milan Triennale of architecture mounted by Rossi and named *Architettura razionale* (Rational Architecture) after the Italian version of modernism during the interwar period. The exhibit proposed a continuity between classic modernists such as Loos, Giuseppe Terragni, and Le Corbusier and a newer, more expressive, and historically based trend documented in urban projects for Naples, Bologna, Trieste, and other European cities.[34] The recent deaths of Piero Bottoni, Hans Schmidt, and Rogers encouraged Rossi to include a segment dedicated to their singular contributions. In another section, he pitted Soviet architecture against projects by Matthias Ungers, Rob Krier, John Hejduk, Michael Graves, and Peter Eisenman.[35] Such a heterogeneous grouping evidently could not hang together for long, and indeed it did not.

Each Italian architect who participated in the exhibit held different views about how to define rational architecture, as well as what constituted the Tendenza, even while each earnestly searched for insights and proposals that could bridge the differences. Scolari, for example, railed against regressive tendencies and the organic architecture movement pushed by Bruno Zevi, who claimed that the only alternative to a descent into "suicide [as] proposed by Pop architecture" was faithful adherence to modern movement dogma.[36] The choices, as stipulated by Zevi and others, seemed stark enough: either deep political involvement or avant-garde escapism, either one of which constituted a death spiral for architecture. Scolari instead argued for establishing "a sense of avant-garde, progress and architecture" to be identified within the "opacity in which [architects were] immersed." The then fashionable avant-gardes in Italy—Archizoom, Superstudio, 999—bereft of theoretical foundations, ended up little more than "comic-book shrieks" with nothing to offer in the way of clarification to counter contemporary "opacity." The primary fault of such groups lay not in being harmful, but rather in being useless. Scolari dismissed the idea that architects should abandon social considerations, instead he proposed rejecting a search for invention, the great "new idea," or "new truths," so that the architect of the Tendenza would instead choose to undertake historical and formal analyses and, echoing Rossi, to study the city as a human product and not as "a series of formal preconceptions." An essential component of this process entailed identifying architecture as an autonomous discipline, not by extracting the architectural project from its social, economic, or political context, but by recognizing the unique tools, traditions, and technologies of the discipline to be able to intervene more appropriately in city building, for example, including for many rupturing the hold of the modern movement on the field.[37] In the definition of naive functionalism that he proposed in *The Architecture of the City*, Rossi had already challenged the regnant orthodoxy in modernist design wherein forms could be deduced logically purely on the basis of objective needs. With such a chaotic mix of ideas, how would it be possible to identify a unifying tendency?

Several years later, in 1979, Rossi offered an even more direct explanation of the Tendenza, where he noted that initially it expressed the difference between their architecture and that of the International Style as well as from standard professional practice. To adhere to the Tendenza meant to insert oneself into the social-political debate, affiliating with the country's reality, rupturing academic and commercial schemes that so dominated Milan Polytechnic. With the rationalist or neo-rationalist exhibit at the XV Milan Triennale he meant to convey such ideas, but he also wryly remarked on how foreign publications completely transformed them.[38] Certainly they missed the poetic dimensions that he believed so essential to architectural design.

Despite the strong desire to fuse the various theoretical and architectural threads of this diverse group, Rossi's aspiration to identify a common architecture, at once logical and poetic, among the works on display foundered on the shoals of paradoxes too numerous to list. One will suffice: under what umbrella could both the Rob Krier of 1973 and the Le Corbusier of the Villa Savoye fit (especially since in inclement weather, one indeed needed an umbrella to navigate the latter)? Nonetheless, the bold effort to identify positive elements in modernist architecture so as to forge a path forward came about in part through an exploration of typology and morphology, without omitting social issues. Precisely the effort to identify a trajectory in terms of form and style proved impossible, Rossi himself being the first to withdraw from an identification with Tendenza. Criticized for not forming a "school," among other things, he above all recognized the impossibility of such an enterprise.[39] Although for the exhibit he minimized the poetic dimensions of his own design process in favor of what the group agreed to describe as "realism," Rossi's truth located poetry at its very heart, the result of an intimate and deeply personal search impossible to duplicate or to hand off as a style. When pressed for an explanation, Rossi clarified that he desired a methodology rather than a set of answers, an approach and a pedagogical practice he hoped would sufficiently captivate architects to set them off on their own journeys of discovery.

While still a twenty-four-year-old student, Rossi elaborated a preliminary assessment of architectural realism in an unpublished article drafted in 1955 with Guido Canella, "Architettura e realismo."[40] The culture of postwar Italy, they argued, was stiff and hermetically sealed within a set of dogmas resistant to change. They unhappily referred to the fact that power—in architectural production as in criticism—remained in the hands of those who, having been valorous servants of Fascism, evinced little interest in undertaking a search for new languages so as not to expose the sterility of their own architecture. In neo-realist film, however, Rossi and Canella found an exception, one in which the tragedies of Fascism, war, and the postwar years received full voice. Nonetheless, they also detected in the work of neo-realist directors a retreat into a new and fatal formalist involution, just as they saw happening in the architecture of Gardella, Franco Albini, BBPR, Quaroni, Piccinato, and others. This new formalism contaminated all of the arts. In the world of architecture as they assessed it then, realism offered the possibility of escaping formalism by exploring specific contexts in far greater depth. They argued for shifting attention away from form toward factors springing directly from the collectivity—cultural, political, economic, and social. And this they believed offered the only path toward a critical perspective on architecture. It entailed an engagement with tradition and with history well beyond a simplistic repetition of forms. Notably, in this early text penned while still a student, Rossi advanced a perceptive critique of the power structure within the architectural academy, one that he developed further in his notebooks, his *Quaderni Azzurri*. In 1989, reading some proposals for the city of Milan, he commented that "the stupidity of architectural culture affiliated with the 'modern' even exceeded the greed of speculators."[41]

Rossi specifically associated realism with key films of postwar Italy, such as his particular favorites Luchino Visconti's *Ossessione* (1943) and *Senso* (1954), Federico Fellini's *Roma* (1972) and *8 1/2* (1963), and Mauro Bolognini's *Senilità* (1962). For the Triennale he organized two short films, *Ornamento e delitto* (*Ornament and Crime*) and *La nuova abitazione* (*The New House*), both of which included selections from several movies. All could loosely be termed "neo-realist" films with dimensions that ultimately attenuated the distance between the "real" and the "poetic." Rossi chose the clips from each film because in different ways each illustrated a dimension of the nexus of the real and the poetic. He pointed to the protagonist's wavering between fantasy and reality in *8 1/2*, or to the dominant and constant presence of the city of Rome in *Roma*. *Ossessione*, on the other hand, recounted the lives of two individuals—an Italian woman and an Austrian officer—trapped in the overpowering panorama of the historic struggle to end Austrian rule in northern Italy in the late 1860s (fig. 1.8). In this, the film proved a parallel to Rossi's firm focus on history, on specific historical context as the rational basis on which to found architecture. In *8 1/2*, the process of filmmaking is recorded as an unstable, transgressive, but marvelously enigmatic alliance between realism and fantasy, a process not unlike that which Rossi, following the indications of Raymond Roussel, repeatedly sought to describe with his architecture.[42] More than twenty years later, Rossi looked back on his "realist education" as having been characterized by a profound passion for life, with a realism that was lyrical, lively, and marvelous, departing from stale academic modernism by instead plunging headlong into the real world of individuals and the collectivity.[43]

During these same years, Rossi and his colleagues on the school council at Milan Polytechnic, politically and culturally in open opposition to the administration and eager to reform the curriculum, found themselves abruptly suspended from teaching in November 1971 by order of then Minister of Public Instruction Riccardo Misasi.[44] Although the group challenged standard practice by voting as a group and by pushing for studies of a socialist city, among other violations of bureaucratic rules the suspension documents revealed what was probably the true reason for the minister's action in its vague reference to the faculty council's decision to admit "external elements" into

FIGURE 1.8
Clara Calamai in *Ossessione*, 1943

the halls of the school. Earlier that year, on 6 June 1971, four thousand police officers violently removed squatters who had been occupying the public housing in Via Tibaldi in Milan, killing a seven-month-old child in the process. Some families fleeing the violence sought refuge in the Polytechnic's school of architecture, where students welcomed them, as did department chair Paolo Portoghesi and some members of the faculty council, including Rossi. As Scolari later recalled, many professors simply ignored the issues, but Rossi remained supportive and very much aligned with the students in their political battles.[45] The squatters resided in the school until the police once again forcibly removed them on 29 June. The university's faculty senate suspended all gatherings and activities other than teaching until further notice. This type of event inaugurated the so-called "leaden years" (*anni di piombo*), when demonstrations, armed struggle, and the brutal suppression of dissent marked universities as well as the streets through the next decade. Until the ministry finally lifted the suspension in 1974, Rossi taught at ETH Zürich, forming fast friendships with Fabio Reinhart among others, and launching studies of traditional Swiss housing.[46]

Today, capturing the flavor of the 1970s and 1980s is a difficult enterprise, for its crackling, contradictory energy eludes facile description. Apart from the devastating political battles in Italian streets, often ignited by corrupt politicians, deviated secret services, foreign intelligence agencies, neo-Fascist groups, and the Red Brigades, architects lived an invigorating, chaotic, and dangerous period.[47] The surge of architectural publications, including magazines and journals, on the continent and in the United States furnishes one easy measure of the fervor that animated the discipline. Numerous Italian publishers produced lavish architecture books, from older houses such as Laterza (founded 1901), Rizzoli (1909), Einaudi (1933), to the newer Franco Angeli (1955), Marsilio (1961), and Gangemi (1962), as well as books and journals published by universities and cultural organizations. The magazine scene flourished even more than it had before the war: in addition to *Domus* and *Casabella* (1928) and *Rinascita* (1941), Italians launched critical and often polemical architectural periodicals such as *Zodiac* (1957), *Lotus* (1964) and *Lotus International* (1970), *Controspazio* (1966), *Rassegna* (1966), *Contropiano* (1968), *Parametro* (1970), *Modo* (1977), and *Dedalo* (1986). Although some soon fell into staid predictability, during the two decades between 1970 and 1990 debate flourished as architects struggled to come to terms with new technologies, exploding cities, and how to negotiate the conjunction of architecture and urbanism. In Italy in particular, people continued to abandon the countryside, and historic city centers strained to accommodate cars, people, and old buildings. What could constitute a contemporary theory of architectural design, Rossi asked, and why was it so difficult to outline one?[48] What, he wondered, should they do with those structures for which one harbored fondness, such as public laundries, cheese houses, or communal rural courts? Above all, they testified to the antique misery of an entire population. So should they perhaps become "museums of such sorrows?"[49] No simple answers emerged, but such questions had to be asked on virtually every occasion an architect confronted an urban building project. Rossi continued to be one of the main protagonists in the debates, as he had been since the late 1950s, but after the XV Triennale in 1973 he built more and published less, in effect choosing that his architecture speak for itself.[50]

THE ANALOGOUS CITY

As the debate over the success—or failure—of the 1973 XV Milan Triennale and what it might mean continued, certain moments stood out as encapsulating the questions it posed. The conclusion of the section on cities consisted of perhaps the exhibit's most emblematic image, a 7-meter by 2-meter (23-foot by 6 1/2-foot) painting by Arduino Cantàfora, "La città analoga" (The Analogous City) (fig. 1.9).[51] This architectural collage assembled in the same fantastic urban landscape Rossi's Monument to Partisans at Segrate and housing at Gallaratese quarter, with buildings such as Behrens' AEG building in Berlin, Loos's Michaelerplatz building in Vienna, and the Pantheon and Cestia Pyramid in Rome. The panel echoed, in a twentieth-century key, Canaletto's famous *Capriccio: A Palladian Design for the Rialto Bridge with Buildings at Vicenza* (1740), where real and imagined Palladian designs defied geography and logic to line the Grand Canal in Venice.[52] Cantàfora's panel summarized the character of the cities documented in the show, along with Rossi's ideas about the city as a complex object, its urban artifacts as expressions of human will and the histories of the city itself, its collective memories liberated in the panel in a vast panorama at once diverse and ordered.

Three years later, at the Venice Architecture Biennale in 1976, for a European-American show that considered possible approaches to questions about central cities and suburbs Rossi presented a quite different, equally provocative panel, also entitled "La città analoga," this one fashioned with Eraldo Consolascio, Bruno Reichlin, and Fabio Reinhart (fig. 1.10). A collaborative project fabricated at ETH Zürich, the panel celebrated Rossi's vision of the historic city as shaped by imagination and by individuals working together, the city as locus of collective memory, imagination, and action.[53] The panel included structures, plans, and images dear to Rossi, those about which he wrote and those he sketched over the years: the Palace of Knossos, Bramante's Tempietto, Borromini's Church of San Carlo alle Quattro Fontane, Piranesi's *Carceri*, Terragni's Danteum; along with fragments of Rossi's own projects: the cemetery at Modena, the Elba cabins, the urban plan for the San Rocco quarter in Turin. Above all and looming over the image stood the figure of David from Tanzio da Varallo's *David and Goliath* (ca. 1625). Tanzio owes his fame in part to the elaborate chapels he devised where he depicted scenes from the Passion at the Sacro Monte of Varallo, either in painting or with sculpture. The new "La città analoga" panel proposed a history of architecture and the city not as rigid and unchangeable but as an entity above all to be challenged, confronted, engaged, modified—and not by treating it as a clean slate but as it is found,

FIGURE 1.9
At the XV Milan Triennale, 1973. Rossi in the center, back row; in the background, Cantàfora's "La città analoga" (Courtesy ETH/Heinrich Helfenstein)

FIGURE 1.10
Aldo Rossi with Eraldo Consolascio, Bruno Reichlin, and Fabio Reinhart, "La città analoga," collage, mixed media, 1976 (MAXXI, Rossi/© Aldo Rossi Heirs)

with all of its memories, real and imagined, intact, overlapping, and superimposing in an apparent disorder much like that of memory itself. In the space of only three years, the analogous city had evolved from a structured, visually diverse landscape to one far closer to Rossi's conceptions of architecture as an apparently chaotic aggregation of richly varied elements presented in random fashion in plan, elevation, section, with an overlay of drawings—Rossi's lone figure standing at a window beneath a lamp. The representation of David and the mythic battle against Goliath suggested a parallel between the architects who waged battles for architecture against the forces of speculation and corruption that blocked their path.

What did Rossi mean by "analogous city"? In an essay published shortly after the exhibition closed, he wrote: "I find it important to show the connections leading from the imagination to reality and from both of these towards freedom. There are no inventions, no complexities, also no irrationality, that cannot be understood by using reason, or at least the dialectic of the concrete. I believe in the power of the imagination as a concrete possibility."[54]

From his earliest years as a student of architecture, Rossi found himself drawn to reflect on the sources of creativity—not only his, but those of other architects. Boullée's treatise gave impetus to ideas already manifest in his writings and early designs, so "La città analoga" merely gave powerful visual testimony to this belief. This concept came to mind when he reread *The Architecture of the City* and urgently believed that having explored methodologies for studying the city, description and knowledge should now yield to a study of "the power of the imagination, arising from the concrete." Rather than pitting them against one another, he believed the focus should shift. He outlined a parallel between his panel and Canaletto's *Capriccio* painting of an imaginary Venice that became more important than the real one. Rossi described his panel as a "creation ... made from designs and from both real and imaginary elements that are cited and brought together to form an alternative to reality." That alternative in turn should be a springboard for imaginative architectural designs. The embodied memories, ephemeral and elusive, built and unbuilt, would issue in something unique yet grounded in the specific site. Jung's description of analogical thought as "a meditation on themes of the past, an interior monologue, ... a sensed yet unreal, an imagined yet silent world," mirrored exactly what Rossi conveyed in his drawings, designs, and his writings.[55]

The third and final major representation of Rossi's theories at a large-scale exhibit came two years later, in 1978, with an invitation from art historian Giulio Carlo Argan, then also mayor of Rome, to participate in a group project dreamed up by Pietro Sartogo.[56] They asked twelve architects to each propose an "interruption" to the city fabric of Rome, with the framework and starting point being the twelve sections of Giovanni Battista Nolli's 1748 map of the city. Nolli's plan illustrated an urbanized area of many parts and monuments, including vast rural areas and expansive private gardens within the city's walls, all blending into a relatively coherent whole that included the ruins of Roman antiquity. Sartogo's intent with the new proposal to "interrupt" Rome entailed pitting the pre-unification city of 1869 against the post-unification urban and suburban nightmare that unbridled speculation (and corruption) had since wrought. With the avowed goal of sparking architectural imaginations, the organizers designated one architect for each of the twelve parts; Rossi received section 10, the area around the ruins of the baths of Caracalla (fig. 1.11). He titled his contribution "Reconstruction of the Antonian Baths and of the antique aqueduct with very modern facilities for heating

FIGURE 1.11
Aldo Rossi, "Roma interrotta," collage, mixed media, 1976 (MAXXI, Rossi/© Aldo Rossi Heirs)

and cooling for use of new bathing facilities, for relaxation, love, and exercise, with adjacent pavilions for use on the occasion of fairs and markets." Along the lower edge, Rossi inserted fragments of tall buildings and of his own architectures, from the Segrate monument to the Gallaratese, with the statue of San Carlo at Arona looming over all. A small version of his Little Scientific Theater, with triangular pediment and paintings of urban scenes on the rear wall, was set out on a stage with out-of-scale glasses, bottles, and coffee. The theme appealed to Rossi especially because it called for him to design as he chose and exactly as Nolli's map presented the city—an entity composed of an architecture of parts assembled into a diverse, complex, yet strangely harmonious landscape. He also slyly referred to the many Lombard architects who had practiced architecture in Rome, including Nolli himself.[57] Rossi's provocative interruption swept away the hand of the modern movement "master" architect and urbanist who presumed to control lives and cities, substituting for them buildings and places fashioned to invite future occupation, to anticipate modifications and alterations rather than oppressive immutability, fragments of a city of parts. Over time his focus on the fragment as fundamental to a contemporary architecture increased and sharpened. Finding the notion of designing everything from "the spoon to the cathedral" ridiculous because it presumed a certain type of order, Rossi instead argued that modern life offers a full range of diverse experiences, best captured by the idea of a city of fragments as expressions not of destruction but of hope. The grand master plans and redemptive promises of modern movement architects were ultimately "anti-human" in his view, in profound contrast with the idea of the city as rich with alternatives that architects needed to recognize and represent in their designs, precisely with an approach that identified the positive in the fragments or individual parts of the city.[58]

In 1975 a collection of Rossi's writings appeared, *Scritti scelti sull'architettura e la città, 1956–1972* (*Selected Writings on Architecture and the City*), including some that had been published in marginal, often difficult to locate publications. With this book Rossi confirmed his profound knowledge of history, the breadth and depth of his knowledge of architecture even outside of Italy, and his ability to navigate all manner of ambiguities and uncertainties with aplomb and originality. For the historian, the collection also affirms the dogged persistence of certain concerns from his earliest writings. In retrospect, it became clear that almost from the beginning of his career, history offered Rossi a perspective from which to contemplate his task as an architect, to understand that it extended well beyond the forms, materials, and other functional features to a point where "the meaning that surfaces at the end of the operation [of architectural design] is the authentic, unexpected, and original meaning of the research. It is a project."[59] As he explained in *The Architecture of the City*, Rossi considered matters of form and technique only a first step, where the content of the project, however ineffable, dominated and completed any work of architecture. Quite simply, Rossi argued, the results obtained solely in a rational key, based on technologies and functionalism, could only end up insufficient and mediocre; instead, this rational construction method must be ruptured from within in a process of continuous contradiction, where meaning and expression exalt and transform the principles into something of substance, something profound.[60] As we will see in the following chapters, Rossi strove to do just that in his own work.

The year 1979 brought Rossi's first major official recognition as an architect, in the form of election to Italy's prestigious Accademia di San Luca. The academy originated in the late fifteenth century as the Università delle Arti della Pittura and, after various phases of development, took on its current form in 1577 when Pope Gregory XIII issued a papal brief officially approving an academy of painting, sculpture, and design. Formal admission for architects came about only in 1634. Although the new Italian state halted the academy's teaching activities in 1874, it continued to promote the arts and architecture through a range of activities, events, and awards. Election to the academy confirmed Rossi's stature within the field of Italian architects, where he joined the ranks of twentieth-century figures such as Pietro Aschieri, Mario Ridolfi, and Ugo Luccichenti, as well as earlier architects Gianlorenzo Bernini, Pietro da Cortona, and Carlo Fontana.[61]

In late 1979 and continuing through much of 1980, the Teatro del Mondo appeared, floating in the waters of Venice adjacent to the Punto della Dogana and the church of Santa Maria della Salute in celebration of the Venice Biennale of Theater, and later of

FIGURE 1.12
Aldo Rossi, Teatro del Mondo, being towed by barge (source unknown)

Architecture (fig. 1.12). It instantly became an iconic image and, as it coincided with the flowering of debates about postmodern architecture, it also became a symbol of the increasingly vigorous debates in the discipline. Following the 1950s-era battles against any departure from modern movement dogmas—such as the Torre Velasca—the postmodern challenge became the new frontier. Three major publications during the 1960s—Rossi's *The Architecture of the City*, Robert Venturi's *Complexity and Contradiction in Architecture*, and Jane Jacobs's, *The Death and Life of Great American Cities*—had posed increasingly serious but diverse challenges to the hegemony of the modern movement, particularly, but not only, in its corporate manifestation in office buildings, residential construction, and urban planning.[62] The debate gathered momentum in the 1970s, in its most public form as the battle between the Whites (dogmatic modernists) and Grays (open to introducing references to history and tradition in architecture) in the United States.[63] The two self-proclaimed avant-gardes each asserted the virtues of their approach, the first by dutifully following Corbusian and Miesian dictates for a purist formalism, while the second polemically touted the importance of color and historical reference in architecture. Michael Graves's project for a public office building, winner of a 1979 competition organized by the city of Portland, Oregon, ideally exhibited the features of the nascent postmodern movement: a brightly, even garishly hued office block containing over-scaled keystones, belvederes, pilasters, and arcades.[64] Publication of the Graves design occurred just as the Teatro del Mondo floated in the waters of Venice's lagoon, with its metal cupola, simple bright yellow and blue wooden structure over scaffolding, announcing the gulf between itself and standard modern movement exemplars.

Not surprisingly, postmodernists often celebrated Rossi as one of their own. To be sure, both Whites and Grays rejected the corporate monotony of postwar modernism, and both instead encouraged the creativity of the individual architect. When he heard he had been classified as a postmodernist, however, Rossi famously (and repeatedly) declined to be so identified since, as he claimed, he had never even been a modernist. Instead, he often teased, a more appropriate classification would be "post-antique."[65] "How provincial was the Modern Movement," he wrote in 1996, making everything from the Frankfurt Kitchen to the "machine for living" moralistic where "progress was only sadness and moralism then crossed sadness to serve [the interests of] speculation."[66] That Rossi also eschewed white in favor of color and employed symmetry and even central planning amounted to nothing more than a gross formal similarity with postmodernists such as Graves, one that dissolved upon closer examination. Exaggeration and facile imitation, along with a penchant for irony and pretentious playfulness as in the Portland Building indeed typified much postmodern architecture of the 1980s, and Graves, Robert A. M. Stern, Charles Moore, Thomas Gordon Smith, Richard Rogers and Renzo Piano, and others pursued that very path. The Portland—emblematic in this respect—like most postmodern buildings such as the Centre Pompidou, reduced to little more than a decorated box. Unfortunately, architecture produced under the rubric of postmodernism often did not hold up well over time any more than have more recent forays into deconstructivist and parametric design. The Portland Building demanded serious renovation only eight years after completion; the Piano and Rogers Centre Pompidou underwent two expensive and extensive restorations within less than thirty years; and Zaha Hadid's MAXXI in Rome needed the same soon after opening.

In the decades following World War II, one of the most significant proposals for negotiating the new demands of industrialized cities and historic centers in Italy consisted of the Directional Centers (*Centri direzionali*), new urban centers to be erected on urban peripheries, thereby shifting demands of traffic, governance, and administration away from historically sensitive areas. Rossi's project for regional headquarters in the Fontivegge area in Perugia (1982) constituted one such Directional Center. Most cities developed plans for them but few followed through, and few of those built achieved the hoped for success other than meeting the basic requirements—Fontivegge being a case in point. Given enough time, even this center remote from the historic heart of Perugia may eventually become a fully active part of the city.

ON THE MOVE

Rossi's fame grew through the 1970s and 1980s, so much that his life began to change dramatically as he traveled the globe, continuing to visit the Iberian Peninsula and maintaining close relationships with Spanish and Portuguese architects. Seville and Santiago de Compostela both attracted him, Seville for its *corrals,* traditional Andalusian courtyards some of which dated back at least to the fifteenth century, and Santiago for its extraordinary medieval cathedral and venerable convents and monasteries. Even if he did not repeat visits to them, in his writings he referred regularly to the Spanish convents and churches, with their beautifully decorated retablos and their remarkable baroque architectures. The translation of *The Architecture of the City* into Spanish came as a result of his Spanish friends' efforts, the first of many publications by Rossi in Spanish. Fortunately, he had a gift for languages and a willingness to study to improve. In the last years of his life, he was studying Japanese, hoping at least to be able to carry on a conversation in a country where he had several projects. His skill in French, Spanish, and English were well known, but he also spoke and read German and Latin.

Rossi first traveled to the United States in 1976, with visits to Cornell University, Cooper Union, and the University of California, Los Angeles.[67] In spring 1977 he returned to the States, teaching at Cooper Union at the invitation of John Hejduk and at Cornell, and he soon began his short-lived collaboration with Peter Eisenman and the Institute for Architecture and Urban Studies (IAUS) in New York. In the following years, he spent time as visiting professor at Yale University and at Harvard, while continuing to travel and lecture at universities throughout the country. His response to U.S. schools of architecture struck a familiar chord: he resisted the drawn-out public juries at the end of the academic year, where jurists vied with one another to celebrate or excoriate the project or to evidence their own presumed erudition. For Rossi, the instructor's sacrosanct duty to advise the student should not be compromised; the juror should only identify one or more elements to praise in a design, and then move on. His lapidary and precise contributions baffled faculty members accustomed to long-winded, excruciating day-long events that, in Rossi's view, accomplished little.[68]

Rossi's drawings began to be published and exhibited during the 1970s, and the IAUS mounted the first exhibition of his drawings in the States in 1976, with a second in 1979.[69] The IAUS also decided to publish *The Architecture of the City* in the Opposition books series with MIT Press, to be followed by the as yet incomplete manuscript of *A Scientific Autobiography,* although ultimately the latter appeared first.[70]

Rossi labored for several years on *A Scientific Autobiography*, one of a handful of attempts he made to draft an autobiography.[71] Not surprisingly, one of his first efforts dates to December 1971, shortly after submitting his competition entry for the Modena cemetery and after he was suspended from teaching at Milan Polytechnic. In that early draft, as in *A Scientific Autobiography*, Rossi avoided a chronological sequence, opting instead for a slowly unwinding series of reflections that curve back and around his projects, buildings, and drawings while exploring his ideas about architecture generally, and the mysteries and joys of life more generally. Where his first book aimed to achieve a rigorously academic analysis of designing in the city as part of a methodology for studying and building in cities, the *Autobiography* explicitly emphasized the poetic dimensions of the same realities. Curiously, the second book appeared in English (1981) and Spanish (1984) nearly a decade before it appeared in Italian (1990).

The book opened with reflections on Dante Alighieri's initiation of the *Commedia* when the poet was about thirty years old, an age by which Rossi argued that one ought to be able to complete something definitive. Max Planck's autobiography, also titled *Scientific Autobiography*, instead had inspired him because of Planck's reflections on discoveries in physics about the conservation of energy, and, like Dante, Plank sought "happiness and death." As the chapters unfolded, Rossi reflected on his fondness for modifications, contaminations, repetitions, and fragments, and his fascination with the relation between exterior and interior in architecture. Certain figures, places, and architectures recurred regularly, such as the Sacri Monti (Sacred Mounts) of Lombardy and Piedmont in northern Italy; the enormous statue of San Carlo in Arona; the convents of Las Pelayas and Santa Clara in Santiago de Compostela; the Lichthof at the University of Zurich (fig. 1.13); St. John of the Cross's Mt. Carmel; Filarete's column in Venice; the abandoned houses in the *golena* (an embankment set below a higher one) of the Po Valley, among many others. Each place or object triggered reflections and memories while also prompting designs and drawings, where he believed the imaginative recuperation of memories and imagination allowed him to communicate beyond language. He recalled his early disparagement of memories and nostalgia, when he had reluctantly rejected history in the practice of architecture as most of his instructors had taught him to do, even while he acknowledged harboring a secret fondness for it. By the late 1950s, he had already begun to distance himself from both the rejection of history and the rigid dogmas of the modern movement and his youthful flirtation with Communist ideas. When Rossi referred to a book, a place, an artifact, or even his convalescence in a Yugoslav hospital following a terrible automobile accident, his reflections rejoined his architecture—an architecture now freshly infused

FIGURE 1.13
Lichthof, University of Zurich

with new material and in a very real sense contaminated by his personal experiences. The roster of Rossi's visual memories intertwined always with his deeper contemplations on life in general and on their meanings for him.

### LATE PROFESSIONAL PRACTICE

With his growing prominence came commissions and projects within Italy and internationally, the latter beginning in the 1980s with housing in Berlin for the IBA and at La Villette in Paris, along with projects in Japan, the United States, Canada, the Netherlands, France, London, Russia, and Turkey. Though many remained at the level of a project—quite common in the world of architectural practice—the drawings circulated widely, attracting more admirers and ultimately more commissions. By the late 1980s, the office had grown to the point where Rossi's longtime headquarters on Via Maddalena (originally a home studio) could no longer accommodate the flood of new work. The move to new quarters on Via Santa Maria alla Porta, though traumatic in some respects, facilitated the office's expansion, which in turn made it possible to pursue an ever-growing list of international projects.

Over the course of his career, Rossi formed several associations with other architects, starting with the Studio di Architettura founded in 1962 with Luca Meda and Gianugo Polesella. The first independent office he formed, with former student Gianni Braghieri, began in the early 1970s, with a shifting cast of architects collaborating on individual projects. Never a true partnership in the sense of handling business, locating clients, and participating fully in design, the association with Braghieri terminated in the early 1980s, with Rossi completing the formal dissolution in 1986.[72] He also formed two ongoing collaborations, one with Umberto Barbieri in Holland and one with Toyota Horiguchi in Japan. The sole successful formal partnership with Morris Adjmi in New York in the Studio di Architettura was responsible for much of the work in Asia as well as in the United States and some in Europe. In addition to architectural designs, Rossi produced prints and other works, particularly for fabrics and jewelry in the States. From the Milan office came primarily designs for projects in Italy and in Europe, as well as some of his prints, and all of the furniture, china service, coffeepots, clocks, wristwatches, and other objects designed for Bruno Longoni, Alessi, Unifor, Rosenthal, and Molteni. Starting with his earliest projects, Rossi collaborated with many architects, including Giorgio Grassi, Luca Meda, Gianugo Polesella and, for the La Fenice project, Count Francesco da Mosto.[73] In all cases, Rossi was the principal designer, as is evident in the evolution of the work itself.

Throughout these years, from 1968 forward, Rossi maintained a set of small blue notebooks, the *Quaderni Azzurri*.[74] In them he recorded his thoughts on architecture, on teaching, on his individual projects, on the books and poetry that he was reading, quotations from books or films, as well as brief notes on his travels. Occasional pauses of as long as five years interrupted them, and in some cases he included drafts of letters, of introductions to translations of his books, and reflections on life in general. Although after 1987 and the sale of the first thirty-two notebooks to the Getty Research Institute, he was always aware that they would become part of his legacy, they nonetheless reveal how his ideas matured and developed over time and how certain buildings and books exerted special influence on his ideas.[75] Notable is the virtually complete absence of discussions of the works of architects such as Le Corbusier and Mies van der Rohe which he appreciated, but from which he drew little inspiration. Instead, he dedicated a great amount of attention to baroque and neo-classical architecture, especially designs by Schinkel, to religious structures, and to his Catholicism. At times he illustrated the *Quaderni* with remarkably detailed colored drawings, only some of which he deliberately intended to be analytical. In short, they reveal a deeply cultured man with an unusually rich interior life, a man of faith, and a man locked in an enduring struggle to bring his ideas into built and written form.

A book entitled *Il libro azzurro* appeared in 1983, published with text in Italian, French, German, and English by a gallery in Zurich. This stunning, long out of print facsimile edition captured a notebook full of beautiful watercolors of some of Rossi's projects, along with his commentary. It also gave expression to his thoughts on drawing and painting, both of which by then constituted a body of work as well known as his architecture itself. After having been discouraged from continuing to study architecture by one of his first-year teachers on the grounds of his poor drawings, it is something of an irony that the drawings enjoyed wild success globally, well beyond the sphere of architecture.

After the Teatro del Mondo's triumph at the Venice Biennale in 1979–80, Biennale president Paolo Portoghesi summoned Rossi to take up the position of director of the Venice Architecture Biennale in 1985. Under the rubric of Progetto Venezia (The Venice Project), Rossi proposed an international competition designed to draw attention to the historic link between the city of Venice and the Venetian hinterland, known as the *terraferma*.[76] Rossi's attention to this area derived in part from his experience working on the new town hall for the terraferma community of Borgoricco, what amounted to the first step in the construction of a new town to be designed and built in the coming decades. Much earlier, he and colleagues had undertaken a profound study of certain parts of the Veneto region, which also served as the basis for the Biennale projects.[77] The competition rules for the Biennale solicited proposals for three sites in Venice (the Accademia Bridge, the Rialto Market, and Ca'Venier di Leoni) and seven sites in the terraferma: the piazzas of the towns of Badoere, Este, and Palmanova; Villa Farsetti in Santa Maria di Sala; Prato della Valle; the castles of Romeo and Juliet in Montecchio Maggiore; and the ancient fortress of Noale. For Rossi, proposing such sites encouraged architects to engage specific historical settings, to reflect on how to design in a complicated urban environment like that of Venice, and to tackle buildings and places long ignored and often in advanced states of decay. Each entrant received a booklet explaining the history and current state of the specific site, complete with photographs and plans. The meticulous presentation of the individual histories invited flights of imagination grounded in real settings—a challenge not picked up by all entrants. The obviously subversive intention in Rossi's Biennale plan came at a still heated moment in the struggle among different approaches to design, and when some of the first signs of the so-called deconstructivist movement had already appeared.[78] Decon, as it came to be known, rejected history, symmetry, and harmony in favor of disruption, fragmentation, and improbable forms. The Venice Project implicitly rejected this new fashion bereft then and later of a theory or even engagement with real problems in the built environment, let alone with tradition and history.

A veritable flood of competition entries arrived, pitting unknown students against prominent designers such as Guido Canella and Robert Venturi. From the nearly fifteen hundred submissions, in April the jury culled out five hundred for exhibition at the Biennale, publication in the catalogue, and consideration for the ten awards. In a decision that many found to be politically motivated rather than merit-based, the jury, headed by Claudio d'Amato (and which did not include Rossi or Portoghesi), awarded the ten Golden Lion plaques (designed by Rossi) to well-known foreign architects such as Raymond Abraham, Eisenman, Venturi, and Daniel Libeskind, and to friends and colleagues of Portoghesi.[79] Despite this unfortunate conclusion, the opportunity to exhibit work at the prestigious Third Architecture Biennale galvanized the imaginations of architects and students around the globe, and the five hundred selected projects appeared in the two-volume catalogue of the exhibit. Other than editing the catalogue, Rossi contributed the design of fanciful gateway arches at the entrance to the Biennale Gardens and along the path to the central pavilion (fig. 1.14). Flyers with images drawn from competition entries plastered the arches in celebration of the many solutions to the ten subjects proposed by architects and students from around the globe.

As director of the Biennale's architecture section, Rossi's choice for the 1986 event of an exhibit of drawings by Hendrik Petrus Berlage (1865–1934) confirmed his insistent pursuit of an architecture grounded in history and real sites. He assembled drawings by the Dutch architect and mounted the show not in Venice but in the terraferma, in the Villa Farsetti (Santa Maria di Sala), one of the ten sites of the previous Biennale. Berlage's focus on building in relation to history reflected the views of Rossi and Biennale president Portoghesi, and like the earlier Architecture Biennales, it countered prevailing facile fashion trends such as Deconstructivism.

A few years later, in 1990, Rossi received the most prestigious award in the field of architecture, the Pritzker Prize, only the thirteenth to have been awarded and the first to honor an Italian architect. In announcing the selection, the jury's citation noted that the theoretical framework outlined in *The Architecture of the City* served as the basis for "designs that seem always to be a part of the city fabric, rather than an intrusion."[80]

FIGURE 1.14
Aldo Rossi, Arch for 1985 Venice Biennale (ASAC, Archivio storico della Biennale di Venezia/ Giovanni Zucchiati)

Describing his work as "at once bold and ordinary," the jury also observed that Rossi "eschewed the fashionable and popular to create an architecture singularly his own." At the award ceremony at the seventeenth-century Palazzo Grassi in Venice, Rossi spoke of his love for architecture, his search for honesty in the making of buildings, and the joy this gave him. Rather than denigrating the infusion of cultural traditions from other places, he celebrated the felicitous contamination of different cultures in architecture just as he believed had happened in the age of Palladio. Memorably, the announcement included a drawing of the Modena cemetery and a picture of the coffeepot he had designed for Alessi, in addition to images of some of his buildings, particularly the Teatro del Mondo that had floated in the Venetian lagoon only a decade earlier. The very next year the United States recognized his accomplishments with yet another award, the Thomas Jefferson Medal, placing him among such luminaries as Mies van der Rohe, Alvar Aalto, and Frei Otto.

Beginning in the late 1980s, Rossi undertook a labor of love to remodel a house on the western shores of Lago Maggiore in the town of Ghiffa. Purchased as a weekend and holiday home for himself, the house originated as a working mill, but its transformation to a residence had long superseded that use. In this vacation house, with its enormous veranda on the upper floor, Rossi painted walls the blue that he loved—"il celeste della Madonna," as he liked to call that clear blue—and filled the rooms with old, comfortable furniture mixed with furniture he had designed, such as the two easy chairs, rug, and fireplace in the living room (fig. 1.15). At the heart of the house was the library and adjacent screening room, where he stored and screened for visitors his collection of movies and which became his private retreat (fig. 1.16). He had long spent summers or parts of

FIGURE 1.15
Aldo Rossi, Villa Rossi at Ghiffa, living room with two Molteni chairs and Sardinian carpet (Palladium)

summers and holidays in a villa on the shores of the small Lago Mergozzo just to the southwest of Verbania and Ghiffa and adjacent to the techno park he later designed in Fondotoce. Once he had purchased the villa, he found himself fondly remembering the earlier era identified in brief asides in *A Scientific Autobiography,* where he had spent family holidays and weekends, and where he enjoyed quiet time to write, to read, and to draw.

These years also saw Rossi taking road trips in the United States, first through the southwest, Texas, and southern California, and then a trip across the northern states to the Dakotas and Montana. Away from big urban areas and freed of the constraints of airplanes, Rossi enjoyed the breathtaking natural landscapes, something always of great interest to him, as well as the small towns, where time seemed to have paused several decades earlier. During none of these road trips was he writing in his *Quaderni Azzurri,* so only anecdotal accounts of some of the strongest impressions remain: his delight in big old American cars, his passion for old wristwatches that he found in pawnshops and antique stores across the southwest, the breathtakingly

FIGURE 1.16
Villa Rossi, library (Laura Fantacuzzi and Maxime Galati Fourcade)

different landscapes, from deserts to fields of grain to towering mountains and Montana's big sky. He experimented with new foods, as he always did when traveling, and he visited legendary sites such as Little Big Horn in eastern Montana, the Alamo in Texas, and Mount Rushmore in South Dakota. Visits to works of modern architecture such as Louis Kahn's Salk Center and Richard Neutra's houses, both in southern California, or the Kimbell Art Museum in Fort Worth, Texas, generally were few and far between. For his travels in the United States, he much preferred immersing himself in the texture of small town and rural life and in the bustle of big cities in an America that still seemed mythical to him.

### ARCHITECT AND FRIEND

Aldo Rossi was a deeply private person; nonetheless he had close friends sufficiently astute to realize how unique he was. Arduino Cantáfora, who painted the 1973 version of "La città analoga," spoke for many when he described Rossi as an extraordinarily fascinating storyteller, a raconteur who could hold a table spellbound like no other. Between him and other famous architects, Cantàfora lamented, yawned a huge abyss.[81] The raconteur manages to tell a tale, or carry a discussion, embellishing, brightening, and enlivening the narrative in unexpectedly delightful ways, with the purpose always being to delight listeners. One evening Rossi was introduced by Frank Gehry to the movie actor Dennis Hopper and the latter's then companion, a South American woman whom Hopper identified as a movie actress. Rossi asked her what films she had been in, and as she listed them, Rossi remarked that he had seen one or two of them. Her face lit up with undiluted joy as they proceeded to discuss the films in some detail. Later, in response to comments about the extraordinary coincidence, he responded that he had seen none of the films, but wasn't it wonderful to see how happy it had made her to think he had?[82] In this he followed one of his favorite ancient authors, Quintilian, who wrote that hyperbole is a common enough practice because everyone seems to want to embellish or diminish facts, for no one is content with the truth.[83] Indeed, in such circumstances Quintilian adjudged hyperbole a forgivable fault.

Perhaps more significantly, Cantàfora and others noted that in many respects Rossi was naive about the world and some of its inhabitants. Being of a "crystalline purity," as Cantàfora put it, he lacked the tools to recognize the exploiters, the manipulators, the malicious gossipers, the jealous hangers on, the liars. When the truth emerged, as it inevitably did about such sordid characters—some of whom stole from him, others who used and manipulated him shamelessly—he avoided confrontation and rarely even displayed anger.[84] Instead, he responded with dismay and disillusion. Though he remained cordial when he happened to encounter them, he simply distanced himself from those who wrap truth in darkness. He maintained strong relationships with Aymonino, Hejduk, Luca Meda, Canella, Portoghesi, and Vittorio Savi, among others, all of whom remained within his orbit even when, as in the case of Savi, Rossi sometimes doubted that he understood his architecture at all. Despite his unflagging courtesy, he soon parted ways with some of his earliest contacts in the States, on the other hand, such as Eisenman, Abraham, and Libeskind.[85] When students asked Rossi, at a summer session in Rome in 1985 with Carlo Aymonino, what architecture other than his own he liked, he responded simply, "I like the architecture of my friends."[86]

This naiveté extended well beyond architecture. When the U.S. visa request form asked whether he had ever been a member of the Communist Party or any related organizations, Rossi duly marked yes. This landed him for decades on the U.S. government list of potential terrorists, requiring him to jump through extraordinary hoops every time he sought a new visa. Although he eventually pursued legal action and managed to resolve the problem, it never ceased to amaze him that his colleagues in Italy, most of whom had been members of the party or related organizations for far more years than he, happily marked no and never encountered problems—Aymonino and Tafuri, among others.[87] Likewise, when the competition for the reconstruction of the La Fenice Theater in Venice came about, almost everyone in Italy soon learned that the destined recipient was Gae Aulenti, though chosen by whom and why never became clear. She collaborated with the firm of Impregilo to enter the competition, Impregilo being the construction arm of the Agnelli family's many business interests in Italy. Gianni Agnelli, family patriarch at the time, had a special fondness for Venice, where he had once employed Aulenti to remodel the interior of Palazzo Grassi—the elegant palace where Rossi received the Pritzker Prize in 1990 from the Pritzkers and the jury of which Agnelli was a member. Long before the La Fenice jury even met, according to some accounts Aulenti was ordering artisans in the Veneto to produce various details and decorations for the building. Nonetheless, Rossi secretly believed that he could prevail over the predetermined results if he produced a stunning design and expended enormous creative energy in presenting it with striking watercolors, model, and elaborately detailed presentation drawings. He may have been the only person in Italy to believe such an outcome possible—but believe he did.

This perennial optimism, even in the face of deeply corrupt and hypocritical academic and public institutions in Italy, marked everything that Rossi did. As is the case for many writers and artists, Rossi gravitated to those in whom he found traces of his own ideas, whether in the present or in history. In writing about Adolf Loos in 1959, Rossi drew attention to the Austrian's deep and remarkably prescient fear about the possibility of a new and more devastating world war—and yet, despite his apprehension, "he worked for a new world in the conviction that in the end, truth would prevail."[88] That Rossi's design eventually did prevail in the La Fenice competition suggests that his persistent optimism was not always misplaced.

Along with his wonder at the world, Rossi also nourished an enormous curiosity about it, eager to travel to new places, to explore and study them, beginning with that early group trip to the Soviet Union. Likewise, he loved to revisit places and discover them anew, always finding something unexpected or previously not understood—much as he particularly enjoyed seeing his favorite films many times because as he remarked, once he knew the outcome, he could enjoy all of the film's intricacies and details unburdened of suspense about the ending. Together, his experiences and passions contributed to that vast treasure trove of images, memories, and sensations from which his creative force issued. In the last years of his life, travel did begin to wear him down, not enough to stop but it became increasingly burdensome. He reflected on his increasingly long stays in Holland, Japan, New York, at times wondering where he actually lived. Nonetheless his delight in discovering new places never abandoned him, nor did that of returning to places beloved and known. On the one hand, he referred to himself as "the last true Milanese" when he cooked risotto alla Milanese for dinner, while on the other he considered himself a citizen of the world. The near constant jetting from Japan to Milan with stops in New York, New Orleans, Amsterdam, and other cities at times began to leave him somewhat disoriented. In 1991 he wrote: "I move about so often that I can no longer separate New York from Milan, that is, the two places where I live. Where do I live? I think of Ghiffa and the Lake, but also because these places by now are abstractions. Or perhaps all places are abstractions."[89] One cannot help but think of

FIGURE 1.17
Aldo Rossi, Molteni furniture: Milano chairs,
Carteggio desk, Momento Clock for Alessi
(Courtesy Morris Adjmi/Alexander Severin)

FIGURE 1.18
Aldo Rossi, Teatro del Mondo brooch for Acme, cloisonné and silver plate, 1988

FIGURES 1.19 AND 1.20
Aldo Rossi, Il Faro, Rosenthal China Service, coffeepot and plate, 1995

the comments on matters concerning a pilgrim such as Rossi by that most perceptive observer Hugh of St. Victor: "The man who finds his homeland sweet is still a tender beginner; he to whom every soil is as his native one is already strong; but he is perfect to whom the entire world is a foreign land.... From boyhood I have dwelt on foreign soil."[90] The pilgrim—as Rossi often described himself—always on the move, was ever on foreign soil, literally and figuratively. The enormous curiosity that drove Rossi made all soil foreign and thus new, ultimately becoming the springboard for his creativity. In his case it signaled his capacity for finding beauty overlooked by others, for finding unanticipated parallels, for being able to recall and juxtapose them in unexpected ways.

The last decade of Rossi's life saw the completion of some of his most important works: the Schützenstraße residential and commercial complex in Berlin; the Palazzo Hotel in Fukuoka, Japan; the Borgoricco town hall; the monument to Pertini in Milan; the Bonnefanten Museum in Maastricht; various projects for the Walt Disney Company. From the mid-1980s forward, however, Rossi became perhaps even more widely known for his product designs: coffeepots, wristwatches, clocks, and kitchenware designed for Alessi; fabrics, sofas, lamps, book cases, dressers, and other pieces of furniture for Molteni, Bruno Longoni, Unifor, and others; handmade Sardinian tapestries (fig. 1.17). For Rosenthal he designed three different china table services, and for Acme, jewelry for men and women, all based directly on his architectural designs (fig. 1.18). His drawings of the beach cabins on the island of Elba from the 1970s, for example, inspired not only pieces of furniture but also brooches, earrings, and the design of Rosenthal plates. The lighthouses that attracted him in Germany and the United States also turned into earrings, pins, and Rosenthal china (figs. 1.19, 1.20). The widely recognized La Conica coffee pot for Alessi (1980–83) combined the coffeepots of his childhood with some of his favorite architectural elements, particularly the cylinder and the inverted cone. In a brief essay on the coffeepot, he noted the simple, solid geometry of the rounded pyramidal form produced by rotating a right angled triangle. He loved the form and its name, also a play on the word "laconic" (*laconica*), which originated as a term describing the speech of the Spartan people in ancient Greece: direct, concise, tight, precisely as in the form of the coffeepot.[91] Designing such objects seemed like a vacation from architecture, he wrote, but also the domestic objects themselves attracted him: coffeepots, kettles, kitchen utensils, watches, lamps in some sense belonged to the abandoned house of childhood, or of senility.[92] Products such as the tea kettle (Il Bollitore) pleased him in part because they entered directly into the intimate, domestic lives of many more individuals than his architectures ever could (fig. 1.21).[93] Their enormous success surprised even Rossi, for whom the steady arrival of requests to design new objects amazed and always intrigued him, for the challenges differed from those of designing buildings.

To some critics, such products spelled a decline of Rossi's work into empty consumerism, surely a misguided understanding.[94] To design an everyday object such as a wristwatch or a coffeepot that differs from traditional models yet still functions superbly

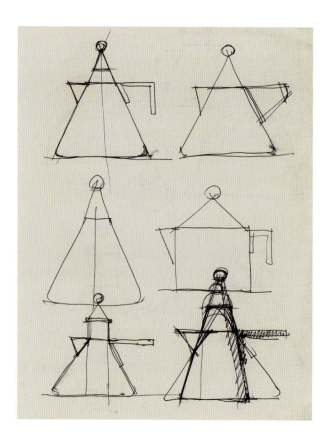

FIGURE 1.21
Aldo Rossi, Sketches for Il Bollitore, ink on paper, 1985 (MAXXI, Rossi © Aldo Rossi Heirs)

demands every bit as much ingenuity as designing a building. La Conica, for example, required three years of design development before the appropriate adjustments had been made for it to function perfectly. The Momento wristwatch (1987), an equally innovative yet functional creation, reflected the irresistible lure of timepieces for Rossi. He proposed an oversized bezel to allow the watch face and mechanism to be removed and placed in another one so that it could be worn either on the wrist or on a fob. Alessi had never manufactured watches, but at Rossi's suggestion the company took on the challenge and later produced watches and clocks by many other designers. While the new coffeepots and watches enjoyed great popularity, both types of objects had long intrigued the architect, as had the beach cabins of Elba and the colorful lighthouses, as documented in drawings some of which go back to his youth. With such an extensive history of drawing these artifacts, it seemed quite natural to take the next step to make them himself. Certainly neither type of product, nor the many others he designed, strayed far from those early and enduring objects of his affection. Why they could be understood as empty consumerism, as some critics disdainfully argued, remains a puzzle, unless the mere fact of popularity diminishes the elite status of other designs.[95] Rossi saw things differently. He saw in the success of his products a response to their simplicity, their ordinariness if you will, but that nonetheless brought beauty into the private domestic realm of many people, a result he found gratifying. Their broad appeal meant that his vision accorded with that of ordinary people, and this pleased him immensely. "I was anxious to see it built," he wrote of the coffeepot, "and above all at home or in people's houses and store windows. In fact I was not disappointed and it seems to me an object of my experience or my daily life.... These objects are presences in many houses and in general (in contrast to architecture) they please quite different [types of] people."[96]

Dismissing his work as melancholy or identifying a negative turn after the triumph of the cemetery at Modena fail to do justice to the extraordinary richness of Rossi's accomplishments as an architect and to the depth of his reflections on life as on architecture. Precisely because Rossi endeavored to explain his ideas, to expose his approach and his reflections to the viewer, we are obliged to take him seriously and ask how he transformed ideas and techniques into creative and compelling works of architecture, into beautiful domestic objects, into compelling drawings. The chapters that follow address specific categories of buildings, or architectural types, in Rossi's work. No attempt is made to produce a complete survey of all of Rossi's projects, and residential design in particular has been omitted and left for a future book. The effort instead remains that of grasping Rossi's theories as transmitted in the different kinds of objects he created, from the smallest brooch to a building covering an entire city block.

He proposed no recipe or new doctrine; on the contrary, typology constituted an analytical approach with which to identify building and urban types and thereby a first step in a long design process.[8] For Rossi the concept of type embraced at once locus and event, form and meaning, with locus understood in the most rich, complex fashion. The objective as he saw it entailed understanding the particular building, street, neighborhood, and district not just with an eye to the forms, but also to their specific histories prior to an architectural intervention, something impossible to anticipate in the absence of such analyses. No dogmas, no prescriptions, no templates: Rossi elaborated the varieties of elements in cities, the diverse forces that produced them, and the need for an architect to study precisely those matters with which, as he spelled out in *A Scientific Autobiography*, the second part of the equation—imagination and creativity—could be figured. In an essay in which he distinguished history from tradition in architectural production a decade after Rossi had won the competition for Modena's San Cataldo cemetery, Robin Middleton encouraged architects to engage tradition, by which he meant as an active agent in the production of their architecture. In his typically astute fashion, he identified the San Cataldo cemetery addition as the only recent architectural project that had initiated precisely that undertaking.[9]

In various writings, Rossi repeatedly encouraged his colleagues to abandon ideologies in favor of concrete facts. "We are far more interested in one page of Hans Schmidt on prefabrication in architecture than we are in the messages and scandals of 'modernism' and the 'monumentalism' of bad scholars," he wrote in 1973.[10] Many of the polemics in the field, he well knew, had more to do with political and personal animosities and posturing than with the real merits of specific works of architecture. Again and again he insisted: that which is specific to architecture commences with an exacting labor of historical analysis, followed by studies of the city, of topography, and of typology.[11] To clarify what he meant by type in *The Architecture of the City*, in 1973 Rossi returned to the point, specifying that "research on type [is the] foundation of architecture . . . above all type as a concrete element, a way of life of people in the city and the countryside through peculiar, specific forms conditioned by cultural and productive levels; typological forms that offer that assemblage of conditions that are not invented by architecture but upon which the architect intervenes only to perfect them, to bring them up-to-date for today's world."[12]

Although modern movement architects claimed to have done research on housing, he continued, their work began and ended in offices closed to the realities of the communities for which they were designing and without even the added grace of invention and imagination. He believed that these could come together in an architectural design neither simply technically sophisticated nor as the product of self-indulgent fantasy, but the result of a deeply informed, personal and socially engaged undertaking. That the results could not be anticipated went without saying; each project, each commission bespoke a new endeavor, beginning with the specifics of the site and its history, from which the solution proposed by the architect should spring. But it must also, in Rossi's view, bring the architect's imaginative capacity into play, and this too should be the object of profound, repeated, and rigorous exploration. Enriched by readings in literature, poetry, philosophy, theology, and art, the design should also arise from close observation of how people live in a particular place, how they understand their world, and how architects understand theirs. Such concepts elude precise definition, Étienne Louis Boullée understood, but he ended up no more successful in explaining them. Rather than dismissing these considerations as unimportant, Rossi knew the need for ongoing research, and he always understood the process of developing a design as involving a dialectical relationship between individual project and creative imagination.

The test, or rather the measure, of Rossi's theory is how he developed it in his own work, how he followed his own method to produce his designs. In this and the succeeding chapters, we will explore projects of several types to do just that, to measure the extent to which his theory did in fact serve as a foundation for his design process. In the following chapters we will consider his commemorative monuments, buildings for culture, theaters, and cemeteries, while in this chapter we begin with the Scholastic Building and consider other urban-based projects for commercial use, combined commercial and residential use, and infrastructure.

❖ ❖ ❖

The Scholastic Company has been publishing children's books, materials for schools, and art supplies, among other things, since its founding in the 1920s by Maurice Robinson. The company had long occupied the old Rouss Dry Goods building at 555 Broadway, but the company decided in the early 1990s to expand into the adjacent space, at the time occupied only by a lumber company and a small garage. Although the founder's son and president, Richard Robinson, considered many architects for what all feared would be a difficult task, when he met Rossi he knew he had found his designer. Within minutes, Rossi had sketched out a solution that sold Robinson, an idea that came together with respect for the Cast Iron District without sacrificing the distinct presence of a new structure.

Preservationists zealously guard SoHo's Cast Iron Historic District, making it one of the most difficult parts of a notoriously difficult city in which to build.[13] The cast-iron façades explain why. Their beauty and rhythms—long appreciated only by the artists who took over decaying, cavernous lofts in which to create their art—became visible to others when the grime of years of neglect began to dissolve slowly at the ministrations of new tenants. Once freshly painted, the prefabricated columns, cornices, arched window frames, elaborate stringcourses, egg and dart moldings, and other splendid details emerged in all their glory and visual richness. Even though builders had quite literally bolted the cast-iron plates onto the framework behind, they appear as firm and dignified as the masonry buildings around them, as solid as the stones of the Parthenon.

FIGURE 2.2
Scholastic Building, detail with adjacent Little Singer Building (1903) (Courtesy Morris Adjmi/Paul Warchol)

On Broadway between Prince and Spring Streets, only two buildings have complete cast-iron façades, but many have cast-iron store fronts on the lower levels. The two of most interest in relation to the Scholastic Building are those adjacent to it, the Rouss building to the south by architect Alfred Zucker, and the Little Singer building by Ernest Flagg to the north. The Rouss building (1889) lost its original storefronts on the first two floors over the course of the twentieth century, but its ten-story, twelve-bay masonry elevation nonetheless stands as a commanding presence on the street. Dun-colored projecting granite blocks capped by elaborately carved capitals frame four large bays, in turn subdivided into twelve smaller ones through to the upper story, where fluted pilasters mark the corners. The building maintains an elegant, austere, even subdued appearance despite the surprising twin gables atop the deep cornice on the top level. Only the colonnettes and spandrel panels framing the windows of the smaller bays are fabricated of cast iron.

The Little Singer building (1903) on the other side does indeed have a cast-iron façade, interspersed with terracotta and glass, one of the most unique in the entire district (fig. 2.2). A taller twelve-story structure, Little Singer's green and burnt umber detailing yields a far lighter, more delicate façade. Elaborate and highly visible ironwork blossoms in the delicate foliate tracery on the balconies and brackets, which then curves over and frames the eleventh-floor windows. Terracotta panels form stringcourses and frame the windows on either end. Lively and colorful, the Little Singer presented the biggest formal challenge as Rossi designed the building next door. As he always insisted, however, the formal aspects followed rather than preceded design choices. To respond to the solid sobriety of the one and the colorful gaiety of the other at once would tax any designer.

By the time Rossi met Robinson, Rossi had lived for ever greater periods of time in New York, with over twenty years spent observing and analyzing its neighborhoods. He had studied the district and how its residents lived, so the quick sketch he produced for Robinson sprang from long and careful analysis. Loft living for artists requires light, for example, and so for the artist residents of the Little Singer he eventually came up with two large light wells to make that possible. Unlike the adjacent Rouss building, this new structure would have more public functions, with a shop on the ground floor and a large theater-auditorium space for meetings and lectures in the cellar level, mostly below ground. Finally, the building would extend through the block to Mercer Street, a

FIGURE 2.3
Scholastic Building, Mercer Street elevation
(Courtesy Morris Adjmi/Paul Warchol)

FIGURE 2.4
Krupp Colliery, Schacht Amalie, Essen, Germany (Ruhrpottler/ Fotocommunity)

narrower and quite different street, with bluestone and granite curbstones lining streets paved with traditional Belgian blocks.

One of the oldest houses in the district sits on this block of Mercer, with its elaborate wood detailing and even an intact, original fanlight. For the most part, however, shops, lofts and small-scale manufacturing buildings, such as for carpenters, line the street. Many of the façades recede behind metal fire escapes, the kind that Rossi loved, and loved to draw, on New York's typical brick elevations. Service entries for larger stores on Broadway can also be found up and down Mercer Street. An elegant public presence did not serve here, so Rossi developed a tougher, more industrial look (fig. 2.3). Metal flanges with outsized rivets march up the full height of the building to frame the same type of pale gray-green I-beams and narrow mullions as found on the Broadway elevation. In great industrial architecture, from Ferdinand Dutert's Gallery of Machines for the 1889 Paris Exposition to the Krupp coal factory of Sälzer-Amalie in Essen (1934), Rossi saw the rare beauty and simplicity of painted steel flanges, so he chose to adopt a brilliant rusty red rather than the bright green of the Essen factory on the Mercer elevation (fig. 2.4).

On Broadway, the Scholastic Building presents the company's public face: pale gray-green quoins enclose the three bays of alternating rusty red and pale gray I-beams up to a deep, three-tier cornice. In between, four rows of simple white cylindrical columns distinguish the tripartite division. At the upper level, smaller cylinders mark the transition from the large bays to the cornice. On the one hand Rossi picked up the rhythm of the stone bays on the Rouss building, while on the other, the colors and window rhythms of the Little Singer building. In short, he negotiated the essential features of the two structures in a less ornate, more modern language. To be sure, some of his favored features appear, such as the Filarete-inspired column in combination with the horizontal I-beam, elements he deployed in many different ways but always with a purpose. Here, respect for the architectural rhythms and living patterns encouraged a contemporary version in harmony with the old. For Rossi, the core of the architect's charge never languished on the level of pure function; instead, he believed architecture expressed a civic consciousness that emerged from a search for common values.[14] Historic buildings expressed those values, as should those of today. While the original Filarete column had by then entered into his architectural vocabulary, more importantly

FIGURE 2.5
Aldo Rossi, Schützenstraße Quarter, Berlin, 1992 (Claudio Davizi)

it was a feature of a tradition which he believed each of his projects would join and thereby enrich. That the elements would be clear and legible to the public constituted the ultimate test of their appropriateness.

The Scholastic Company acquired fame and riches nearly instantly when it joined with Bloomsbury Press in London to gamble on an unknown writer, a woman on welfare—J. K. Rowling—to publish her Harry Potter book series beginning in 1997. Scholastic's new image on Broadway could not have come at a better moment.

A comparison of the Scholastic project with a residential-commercial complex in Berlin, the Schützenstraße Quarter from 1992, helps clarify the ways Rossi's theories about cities and architecture cohered with his architectural designs (fig. 2.5). Only a few dozen meters separate this block from the Checkpoint Charlie of the old divided city, in an area formerly known as Berlin's newspaper district, home of most of the dozens of daily newspapers that flooded Berlin prior to World War II.[15] Thoroughly bombed during the war, the district suffered its next grievous blow with the erection of the Berlin Wall in 1961. The block bounded by Schützenstraße, Markgrafenstraße, Zimmerstraße, and Charlottenstraße was located in East Berlin and had remained empty of buildings until Rossi received the commission in 1992. He had visited Berlin many times since his early years as an architecture student, and by the time of the Schützenstraße Quarter project, he had already built or designed several important works in the city, including the house on Verbindungskanal (1976), the southern Friedrichstadt IBA residential complex (1981), the house in Rauchstraße in Berlin Tiergarten (1983), and perhaps most important, his winning competition entry for the German Historical Museum (1988).

Berlin's urban texture in this historically dense part of the city suffered interruption with the division of the city from the 1960s forward, in effect meaning that speculators and real estate brokers were shut out of East Berlin for more than thirty years.[16] At the same time, Berlin's post–World War II urban fabric contained large areas of run-down buildings and a lively alternative culture, some of which drifted to the older areas of the east city after the wall collapsed, attractive also to pensioners and other low income groups primarily for the low rents but also for their decidedly nonbourgeois appearance.[17] That the two forces—speculators and alternative cultures—came into conflict should have surprised no one. New York's SoHo district had a similar history of struggle and alternative cultures, artists' lofts and cheap rents, and its own successful battle against a freeway, but in neither case could the juggernaut of speculation be stayed. For the real estate market, updated, renovated, and new buildings signaled prosperity, growth and exceptional profits; for alternative culture groups, "dilapidation is worn on the face of buildings as a mark of distinction from mainstream landscapes."[18] The not unreasonable dream of such groups has been to create more democratic urban spaces, with more affordable housing and shops for larger numbers of people, rather than enclaves of wealth and gentrified privilege. To be sure, alternative cultures in cities such as New York and Berlin may celebrate dilapidation, but cities where huge populations live in squalid shanties, as in São Paolo, Brazil, rarely share romantic views about grit and rough-looking areas. This perhaps is because such communities have fewer choices than those of more prosperous societies, which have social safety nets, where occupants are often there by choice, and in some cases they enjoy the opportunity to move elsewhere.[19] In any event, groups in Berlin waged a steady war on efforts to substitute chic restaurants, art galleries, and the like for low rent and unrestored buildings.

Rossi wrote repeatedly about the negative effects of speculation on cities and on the inequities of capitalist cities.[20] He also confronted the question of how to treat old cities in the aftermath of the devastating bombings of World War II. By the time he wrote an essay entitled "What to Do with Old Cities?" in 1968, hasty and poor decisions abounded in what had been some of Italy's most beautiful cities. Earlier, in his 1956 assessment of Milan's architecture, Rossi sharply criticized the quality and character of the buildings then being erected hastily to repair wartime damage. He sympathized with the concerns expressed by those who resisted the changes taking place before their very eyes, but perhaps for different reasons:

> By now the theme of an Italy or a Europe to save with absolute respect for the environment seems accepted.... Continually and fatally, the environment formed of small structures, of old buildings, of the houses of the past dear to memory, of colors, of peeling stucco, [that] crumble, alter, change, are transformed into something... thus cities change before our eyes.... We do not know how to justify losing this lesson of ancient misery dear to us as testimony to the pain of a people; so we

preserve the laundries of Lodi or Milan along the canals, and the courts of the farmhouses as a museum of this pain.... I believe that when the image of the old streets of misery has entirely disappeared even from within ourselves, we will have lost the meaning of the beauty of these environments.[21]

Perhaps Rossi glimpsed the problems and contradictions too clearly to accept the idea that a certain, single answer could prevail in different conditions. Could application of the theory and methodology outlined in *The Architecture of the City* result in better cities? In the end, it came down to choices to be made in specific settings, on specific sites, with their unique circumstances and problems. His public housing projects such as the Gallaratese and the Berlin IBA, all erected on the periphery of their respective cities, afforded ample opportunity to counter some of the forces of speculation. Notably, the Schützenstraße Quarter did not uproot communities, nor destroy or take over buildings occupied by squatters: the war and the Wall had already taken care of that. The street's early history also lacked great architectural distinction, but that old quixotic streetscape offered clues for rebuilding in the area (fig. 2.6). A 1905 photograph documents an urban fabric of shops with housing above, perhaps some small-scale manufacturing, but also buildings with pretensions to grandeur on the left and right, with quoins, deep classical cornices, pedimented and segmental arches for window frames. Over the next decades, this and adjacent streets were built up, replacing the low-scale live-work structures with more elaborate, five- to six-story residences and office buildings, which were then destroyed during World War II. With the Scholastic Building, the questions involved fitting into an existing, lively historic setting, while with Schützenstraße, Rossi would have to create a new setting. Other than the old photos of the street, where should he start?

FIGURE 2.6
8 Schützenstraße, 1905

The city's traditional *Mietskasernen*, rental barracks, paradoxically provided the best opening. These full-block buildings arose to meet the housing needs of a continually expanding urban working class in the early phases of industrialization in Berlin.[22] Symbols of the rise of industrial capitalism, the *Mietskasernen* usually consisted of tiny apartments that provided the bare minimum for existence. Poor ventilation and lighting made them unusually unhealthy by comparison with other Berlin housing schemes for more prosperous groups, even if both lacked adequate sanitation facilities. Indeed, Rossi remarked that these and other complexes needed to be neither "machines for living in" nor to have the Frankfurt Kitchen, when adequate sanitary facilities and more space would have sufficed.[23] Poverty remained the problem. Landlords repeatedly flouted building regulations that

48  ARCHITECTURE AND THE CITY

required maintaining adequate courtyards for both ventilation and light, with building inspectors fighting against landlords' desire to keep squeezing additional units into the courtyards and collecting more rents. Spacious apartments for the upper classes often lined the street fronts, while miserable tiny units spread out behind them in rabbit warrens of passageways and courtyards. By the second half of the twentieth century, and especially after 1980, these blocks slowly underwent transformation, with small apartments merged to form larger ones, accompanied by running water, sanitation facilities, and other amenities common to modern urban housing.

Rossi chose for the Schützenstraße site a full-block scheme with three courtyards, one of which is octagonal, all accessed by the traditional long passageways that cut through the entire block (fig. 2.7). The complex covers almost 8,500 square meters (more than 91,000 square feet), accommodates both commercial and residential uses, and includes up to four floors underground. For the four street elevations Rossi crafted twelve different façade types, repeating and varying parapets, attics, thresholds, and window treatments. Colors drawn from a rich and varied palette—from bright primary colors such as red, blue, and green to more muted terracotta red bricks, two tones of stone, pale yellows, ruddy oranges, and baby blue—define each unit in an orchestrated harmony of style and color. Too brash for some, luminous and cheerful for others, for Rossi, the colors brightened a city often shrouded in low, gray clouds. Precisely because of the site's rawness, Rossi could freely turn for inspiration to strategies common to architects around the globe: copying the design of a past master. In this case, for the old 8 Schützenstraße, Rossi substituted a bay of the Palazzo Farnese in Rome, as designed by Michelangelo and Antonio Sangallo the Younger (fig. 2.8). The grand section framed by pale gray pilasters rises to a deep cornice modeled precisely on the Roman one, with the other details—triglyphs, garlands, segmental and pedimented window frames set within arches and entablatures—in gray stone against a white stucco backdrop. With his love for historic architecture, reproducing a classic and elegant façade for a structure with more modest pretensions made it worthwhile; for Rossi, this was an exercise in pure joy. While Schinkel had brought the ancient Greek stoa into the heart of Berlin with the elevation of the Altes Museum in 1830, Rossi introduced an element of the Renaissance not far away in this urban block. And the choice was not frivolous. Rossi found that the long, tunnel-like passages through the historic *Mietkasernen* bore striking similarities to the long *androni* (entrance halls) into and out of the Palazzo Farnese's courtyard, prompting him to adapt one bay of its façade for one of the bays on Schützenstraße.

Reference points for the lively collection of façades Rossi assembled in the Schützenstraße complex extended well beyond Italy; they abounded closer to home, specifically in many of the nineteenth- and early-twentieth-century buildings in the former East Berlin. The faded beauties of residential and office buildings in Kollwitzkiez on Straßberger Platz reveal splendid *serliane* over doorways, slender columns beneath I-beam entablatures, tight, two-bay elevations with varied window patterns. On a

FIGURE 2.7
Schützenstraße Quarter, entrance to courtyard
(Nina Aldin Thune)

FIGURE 2.8
8 Schützenstraße (Julie G. Woodhouse/Alamy)

high-rise on Weberweise, ceramic tile revetments rise between decorative columns. Rossi's elevations draw upon such richly varied remnants of old Berlin.

The methodology Rossi pursued varied not at all between the two projects, one in New York's SoHo and one in Berlin, and this is precisely the reason the results differ so markedly. Considering each site, its history, its living patterns, its role in the larger community, constituted the first step in both instances, only afterwards to be followed by the development of a new, creatively fabricated type. Each was tailored to the setting but open to the architect's lyrical engagement with the site's unique features and with the same types of historic architecture that inspired the existing urban structures.

In a similar mixed-use project on the periphery of Verona at Ponte Crencano dating from 1993 and also on an unoccupied piece of land, Rossi referred back to his long-ago studies of the cities of the Veneto region to consider various types, materials, colors, and building patterns.[24] This extended research into the urban and architectural history

FIGURE 2.9
Aldo Rossi, Ca' di Cozzi Complex, Ponte Crencano, Verona, 1996

of cities such as Verona afforded an opportunity to identify and compare their chief characteristics, isolating the singular aspects of each. Verona retains a remarkable group of Roman ruins—amphitheater, theater, bridge, and, equally important, the street network, including the piazzas and the sites these and other monuments occupy. Verona also became a powerful center in the middle ages, as evident in the walls constructed by the Scaligeri and Visconti overlords, in the Duomo erected and transformed over the centuries, in the market structures and squares still vibrant today. These august remnants of past glories nonetheless remained distant from Via Ca' di Cozzi, its semi-rural site remote from such remarkable structures. Instead, the architect confronted an open, empty field; to create a place became the challenge.

The complex now situated on Via Ca' di Cozzi, just north of Verona not far from the Adige River, includes residential and commercial properties and administrative offices (fig. 2.9). For this site in Borgo Trento on the periphery of the city, Rossi chose to emphasize views of the northern hills and to use strictly local materials, stucco and brightly tinted tiles, alternating bands of the typical red Verona marble with *biancone*, a lightly veined, very strong local marble, exactly as found in traditional Veronese architecture. The two primarily commercial/office buildings recall the barrel vaulting of nearby Vicenza's Palladian Basilica, and the white stone columns along the front elevation set on high bases follow Palladio's model for columns on church façades. The references to local and regional traditions underscore how an element as simple as a cylindrical column can achieve quite different effects (fig. 2.10). In this setting, with its unique history and traditions, Rossi deployed I-beams, cylindrical columns, square windows, and pediments in ways that recalled the architecture of the Veneto region, where similar elements at the Schützenstraße Quarter or the Scholastic Building instead spoke directly to their individual settings. In other words, here Rossi emphasized local building traditions and materials, and rather than emulating the city's rich architectural heritage he elected to privilege harmony with the surrounding landscape. The simple architectural forms accomplished what Rossi sought, for he wanted them to be legible to everyone. A comparison with those of the indifferently mediocre structures erected over the succeeding two decades most tellingly reveal the strength of Rossi's ideas.

Rossi designed or completed several other office buildings or mixed-use complexes during the 1980s and 1990s, including a nearly contemporary office building on Landesberger Allee in Berlin (1992), a new administrative center and renovation of the old hospital in Hasselt, Belgium (1992), and the GFT office building, called Casa Aurora, in Turin (1984), each unique in its expression even while including some of Rossi's most cherished elements. The Casa Aurora, for example, replaced a smaller office building

51  ARCHITECTURE AND THE CITY

FIGURE 2.10
Ca' di Cozzi Complex, portico

on the corner of Corso Giulio Cesare and Corso Emilia at a site just north of the Dora River and Turin's historic center, in a Borgo Dora district known as Aurora (dawn; fig. 2.11). Historically, Borgo Dora contained many of the city's manufacturing facilities, a tradition dating back at least to the late middle ages, when the area began to be noted for its production activities. Leather, hemp, oil, and silk factories along with granaries, water mills, and foundries dominated for several centuries, with the city's textile production largely centered here. With industrialization came factories, and with factories came workers and worker housing, much of which no longer exists; squalor and poverty dominated for people poorly paid for their labor and who therefore lived in ramshackle housing.

The Gruppo Finanziario Tessile (GFT) commissioned Rossi's building for its new headquarters to replace one on the same site that had been demolished. Famous for having brought ready-to-wear clothing to Italy, the GFT also launched some of the country's most famous fashion brands, from Giorgio Armani to Valentino. Like much of Turin, the area mixes residential and office buildings, with a late-nineteenth-century elementary school just across the street on Corso Giulio Cesare and residential buildings with shops on the ground floor on the other two corners. A large garden with playground equipment, trees, and benches, dedicated to Mother Teresa of Calcutta, occupies about a third of the block behind Rossi's building. No particular architectural style distinguishes the area, which had undergone a nearly complete transformation over the previous century by the time the GFT decided to erect new offices. Nonetheless, certain elements of the surrounding buildings and of Turin's architecture more generally offered possible references for Rossi's design. In the nondescript apartment block across the street on via Emilia as well as the elementary school, for example, we find the same division of darker base, lighter middle block topped by either an elaborate stringcourse or a projecting cornice. Rossi inverted the pattern by setting the L-shaped Casa Aurora on a base of a pale local stone, topped by two brick-clad floors, with stone and green painted I-beams forming porticoes along the Corso Emilia and Corso Giulio Cesare elevations. Unfenestrated brick towers anchor the building at each of its three corners, while a pair of giant white columns extending to the second floor, topped by a deep green I-beam lintel, marks the entrance. The corner treatment of the GFT also mirrors that of the nearby elementary school, with the elbow of the complex set at an angle.

FIGURE 2.11
Aldo Rossi, GFT Office Building, Casa Aurora, Turin, 1984 (Palladium)

FIGURE 2.12
Adolf Loos, Looshaus, Michaelerplatz, Vienna, 1909 (Gugerell)

Once again, Rossi's first step was to respond to the site, its history, and its current character. In this instance, he also turned to the history of architecture, specifically to the Looshaus (formerly the Goldman and Salatsch building) in Vienna (1909–11).[25] Some ten years earlier Rossi had described the blurred frontier between his architecture and that of Loos, so deeply had he absorbed the Viennese master's lessons.[26] The Casa Aurora illustrated what Rossi had learned from Loos by referencing the Looshaus on the Michaelerplatz, one of Vienna's historically richest sites (fig. 2.12).[27] Anchoring this plaza on the south end was the Hapsburg dynasty's vast Hofburg palace, dating from the thirteenth through the early twentieth century, and directly to the east stands the venerable Michaelerkirke. A Roman-era villa whose remains archaeologists had recently unearthed provided the foundation for the Michaelerkirke, and documents attest to a church on the site at least in the eleventh century. Joseph Fischer von Erlach redesigned the plaza in the early eighteenth century, giving regularity and order to a formerly haphazard street arrangement. Having published *Ornament and Crime* only two years before receiving this Looshaus commission, Loos remained true to his dictum and designed a largely unornamented structure with a dark base for the ground and mezzanine levels dedicated to commercial activities, four stories of whitewashed walls punctuated by regular window openings for apartments, and above the cornice a green copper roof. At the entrance, four grand, deeply and colorfully grained marble columns set on black bases hold aloft an I-beam, with bow windows framed by smaller columns above. For Loos as for Rossi—and in direct opposition to the strident avatars of the modern movement—columns informed the European urban landscape throughout history, and, as such, they functioned appropriately for such a building. From Loos then, Rossi drew the colonnaded entrance with I-beam, though tightened and blazed with bright colors for the site in Turin. Nonetheless, the references remained only that: among other differences, two white cement columns rather than four richly colored marble ones, no piers,

54   ARCHITECTURE AND THE CITY

and Rossi provided simple square windows for the upper stories in contrast to the bow and rectangular ones at the Looshaus. But that Rossi paid homage to Loos in his Casa Aurora project simply affirms what Rossi brought to every project: a rich understanding of architectural history and of the history of each specific setting, including the fact that both the Goldman and Salatsch Company and GFT produced clothing, which renders the subtle homage to the Looshaus doubly appropriate.

One of the most controversial office developments for Canary Wharf in London's Docklands remained unbuilt. East London enjoyed a long and colorful history of riverside industries that late-twentieth-century revolutions in shipping such as containerization truncated abruptly in the second half of the century. A vast area of basins and abandoned wharves and buildings, renamed an "enterprise zone," enticed financial capital to invest in reconstructing part of this area, the Isle of Dogs, into new headquarters for London's burgeoning financial industry. Canadian developer Olympia and York commissioned giant corporate architectural firms such as SOM, Cesar Pelli, Pei Cobb Freed & Partners, and Kohn Pederson Fox to produce buildings for the Docklands, but the company also selected Rossi to design two buildings. As unabashedly colorful and original as the Scholastic Building, the Schützenstraße complex, and the Il Palazzo Hotel in Fukuoka, Japan, the two barrel-vaulted structures bore the familiar oxidized green copper roof, paired cylindrical columns at the main entrances, along with the I-beams as lintels typical of much of his later architecture. Had they been built, they would have cast into high relief the conventional tedium of the neighboring buildings. In an essay on his design, Rossi outlined the reasons the project intrigued him—chiefly, the opportunity to participate in "the creation of 'the city.'" He linked the two structures with a gray and white stone colonnade, and he named the larger of the two buildings facing the river a basilica, presumably in part because of the classicizing details and also the red and pink stone (a rose red Indian sandstone) of the base set against white Carrara marble. Here Rossi drew on a tradition of cathedral and baptistery building in Italy where delicately veined white Carrara marble was often set against a darker stone, such as in the baptistery at Parma. The barrel-vaulted structures also summon references to the secular version of a basilica, the Basilica Palladiana in Vicenza. The colors, especially the red sandstone imported from India, he imagined as rendered austere by London's overcast skies and the mistiness that casts a sheen on everything, while the Portland yellowish white sandstone blended with the city's gray skies. He imagined the project oriented primarily toward the water, to the memory of the port, urging the developers to imagine walkways not unlike Venice's Riva degli Schiavoni, amplified by the parks and gardens so typical of London.[28] A financial downturn led Olympia and York to abandon the project, even though the underground parking had been completed.

Rossi's Italian projects enjoyed great success, as did most of those discussed above, but did this repeat elsewhere? How did his methodology and analyses apply with quite different types of structures, those dedicated to transient populations such as airports, port facilities, hotels, or shopping centers? What, finally, can we understand of his theory of architecture and the city from his built work? And especially, what happened when he left cities and countries with which he enjoyed long familiarity to essay projects in places with cultural traditions remote from his own?

### ARCHITECTURE FOR TRANSIENTS

By the time he received the Pritzker prize, Rossi had lived much of his life traveling the globe, so he took great delight in receiving the commission to enlarge Milan's Linate airport (1991–93); it seemed only fitting that he too should design a building type with which he had accumulated so much experience. Linate as the smaller of Milan's two airports primarily supports national and European flights (fig. 2.13). In 1933, Gianluigi Giordani designed an elegant streamlined modern airport that soon lost its architectural identity in a sequence of poorly planned additions. Rossi's charge included providing a new gateway to the city. Changing technologies, increasing numbers of passengers, and heightened security apparatus all had contributed to a broad rethinking of some aspects of airport architecture over the previous half century. To be sure, the events of 9/11 in 2001 and the consequent new requirements for security facilities helped transform airport design even more, as did the ruthless initiative of airport operators to force passengers to traverse interminable halls of luxury and other goods before arriving at their gates. In any case, even before that calamity, changes in airport design had not always improved matters. Eero Saarinen's TWA terminal at JFK airport in New York (1962) proposed the form of a bird in flight so faithfully that it soon became a white elephant, but not soon enough to discourage others from adopting a similar strategy: Santiago Calatrava with the Sondika Airport in Bilbao, Spain (2000), and even as recently as 2015 with Zaha Hadid's Beijing airport. Most architects have chosen instead the oversized shed model (Murphy/Jahn, United Airlines Terminal, Chicago O'Hare, 1987; Foster and Partners, Stansted Airport, U.K., 1991; Renzo Piano Workshop, Kansai International Airport, Japan, 1994). This architecture—resolutely white—lays claim only to gigantism, glass, and glare.

Not surprisingly, having spent considerable time in such airports, Rossi did what he always did: he looked and learned. He flatly rejected the pretentiousness of some and the blandness of the others, proposing instead a far more traditional and colorful facility. Marked by slender piers to form a colonnade at the entrance, the cheerful green and yellow painted steel columns abut revetments of richly grained Candoglia and Baveno marbles. Rossi, working with Uniplan (Virgilio and Matteo Vercelloni), also treated the windows like those in a house or a studio. Though not completed as planned, the rest of the interiors would have come alive with images of Milan, producing inside and out an almost magical rhythm of color and form, vibrant and lively without succumbing to either the kitsch or the tedium of most contemporary airports.

FIGURE 2.13
Aldo Rossi, Linate Airport, Milan, 1989 (Marco Introini)

Unfortunately, transit facilities tend to be among the worst, most poorly maintained structures in many cities—New York's subway system being a prime example. Occasionally opportunities to rethink some aspect of public transport do appear, as was the case with the Whitehall Ferry Terminal competition (1992) for the Staten Island ferry. It presented a set of problems quite different from those of an airport.[29] For one thing, the long tradition of urban waterfronts as shipping centers for loading, unloading, and storing goods historically determined their shape and character across the globe, with passenger comfort not high on the list of priorities.[30] As technologies shifted from sail to steam to oil, so too did shorelines undergo transformation in the nineteenth and twentieth centuries. The advent of railroad tracks terminating directly at ports also inaugurated major changes. In sum, steady modifications led finally to the gradual loss of shorelines to public view—to say nothing of the highways that further eroded the urban coast's visibility, such as the famous Embarcadero Freeway in San Francisco (1968; demolished 1991).[31] Landfill extended along the urban shorelines of New York as of other

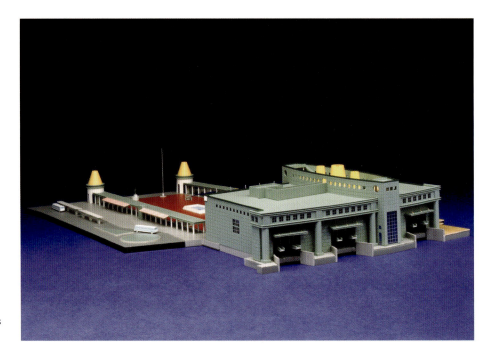

FIGURE 2.14
Aldo Rossi, Whitehall Ferry Terminal, New York, 1992, model: painted plexiglas, wood, brass (Courtesy Morris Adjmi/Ned Matura)

American port cities, with those of New York dating back to the city's seventeenth-century origins. Over the intervening centuries, as public and private entities negotiated jurisdictions and rights, piers and other facilities expanded along almost the entire coast of Manhattan. In 1992, while the city considered new strategies for accommodating ferries at different points on the coast, a fire devastated Manhattan's Staten Island ferry terminal, the Whitehall Ferry Terminal, prompting the decision to mount a competition for a new, modern facility. This ill-fated venture brought proposals from six architects, including Rossi. Venturi Scott Brown was awarded the project, but the toxic combination of politically motivated mayors (Rudy Giuliani of New York and Guy Molinari of Staten Island) and an ambitious and vocal architect (Peter Eisenman) engineered opposition to several aspects, including the oversized clock the firm proposed. In response, the Port Authority demanded such major changes that Venturi Scott Brown withdrew, leaving the task in the hands of a former employee, Frederick Schwartz. In return, Eisenman received—briefly—a commission for a new terminal on the Staten Island end, the St. George Terminal, courtesy of mayor Molinari.[32]

How did Rossi choose to address the problem of a major waterfront site in New York, where virtually every real estate transaction—with the remarkable exception of the Scholastic Building—turned into a pitched battle among residents, funds-hungry city agencies, and profit-hungry developers (fig. 2.14)? If the project could both serve the daily flux of commuters to and from Staten Island as well as forge a link between the financial district and the waterfront, then it would be a success, rendering at least this part of the shoreline publicly accessible again. By extending the terminal out to align with the Battery Maritime Building (1908), Rossi proposed linking his structure to its closest neighbor, a distinguished building listed since 1976 on the National Register of Historic Places. Ferries to Governor's Island leave from this Beaux Arts structure crafted of several types of metal, including cast iron, rolled steel, zinc, and copper. One of its chief beauties, Guastavino tile vaults set under the porch, consists of an arch system patented by Valencian architect Rafael Guastavino in the nineteenth century.[33] Unique features of the technique include the fact that the vaults of thin terracotta tiles with an even thinner layer of special cements can be constructed without centering, rendering them both more economical and structurally more sound than traditional stone vaults. Rather than ignore this outstanding neighbor as the other competition entries did, Rossi chose to engage it, with three ferry slips facing the river responding to the elegant metal columns and earthen hues of the Maritime Building. The green columns, cornices, and square windows harmonize with rather than duplicate those of the Maritime Building, while the piazza framed on two sides by porticoes opens to the city's financial district (fig. 2.15). Once again, Rossi let subtle ties to the surroundings and to the history of this particular site guide his design—remarkably, the only one of the six architects to do so.

FIGURE 2.15
Aldo Rossi, Whitehall Ferry Terminal, watercolor and markers (Courtesy Morris Adjmi © Aldo Rossi Heirs)

59    ARCHITECTURE AND THE CITY

FIGURE 2.16
Aldo Rossi, San Cristoforo Rail Station, Milan, 1983, left uncompleted (Marco Introini)

Over the course of his career Rossi tackled several other port or shoreline facilities, for cities as remote as Marseilles, Zeebrugge (Belgium), Rotterdam, Naples, and Neuruppin (Germany), none of which left the drawing board. This last project (1999) was particularly close to Rossi's heart. Neuruppin, Karl Friedrich Schinkel's hometown, burned nearly to the ground in a 1787 fire in which Schinkel's father lost his life. In the seven years he lived there until the family moved to Berlin in 1794, Schinkel watched the city being rebuilt with neo-classical buildings, something that no doubt influenced his own architecture in the ensuing decades. Rossi received multiple invitations to work in Neuruppin, some for new buildings, but also for other types of projects, such as restoring the old wooden Pfarrkirche and a master plan to develop the lakeside area. Although he had become quite familiar with the small town over the years, he declined the church restoration project because he believed it needed only accurate maintenance and therefore should be assigned to a local architect skilled in wood construction. For the lakeside area he suggested an enclosure with simple, gable-roofed structures in bright colors, with nearby equally modest structures for leisure and tourist facilities, including guesthouses.

Although it is common for architectural projects to remain unbuilt, those where construction begins but is halted are less common. In 1983 the Italian State Railway elected Rossi to design a new train station near some historic working class districts in Milan such as the Barona and Giambellina districts, with the idea of facilitating transport to the city and to the connection for trains bound for France (fig. 2.16). The prospect of Italy as host of the 1990 World Soccer Cup also lay behind the project and, like many initiated under the same pretext, came to an ignominious end. Some thirty-five years later, San Cristoforo Rail Station remains a slowly corroding, skeletal structure, abandoned to its fate in a peripheral wasteland. Rossi occasionally visited the site over the years, dismayed at the waste of money and energy, but more at the lost opportunity for the district.

In each of these projects, Rossi elaborated his basic theory of the city as assembled of parts, an urban tissue into which new work would be inserted by an architect who had undertaken the laborious study outlined in *The Architecture of the City*. Nonetheless, in each case Rossi had dealt with a location in Italy or in a European or American city that he knew well. Would his theory hold up in a radically unfamiliar culture? We will explore this in the projects that follow, all but two of which address the needs of transient populations. Rossi's first commission in Asia, the Il Palazzo Hotel (1987), arrived shortly after the 1985 and 1986 Venice Architecture Biennales had been completed. Images of his projects and books about his architecture had been best sellers in Japan

FIGURE 2.17
Aldo Rossi, Il Palazzo Hotel, Fukuoka, Japan, 1987 (Courtesy Morris Adjmi/ Nasca Partners)

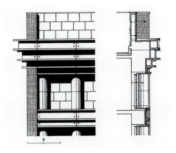

FIGURE 2.18
Il Palazzo Hotel, detail drawings (Courtesy Morris Adjmi)

for over a decade, but how would his architecture work in such a dramatically different culture? Fukuoka is the gateway to southern Japan, a port city bustling with traffic on land and water. Staying in the comfort zone of conformity never appealed to Rossi; a project for a hotel along—or almost along—the Naka River in Fukuoka presented a tempting challenge.

In fact, a row or two of small single-family homes stand between the hotel and the river, blocking views to and from the stepped entrance plaza (fig. 2.17). The developers wanted a boutique hotel, the first of its type in Japan, and they chose an area not exactly at the high end of the city. But the gamble worked. As Rossi's colleague Morris Adjmi reported later, their Japanese partners supplied them with two huge books of glowing newspaper accounts of the hotel's overwhelmingly positive reception. What had Rossi done that achieved such success?

The seven-story hotel block sits on a plinth flanked on either side by two-story structures housing specialty bars, a restaurant, and a disco. As revetment for the masonry construction, Rossi chose to place rows of seven amber-hued, Persian travertine columns atop copper lintels aged to a deep, rich green, and at the top, a three-lintel deep copper cornice (fig. 2.18). Notably, no windows interrupt the waterside façade; instead, they have all been reserved to the lateral walls. Although unusual in approach—most hotels privilege spectacular views when they can—the low-scale, not particularly compelling port invited reflection on just where the vistas should be located, and Rossi chose to place them with views back into the city. Compact, rich in color, appealing to the elegant simplicity of Japanese architecture, Rossi thought he had produced a profoundly Japanese building. The developers, however, were thrilled that he had given them an Italian building! The combination reaped immediate rewards, as the hotel remained successful following its opening. Indeed, it arguably helped lure others into building in the area.

Rossi only designed one bar in the hotel. There, as a backdrop to the bar he inserted a floor-to-ceiling wooden model of the façade, flanked on another wall by a Rossi drawing that included the hotel. As we will see in the chapter on theaters, Rossi used this device repeatedly, turning the building in upon itself for the viewer.

The second hotel he designed in Japan, the Mojiko Hotel (1993–98), towers over the Kanmon strait in another port town, Moji, a ward in the city of Kitakyushu, just a short way up the eastern coast of Japan's southernmost island, Kyushu (fig. 2.19).[34] Builders had finished nearly all of the construction work at Rossi's death, with final completion in 1998. At 134 rooms nearly three times the size of the Il Palazzo Hotel, it sits on a piece of land jutting into the strait but also looking back at the town. The public-private partnership intended the hotel to be the first step in an upgrade for the entire port area, a gamble that proved effective. Rossi, partner Adjmi, and the interior architect Shigeru Uchida explored the small city on foot, seeking traces of its history and fragments of the past. Some of the buildings they found amazed and intrigued them, such as the wooden train station apparently modeled on a French chateau, complete with mansard roofs (1914). Or the Chinese Eastern Railway office, a replica of a part half-timbered, part brick and stone, more or less neo-Romanesque Russian building erected in China (1995); the Osaka Shosen Mercantile Steamship Company building in the Secession style (1917); or the Romanesque customs building in brick and stone (1912). With such a rich mix of buildings and stories—all exuberantly expressive of anything but Japanese domestic architecture—Rossi decided to insert the new hotel into the city's traditions by telling a new story, with elements both new and old, as he reflected on how a design could help fulfill the aspirations of the city and its partners in the hotel project. The town certainly did not enjoy a flourishing economy, so as was the case with all of the projects in Asia reviewed here, the developers depended upon these buildings to be anchors and promoters of future development.

The team labeled the building "the shark" because of the form of the central section of the tripartite structure: the brick-clad, eight-story hotel follows the general form of a boat, or a fish, with the bow containing guest rooms pointing in the direction of the harbor and the stern nestled between lateral, six-story stone-clad blocks. Toward the town, two stacked towers of brick and stone respond to the texture and architecture of the building on the corner, now a restaurant; the towers almost seem to belong to the area independent of the rest of the building.

FIGURE 2.19
Aldo Rossi, Mojiko Hotel, Moji, Gifu, Japan, 1993, view from town (Morris Adjmi)

Rossi's approach at Moji, Fukuoka, and at a third hotel in Osaka, Il Monte, conformed to the strategy he had pursued for the remodeling of the Hotel Duca di Milano (1988, now called ME Milan Il Duca; fig. 2.20). Construction of the Milan subway line disrupted the city for years, but it also made it possible to reconfigure streets and squares and prompted some of the city's major hotels to undertake exterior and interior renovations. The looming arrival of the World Cup finals in Italy scheduled for the summer of 1990 also lay behind the desire of the owner, the Reale Mutua di Assicurazioni insurance company, to undertake a renovation and enlargement of the post–World War II structure. On the same piazza, Rossi acknowledged the architecture of his distinguished predecessor Giovanni Muzio, his Casa Bonaiti apartments (1935), and the dreadfully out of place Torre Breda (Luigi Mattioni, 1954), Italy's first skyscraper and the first building in Milan to exceed the height of the statue of the Madonnina on the Duomo.[35]

He noted too the nondescript architecture of the existing Hotel Duca di Milano and its poor condition after only a couple of decades of use. Given its proximity to the central train station and to downtown Milan, the owners anticipated a clientele largely consisting of business people, plus others attending important occasional events such as the World Cup or one of Milan's fashion or design fairs. The remake entailed applying a new stone façade, organized in long piers to frame windows, with the last three floors faced in brick. For the two-story reception and restaurant pavilion, he chose white Carrara marble columns topped by a green I-beam lintel, with *beola bianca*, a local white granite, for the pilasters on the main building, and the same scheme for the new wing.

ARCHITECTURE AND THE CITY

FIGURE 2.20
Aldo Rossi, Hotel Duca di Milano, Milan, 1988 (Marco Introini)

He insisted that the rear elevation facing Via Galilei and Via Marco Polo should receive similar treatment for, as he specified, reasons of urban decorum.

For Rossi, leaving the upper floors with simple brick facing followed a long tradition of unfinished buildings, especially cathedrals, in Italy, sometimes for lack of funds but often, he believed, because of "a liking for unfinished works," such as the façade of Milan's Duomo, begun in 1386 but not finished until the nineteenth century.[36] An inveterate walker, Rossi's strolls in downtown Milan often terminated in the Duomo, which he considered the most beautiful architecture in all of Milan. Visitors often found themselves led to the cathedral for a walk down the long nave flanked by enormously tall bundled columns with their distinctly non-classical capitals fading into darkness above. Light suffuses the altar from the apse windows, on many days, so that to walk to the altar means walking toward the light both physically and metaphorically. Always moving slowly, always looking, Rossi claimed to discover something new in the Duomo with each visit. So often had he drawn the cathedral that he could do so from memory. He inserted the Duomo or fragments of it into many of his drawings and prints, either as a backdrop toward which a viewer could peer from a window, or simply what he described as the quintessential public building that welcomed everyone (fig. 2.21).

So too, in his view, should the most recent version of public space, the shopping center, be a welcoming place. As with hotels, the transient population of malls has but one purpose, in this case to consume—or at least, so the shop owners hope. Milan's own Galleria Vittorio Emanuele II (Giuseppe Mengoni, 1877) by the second half of the twentieth century became the model for shopping centers around the globe, many of them being named Galleria in its honor. Alas, none can compare with the original's grand architecture, with its glazed octagonal dome and two four-story-high barrel-vaulted arcades of glass and iron. While the lessees in Milan have almost always been upscale, shopping remains confined to the ground floor, by contrast with most American malls, such as the Houston Galleria (1970), where three stories of shops, offices, and other amenities spread out over 22,300 square meters (2.4 million square feet). Though ostensibly paying homage to the Milan precedent, doing so on steroids certainly diminishes any visible parentage. More importantly, Houston's Galleria is a suburban complex remote from the city while Milan's sits directly in the historic center, adjacent to the Duomo and just a couple of blocks from the famed La Scala opera house—that is, part of the city that draws visitors to the center rather than to the periphery.[37]

FIGURE 2.21
Aldo Rossi, "Milanese Interior with Person Observing the Duomo. With Fog," lithograph and serigraph, 1989 (Private collection/Alexander Severin © Aldo Rossi Heirs)

FIGURE 2.22
Aldo Rossi, inauguration of Uny-Gifu Mall, Nagoya, Japan, 1993 (MAXXI, Rossi)

Two shopping centers in Japan set directly within dense districts activate their surroundings much as the Milan Galleria does. The developers and the city specified that Uny-Gifu Mall (now Apita Shopping Center, 1988–93) in southern Gifu should function as a large plaza, with restaurants, cafes, shops, and space for cultural activities and all of the other features one would want in a depoliticized space (fig. 2.22). The name originally given to the mall—Centro Città (Center City)—reflected precisely that aspiration. The surroundings consist of a mix of low-rise housing and low-scale office and commercial space, with an occasional apartment tower, and while the adjacent road network discourages pedestrian traffic, the mall owners actively encourage bicycles and cars. In the original design, Rossi proposed a large tower to accommodate cultural activities, though it was never built. As his inspiration, he spoke of having in mind Diocletian's fourth-century palace in Split, Croatia, at once a fortress and residence for the Roman emperor that became a complete city after the fall of the empire, and still constitutes the urban core of the city. With the corner towers, scale, grand fortified entrances (although with brightly hued metal flanges framing the portals at Gifu), and the cavernous spaces below level, the parallel with the beautiful city on the Adriatic coast, where a lively market fills some of the massive vaulted spaces of the palace's foundation, becomes apparent.

The Tochi shopping center (now Port Walk Minato, 1989), located not far away in Nagoya, follows some of the same principles of the Uny-Gifu Mall. Both rise three stories and both have their entrances marked by bright yellow–painted steel flanges of the type Rossi also used on the Mercer Street elevation of the Scholastic Building. The Tochi mall, also located in a low-scale area, sets the stage for urban growth as at Gifu. Rossi employed brighter colors and stronger forms, with luminous primary colors—yellow, blue, and red-orange—originally rising up from a sea of asphalt but now tightly packed in among other buildings. Rossi divided the mall into four quadrants—one for shopping, one for the food court, one for health and culture, and one for fashion and entertainment—each signaled by an unfenestrated corner tower. Though not completed as originally designed, both malls were intended to generate development around them as propelling forces in the city, much as Rossi argued in *The Architecture of the City*. The latter shopping center did so more effectively than did that at Gifu, but given time the Gifu mall may also fulfill its promise.

The nineteenth and twentieth centuries saw numerous instances of the wanton destruction of a historically significant part of a city's history, including in Paris, in Milan, and in many other Italian cities. But however noxious and devastating to the people evicted from their homes, the changes nonetheless transformed these, for better and for worse, into the modern cities we see today. Repeating such vast, so-called urban

FIGURE 2.23
Aldo Rossi, Centro Torri
shopping mall, Parma, 1985

renewal schemes seems at best difficult today, and indeed, developers normally erect shopping malls on cheaper land outside of city centers, thereby drawing people out of rather than into urban areas. In the process, shops and services in city centers gradually lose their clientele and ultimately close down, leaving empty stores and urban desolation in their wake. Although the phenomenon occurred virtually everywhere, it may have been most visible in rural areas, where new regional malls drained the life out of surrounding small towns. With the advent of e-commerce, many of the ambitious malls of the second half of the twentieth century are now suffering the fate of the downtowns they so ruthlessly eviscerated just a few decades ago.

Italy proved no more immune to this pattern than other advanced economies, and as happened in the United States, rural areas may have been the most visible victims, but the economics did not spare larger cities. Nonetheless, the situation differed somewhat in Italy. Over the course of the twentieth century, families moved out of dense city centers and their usually small apartments into larger units, duplexes, or even single-family homes outfitted with more rooms, convenient parking, and gardens, farther and farther from urban centers.[38] At the same time, cities increasingly closed historic centers to automobiles, rendering shopping and other activities more difficult due to often inadequate or unreliable public transportation—a condition that afflicts Rome, Milan, Naples, Palermo, Trieste, and Turin, and other cities. By the 1980s, shopping centers were popping up throughout Italy, but especially in two regions: Campania (with its regional capital at Naples) and Lombardy (regional capital at Milan), many with more than a hundred stores. In the thick of preparing the Biennales of 1985 and 1986, Rossi received his first commission for a shopping center on the outskirts of Parma, an ancient city about 130 kilometers (80 miles) southeast of Milan at the westernmost part of the Emilia-Romagna region. The city owes its worldwide renown to its historic cheese, *parmeggiano*, and its university, one of the world's oldest, founded in the tenth century. Sixty-seven percent of the town's buildings have been erected since the early 1990s, an expansion of enormous proportions.[39] The new mall, Centro Torri (Towers Center)—with around fifty shops, including a huge supermarket and a bargain electronics, appliances, and computer store—serves suburbanites and rural residents scattered in the ever less populated countryside (fig. 2.23). Even thirty years after opening, the center still celebrates its "avant-garde" architecture on its website. And so it was.

During the middle ages, pilgrims from throughout Europe descended on Italy in droves to celebrate jubilees and visit sacred shrines. They encountered urban textures unlike those at home, especially the dozens of towers crowding the skylines of Italy's cities—highly visible especially along the long flat reach of the Po Valley that traverses the Piedmont, Lombard, and Emilia-Romagna regions. Over time, many of the privately owned towers were reduced in height by command of civic authorities, who viewed them as symbols of private political and military power in opposition to that of the collectivity. The community in turn expressed its power with a tower on the communal town hall.[40] Indeed, the collectivity swept away symbols of individual might precisely in order to distribute power more democratically, with the municipal tower literally towering over all others and asserting the dominance of the people as a whole over that of individuals. In this new order, families could no longer claim control over streets, squares, and districts; the entire community—or at least, the entire property-owning, male community—now affirmed that right; public spaces in theory would be open to all. However far towns fell from this ideal, the association of the tower with the collectivity endured, just as the campanile of the medieval cathedral or church signified all Christians. The bells of each summoned the two communities to festivals, announcements, rituals, and everything else that involved a town or parish as a whole. Rossi's choice of towers as the most visible and significant emblem of Parma's new mall appealed to that tradition and promised a comparable openness for the entire collectivity—a promise often not maintained, in the present as also in the past. Evoking not only ancient symbol but also future aspiration, if shopping centers indeed were to become the new civic centers, then they ought to beckon all, as did the towers of yore and as do those of Rossi's Centro Torri.

Multiple brick and terracotta towers—with "Centro Torri" inscribed near the summit of each—signal the mall's presence to those passing on the Milan-Rome freeway, and they also frame the entrance from the parking lot. A low, rectangular brick structure serves as the formal entrance, and shortly thereafter the visitor begins the stroll through the mall itself, beneath gabled metal roofs with clerestory lighting, through twin rectangles in plan, one lined with shops with another block of shops set in the middle, the other housing various facilities and the larger anchor stores such as the supermarket.

Rossi's favorite shopping center project, however, never proceeded to detailed drawings: a market in Pallanza, in Verbania, a town on the shores of Lago Maggiore, not far from his villa at Ghiffa (1993). Formerly the site of a slaughterhouse and the town's public baths, and adjacent to a small river, here Rossi imagined a project that responded to the requests of the city and of the Catholic Curia—the former for the piazza, the latter for a church—to enclose shops and offices, with the prospect of a footbridge linking the market with the new buildings across the river. His solution—imagined with trees, wings both gabled and barrel-vaulted, and a six-story tower—sprang from long familiarity with the town due to summers spent at a family villa on Lake Mergozzo just a few kilometers northwest of Pallanza. He envisioned gardens such as those found at many lakeside villas and hotels on Lago Maggiore, with a neo-classical building also consistent with local tradition. The project never advanced beyond a preliminary stage, to his dismay for he had anticipated the joy of designing a public space in an area so close to his heart.

❖ ❖ ❖

With choices such as those we have seen in these mixed-use and commercial projects, did Rossi fulfill the expectations spelled out in *The Architecture of the City* and other writings? In the projects reviewed above, I believe that he did, to varying degrees. In what ways? In a 1968 essay, "Architettura per i musei" (Architecture for Museums), Rossi wrote about his approach to architecture beginning with formulating a theory of design. The fundamental points of a design theory, he argued, "are in the first place a reading of monuments, in the second, a study of the form of architecture and the physical world, and finally, the reading of the city."[41] The city as a collective creation and architecture as a technique or art, he continued, pass down from hand to hand, in traditions hallowed and refined over time, the first comprising a slow evolution, while architecture, he wrote, becomes a meditation on things. Only a handful of basic and unchanging principles can be identified in architecture, to which the architect and the collectivity have an abundance of possible concrete responses, depending upon the nature of problems that arise over time. To address them, Rossi did not ask the architect only to study history; he asked also that the architect study architecture, and especially monuments, by drawing them, which requires observing them closely, looking and asking questions. The slide show of the movement of shadows across the face of a building in his class in Zurich with which we began illustrated the kind of attentiveness Rossi encouraged in his students. He drew, insistently, always, what he saw, what he imagined, what he remembered—even if he could not always fix them as memories or as figments of his imagination. But above all: he drew. He urged the architect to study the urban context, and much more than that, he urged the study of the physical form and essence of the city and its architecture, and never to fail to register the city and its buildings as dynamic, changing entities. In the urban projects reviewed above, Rossi accomplished precisely that, not just a close study of the physical context of a site but also the more comprehensive and difficult understanding of the city as a human creation, as a *fatto urbano*. Numerous sketches accompanied each project, sketches in which his design ideas emerged from and responded to those ideas he intuited, analyzed, and documented around the site, the city, the evolving character of life as played out in public—in short, the essential elements from which a design finally began to take shape.

Perhaps the best approach to unraveling the enigma of the movement from theory to practice for Rossi sets out from the 1976 "La città analoga" exhibited at the Venice Biennale (see fig. 1.10). In this collage, Rossi inserted fragments of various projects such as the Monument to Partisans at Segrate and the San Rocco Directional Center superimposed on or mingled with fragments of Piranesi etchings, from which springs a sacred sanctuary, then a Doric entablature, then Rossi's drawings of the cabins of Elba, and coffeepots, all in a crescendo of apparently unrelated items. Some appear in elevation, some in plan, geometric forms tumble down from the Russian walls, and so forth. In this heady disarray, no organizing mechanism appears available, or even possible. And yet the drawing speaks of Rossi's ideas about architecture. First, it is an architecture assembled of parts, not a grand whole set up to contain all of human life. Recognizable fragments jostle with less well-known bits or even imaginary shards of possible architectures, even though unrelated in formal terms. They slide along the edge of consciousness like a memory too flimsy to summon fully to mind. From such pieces, in the interstices between such pieces, the collective begins to form the city, argued Rossi, and the architect simply joins in that process—though "simply" may not be the best word, because the architect's labor did not end there.

The second point thus arises, concerning exactly the place of architecture in the city's landscape, as a civic architecture, the embodiment of the values and history of the collectivity. What did he mean by this? He spoke about this repeatedly in *The Architecture of the City*, for example, when he discussed the Palazzo della Ragione in Padua. Even prior to the construction of the current building (begun 1218), the ground floor consisted of merchants' shops, while above an enormous room (Il Salone) served for the city's law courts. Here the collectivity issued its first decrees—regulating the administration of justice, the honest operation of markets, and public life in general for the benefit of all. The form and scale of the structure testified to this role: only the cathedral and its campanile contended with the palazzo for dominance on the city's skyline; the community asserted its privilege even against that of the bishop. The grand vaulted space of the Salone, constructed of wood in the form of an overturned ship's hull, answered the problem of how to span such a wide space by turning to the accomplishments of Venetian shipbuilders, whose work lay behind the wealth accumulated by Venice and the Veneto in maritime trade. In these and many other ways, the palazzo testified to a history of shared values, indeed embodying them in its very architecture—an architecture that inventively transformed shipbuilding practices into a grand communal space.

There is more. The architecture envisioned by Rossi remained an artifact also of service, in that the values it embodied should be recognizable to the collectivity as expressions of their shared values, reinforcing and clarifying them at the same time.[42] As "La città analoga" evidences, a civic architecture comes not from without—not from the delirium of an architect's egocentric psychic rampage as a prelude to a "signature" work, or the impoverished fantasy of crumbling a bag and calling it architecture, or the deployment of a series of grids systematically out of synch with one another to produce an inchoate mess of intersecting grids—but from history itself. And so "La città analoga" binds the old to the new as the new emerges from within, at once rupturing with the very past from which it springs. This, to Rossi, constituted the greatest honor for an architect: to produce, as the Pritzker award stated, an architecture at once "bold and ordinary," designs "that seem always to be a part of the city fabric, rather than an intrusion."

One might protest that the buildings and projects discussed above appear not to have had great ambitions with regard to their significance for the larger community; for the most part they were largely driven by function, either as sites of labor, living, or consumption or as transit points for a transient population flowing irregularly through them. And yet, they do serve their communities. An architecture like that of the Scholastic Building, that recognizes and honors the surrounding urban fabric even while proposing something bold and new, already speaks to a relationship with the past as well as the present and the future. Much the same holds true for the Schützenstraße Quarter, which accomplishes the same ends, also for a stable population. Could we not say the same of the simple pleasures of Linate airport, or the aspirations about the character of the community so clearly evidenced in Parma's Centro Torri?

Each in its own way becomes a *fatto urbano*, the structures Rossi described as fabrications of the collectivity in any city; they are architectures of the city. The next chapter, where we reflect on some of Rossi's designs for monuments, will further clarify what he meant by architecture as an expression of civic values, architecture as a testimony to a civic conscience.

# 3  Memory and Monument

> Greatness out of small things.
> —OVID

Via Montenapoleone in Milan, one of the most expensive shopping streets in Italy, terminates at a piazza designed by Aldo Rossi and dedicated to former Italian president and resistance hero Sandro Pertini (fig. 3.1). In April 1990, following the inauguration of a new Metro stop, the piazza called Via Croce Rossa replaced a formerly messy urban intersection of five streets (fig. 3.2). To the dismay of nearby merchants, instead of an innocuous statue of a beloved president, they found themselves facing a large marble cube carved away on one side to accommodate a steep staircase, an exercise in abstraction they found distinctly unappealing. They complained as well about water splashing from the triangular fountain at the rear of the block. In his private notebooks, Rossi puzzled at the reactions to a monument often referred to as cold and inhuman, but he also mused about his inability to convey the joy he believed it embodied.[1] Nonetheless, as he predicted, the monument aged, the mulberry trees grew, and opposition mostly faded away.

The incomprehension did not surprise Rossi, because many of his projects, including the most famous, such as the Modena cemetery and the Gallaratese housing, prompted similar reactions from some critics. If not surprised, he was still often dismayed, because he wrote extensively and produced thousands of prints and drawings that he believed helped clarify his ideas. For many, however, the abundance only added to the puzzle. Rossi's reflections on architecture matured and developed over time with remarkable consistency and coherence. The monument to Pertini drew on a competition entry that Rossi assembled with Luca Meda and Gianugo Polesella nearly thirty years earlier for a monument in Cuneo, and from a second for the town of Segrate in 1965.[2] With their remarkable formal similarities, these three projects offer a compelling introduction to the convergence of theory and imagination in Rossi's architecture.

FIGURE 3.1
Aldo Rossi, Monument to Sandro Pertini, Milan, completed 1990 (Palladium)

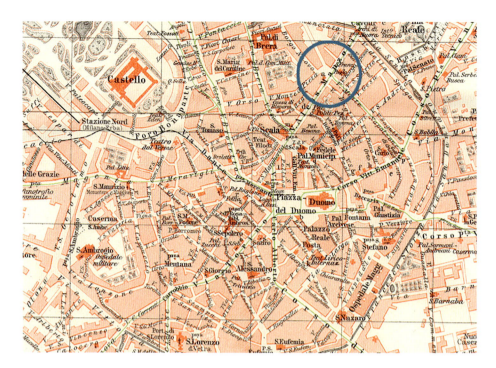

FIGURE 3.2
Map of Via Croce Rossa area, Milan (TCI Guide to Milan, 1904)

MONUMENT TO SANDRO PERTINI, VIA CROCE ROSSA, MILAN

Pertini, a famous opponent of Fascism, socialist, and partisan who fought against the Germans, was perhaps Italy's most beloved president and therefore a popular choice for a person to merit a monument in the heart of one of Italy's busiest cities. Rossi's monument to Pertini, completed in 1990, sits deep within the historic center of Milan, north of the Duomo and the Galleria Vittorio Emanuele, and but a few blocks from La Scala opera house. Far more than in the earlier two designs, Rossi here was able to explore ideas about collective memory, permanences (as discussed in chapter 1), and the role of a monument in greater depth.[3] Work on the Pertini monument also enabled Rossi to bring wonderful clarity to thoughts he had expressed years earlier about the design process itself, in particular as he framed them in his 1967 introduction to the Italian edition of Étienne-Louis Boullée's eighteenth-century *Architecture: Essai sur l'art*.[4] Nonetheless, precisely because of its location in the heart of the city, the Pertini monument triggered conflict, incomprehension, and opposition.

The completion of one line of the Milan Metro system opened up the question of what to do with a dozen intersections in Milan that had been closed for five years to permit subway construction. Because the purpose for expanding the Metro was to reduce automobile traffic, closing such intersections to all but pedestrian traffic presumably would help discourage the use of private automobiles. The mayor of Milan at that time, Paolo Pilliteri, decided that the intersections disrupted should be transformed into plazas to be designed by an artist or architect. Rossi received the commission for the new piazza called Via Croce Rossa after its former central street. Although one of many such sites now freed of barriers after the subway's completion, Via Croce Rossa in the Brera district presented a particularly difficult set of problems. Four streets converge on the new piazza, all associated with wealth and power: Via Borgonuovo, Via Alessandro Manzoni, Via Montenapoleone, and Via Giardini-Monte di Pietà. Wealthy and aristocratic families from the seventeenth century forward chose Via Borgonuovo as the site for family palaces, still today notable concentrations of wealth and nobility, including the Orsini, Bescapé, Taverna, and Perego palaces.[5] Hence the common reference to Via Borgonuovo as "the street of the nobles."

Via Alessandro Manzoni, named for the nineteenth-century author of the classic *I promessi sposi* (1827), also boasts elegant seventeenth- and eighteenth-century palaces as well as the prestigious Poldi-Pezzoli Museum.[6] Apart from some of Milan's most elegant family palaces, since 2011 the Armani Hotel also sits on this street. The luxury fashion house replaced the Assicurazioni Generali insurance company in the office-residential building designed by rationalist architect Enrico Griffini (1937–38, 1947–48), a reinforced concrete modernist structure boasting abundant green marble to frame doors and windows.[7] The city opened Via Giardini in 1938 as an artery to bypass Via Manzoni and arrive more quickly at the new train station. Its name springs from its route through and adjacent to some of the city's most elegant and spectacular private gardens, including those of Palazzo Borromeo d'Adda.[8] The last street to converge at Via Croce Rossa, Via Montenapoleone, follows the route of the ancient Roman walls and the Seveso River. Until the end of the eighteenth century the area contained convents for Benedictine, Augustinian, and other nuns, but aristocratic families gradually drove them out, turning the spacious cloisters into private gardens. During the nineteenth-century revolt against the Austrian government, the upper-class rebels located their headquarters on Via Montenapoleone. By the end of the century, however, the street had become the center of luxury shopping in Milan, and today it remains one of the most famous and expensive shopping streets in Italy, if not in Europe.

The name of the fifth and central street in this intersection, Via Croce Rossa (red cross), recalls the flag carried by Milanese soldiers during the wars against Federico I Barbarossa in the second half of the twelfth century, and more recently, the red cross on a white field served as the emblem and street sign of an inn once located on the narrow street. Only after World War II was the little passage widened to accommodate the needs of the Griffini building, with its offices, apartments, and a new movie theater, the Capitale Cinema, which subsequently closed in 1984.[9]

Placing a monument, and especially a structure like Rossi's, in this upscale neighborhood could hardly fail to trigger debate, especially because it cast unrelenting light on the conflicting interests battling for access to and control of the historic center. The entire organization of the piazza and the monument ruptured the solidly upper-middle-class and aristocratic pretensions of the surrounding district. Rossi designed a simple cubic block 8 meters high and 6 meters square (26 by 20 by 20 feet) set toward the Via

FIGURE 3.3
Aldo Rossi, Sketch for a fountain in Feltre, Belluno, pen and pastel on paper, 1965 (MAXXI, Rossi/© Aldo Rossi Heirs)

Borgonuovo end of the site. The gray and pink marble-revetted block refers directly to the Cuneo project in a number of ways. The block is closed on three sides, but the fourth opens to a broad and steep flight of stairs that leads to a viewing platform with a bronze-framed rectangular opening from which to peer at the city, even to a glimpse of the Duomo a few blocks away. To the rear, from a bronze-framed triangle a sheet of water fell to a bronze grid below. Rossi had experimented with this particular design for an earlier unbuilt project for a fountain in the town of Feltre in the Veneto (fig. 3.3). Certain features appeared in both the design for Feltre and for Segrate: the white unadorned column supporting a triangular channel from which a fine sheet of water flows, staircase to the rear, though at Segrate, Rossi eliminated lateral seating.

As for materials at Via Croce Rossa, Rossi specified a pavement for the piazza fabricated of rose granite squares that had been extracted from Milan's streets for subway construction. Six graceful mulberry trees alternate with 6-meter-tall (20-foot) light standards to line the lateral approaches to the monument, punctuated with granite benches in the intercolumniations. Milanese traditions pervade more than the paving, for the marble revetment of the cube comes from the same quarry as that from which the marble on the Duomo was extracted, and mulberry trees, destined to grow to 12–15 meters (40–50 feet), are a typical but increasingly rare thick-foliaged tree in Lombardy. The colors of the mulberry trees evolve through the seasons from the stark brown branches of winter to the pale, bright green leaves of spring and finally, the deep green hues of late summer

FIGURE 3.4
Monument to Pertini

and early fall (fig. 3.4). Adding to nature's bounty, Rossi managed to join that subtle but rich polychrome with deep green lamp standards, pale rose paving, bronze I-beam, and gray and pink marble panels to achieve a display of maximum visual texture.

What most vexed the good burghers of the Brera district—and especially Giorgio Armani—was that the benches, shade, and stairs ideally accommodated everything from lingering for eating ice cream, reading a newspaper, meeting friends, or soaking up summer sun to horsing around with friends—not to mention impromptu skirmishes with a soccer ball. Worse, they feared that drug users would flood the piazza.[10] As the moon draws the tide, the piazza attracted people otherwise unwelcome in the district, from foreign immigrants to rowdy adolescents. This oasis of calm amidst the noisy traffic speeding by on either side irritated local storeowners for that very reason. Spending money in expensive stores hardly drew visitors to the piazza, and in the logic of the merchants, if not buying they should not be there. Otherwise rare in this part of the city, the stairs and benches especially irked shopkeepers like Armani, who even promised to pay for its removal to some remote site.[11] With the completion of Rossi's project, to pause and linger in Milan's upscale Manzoni and Brera neighborhoods no longer entails spending money in a restaurant or shop. The latter practice contracts the field of legitimate users of the neighborhood to those few with fat bank accounts. Rossi's stairs and benches, free and open to all, ignore economics. Over the decades, merchants made every effort to push out anything other than luxury stores, but three still survive at this writing, a fruit and vegetable store, a delicatessen, and a grocery store—plus the monument. In short,

Rossi's piazza brought the groups that had steadily been edged out right back, with comfortable seating and shade for all. Not surprisingly, aesthetic arguments mask the more venal and discriminatory reality of the opponents' motives.

Merchants advanced an alternate proposal for the piazza consisting of a fountain and three trees, with no benches or stairs for sitting, a proposal that never gained traction with city authorities. The merchants then launched complaints about every aspect of Rossi's project. For several years, a sign forbade climbing the stairs, and the city obliged Rossi to add a large bronze box to catch the water from the fountain because of neighbors' complaints about splashing. They tried every trick imaginable to prevent anyone from lingering in the square, ultimately to no avail. Clearly the piazza design brought to the fore questions about who owns the city, who controls its public realms, what factors trigger conflicts, and especially, whether it would be possible to create a setting that resisted the overwhelming power of capital to transform cities into centers of undiluted consumption, to transform every encounter into a financial one. While many of the complaints about the monument's design concerned its aesthetic, on the whole they were little more than masks for the underlying desire to avoid giving space to all but the wealthiest shoppers—in effect, to edge further out those already on the margins.

The aggressive desire of merchants, corporate giants, and upper-class institutions in Milan to erase the presence of other groups in the city involved not only the monument to Pertini. After having occupied a shop in Milan's Galleria Vittorio Emanuele II for twenty years, in 2012 McDonald's successful fast food restaurant found its lease renewal proposal rejected, following which the city booted it out of the Galleria and substituted it with a second Prada store.[12] Whatever one's judgment of McDonald's, that the city replaced it not with a different or better hamburger joint but with an extremely expensive fashion house reveals all we need to know about who officials believe has a right to the city. The Galleria does not belong to a private company; from the beginning it has been the property of the city. And city officials—a presumably left-wing government putatively representing all of the city's residents, not some corporate giant of luxury goods—elected to substitute expensive fashion for inexpensive food. That the effort to remove or demolish the Pertini monument has not succeeded despite the unremitting opposition of rag trade denizen Giorgio Armani remains something of a miracle.

Rossi acknowledged the political dimensions of his project; to him, public space should accommodate everyone, without reservation. He often recounted the story of San Carlo Borromeo's repeated, unsuccessful attempts to banish gambling and prostitution from inside the Duomo.[13] Borromeo enjoyed no more success in the late sixteenth century than more recent politicians have at the end of the twentieth century, Rossi wryly noted. Our societies are complex, full of individuals and groups who resist easy classification. Politics, he observed, "is of primary importance and indeed, [is] decisive. *Politics constitutes the problem of choices.*"[14] With the Pertini monument, Rossi chose to design a structure open to all, without a program or a definite purpose, a site of collective memory that visitors could explore and experience for themselves, thereby helping form collective memories for the future. What did "collective memory" mean to Rossi?

### CUNEO, SEGRATE, AND COLLECTIVE MEMORY

In two earlier designs for monuments, at Cuneo in Piedmont (1962) and at Segrate, outside Milan (1965), Rossi confronted quite different aspects of memory. Following World War I, cities and villages throughout Italy erected monuments in honor of soldiers who fell in battle (fig. 3.5). After World War II, Italian cities often commissioned similar monuments to emphasize the partisans who fought to rid the country of Mussolini's Fascist Republic of Salò and Nazi Germany's armed forces, rather than the soldiers who fought in Mussolini's armies. The first Nazi destruction of a town in Italy as reprisal for partisan activity took place 7 kilometers (4.3 miles) from Cuneo, in the village of Boves, on 19 September 1943, just days after Italy's unconditional surrender to and subsequent alliance with Allied forces. The Cuneo project embodies the themes that became central to the Italian resistance to Nazi-Fascism in the following eighteen months and the devastating response of the Nazi-Fascists, from the tricks and dishonesty of the Schutzstaffel, the infamous SS, to persuade the priests at Boves to cooperate in obtaining the release of German soldiers held captive by the partisans, to the decision to burn the town (along with many of the residents, including the two priests). A second scorched earth attack by the Nazis in 1943 destroyed many of the remaining houses and killed still more people.

The competition for the Monument to the Resistance at Cuneo specified a site neither in the city nor at Boves but rather in a park on the outskirts of Cuneo. The 1965 Segrate competition, on the other hand, called for a reconfiguration of the municipal plaza (Piazza Ugo La Malfa) and the addition of a new monument in honor of World War II partisans. Rossi's winning project (with Luca Meda) for Segrate drew on but departed notably from the earlier, unsuccessful competition entry for Cuneo. During the design development phase of both projects, Rossi was tinkering with the final touches on the first Italian edition of *The Architecture of the City*, which encouraged him to reflect on cities and monuments together with the pragmatics of an actual design.

With the Cuneo design, Rossi began to explore the ideas about monuments already taking shape in his book, but now through a project proposal for a real site. The competition for Cuneo unfolded with the tragic events of nineteen years earlier still fresh in the minds of the population, and so they were to the designers.[15] The site, located on the eastern periphery of Cuneo, flanks the Gesso River in a wooded park dedicated to the Resistance. In effect, the monument could not serve as a propelling force around which other activities and events would grow, as Rossi believed monuments could do in cities, but in its setting in a park, it would also not exert a negative influence on its surroundings. Although the competition did not require special reference to the reprisals at Boves, for Rossi this became the design's guiding principle. Like many Italian architects who

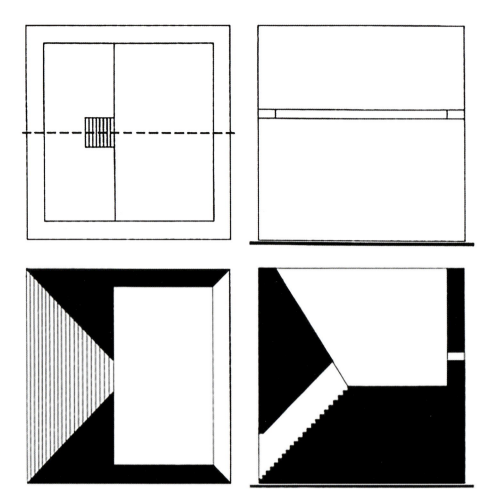

FIGURE 3.5
Aldo Rossi, Gian Ugo
Polesello, and Luca Meda.
Monument to the Resistance,
Cuneo, 1962, project drawing
(drawing by M. Bortolotti
after *Casabella-continuità*)

FIGURE 3.6
Giovanni Greppi, Sacrario
Militare, Redipuglia, Gorizia,
1938

FIGURE 3.7
Giuseppe Terragni,
Monument to Roberto
Sarfatti, Asiago, 1935

designed World War I memorials, Rossi chose to allude to the monument's meanings, to what it represented, both by reference to earlier monuments and to the specifics of the events memorialized.

That delicate balance would have transpired with the construction of a cube poised on a low pedestal, with internal stairs leading to an open-air terrace with its framed view toward Boves, a deceptively simple solution rich with meaning. For Rossi, the most significant and profound monument created to honor Italian soldiers who fought and died in World War I remained that created by Giovanni Greppi at Redipuglia, near Gorizia (1938; fig. 3.6).[16] This extraordinary memorial consists of monumental, open-air stairs along the western flank of Mont Sei Busi, leading to three crosses on the crown of the hill. The names of 100,000 soldiers who perished nearby engraved on the risers recall with painful immediacy the lives of young men sacrificed in a desperately stupid and destructive war. In Cuneo, instead the lives of civilians, including the two priests assassinated by the Nazi SS and anti-Fascist partisans, were to be memorialized, implicitly inclusive of other towns and people in Italy who suffered similarly brutal reprisals over the subsequent nineteen months before the war ended. Enclosing the stairs and focusing the only external views on the distant commune of Boves to the southeast would commemorate just that—emphasized by Rossi's decision to place the cube not on axis with the road from town but shifted precisely to accommodate a direct view toward Boves.

Rossi could find a second source of inspiration in Giuseppe Terragni's Monument to Roberto Sarfatti (1935), a monolithic series of blocks with a narrow staircase.[17] Rossi and his friends appreciated the work of a few Italian rationalist architects from the interwar period, in particular that of Terragni (1904–1943). The Sarfatti monument in Asiago, north of Vicenza not far from Bassano del Grappa, was well published in the 1960s (fig. 3.7). Its plan essentially repeated that of an early Christian basilica, with lateral transept and framed staircase leading to an altar-like structure, but it also evoked the struggle in which Sarfatti lost his life in the attempt to conquer the hill. Both aspirations responded to Terragni's passionate patriotism as a deeply dedicated Fascist, and to his equally profound Catholicism. Terragni, in Rossi's view, proposed not an abstract rationalist work but rather "a concrete, historic rationality," and in his embrace of local materials and traditions he offered a rare alternative to arid, abstract modernism.[18]

Nonetheless, Rossi did not need to turn to such recent monuments for inspiration. A complex range of associations of specific sites with historical memories underlay much of Italian culture since the Roman Republic, but likely even further, to the archaic Greeks, who understood memories of events at particular sites to be conserved by the site itself, only awaiting the presence of a visitor to spring back to life. In these ancient cultures, one even acquired the skill of memorizing speeches by reference to places.[19] Though we no longer use those same strategies, we acknowledge the potency of sites every time we visit a battlefield from a long-ago war, the home of a respected figure, or a monument such as the Vietnam Veterans Memorial in Washington, D.C. We activate those distant events, bring them into the present, through our imaginative recreations of the long-ago events.[20] Rossi's idea for Cuneo entailed fostering reflection on that not so remote past through the architecture, through the stairs and the viewing platform.

The distance between Rossi's project and the one eventually built could hardly have been greater. The winning proposal by prominent sculptor Umberto Mastroianni sits as a traditional, though decidedly abstract, object in the park.[21] It consists of a grid of intersecting steel bars supporting a burst of bronze wedges understood to mimic an exploding crystal. Mastroianni designed the sculpture as an object to be gazed at from afar as an object of admiration. Daniel Libeskind's memorialization of the Holocaust with the Jewish Museum in Berlin provides another instructive comparison with Rossi's three monuments, for Cuneo, Segrate, and Milan. Designed in 1989 as an addition to the Berlin Museum, the zinc-titanium–clad zigzagging structure (following historian Kurt W. Forster's suggestion to adopt a broken Star of David for the plan) is traversed by irregular, apparently random apertures and ruptures.[22] Libeskind drew the trajectories of the building and the window openings, among other things, by plotting the addresses of apparently randomly selected prominent Berliners on a map. Openings within the structure known as "Voids" devolve from the intersections of two axes (one straight, one zigzag) for no otherwise apparent reason. These Voids extend from floor to ceiling, are crossed by diverse bridges, and lack both air conditioning and heat. Texts explain to visitors that Libeskind meant the Voids to address the physical emptiness of Berlin after the expulsion of the Jews. Other texts describe features such as three axes—the Axis of Exile, the Axis of the Holocaust, and the Axis of Continuity—meant to encapsulate the Jewish experience of Berlin.[23]

Through all of this, the scheme ushers the visitor along a one-way trajectory through the structure, experiencing heat, cold, darkness, dead ends, disorienting loss of direction, and other potentially disruptive moments. Outside, a pleasant garden is set on a steep slope that precisely prevents access and hence first-hand enjoyment. Everything about the programmed movement through a tightly controlled sequence of carefully staged scenes meant to trigger specific emotions eerily recalls the Disneyland amusement park ride Pirates of the Caribbean. Visitors sit in small skiffs set on tracks that carry them, willing or not, along a journey where the boat drops suddenly down a waterfall and elsewhere abruptly confronts some menacing event. The promenade's supposedly threatening ambience is enhanced by voices warning of forthcoming calamities, signs indicating dastardly pirates lingering in the shadows, scenes of somber oppressiveness and looming danger. Just as Libeskind's Voids and Axes of Continuity, Exile, and Holocaust exhort the visitor to experience certain specific emotions, so too the Pirates ride meanders through Dead Man's Cove, a dark and menacing tunnel, Puerto Duerto being sacked and looted by pirates, weeping women being auctioned off to the highest bidders, and so forth.[24] Of course the ride is a caricature of real experience, much as is the Jewish Museum. In both the Libeskind project and the Pirates ride, visitors must follow a careful, authoritarian choreography with what can only be described as bovine submissiveness, where the spatial sequences are carefully calibrated to achieve dismay, disorientation, and disquiet—the latter playfully, the former not. Whatever one thinks of the oppressive control of visitor experience as at Libeskind's project, it stands worlds away from the sensibility of Rossi's monuments for Cuneo, Segrate, and Milan.[25]

Rossi envisioned a quite different experience for the visitor than those offered by Libeskind and Disney. The white, stone-clad cube proposed for Cuneo functioned as a vehicle, a device to guide a visitor to the act of contemplation, to be lived from within the memorial itself, standing on a terrace from which to gaze at the distant site of the reprisals. The only programming to the visitor occurred in the subtle prod to shed quotidian cares through the ascent of stairs, through darkness to a light-suffused space open to the sky. Rossi intended it as a place where, raised above the surroundings and looking beyond the park and the Gesso River to Boves, meditation on the events commemorated and their import could, if desired, take place. In his Redipuglia monument to World War I soldiers, Greppi appealed to individual and collective memories through the 100,000 soldiers' names engraved in the stairs and the response "Presente!" to the roll call repeated along with them. Rossi's proposal summoned both collective and individual memories in a different way, precisely by directing each visitor's passage up the tightly framed and steadily narrowing staircase to a singular, deeply personal moment on the viewing terrace which would be, nonetheless, the site of a powerful, collective memory. That same year, Rossi and Meda also proposed a cubic fountain set in a shallow pool for Milan, adopting the same crisp geometry as at Cuneo, though with some adjustments.[26] Three of the four walls of this cube would have sheets of water flowing into a channel below the pedestal; this, along with the view of the sky from the open-air terrace, would summon reflection on the rhythms of nature, the passage of time, and the "human passions" of joy as well as suffering that ebb and flow over the courses of our lives.[27]

Although the team did not prevail in the Cuneo competition, the project constituted a benchmark in Rossi's designs, condensing his reflections on memory, monuments, and personal experience while foreshadowing richer and more complex development over time. The two most significant architectural features carried forward to the later projects are the staircase framed by high walls and an open-air viewing platform. That he was working on his first book and the monuments for Cuneo and Segrate contemporaneously contributed to the way his thoughts evolved in the ensuing years. While he and his team developed the first competition submission, Rossi also worked on the book's final draft, and this provides an important key to understanding how his thinking matured between 1962 and 1965. Born as a critique of the hegemony of the modern movement in architecture, the book both criticized the architectural and the urban theories dominant in mid-century America and Europe and also proposed different methodologies for understanding cities and architecture. Of the many topics he considered, one addressed the monument, its character, significance, and role in the community. For Rossi, among other things a monument expressed the collective memory of a community and as such formed an essential link between the present and the group's past.

As he divided his time on the book and the Cuneo project, he mulled over the varied meanings of monuments. He found Maurice Halbwachs's 1945 (posthumous) book *On Collective Memory* particularly informative.[28] Halbwachs identified what he termed collective memory, like all memories, as springing from the dynamics of group interpersonal relations. In effect, Halbwachs argued that groups assemble personal memories to form a body of collective memories, even if each individual member will nonetheless conserve a particular view of that past and of its single events. Collective memories, distinct to a group, continually shape and reshape the group's shared experiences. Halbwachs embraced the theory of his mentor Henri Bergson on the subjective origins of memory, without entirely rejecting the ideas of Emile Durkheim, for whom the role of society in the formation of collective memory far exceeded the subjectivist approach of the former.[29] In part by referring to groups instead of a rather more vague "society," Halbwachs rejected those aspects of Durkheim's theory that ignored the role of the subjective even in the formulation of group memories. For Rossi, Halbwachs's concept of collective memory underlay every monument commissioned or preserved by a community, each one fashioned of both group and individual memories. Those collective memories did not end with the construction of the monument.

Halbwachs's chapter on space and collective memory particularly attracted Rossi, where the sociologist wrote, "The group's image of its external milieu and its stable relationships with this environment becomes paramount in the idea it forms of itself, permeating every element of its consciousness, moderating and governing its evolution."[30] How this milieu took shape, how a monument figured in this process, and what role it could play in a particular city, intrigued Rossi. The architecture of the city, the sign on the walls of the town hall, Rossi wrote, its very soul, its character, its memory, become the city's history.[31] The forms never stood alone for Rossi; they took shape in specific places, each with its own unique history and collection of memories. In speaking of *genius loci*, or the spirit of a place, Rossi wrote to his colleague and friend Paolo Ceccarelli in 1965 that he considered it like the space of the Catholic Church. "The universal space is defined as the communion of saints; [the space] is undifferentiated. But sanctuaries, pilgrimage sites are particular, recognizable acceptances of space, even if they have nothing to do with the space of the [universal] church."[32]

From Halbwachs he understood that when groups enter a space, they at once transform it and adapt to it. In turn, that exterior environment and the relationships it conserves come to form the image the group retains of itself. The city thus constitutes the collective memory of its peoples as found and embodied in objects and places. Rossi referred to this as the city's locus, which together with the architecture, the history, and what Rossi described as *permanences*, constitute some of the most compelling features of the city as a human-made object, an urban artifact. By permanences, Rossi indicated those features that remain constant over the city's history, such as streets, the general plan, and individual historical structures of various types, all of which could either be propelling and positive or negative forces.[33] Into this category, Rossi inserted monuments, with memory the most essential unifying element for a community. The architectural monument both exceeds and differs from a work of art, because while art exists for itself alone, Rossi argued, the monument is intimately, permanently, bound up with the city. It should trigger celebration, he wrote in 1956, but also "severe remembrance" and "the comprehension of human passions."[34] It is, he wrote, "the paradigmatic architectural expression."[35]

When city officials launched the competition at Segrate, twenty years had passed since the end of the war, twenty years during which ravaged cities cleared out rubble left behind from bombings and families put their lives back together despite the loss of loved ones. Segrate is a small center of about 33,000 people on the eastern outskirts of Milan, its origins lost in the mists of history but probably dating back at least to the period following the Gallic Wars at the end of the third century BCE. Still an agricultural center at the beginning of the twentieth century, the town is now largely a bedroom community for Milan. In 1965, Italy's Economic Miracle still powered industrialization and development, and Segrate's building boom was in full swing.[36]

The competition for the piazza and a monument to Italy's partisans gave Rossi a second opportunity to develop further his thoughts on monuments and collective memories, this time on a site across from a new town hall designed by a team headed by one of his university friends, Guido Canella (1963–66, now the town's library).[37] At Segrate, the monument would be the main ornament of a newly reconfigured piazza adjacent to the town hall, and as such, a daily reminder of a not so distant past (fig. 3.8). No evoking of memories of noncombatants who died as "collateral damage" and no privileged gaze toward the site of disgraceful Nazi war crimes guided the competition rules. The remit at Segrate simply entailed honoring all partisans who had fought against Nazi-Fascism throughout Italy; this, and its location within a future residential quarter of no particular historical significance, presented new challenges for Rossi. In some way, the piazza and monument also had to enter into a dialogue with the new town hall (known as the Giuseppe Verdi Civic Center), a challenge because of its formal distinctiveness. It consists of a generally circular form that unfolds in plan almost like a chambered nautilus, with one rectangular entrance block angled and more or less facing the space set aside for the new piazza and monument. The full-size fenestration of the cylindrical sections is marked by irregular groups of two to four cement columns, while a giant order of

FIGURE 3.8
Aldo Rossi and Luca Meda, Monument to Partisans, Segrate, 1965 (Federico Torra)

columns is disposed regularly along the entrance façade. With an architectural language neither modernist nor historicizing but rather springing from the formal principles possibly associated with the organic architecture movement introduced into Italy after the war by Bruno Zevi, the town hall stands out from the surrounding—largely speculative and conventional—residential housing.[38] Rossi had to work out a design autonomous from the town hall, something with a distinct presence and power all its own. And he did.

Though difficult to imagine today, when erected the Monument to Partisans indeed stood in the middle of a field, with only a couple of ancient farmhouses and the new town hall as neighbors. New, large buildings (see fig. 3.8) did not appear for several more years, so Rossi had to imagine a future for the monument. He proposed surrounding the piazza with a wall (not built) to close it off from the adjacent fields but punctuated by doors. He framed the site with trees, low stairs leading toward the town hall, and fragments of cylinders set on square bases, objects Rossi described as "fragments

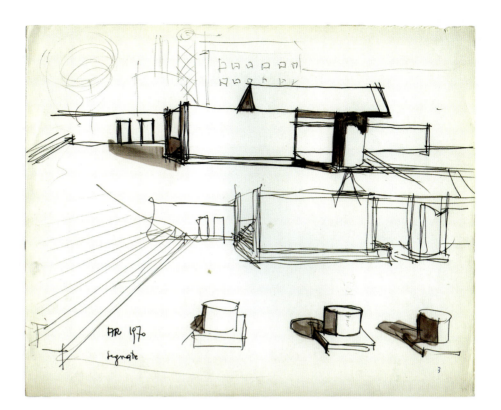

FIGURE 3.9
Aldo Rossi, Monument to Partisans, Segrate, ink drawing, 1970 (Fondazione AR/© Aldo Rossi Heirs)

of other architectures" (fig. 3.9). For the stairs leading into the piazza he chose cement, while for the paving he ordered red porphyry cobblestones, positioning the monument within a long tradition of porphyry monuments on the Italian peninsula. Pliny the Elder spelled out imperial porphyry's origins in Egypt; Romans knew it as the hardest of stones, particularly prized for monuments, especially for drapery on busts of historical figures.[39] At Segrate, the monument itself consists of a podium and a fountain, once again a deceptively simple scheme. High concrete walls frame a narrow staircase. A triangular section that appears to have slid off of the podium extends out to a single, white cylinder set on a shallow base. One peers through the open triangle not at the countryside, nor at the town hall, but at the residential blocks before it, as if in mute acknowledgment of the types of ordinary people from whose ranks the partisans who battled Nazi-Fascism came. The triangle, Rossi wrote, "is a permanent element as form, and in the composition [it is] substantially a canal, a covered passage, a cantilevered link, more or less a pediment."[40] Rossi described the monument as a machine, in that from the cylinder and triangular element a fine sheet of water flows to a cement channel set perpendicular to the monument. Both the cylinder and the triangular canal were to be painted a bright and shiny white, with the remainder unpainted concrete.

Rossi variously described the scheme as an assemblage of parts and fragments, as a machine of architecture, as an architecture of shadows. In exploring the implications of these concepts Rossi availed himself of multiple sources. He referred to the metaphysical paintings in the *Piazze d'Italia* series of Giorgio de Chirico, often described as conveying mystery and melancholy. From early on, Rossi included a tower or chimney in some of his drawings, a tower that in one case he described as an homage to de Chirico because of the resemblance to towers in the *Piazze d'Italia* series.[41] The homage ended with the tower, however, for while de Chirico's paintings indeed constituted part of Rossi's visual archive, arguably Mario Sironi's paintings of Milan's industrial suburbs held greater potency for him. Bereft of people but populated by largely utilitarian, modern structures remote from the city's architectural traditions, the city's expanding periphery nonetheless constituted an important challenge, one that Rossi addressed in his earliest publications on the socialist city and the expanding metropolis.[42] Nonetheless, images from art works on canvas formed only a small part of his repository of visual sources; Rossi primarily looked elsewhere for inspiration.

Assembled of parts, pieces and fragments, the monument and piazza deliberately summoned references to other piazzas, other architectures. The column fragments set between the town hall and the monument, like the porphyry pavement, recall the town's remote Roman origins, but also other, nearly forgotten architectures that, with a bit of imagination, come to life. Rossi knew the rich history of columns of infamy (*colonne infame*), with which those guilty of betrayal or heinous crimes were punished severely. Among the methods chosen to damn the miscreant's name in perpetuity, governments confiscated and destroyed their houses, replacing them with a single column inscribed with their crimes. A column of infamy figures in the tale recounted by Alessandro Manzoni in *Storia della colonna infame* (1840) in an appendix to his novel *The Betrothed*. In its solitary setting empty of buildings, such a column spoke to citizens even if they were unable to read the inscriptions.[43] When a monument lacks figures, such as at Segrate and at the Vietnam Veterans Memorial in Washington, D.C., many theorists argue that more imaginative reactivations of the events or people memorialized take place than in others that include figures.[44] For Rossi, where rationality and logic end, what he described as an exalted rationalism steps in to allow the imagination to take wing. Those blunted columns invite the viewer to restore the absent parts, and with them to imaginatively summon forth a full range of associations and memories. So too for each piece of architecture in the piazza: we believe in what we can imagine, and Rossi asked us, the viewers, simply to imagine. He often referred to André Breton's wry salute to imagination, which never forgives.[45]

Cylinder, triangle, square, circle, portico: the most primitive of architectural forms, from which Rossi fashioned the monument he never intended as appeals to the architectural archaic or as some residual purist impulse. Rossi envisioned meaning in architecture as far more expansive and open-ended—which also explains why facile formal comparisons to other works will never help unlock the richness of Rossi's thought. In annotations to sketches of the basic forms in his designs, he observed that the circle,

FIGURE 3.10
Church of Santa Clara, Santiago de Compostela, Spain, façade by Simón Rodriguez, 17th c.

or the cylinder, represents infinity, the basis of everything, with the triangle as the fixed and inalterable natural law from which all other forms spring. Doubled, the triangle becomes a square, and doubled to infinity it brings multiplicity leading, finally, even to man.[46] In the original scheme for the monument at Segrate, the brilliant white varnish of the triangle and water canal emphasized their singularity, from which water flowed endlessly, and from the three forms—triangle, cylinder, and podium—fell the shadows that Rossi embraced. In Italy's piazzas, he remarked, the shadows belong to the architecture; in effect, he anticipated the shadows even as he designed. To the fixed and static shadows in de Chirico's paintings, Rossi counterposed a concept of shadows that marked the passage of time, of the seasons; dynamic and expressive, they embodied becoming, a future still unfolding, as yet undefined.[47]

A few years after having completed the Segrate project, Rossi took a trip through Galicia in northern Spain, where he found himself enthralled by the baroque façade of the convent church of Santa Clara at Santiago de Compostela (fig. 3.10).[48] He viewed the grand cylinder that crowned the façade as particularly compelling. He described the powerful upward thrust of the various elements, including two smaller cylinders disposed laterally that terminate with the central cylinder that, despite its horizontal position, continues as a powerful force. In his exploration of geometries and forms in earlier projects, such as the town hall for Scandicci and the Gallaratese housing, he admitted that this potential had escaped him, both for the upward thrust and for the power of the additive nature of the individual forms. The cylinder reappeared in many subsequent projects after this first appearance at Segrate, a form that interested him beyond any structural or functional exigencies.

THINKING THE MONUMENT

The monument to Pertini, springing as it does from the two earlier monuments at Cuneo and Segrate designed while he was writing *The Architecture of the City,* though more than two decades later summarizes and clarifies some of the themes he had explored at Cuneo, Segrate, and for other projects in the intervening years, such as the new municipal buildings in Perugia, the Bonnefanten Museum, the school at Broni, even the Gallaratese. Clues to his design thinking and to the resources upon which he drew for his reflections abound in his drawings and writings, one of the most important being his introduction to the first Italian edition of Boullée's *Architecture: Essai sur l'art.* Boullée's severe but simple geometries appealed to Rossi less as examples of artifacts shorn of specific historical associations than as simple forms that permit imaginative reflection and allow meanings to accrue over time. After discussing Boullée's thoughts on the role of rational design principles in general, Rossi turned to the question of how a design evolves, proceeding from the earliest moments to the finished product. He referred to Boullée's design for a metropolitan library, where for Rossi the key to understanding the design and its meaning was to arrive at its ineffable origin, "an emotional reference point that eludes analysis; it is bound to the theme from the outset and it will grow throughout the design process."[49] Boullée began with an understanding of a library as a repository of the spiritual inheritance of past culture, Rossi wrote, and in developing a formal solution he associated his design with Raphael's fresco in the Vatican Palace, the *School of Athens*, not only for the grand space and the vibrant figures depicted, but for the technical mastery it evinced. From here, Rossi reflected on Boullée's engagement with the compositional, technological, structural, and stylistic character of the architecture. Without denying the importance of any of those matters, Rossi repeatedly returned to that initial, emotional reference point that eludes analysis yet clearly stands at the heart of any design. No matter how persuasive and complete the rational character of a project, for Aldo Rossi a design based solely on that would always be inadequate.

"There is no art that is not is autobiographical," wrote Rossi, as he struggled to explain how the artist unlocks individual, human, deeply personal experience—that is, that of the artist, in the process of inventing a technique, *una tecnica*.[50] Certainly as he was exploring these matters in his reading of Boullée, Rossi was also negotiating them in his own design processes, whether for a building or for a drawing, and he especially found Boullée's reflections on shadows evocative. Even during his university years Rossi mused about the meaning of a monument, the emotions it was destined to spur—at once "severe remembrance" and a "comprehension of human passions."[51] Does this help us understand that "emotional" or "spiritual" core from which the three designs at Cuneo, Segrate, and Via Croce Rossa unfolded? In part, yes. Take, for example, the shadows of which he wrote frequently, the dynamic shadows at Segrate and at the Pertini monument. Shadows, Rossi noted, "alter the relation with reality."[52] They participate in the double sense of the word *tempo* in Italian, which can mean both duration and atmosphere. Shadows mark the passage of time (*tempo*) in the piazza, and even changes in the weather (*tempo*). The piazza and the monument, alive in the most fundamental ways, radically differ from the static melancholy of de Chirico's *Piazze d'Italia;* indeed, Rossi quite explicitly rejected those references:

> For this [reason] I don't think I am interested in silence, in an architecture of silence, as is often said [of my work]. In these walls, in the walkways of the Gallaratese, in the courtyards, in all [of it] I am attentive to this tumult that is life: it seems to me that I prepare it, that I observe perplexed everything that will happen.[53]

Rossi's perplexity about the inability of others to perceive the joy in the monument to Pertini, for example, certainly sprang from his belief in the capacity of people

FIGURE 3.11
Giovanni Battista Crespi (designer), Siro Zanella and Bernardo Falconi (sculptors), San Carlone, Arona, 1614–98

to imagine the lives and activities that would unfold in their spaces, that would animate them with surprise and delight. To this add those personal, autobiographical experiences of which he also wrote repeatedly. One of his favorite poets, Carlo Pòrta (1776–1821), provides clues for how Rossi imagined the monument as embedded in the richly complex and varied mix of the quotidian.[54] Pòrta explored the power of the intimately contemporary world of early-nineteenth-century Milan particularly as transmitted through poems in the Milanese dialect and through an intense attention to the ordinary people he found in that world. For Rossi, these at times sad, at times rollickingly humorous poems appealed to his own sense of the importance of the ordinary and the real in his own work, particularly monuments such as at Segrate and in Milan.

All three projects—Cuneo, Segrate, Pertini—center on a staircase and viewing platform as the most meaningful and immediate expression of the monuments' significance. Other than the Redipuglia Memorial and Terragni's Sarfatti project, monuments consisting primarily of a staircase are not common, so how to explain Rossi's decision to use it as a solution for projects spanning nearly thirty years?

Rossi's drawings shed light on this, particularly those that include the statue of San Carlo Borromeo at Arona (1614–98), known affectionately as Sancarlone or San Carlone (big San Carlo), which figured in his drawings from 1968 forward but in his writings even earlier. As a child, Rossi's aunt took him to visit the enormous 35-meter-tall (about 115 feet, including pedestal) copper-plated statue overlooking Lago Maggiore in northern Italy (fig. 3.11). Sheets of hammered copper fastened with nails and tie rods are bound to a hollow-core structure fashioned of stone, brick, and iron that is accessible on the interior. The arm extended in blessing required a complicated structural system to enable it to withstand the area's often violent winds. Rossi delighted in these practical, technical accomplishments, but again, they could not explain the statue, nor could they clarify the contours of the pilgrim's journey inside the statue (fig. 3.12). Rossi recalled entering the body of the saint at its base, then climbing a combination of vertical and spiral staircases to arrive at the top, where he could then peer through the saint's eyes at the panorama of Lago Maggiore, the mountains, and the sky. Rossi described this experience: "As with the Homeric horse, the pilgrim enters the body of the saint as he would a tower or a wagon steered by a knowing technician. After he mounts the exterior stair of the pedestal, the steep ascent through the interior of the body reveals the structure of the work and the welded seams of the huge pieces of sheet metal. Finally, he arrives at the interior-exterior of the head; from the eyes of the saint, the view of the lake acquires infinite contours, as if one were gazing from a celestial observatory."[55]

Rossi's account of the upward movement inside the statue parallels precisely what

FIGURE 3.12
San Carlone, Arona, postcard from the 1950s

he emulated in the three monuments: a narrow, walled, and steep ascent to a viewing platform where architecture frames and controls the vistas (fig. 3.13). Even more germane, at Cuneo, entry into a covered, enclosed space only opens to the light as one ascends the stairs, in effect recreating the experience of climbing San Carlone.[56] Rossi here discovered what the Greeks long ago understood about such ascents. During the passage from the agora (marketplace and public assembly area) to the propylaea (ceremonial gateway) to the acropolis and the temple precinct in Athens, the arduous climb encouraged the pilgrim to shift attention from quotidian affairs to reflect instead upon the sacred rituals about to take place in the temples. Architecture framed and guided the entire journey, up the steep stairs to the Doric portico and the adjacent rooms set aside for refreshment or a pause to admire works of art on display. The trajectory continued through a narrow passageway lined by high Ionic columns, the tight, cool space only faintly lit by clerestory level openings, altogether conveying a sense of mystery, of anticipation, until arrival at bruising light upon entering into the second Doric portico and its dramatic opening to a panoramic view of the Parthenon, the colossal statue of Athena, the Erechtheion, and the sacred precinct of the Acropolis. The ascent to a sanctuary, from the time of the Greeks through to the era of Christianity, always entailed a notion of purification while moving toward something greater than the self. The architecture of the propylaea deliberately urged just such a cleansing on the part of the pilgrim, to detach emotionally and intellectually from ordinary matters and to engage with the spirituality embodied in the rituals about to be enacted. Rossi knew this journey well. An often published photograph shows him standing amid the Parthenon's grand fluted columns in 1971, having completed the same ritual climb as the Athenians had done thousands of years earlier. As a schoolboy, Rossi's visits to the sanctuary, near his boarding school, dedicated to St. Jerome Emiliani entailed the same kind of ascent, with high steps initially framed by flanking walls much as in the three monuments discussed here (fig. 3.14).

That Rossi mused on the significance of stairs and upward movement more generally is clear from entries in his *Quaderni Azzurri*. In later years, after moving his office to be across the street from the eighteenth-century church of Santa Maria alla Porta (Francesco Maria Richini, 1652), or more properly, Santa Maria Annunziata, he frequently studied the church's elegant baroque façade, specifically reflecting on the words engraved on the entablature: *Ascendit quasi Aurora consurgens* (Who arises like the Dawn).[57] After identifying the source of the inscription as the biblical Song of Songs 6:10, Rossi detected an error in the inscription. The church was dedicated to the Virgin Mary at the Gate, in reference to the Vercellina Gate which the church replaced on the

FIGURE 3.13
Aldo Rossi, San Carlone, mixed media (Fondazione AR/
© Aldo Rossi Heirs)

FIGURE 3.14
Sanctuary of St. Jerome
Emiliani, Somasca,
Holy Stairs

ancient Roman *decumano massimo* (main decumanus). The inscription referred to the assumption of Mary into heaven, but Rossi took issue with the use of the word *ascendere*. He noted that to ascend (*ascendere*) differed from to be assumed (*assumere*), in that the Virgin Mary was "assumed," or admitted or brought up into heaven (at the feast of the Assumption), while Christ ascended into the heavens from which he originated, that is, *ascensionis in caelum domini nostri Iesu Christi* (Our Lord Jesus Christ ascended into heaven). In stairs such as in his three monuments, even though we ascend them, as pilgrims we seek to be assumed by a loving God, he believed, extracting us from our earthly distractions.[58]

Lessons from the Greeks did not escape the attention of later architects, including Karl Friedrich Schinkel in his design of the staircase and portico at the entrance to the Altes Museum in Berlin (1830), a building Rossi had first visited in 1961.[59] In Schinkel's view the museum constituted a repository of the highest accomplishments of human civilization, and thus a sacred space in its own right. Passage into the museum involved ascending a double, royal staircase with landings upon which to pause, either to look back at the city receding in the distance, or ahead at the portico behind which lay an abundance of treasures (fig. 3.15).[60] The art on the walls at the same scale as the urban panorama glimpsed through the columns locks in the parallel Schinkel drew between the two. In both cases, the giant Ionic order mediated vistas both entering and leaving, a reminder of the journey undertaken from day-to-day life to the prospect of meditating on the extraordinary achievements of human civilization. Rossi did not forget that one both ascends and descends heights, and indeed, a photograph he snapped from inside the San Carlone statue in 1991 looks down at the religious structures below, with the only part of the statue visible being the saint's hand (fig. 3.16). In his epistolary exchange with Alexander van Grevenstein, director of the Bonnefanten Museum at Maastricht, Rossi lingered over the notion of descending or even falling down stairs more than he did ascending them.[61] He referred to the long-standing tradition of achieving purification in ascending stairs, but also, as in the case of the underground temple at the Santa Cristina archeological site of nuraghe in western Sardinia, a descent into ritual purity (see fig. 4.21).[62]

At a much smaller scale, Rossi explored these concepts in his monument projects. Each visitor embarked on a comparable journey, with a trek up narrow stairs to a terrace with a framed viewing aperture, a collective experience made up, as Halbwachs noted, of the assembly of shared and individual memories. Rossi's monuments also prompted

FIGURE 3.15
Karl Friedrich Schinkel, Portico of Altes Museum, Berlin, lithograph (from *Sammlung Architektonischer Entwürfe*, issue 17, 1831, pl. 103)

FIGURE 3.16
Aldo Rossi, Photograph from inside the San Carlone statue, 27 December 1991 (MAXXI)

the visitor to engage with a personal lived memory as much as with a collective one, and each in its own way responded to the site of memory, the *locus memoriae*. At Cuneo, the visitor would have ascended the stairs to reflect on the events that unfolded at Boves, now an eternal repository of painful but highly explicit collective memories, yet with no visible signs recounting the story. At Segrate, the monument summons nonspecific memories of unnamed partisans who fell during World War II, with no particular events or sites being recalled. Classicist James Porter wrote, "Nowhere are sites of memory more compelling than where they are least visibly supported, as in the example of empty sepulchers, which are literal monuments to memory ... or else in those unmistakable signs of absence—that is, by pure loss—that thus designate *the very loss of loss.* Remains like these, overwhelmingly oppressive in their felt material presence, are the most resistant to the project of description and therefore the sublimest sites of all."[63]

And this Rossi understood to be an essential aspect of architectural form: "The most precise form is also the one most absent, and something of this is expressed perhaps in the desire to imitate to which my projects submit."[64] From some perspectives, Segrate even alludes to a nude, undecorated modernist sepulchre with its top slid forward, partially opening the interior. The ancient Greek town of Assos in northwestern Turkey comes to mind, where Aristotle founded a school of philosophy in 340 BCE and where the apostle Paul walked (Acts 20:13–15). Despite its breathtaking panorama over the Aegean, the ruins of an important sixth-century BCE temple to Athena, and a stunning Greek theater of volcanic stone nestled into the hillside, for the visitor it can be the empty plundered sarcophagi scattered on either side of the road between the citadel and the harbor below that remain in memory–enduringly, powerfully captivating.[65] The Segrate memorial, too, without an individual or unique event to commemorate, evinces the signs of absence, of pure loss, and hence in Porter's terms, resides among the most sublime of monuments.

The decision to dedicate the Milan project to Pertini arrived as an afterthought, when Rossi had already designed the piazza and the monument. Since no specific purpose guided the design other than transforming a former intersection into a public square, Rossi's inspiration necessarily sprang from elsewhere. Like many cities in Italy, Milan's origins predate the arrival of the Romans, though Roman troops conquered and annexed the city in 222 BCE.[66] Milan's thick tapestry of memories quite literally litters the city with a millennial accumulation of sacred sites, against which the Milanese brush in the course of their daily lives. Rossi intended his project as a new element slipped into that rich tapestry, one destined over time to become as much a part of the everyday as were Milan's other memories. For Rossi then, the monument itself would become a celebration of life and of the city in all their reciprocal complexity.

How did his design accomplish this? Just as the column fragments at Segrate encouraged viewers to complete them imaginatively, so too in Milan do the stairs, benches, trees and lampposts, viewing platform, and aperture induce active engagement. In reflecting on public buildings in an essay Rossi prepared for an exhibit together with photographer Luigi Ghirri, he wrote of Leon Battista Alberti's church of Sant'Andrea in Mantua as a structure "bound to the light and to the fog. Sant'Andrea is a forum and a covered piazza, interior/exterior again, city/country, almost undefined in its precise design."[67] Even earlier, in 1974, Rossi had described a church as a covered piazza, a single space within which diverse activities occurred.[68] When he designed the Via Croce Rossa site a dozen years later, he reversed the order, in effect producing an outdoor, cathedral-like space recalling the plan of a Romanesque church, with colonnades of alternating trees and light standards framing the nave, trees with branches that seasonally form a vault over the nave, the cube as a raised, altar-like structure, and benches for seating (fig. 3.17). The basilica church form, modified and essential, springs into robust temporality by means of the elegant colonnade of alternating light standards and trees undergoing seasonal and temporal changes, by the evening light flickering through the leaves, by the benches interspersed between the trees facing not the cubic monument but one another, by the rush of water from the triangular fountain to the rear of the cube, and by visitors who animate and summon new memories to the site. They climb and sit on the stairs and reflect on the spectacle unfolding before them in the cathedrallike space, or they can turn around and peer through the I-beam-framed opening at a slice of the Milan Duomo itself (fig. 3.18). Rossi's experience ascending the interior of San Carlone, where the final view through the saint's eyes evoked reflections on infinity, "as if one were gazing from a celestial observatory," helps explain his aspiration for these monuments. Rossi kept the tumult of daily life in the forefront as he designed, with all its vitality and excitement. But with the monuments, and not only with them, he encouraged meditation on what lies beyond the quotidian, that which the celestial observatory seems to offer, a glimpse of the infinite unfolding before us. At the same time, however, Rossi rejoiced at the tumult that he eagerly anticipated filling the square over time, burnishing the marble and bronze with an ever-thickening accumulation of collective memories. The two necessarily go together—the tumult and the infinite.

FIGURE 3.17
Aldo Rossi, Monument to Pertini with Milan Duomo, photocopy plus ink and felt tip pens (Fondazione AR/© Aldo Rossi Heirs)

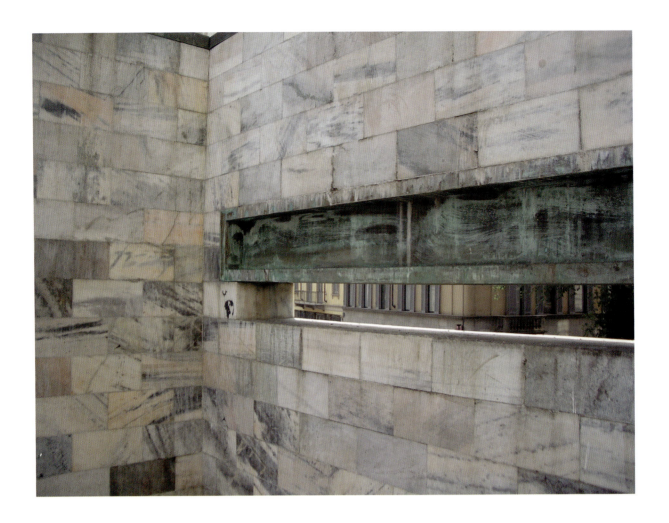

FIGURE 3.18
Monument to Pertini, viewing fissure

The projects considered here, particularly the monument at Segrate but also the cubes at Cuneo and Milan, reappear in part or in whole in Rossi's drawings and prints throughout his career. Often registered as disparate elements adjacent to one another, the forms also confront the many issues that engaged Rossi in his writings and designs. The earliest drawings of the three projects disclose how each design took shape, but the later ones illustrate Rossi's habit of returning to an apparently infinite wellspring of images, memories, and desires, shuffling them among fragments of other projects, such as Gallaratese and the Modena cemetery. Indeed, the staircase from the ground to the first floor at Gallaratese repeats that at Segrate on a larger scale, while the stairs for the fountain at the Fontivegge regional government complex in Perugia (1982) almost painfully tighten and narrow the passage (fig. 3.19). In the drawings, among the most constant features, the partial figure of San Carlone—or even just the hand—participates in the narrative of the personal and the collective nested within one another, as memories always are.

FIGURE 3.19
Aldo Rossi, Regional Offices and Centro Direzionale,
Fontivegge, Perugia, 1982, detail of fountain

FIGURE 3.20
Aldo Rossi, "L'architettura assassinata," lithograph, 1974 (Private Collection/© Aldo Rossi Heirs)

Drawings related to the Segrate and Pertini projects reveal other aspects of Rossi's ideas. In general they are impressionistic rather than documentary, and indeed, as in some where he transformed the monument's scale and even its color or, as in his fanciful composition "L'architettura assassinata" (Architecture Assassinated, 1974), he shifted the triangular channel off axis from the cylinder (fig. 3.20). As with most of his drawings, they are open-ended and generative, assembled of real or fictional fragments to make space for innumerable narratives for himself and for visitors. In "L'architettura assassinata," or at least this version of the subject, quotidian household objects and the buildings at the same scale jostle for space on a yellow field of destruction against a backdrop of stability, where construction cranes stand ready to erect new structures.[69] Critics focusing on a reading of melancholy or despair often see only the foreground, but not even all of the foreground: the household objects such as coffeepot, wine bottle, cup,

FIGURE 3.21
Aldo Rossi, Monument
to Partisans, Segrate
(Federico Torra)

silverware, and pot rest calmly on the yellow field and do not join the little architectures that jump, fracture, and tumble. Never fixed solely on the visual, Rossi also apprehended his memories with a profound tactile sensibility such that they remained enfolded within a spatial and temporal expansion wherein he perceived himself poised between time and eternity. Those objects of daily life illustrate Rossi's endless "nexus with the things that surround [him]," their shadows suggesting the tranquil passage of time in the face of the stability of a civilization greater than the temporary noise before it, the tumult, that which, in Rossi's words, he anticipates in all of his projects.[70] The three monuments, in drawings and in reality, rest poised on that sweet tension between the rough and tumble of daily life and a glimpse of the elusive horizon that we call infinity (fig. 3.21).

# 4   Building for Culture

> Wisdom shouts in the streets, in the square,
>   ... in the city she raises her voice.
>   —PROVERBS 1:20

In 1987, as the Borgoricco town hall slowly rose from the fields north of Padua, Aldo Rossi wrote in his *Quaderni Azzurri*, "I love this project."[1] He followed its construction more closely than he had other projects, even though inadequate funding meant it lacked furniture and sat open and unused until a decade after completion. Rossi did not explain his particular fondness for the town hall then, but four years later he characterized Borgoricco as emblematic of his architecture, or even of architecture more generally.[2] Why he made this claim both confirms his unique contribution to late-twentieth-century architecture and differentiates his approach from that of his contemporaries, and indeed from most architects today. Borgoricco also introduces us to Rossi's designs for public architecture, from schools to libraries to museums to municipal buildings. They set out from the same premises that undergirded the monuments considered in the last chapter, and they illustrate another dimension of his understanding of the multiple roles of monuments in the life of the city.

### BUILDING FOR EDUCATION

In his medieval treatise on education, *The Didascalicon*, Hugh of Saint Victor wrote to his students, "Learn everything that you possibly can, and later you will find that none of it was superfluous."[3] Rossi's words to students sounded the same note. A voracious reader in subjects from theology to poetry, Rossi possessed a curiosity that probed everything, from music to film to cultural artifacts of all types. In looking back on his own education, especially in the Somascan Fathers' boarding school near Lake Como, his appreciation and joy in his education never wavered. In the draft of an autobiography from late 1971 he expressed his gratitude for the Catholic education "that enabled me to choose extremely different types of logic and beauty inasmuch as they referred to something

Detail, figure 4.20

beyond themselves."[4] As an adult he also spoke of the sadness of leaving the hills around Lecco and the memory of Somasca, areas that had by then become "autobiographical, without discoveries but confirmed by life."[5] In the area of Lombardy near Piedmont familiar to him since childhood, he managed to design a school he believed extremely important, in the small town of Fagnano Olona (1971).

The previous year, Rossi had finished remodeling and enlarging the De Amicis elementary school in the southern Lombard town of Broni, although he only designed the entrance portico, stairs, some new classrooms inside the early-twentieth-century structure's courtyard, and the fountain framed by a colonnade. The latter became one of the most well-known images of the school in his drawings and in photographs. Here too could be found the square, four-light windows and the colorful frames common to many of his later projects. With the commission for a new school in Fagnano Olona, the Salvatore Orrù Elementary School, Rossi now had the opportunity to elaborate a complete design for what he described as a place of life: the school.[6] This small town near Varese sits on the banks of the Olona River, in a province tucked between Switzerland, the Piedmont region, Lake Como, Milan, and the eastern Po Valley. The community enjoys a unique history and some important monuments (a Visconti-era castle, the sanctuary of the Madonna of the Selva). Germanic tribes known as *longobardi* (or longbeards) conquered northern Italy in the sixth century, but after two centuries the area regained its autonomy for six hundred years until the fourteenth century, when the Visconti family took control of the area and established the duchy of Milan.[7] Italy's nineteenth-century industrial revolution centered in part in the Olona valley, where the river's mills powered a burgeoning textile industry. Only 5 kilometers (3 miles) from one of the province's chief industrialized cities, Busto Arsizio, Fagnano's residents labored in the new factories, especially in the second half of the century, and women also did piecework at home for textile entrepreneurs.

The most recent census in 2011 recorded the population's steady increase to nearly 13,000 people, and it continues to grow as a bedroom suburb for the larger cities of Busto Arsizio, Gallarate, Legnano, Saronno, and Milan. A new elementary school became a necessity already by 1971, the year Rossi received the commission.[8] Not unlike the recent Broni project, he conceived of the Salvatore Orrù school as a small city organized around a piazza, with the classrooms branching off from it (fig. 4.1). Obscured by trees on Via Pasubio and Via Legnano, on the other sides the school opens to playgrounds and more greenery. He described the plan as evolving from a central axis extending from the entrance to the library through the courtyard to the stairs and to the gymnasium. Off of this axis branch three wings on each side, one-story structures with Rossi's preferred large square windows. Here, as in the Modena cemetery, he envisioned a cylindrical structure, in this case the library, as the heart of the school. Its glazed and metal roof bathes the interior with light but leaves in shadow the bookshelves subsequently tucked under a smaller drum. The metal stairway from the ground to an upper passageway

FIGURE 4.1
Aldo Rossi, Salvatore Orrù Elementary School, Fagnano Olona, completed 1975, pergola

presumably anticipated a time when the library would serve the larger community (fig. 4.2).

In choosing a centrally planned structure, Rossi returned to one of his earliest major projects, for the Paganini Theater in Parma (1964). In both cases he referenced a typical feature of medieval Italian cities—either an octagonal baptistery, such as at San Giovanni in Laterano, Rome, or a round one, such as San Giovanni in Florence—but to a different effect in the school. The centrally planned library here evokes another liturgical meaning, for with the invention of baptisteries, the sacrament signifying entrance into the Christian community became a public rather than a private event, one witnessed by the community at large quite apart from the significance to the individual being baptized. In selecting a centrally planned structure, Rossi emphasized its role in presenting young students to their culture, in effect offering them an introduction to the history and traditions of the global community by means of the library. Not surprisingly, Rossi repeatedly called on this concept for other school facilities—notably at the second school in Broni a few years later, but even for the new building for the architecture school at the University of Miami some fifteen years later.

Rossi thereby adapted a building type imbued with sacred or liturgical meaning in Italian culture to a secular purpose, where the aspirations of the new structure cohered with those of the original type. But he was not the first to have done so. Significant modern examples include the reading room at the British Library (Panizzi and Smirke, 1854), and in the twentieth century, Gunnar Asplund's Municipal Library in Stockholm (1925), a grand cylindrical structure with clerestory lighting and books lining the walls, all of which Rossi particularly appreciated. What distinguished his libraries from these

FIGURE 4.2
Salvatore Orrù Elementary School, library

splendid earlier exemplars was precisely his unique decision to insert a grand, essentially nineteenth-century building type into a far more humble setting, reduced in scale but not in ambition. With the beneficiaries no longer prosperous and literate men but children of all backgrounds, these exquisite little libraries transcended barriers of class, gender, and education, thereby ennobling both the school and the library type itself.

Rossi's selection of this motif, neither banal nor hasty, also sprang from his reflections a decade earlier on the writings of Boullée, as well as the National Library that Boullée had proposed for Paris. Rossi later designed a library in Seregno (1989) with a vast, barrel-vaulted space soaring above book-lined walls and terminating in a grand triumphal arch. It amounts to a direct homage to Boullée, underscoring the shared views of the two architects about the significance of libraries for their cultures. Boullée had announced his design for the National Library with the observation that in a library one could encounter the masterpieces of great men that "would evoke a desire to follow in their footsteps and give rise to lofty thoughts. . . . The building that is most precious to a Nation is undoubtedly one which houses all its acquired knowledge."[9] This twofold observation—the importance to the collectivity of its heritage of accumulated knowledge conserved within and the inspirational effect that knowledge would bestow on others—underscores Rossi's understanding of a library and his choice of a centrally planned structure. Like the baptistery, it emphasized the building's public dimension as a public school, and at the same time it evinced what Rossi believed about young minds, whose study "is larger, positive, progressive," and hence fully open to the treasures of the culture offered in libraries. The courtyard, which Rossi defined as its public square, its piazza, likewise affirmed its public role.

At the opposite end of the piazza from the library a broad staircase ascends to a smaller piazza, flanked by the gymnasium, where Rossi imagined children would gather for the annual class photograph (fig. 4.3). He also drew attention to the industrialized environment surrounding Fagnano, and he acknowledged it with his choice of the brick chimney for the school's incinerator, recalling the tall brick chimneys of the area's industrial plants, fortunately for the environment now largely abandoned but with their tall towers still dotting the landscape. Despite the care with which Rossi developed the scheme, some of the most notable features—the pergola, the bike deposit, the glazed cupola, and the blue portico—came about in the course of construction, which delighted Rossi because they echoed the variations and incidental changes of life itself.[10]

Beyond these fairly straightforward observations, Rossi's work on the Fagnano school and his writings about it allow us to glimpse the wide range of his reflections, and how things he saw and read came together in remarkable ways as he worked out or thought back to a particular design. In comments drafted in 1972, he noted the importance of the school's entrance, bound up for him with our "anguished memory" of school, a shared stress associated with exams, recitations, and memorization.[11] Such childhood fears remained impressed on his memory; passing through the school's door eerily

FIGURE 4.3
Salvatore Orrù Elementary School, stairs (Federico Torra)

FIGURE 4.4
Salvatore Orrù Elementary School, plan, site and massing studies, pen and marker on paper (Drawing Matter Collection/© Aldo Rossi Heirs)

resembled entering the whale's mouth in the story of Pinocchio. Although the whale swallowed both Pinocchio and his father Geppeto, their great fear finally receded, for the two ultimately escaped while the beast slept, just as the terrors of the school ended with the student's successful passage to the next academic year.

In other notes Rossi mused over how the plan at Fagnano in some way also reminded him of a human body laid out flat on the ground (fig. 4.4). Both the Fagnano school and the cemetery of Modena bore layouts vaguely reminiscent of an inert body (fig. 4.5) but were also similar in his mind to the plan he drew in his notebooks of the ascent of Mount Carmel on the basis of the description offered by St. John of the Cross.[12] The sixteenth-century Spanish mystic and poet wrote a tract in which the saint set out the path by which the humble pilgrim should follow the arduous path marked out by the mystic to reach the summit of perfection. That Rossi reflected on and reread *The Ascent of Mount Carmel* while he spent time in a hospital in Bergamo in July 1979 may explain why the form and substance of the mystic's way, the vagaries of Rossi's own ill body, and the layout of the school and the cemetery seemed to Rossi all of a piece.[13]

Four years after completing the school at Fagnano Olona in 1975, Rossi submitted his final proposal for another school in Broni, the C. Ferrini Middle School. With the

FIGURE 4.5
Aldo Rossi, Study for a Pietà or Deposition, pen and watercolor (MAXXI, Rossi/© Aldo Rossi Heirs)

FIGURE 4.6
Aldo Rossi, C. Ferrini Middle School, Broni, 1979, pen and marker on paper (Fondazione AR/© Aldo Rossi Heirs)

opportunity to start afresh, Rossi turned again to the idea of a city, but this time to a smaller, more exclusive one that resembled, more than anything, a monastery (fig. 4.6).[14] Shortly after he consigned the definitive scheme, he commented on how the design process for the school at Broni evolved: "[It] started from developing the central element of Fagnano, [and] it became a great interior courtyard and garden."[15] His words implied that the design itself took over almost independent of his will. Recalling his reading of Boullée's emphasis on the unknowable and the overwhelming importance of the internal source from which a design springs, it seems as if Rossi felt himself impelled by this powerful, mysterious force, almost beyond his control. It should not be surprising that he frequently turned to the monastery as a model because in his earliest *Quaderni Azzurri* he wrote about the monastery as an ideal type.[16] In the monastery he found a direct correlation between form and ideology, or perhaps better, between form and the organization of the community. The Rule of St. Benedict set out the monastic way of life, thereby constituting its very architecture: church, cloister, garden, workplaces, dormitories, refectory, and so forth.[17]

This organization of a type, so exquisitely apparent in monasteries, had already figured in his thinking in the design of the school at Fagnano Olona. During a visit to the Cistercian Royal Abbey of Santa Maria de Poblet at Poblet, Spain, in 1974, he recognized a parallel between the tension created by the compression of the fountain centered in the monastery's patio in opposition to the vertical façade of the church, and the adjacent building with Fagnano's library set in the piazza-like space of the school.[18] In retrospect he realized that the same concept underlay all of the schools he designed in Italy in that for him the school was a "site of life," and as such, it always summoned parallels to the monastery, where the architecture itself springs from the organization of life within. The octagonal theater-auditorium in Broni, with its wood and metal cupola positioned in the center of four small courtyards, Rossi planned as a site for theatrical performances, films, and similar activities, in effect the beating heart of the school and the larger community (fig. 4.7).

For the Tibaldi Middle School in Cantù (1986), instead of adopting the monastery type Rossi chose to place two parallel classroom wings with an intersecting block and a circular structure known as "the planetarium." The gymnasium, auditorium, library, and other facilities are situated between the two classroom wings, and all are topped by shallow copper barrel vaults. The circular brick structure lends grace and character to this

FIGURE 4.7
C. Ferrini Middle School, detail of library ceiling

school, as in the others, as a symbol of the life of the mind ideally to be cultivated in this public facility. Rossi hoped to surmount the circular structure with a dome, but it unfortunately was not completed according to his design.

The town of Broni had long ago decided to enclose three schools within the same precinct, with the elementary, middle, and high schools set adjacent to one another. Yet the way the Ferrini Middle School dominates, even though the other two are larger and taller, is nothing short of a remarkable illustration of how to create an eloquent presence even in a small building. How did Rossi manage to achieve such a compelling presence in such a modest project? Quite simply, the elegance and clarity of the forms stand out against the other two busier yet bland structures. He tailored the scale of the Ferrini school to that of the children, but that only explains part of his achievement, attributable in the end to a combination of scale and the judicious selection of a few simple architectural elements organized into a coherent whole. Even the cupola—the school's most impressive architectural feature—only becomes visible from a distance; children walking up to the front door only briefly glimpse it. Instead a large clock at the entrance greets them, a regular reminder of the bells that mark the passage of time in the classroom, of the order and discipline in the organization of the school day (fig. 4.8). For Rossi, the clocks in effect "marked the time of school, every hour."[19] He loved this school, and all of the schools he designed, because it seemed to him that in them "everything he had never loved about school was redeemed."[20] Although he did not explain further, presumably he referred at least in part to the accommodating plan, large windows, the cheerful theater space and bright colors.

Clocks loomed large in Rossi's inventory of significant images, almost as large as coffeepots. Apart from wall clocks and wristwatches designed for Alessi, Rossi's fascination with watches led him to become a desultory but regular collector of old watches—the hobby that prompted him to persuade Alessi to manufacture wristwatches. The wall clock he designed for Alessi named "Tempo" figures in so many of Rossi's buildings that we too must attend to it (fig. 4.9). Mystery shrouds the devices we use to track time's passing; despite their apparent clarity, unknowables suffuse what they mark to such a degree as to render them more metaphors than measures. Rossi understood this. The intrinsic tension and fragility of the moment, he observed, demand that the wristwatch be robust, hence the steel body protects this index of time's inexorable passage. Records on paper are full of gaps and treat time as if something discontinuous in which we note only the anomalies. The steel-framed clock instead signals continuity even as we know that the quality of the specific moment "undermines the presumed opacity of its continuity."[21]

FIGURE 4.8
C. Ferrini Middle School, façade and cupola behind (Palladium)

FIGURE 4.9
Salvatore Orrù Elementary School, clock inside, chimney through window (Federico Torra)

Critics dismiss Rossi's repetition of clocks as an indicator of a melancholy obsession with the passage of time, with death. Instead, Rossi saw them as reminders of the importance of remaining alert to time, or the attentiveness it demands of us. In a school, he commented, clocks remind us of the order and regularity of the school day, its shortened hours, but more generally the clock always, inevitably, signals our inexorable march toward our common fate. This need not be understood as negative, however, or even melancholy; instead, it tangibly evokes a recognition and acceptance of haphazard but definitive destiny. As Rossi developed the Ferrini school at Broni, he maintained in the forefront of his thoughts the passage of time in schools, at mid-day "the [empty] classrooms and the corridors, stairs and spaces and everything seemed marvelous and lost," that hour when students no longer filled the school, almost like the complete abandonment of schools over the summer.[22] Such ruminations, as we have seen, permeated Rossi's writings; as he designed he imagined the future spaces in various moments, how people would move about in them, the activities they would engage in, and the full range of possible events that the spaces might host. As such, they emphasize Rossi's way of thinking about architectural design that relegates function to a circumscribed role and instead favors bearing in mind unpredictable human activity and the inevitable surprises that follow. Far from signifying a morbid obsession with death, the clocks celebrate the vivacious, diverse, ever changing abundance of life itself. There is much more to consider about Rossi and time, a topic to be considered in more detail in chapter 6, in exploring the cemetery projects.

As a building type, the monastery continued to appeal to Rossi in subsequent years, even across the Atlantic, as in the commission to design an academy for art in a run-down area of the South Bronx in New York (1991; fig. 4.10). The program requested an architecture that demonstrated "an engagement with the life and death of a community as expressed through its spaces, streets, and buildings; a desire to reinterpret the forms of history in order to transcend their tyranny." School head Tim Rollins asked for more than a home for the school. He dreamed instead of "a sanctuary, an architecture that understands the tragic history of this area yet—stubborn—celebrates the neighborhood."[23] He believed Rossi would respond especially to the call for a monument, a memorial, a beacon of hope; as Rollins commented, "Aldo Rossi is a great architect because he understands . . . this bittersweet and silent beauty of abandonment. . . . He sees beginnings where others see The End."[24]

Rossi walked through the area, studied it, and appreciated its beautiful if shabby buildings and urban landscape. At first he reported uneasily that, "I don't have even the embryo in my mind of what I'm going to do. I haven't spoken with anybody about it yet, whereas in other cases I can foresee more immediately how the design will progress."[25] Nonetheless, when it came time to sketch out ideas for the site, Rossi reverted to a familiar type, the monastery, laid out in a fashion similar to that of the school at Broni. On a long narrow lot, Rossi shifted the academy to one end, leaving a large area open

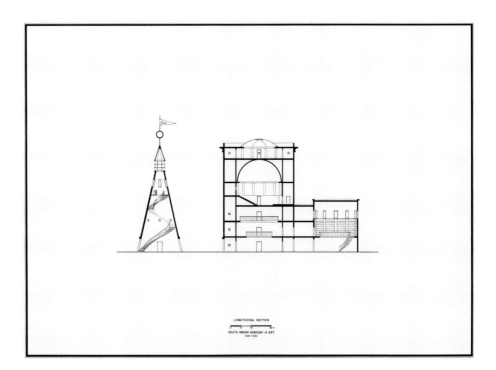

FIGURE 4.10
Aldo Rossi, South Bronx
Academy of Art, New York,
1991, section (Morris Adjmi)

for a neighborhood park. The academy would extend laterally from a domed enclosed courtyard-type space lined with offices and infrastructure, with the classrooms, science lab, studios, library, and auditorium extending out to either side for two floors (fig. 4.11). The double-height auditorium-theater on the fourth floor would rise to a glazed and metal ribbed dome. At one end of the main axis he planned a colorful *torre-faro* (tower-lighthouse) as a beacon welcoming the community into its precinct, which also recalled a childhood memory of Rossi's reading of the classic *Moby Dick*, where the lighthouses on the Maine coast partake of a fantastic landscape.[26]

Rossi completed an addition to one other major educational institution in Italy, the University of Castellanza Carlo Cattaneo near Milan. In the late 1980s, a group of entrepreneurs decided to establish a new university with the goal of training students to meet the needs of contemporary industry, including management engineering, business law, business, and economics. For the school they chose to take over an enormous abandoned textile factory, the Cantoni Cotonificio, erected in the late nineteenth century, and they invited Rossi to remodel some parts for classroom use and to add a small section of new structures to meet additional needs: two brick towers, a three-story L-shaped building, and a high-rise structure.

Rossi's proposal for an addition to the University of Miami School of Architecture (1986) was more significant as a work of architecture than the Castellanza renovation. Old dormitories housed classroom and studio space, but the school lacked a gallery, an auditorium, and a multimedia center; it also needed new office space. Rossi's proposal

BUILDING FOR CULTURE

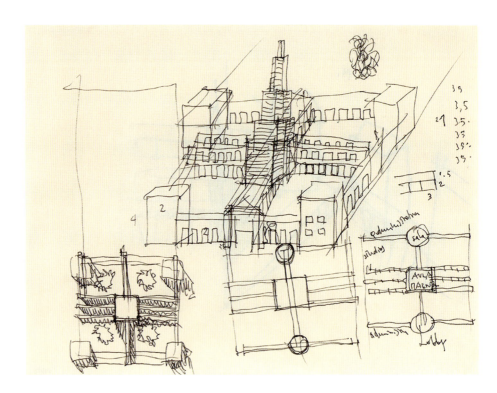

FIGURE 4.11
South Bronx Academy of Art, ink sketch on mylar (Morris Adjmi/© Aldo Rossi Heirs)

FIGURE 4.12
Aldo Rossi, School of Architecture, University of Miami, Florida, 1986, pen and ink on tracing paper (Morris Adjmi/© Aldo Rossi Heirs)

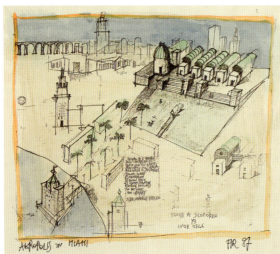

took care of those needs by proposing an entirely new complex that unified the school, in some versions with the addition of a long pathway leading to a reconstruction of his Teatro del Mondo at the end (fig. 4.12). A tower anchored one end of the complex, while at the other a series of five parallel blocks included an administrative complex with auditorium and a centrally planned structure similar to those we have seen in most of his schools. Construction began in 1991, but financial difficulties halted the project, and after Rossi's death, the university turned to Leon Krier to design new facilities.

Schools accommodate specific groups—children in the elementary and middle schools, young adults in the universities. Even though in Italy, as in the United States, schools also often fill in as polling places during elections, and in smaller towns they also host events for community celebrations of various types, their public functions are generally limited to education. Buildings for the entire community present other types of problems.

REPRESENTING THE COMMUNITY
Since the middle ages two building types historically have represented the community in Italian cities: the cathedral and the town hall, each congealed over centuries into its own

116  BUILDING FOR CULTURE

historically refined type. The medieval town hall took shape over the course of several hundred years, in a pattern similar to what occurred in Fagnano, where the town gained independence from Longobard rulers and regained its autonomy for six hundred years until the thirteenth century, when the Visconti took control of the area, establishing the duchy of Milan a hundred years later.[27] Many central and northern Italian cities underwent a similar process of liberation from external control and the establishment of autonomous civic government beginning in about the tenth century. Part of the movement for autonomous communal governance also entailed curbing the power of individual families, who erected towers as defensive, but also often offensive, bastions within the cities. Communal authorities gradually established a building within which to hold civic assemblies and where a mayor, usually brought from outside to avoid the risk of partiality, governed and maintained order. The type contained a few key configurational elements: an unfenestrated campanile usually with a clock; an *arengario,* balcony, from which the citizenry could be summoned; a loggia within which citizens could meet informally; a large assembly hall, usually on the first floor above ground; and a ceremonial staircase leading to the assembly room. These components could be arranged in many ways without undermining the authority and visibility of the type. Towers could be detached, centrally placed, or asymmetrically placed on the building; they could be of unfinished stone or brick, short or tall. The ceremonial staircase could rise from within an interior courtyard, as at the Palazzo Vecchio in Florence, or from without, as in Bevagna in central Italy. In short, infinite variations could be found throughout central and northern Italy, and elements could be missing entirely, yet the type held firm. The most emblematic town hall was in Rome on the Campidoglio before Michelangelo's sixteenth-century intervention, the palace known as the city's senate, where corner towers, ceremonial staircase, tower, and location on a hill signaled its representational functions. As Rossi well knew, each component or configurational element derived from a particular history and had therefore specific relevance for the town hall. The assembly room, for example, descended from the baronial hall, the tower from the private expression of power and the church campanile; the loggia had long served as a market and informal meeting space for men.[28]

For the town halls that Rossi designed, from Scandicci (1968) to Muggiò (1972) and Borgoricco (1983), he elected not to adopt this hallowed type and instead approached the problem from different perspectives. Scandicci, a town of about 50,000 people in a hilly region about 6 kilometers (less than 3 miles) southwest of Florence, since the early Renaissance had appealed to wealthy Florentines as a setting for rural estates and villas such as the spectacular sixteenth-century Villa Collazzi.[29] More recently the town has become a bedroom community for Florence. In 1870 the city had inaugurated a new town hall designed by Francesco Martelli, and in 1968 held a competition, which Rossi entered, calling for ideas for a new one.[30] Though Pietro Grassi emerged victorious in the competition, Rossi's designs provide ample evidence of his approach to the town hall building type. The demands of a swelling population had encouraged city officials

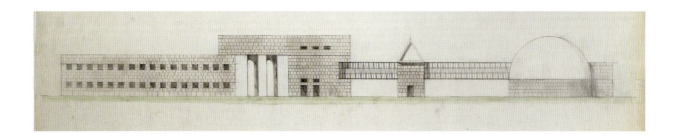

FIGURE 4.13
Aldo Rossi, M. Fortis, and Massimo Scolari, Competition entry for Scandicci Town Hall, 1968, photocopy plus watercolor on paper (Fondazione AR/© Aldo Rossi Heirs)

to erect a new town hall in an area between the historic center and the expanding periphery. Rossi put into play his theories about an architecture of parts by aligning a sequence of volumes along an axis, what he described as a complex structure. The use of specific typological forms—the courtyard type, the centrally planned structure, the dome, axial organization—underscored the goal of avoiding mammoth buildings and experimenting with unifying diverse elements in different ways.[31] Departing from the strict, bilateral symmetry of the rest of the design, for the garden connected to the new town hall Rossi quoted the winding path and house designed by Karl Friedrich Schinkel at Charlottenhof.

Of the volumes assembled along the main axis, one contained administrative offices that maintain regular contact with the public; linked vertically and also at the ground level were the mayor's suite, reading rooms, the bar-restaurant, and the city council chambers.[32] Rossi decided to treat the office building's interior courtyard like a piazza, therefore an urban element, where he inserted a colonnaded portico, much as could be found in the historic centers of many Italian towns. At Scandicci, he again adopted the thick, white cylindrical column to hold aloft one structure placed to one side of the axis. This was the only element (except for elevators and restrooms) not aligned with the other volumes, and one of two subtle concessions to the historic type, for the space around the columns could be understood as an open-air loggia, while the modest pedimented structure is a small tower (fig. 4.13). Finally, an elevated passageway connects the mayor's suite to the council chambers, interrupted by a small rectangular block topped by an equilateral triangle, much like the channel at the Monument to Partisans at Segrate. The radically simple volumes, strict bilateral symmetry, and unusual triangular form all flew against the tenets of the then dominant modern movement, and, inevitably, worked against a victory in the competition; only with the Gallaratese housing and the Modena cemetery did his independence from the modern movement achieve recognition and begrudging acceptance in Italy's architectural community.

In short, the distinguished and important history of this building type as both a symbol of civic independence and of local autonomy and pride—*campanilismo*—shrank to virtual invisibility in Rossi's project and those of most competitors. Why? The answer can be found in the years of Fascist hegemony. In an effort to capture the prestige associated with the traditional town hall, officials of the Fascist Party (PNF, Partito Nazionale Fascista) revived the type as the basis for the designs of PNF headquarters throughout

Italy. Although emptied of its associations with local autonomy, the PNF did as many others had done in the past in laying claim to the type's associations and history. Even today, a tour of Italian cities reveals an abundance of former PNF headquarters still sporting the tower, arengario, loggia, and ceremonial staircase rendered in a modern language. Whatever the medieval origins of the building type, in 1968 the memory of the destructive years of Fascism effectively excluded it as a contemporary solution. Only with a proposal in 1995 for a new town hall in San Giovanni Valdarno did Rossi incorporate a tower, in this case a stacked brick tower reminiscent of Filarete's design for the tower of the Sforza Castle in Milan—decidedly remote from the traditional town hall type. The stacked and receding tower form fascinated Rossi, recalling not just the Sforza Castle but those of Schinkel, and his own in many other designs.[33]

Only four years later, Muggiò, a town just 15 kilometers (9 miles) northeast of Milan near the city of Monza, also held a competition for a new town hall. The existing elegant sixteenth-century Villa Casati Stampa, remodeled to become a neo-classical villa in the eighteenth century, in the twentieth century became the town hall. Rossi's project entailed a complete restoration of the Villa Casati and a new structure for additional offices and service facilities. He chose not to follow the scheme proposed at Scandicci; instead, he turned to the Parma theater competition entry to develop the solution. Two buildings face one another, each shaped in plan like the letter E with four bars rather than three, one block to serve as offices for councilors and the other for public offices. They pivot apart on an angle away from a conical structure that Rossi envisioned as an art gallery or exhibition space, with council chambers on the upper floor that could be exchanged for exhibits or public events. The new buildings, the villa, and another historic building, the Casa Gasparoll, together formed a new public space, a piazza that Rossi planned to pave in red porphyry as a unifying element. He won neither competition, and it took another decade for Rossi finally to be able to build a town hall.

Uninterested in positioning himself on the cutting edge of fashion, for the new town hall at Borgoricco, Rossi instead studied the province of Padua and its rural building traditions. Apart from the nearby church, the town hall site was isolated in an agrarian landscape scored still today by the ancient Roman centuriation land division system. For such a setting, Rossi looked first at the region's historically consolidated rural building traditions for farmhouses and Palladian villas. From the farmhouse and its later Palladian villa variation, Rossi derived a scheme for a central block flanked by porticoes in *barchessa*-like wings (fig. 4.14).[34] The public buildings of the Palazzo della Ragione in Padua and Vicenza, themselves referring to the overturned wooden hulls of Venetian ships, inspired the grand ribbed and barrel-vaulted council chambers on the upper floor (fig. 4.15). From the central and northern Italian medieval town hall came the idea for two low, flanking towers framing the central block, here containing modest staircases giving access to the council chambers. By adapting the concepts but not the

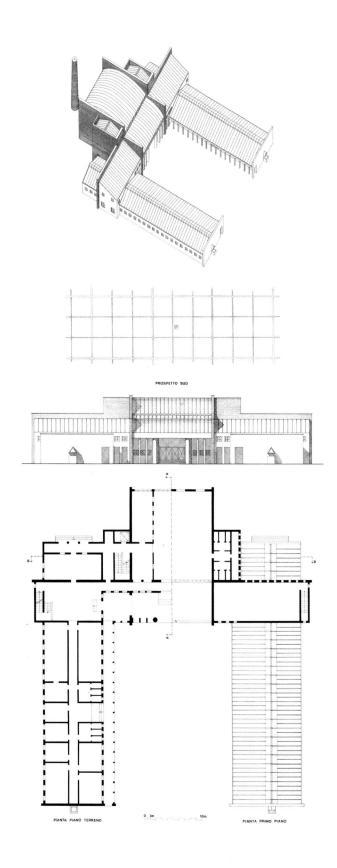

FIGURE 4.14
Aldo Rossi, Borgoricco Town Hall, 1983 (Commune of Borgoricco)

FIGURE 4.15
Borgoricco Town Hall,
ceiling of Council Room

FIGURE 4.16
Borgoricco Town Hall

architectural language of traditional designs, Rossi nonetheless fashioned an unequivocally modern building.

For the details, the architectural language, and the materials, Rossi turned to many other sources, such as the traditional deep red bricks typical of Milanese building for the two walls framing the central block. The simple, unadorned column of Filarete's unfinished fifteenth-century palazzo on the Grand Canal in Venice inspired the twin columns at the entrance, while the triangular fountains in pietra d'Istria at the end of each *barchessa* wing recall Rossi's own early design for the fountain at Segrate. In all cases, however, Rossi encouraged the variations proposed by artisans who worked on the building; he enjoyed the exchanges with them, and he understood their suggestions as enrichments that deepened the project as a whole.[35]

As gracefully as the design tapped into a range of traditions, for Rossi architecture was more than a catalogue of elements to adapt to a new setting, more than the self-expression of a single architect, more than a competent assemblage of functions. Architecture, as an emblem of civilization, in Rossi's view was at once its finest expression and its most exalted aspiration. Thus Rossi's design embodies some of his own deeply cherished ideas about culture and civilization, and therefore history, a belief embodied in his decision to place the library and the museum at the center of the complex. Virtually every other town hall in Italy opens to a reception area, a foyer giving onto offices and council chambers. At Borgoricco, however, after visitors enter a narrow hallway extending laterally to the two office wings, they find themselves facing the library (fig. 4.16). This core block also housed the town's Museum of Roman Centuriation until the theater and museum (also designed by Rossi) opened in 2002. Visitors do not access the council chambers on the upper floor by a ceremonial staircase, typical of traditional Italian town halls, but rather by two smaller, modest stairs situated in the twin towers.

Position alone indicates the importance Rossi dedicated to the library, which forms the center, the very heart, of the entire complex. And what is a library if not the repository of human civilization in all of its aspects and all of its aspirations? A voracious reader, Rossi had a personal library that extended throughout his apartment on Via Rugabella, in addition to the architecture collection in his office. It is no accident that Rossi singled out the library as the core of most of his designs for schools, placing it at the center (Broni, Fagnona Olona); it bears witness to his belief in the vitality of a library as a repository par excellence of knowledge and accomplishment. By placing the library as a base for the council chambers above, Rossi gave built form to a concept of the primacy of culture and of memory embodied in the library without which all other aspects of communal life—including deliberation and debate—the future cannot be imagined. For Rossi the library, as a type, constituted one pillar of human accomplishment, the museum a second. Rossi would not manage to design and see a museum built until 1988.

CONSERVING THE PAST

At the end of 1986, Rossi wistfully wrote in his *Quaderni Azzurri* that missing from his body of work was a museum project.[36] In 1971, he began a design for the competition in Paris for the new Place Beauborg museum (now Centre Pompidou), eventually won by Richard Rogers and Renzo Piano. The solution Rossi proposed resembled that of the Scandicci town hall, with a sequence of volumes extended along what he described as a spine.[37] Because the competition called for exhibition space, library, offices, and storage space, the preliminary designs evinced a complex group of buildings more closely connected than he had envisioned for Scandicci. He proposed a truncated conical tower likened, in his mind, to coffeepots, a series of stacked cylinders also linked to industrial chimneys and cement factories.[38] He already had begun to enrich his concept of an additive process of design—that is, design by parts, by perceiving his architecture as broken parts subsequently recomposed again.[39]

Just a week after beginning to elaborate his ideas for Beauborg in greater detail, he ended up in a hospital in Slavonski Brod, Yugoslavia, after a terrible automobile accident and, as he noted in the *Quaderni Azzurri*, "among other things, [this led to] the failure [to complete] the competition for Place Beauborg."[40] For a time after the accident, he even found it impossible to design; instead over the next few weeks he read books, rereading Joyce and *Hamlet*, but also Helen Rosenau's publication on public buildings in London and Paris.[41] He restlessly mused on the architecture of the Enlightenment and its failures; on Jean Itard's account of the wild boy, Victor of Aveyron, a book Rossi found enormously sad; on the old and new hospital buildings at Slavonski Brod; and on the work of Keven Lynch, which he found silly in many respects because Lynch seemed not to grasp how remote feelings and emotions are from aesthetics.[42]

More than a decade passed before he could tackle the problem of the museum again, when he accepted a commission for the German Historical Museum to be erected in Berlin (1988–89). During the design process, the Berlin Wall came down, transforming how it would be possible to think about the newly united city—and raising new questions about the formation of the museum. The massive change for Germany, but especially for Berlin, delighted Rossi, who praised the fact that Berlin's profound wound was now being healed, and indeed, the project for the German Historical Museum had become particularly dear to him.[43] Even if politics dashed his hopes of seeing the building erected, Rossi believed that his design shared the joy of Germans who were greeting the earthshaking events unfolding. This museum, he believed, would have become a democratic center at the core of the new united Germany.

The committee formed to consider founding a museum dedicated to German history began to meet in 1985, soon settling on a site near the Reichstag, at the time still largely empty after the World War II bombings, and also establishing the basic principles underlying the museum.[44] The museum would have chronological sections dedicated to

FIGURE 4.17
Aldo Rossi, German Historical Museum, Berlin, 1988, model: wood, glass, plastic, metal, copper, and brass

key years in German history—such as 1200 (the reign of the great emperor Frederick II of Svevia) and 1945 and the end of World War II—while other sections would be thematic in nature. Officials hoped that the museum would become a major tourist destination in the city. The endeavor was funded by the Federal Republic as well as various German regions and the city of Berlin, and in August 1987 the committee announced the competition for the museum, with the understanding that it would be a key element in the development of the entire district. An earlier competition in 1986 for ideas on how to develop the area resulted in the Berlin Senate outlining an urban project between the Spree River and the Reichstag and the Tiergarten, with buildings more or less following the prewar lines. The museum would face the river with its entrance on the main crossroad of the Tiergarten. Open to all architects licensed to practice in Germany (Rossi being among them) and to some distinguished foreign firms, the competition concluded in March 1988, and in June the jury awarded first place to Rossi's project.

Rossi's team completed a 1:200 scale elaboration of the museum by May 1989, although revisions and in many cases reductions continued throughout the year (fig. 4.17). In November 1989, the wall that had divided Berlin and Germany since 1961 began to tumble down, as Rossi continued to adjust the design to meet the demands of the building authorities. Although the foundation stone for Rossi's design had been placed, with reunification in 1990 came a number of changes, including the decision to house the new museum in the city's three-hundred-year-old armory on Unter den Linden, and much to Rossi's chagrin, the government decided not to erect a new building. After Rossi's death, architect I. M. Pei received the commission to build an exhibition hall, which opened in 2003.

Winning had surprised Rossi; he had not expected it, he noted in his *Quaderni*, and he offered bemused responses to questions from the press about an Italian architect designing a museum to German history and about his intentions. "I don't want to seem like a tourist," he wrote, "but it is increasingly difficult for me to discern differences in living, customs, and even language [in Europe])."[45] So deeply imbricated are the histories of European countries, both negatively and positively, that it almost seemed silly to ask the question, and of course, by this time Rossi had completed projects in Germany and specifically in Berlin.

The lost opportunity dismayed Rossi, but the loss to Germany was even greater, for his graceful, elegant, and thoughtfully planned design may have been one of his strongest. During the design development phase, as officials reduced the budget and Rossi undertook the necessary revisions, the architect's ability to elaborate clear and persuasive alternatives became obvious, as he managed to address budget and functional concerns with ease.[46] His solution set the main building on an angle, like a right triangle in respect to the future structure on the corner, where each of the themes and focus years occupied separate pavilions. For the entrance, Rossi chose a cylindrical structure from which the others branched off. Apart from its distinguished history in Italian architecture, the centrally planned entrance paid homage to Schinkel's grand rotunda in the Berlin Altes Museum, each conveying the notion of a secular, sacred space, though Schinkel's stood at the center of the museum, while Rossi's rotunda sat at the entrance.[47]

How did Rossi conceive of his project? In his competition statement, after having listed some of the world's most significant museums and the importance of the site, he then characterized the design "architecturally as a cathedral, or an enormous hangar with apses or adjoining structures." On the Spree side, it offered a continuous elevation as if it were a dock, while the side facing the city consisted of structures that flank the main hall, as in a medieval city. For the study of German history, the spaces would be both analytical and analogical.[48] By this he did not intend to propose a symbolic architecture; rather, he argued that architecture issues from a time generated by the site and its history. The modernity of the colonially inspired buildings of nineteenth-century London, for example—despised by modern architects—in the end coheres with their testimony to English culture at a particular moment, an analogical architecture much like the analogical Venice John Ruskin fabricated that became as real as the city. Rossi also acknowledged that he could not even provide an image of German history, because the capacity to produce syntheses in the modern age has been ruptured; he could only offer fragments of life, of history, of buildings. Having abandoned both romanticism and nihilism, today the architect could compose fragments in such a way as to trigger a general vision, to be completed imaginatively by the collectivity and by each individual viewer.

For some time, Rossi had been musing about fragments. Increasingly he glimpsed fragments in his recent architecture, fragments associated with a particular site, and he wondered whether it was a kind of nationalistic symbolism, or was it more a search for tradition? Conditions differed remarkably among different sites, some remarkably so—for example in the case of the roof of the project for Park de la Villette in Paris, where the shallow, zinc-covered barrel-vaulted roofs articulated with dormers and chimneys summon references to the traditional Parisian mansard roof without directly copying. In other cases it became difficult to locate a precise reference upon which to build. Yet he wanted to do exactly that, to identify quotations and apply antique or new elements that could signify the place. He had not been able to do so with the Tibaldi School in Cantù, he observed, where the absence of any "exotic" feature signified the search for local references.[49] What did he mean by this? He referred to a design being developed for a museum in Marburg, where he saw the site as having become more powerful than the architecture, and to a project in Japan, where the uniqueness of materials and construction constituted another example. The GFT building in Turin, with its columns, architrave, and corner, along with references to the topography and the materials, comprised fragments that issued from the same type of search. He questioned how to do this in improbable places such as Miami, Florida, for example, or some unusually exotic parts of southern Japan. He foundered here, as he often did, on the limits of language and description, where the readings of his projects seemed to him at once rigorous and crazy. In this he followed Schinkel, who substituted an urbanism of fragments for a baroque urbanism of unity. Emblematic, as Rossi well knew, were Schinkel's planning and buildings in Berlin, and models as well for him to follow in Berlin.[50] Rossi did not adopt a strategy of fragmentation in the designs casually, for it could not be separated from his own approach to history, much as was true for Schinkel. Where for Karl Marx "the tradition of all past generations weighs like an Alp upon the brain of the living," for Rossi the past, an abiding presence in the present day, gifted us with a legacy to respect and preserve.[51] As becomes apparent in his architecture, Rossi understood the challenge of conserving this legacy not as exercises in copying styles and forms but as a resource from which an architecture of today could emerge.

As we have seen, Rossi repeatedly emphasized a concern for meaning, above all in memorials and theater projects. How are we to understand this in the works we have reviewed? Vittorio Savi argued that Rossi configured the cemetery, the house of the dead, as an architecture deprived of life and of things, and "the true museum is the void, so the museum symbolizes isolation, and when we think of the museum, in reality we linger on museification, on the void, on squalor."[52] Rossi demurred, rejecting the idea that an abandoned house exemplified squalor; rather he believed that in living outside of time it "personifies architecture just as empty theaters represent the theater."[53] In the same way, the museum as the repository of culture, of civilization, of our shared past, places artifacts on display to make them available to all. Rossi underscored repeatedly the library's centrality to individual and communal life just as he believed in the museum's role of presenting the past as a resource, and the school as one of the sites where students become acquainted with the past. The title of the 1980 Venice Biennale, The Presence of the Past, nicely summed up the vision that guided Rossi in all of his designs.

We will return to the question of history in the next chapters; here we consider the ways Rossi engaged the past in his architecture for museums. He specifically rejected the reduction of the museum to a "clinic for history or art, with aseptic white walls, anonymous glazed surfaces, repeated, and repetitive galleries indifferently displaying this or that object as if in an antiseptic and efficient hospital."[54] Materials instead constituted the core of the German Historical Museum project: the bricks of old Berlin with strips of blue and yellow tiles, the white stone of Schinkel's colonnade at the Altes Museum. Even the Romans had learned that changing a material could alter a structure and achieve radically different effects bound to other meanings.[55] The hinge around which the project pivoted, the rotunda, he conceived of as a both a lighthouse and an atrium, perhaps the most important element of the project. Skylights flooded the corridor with light as if dispelling the darkness that shrouds truth.

By the time Rossi completed the revisions of the history museum the following year, certain elements had solidified, even if the general scheme remained unchanged. Revisions adjusted lighting in the galleries and in the use and lighting of the corridor, but the committee also decided to add facilities for additional activities. The tower-lighthouse so much a part of Rossi's imaginary still looked out over the river, with exhibition and leisure facilities inside, and a belvedere offered a panoramic vista over the river. Rossi paid particular attention to the materials, always those outlined in the competition entry but carefully studied to keep costs low. At that point, in late spring 1989, the senate and Rossi agreed on two phases of construction, with the administrative and didactic structures first, the tower-lighthouse and the colonnade to be completed in a second phase. Even so, he believed that many of the didactic activities could be held in the main wing until the building had been completed, so the building ended up more than a work in progress. It could be described as the progression of "a work erected formally and functionally, the creature of German time and the thermometer of the *Zeitgeist* of Germany and Europe."[56]

And then the Berlin Wall came down.

During that same year, 1988, Rossi was also designing a contemporary art center in Vassivière, France, the *Centre international d'art et du paysage*, CIAP (fig. 4.18). He later wrote that he was not fond of exhibition spaces and ephemeral exhibits, much preferring a true museum with a diverse collection that might include artifacts such as an ancient iron crown, manuscripts, a Greek statue.[57] The CIAP instead provides a place for artistic experimentation, an opportunity for artists to try out ideas difficult to accomplish in traditional museums. It sits on a 70-acre island in Lake Vassivière devoted entirely to the arts, where sculptors and landscape architects display their work in the landscape, painters and others within the building. Artists and researchers in residence also live in the castle on the island and in nearby Domaine d'Abbadia. Rossi found the prospect of designing a building on an island intriguing, particularly because it allowed him to erect a true tower-lighthouse, with a belvedere providing panoramic views of the lake and the heavily wooded island. He chose a steeply sloping site almost in the island's center for many reasons, but chiefly because it nestles in a hilly cleft high enough to

FIGURE 4.18
Aldo Rossi, Centre international d'art et du paysage, CIAP, center for contemporary art, Vassivière, France, 1988 (Scott Hortop Travel/Alamy)

allow for the lighthouse and the vistas it offers. Other than the tower, the CIAP consists of a long, barrel-vaulted, metal-roofed structure with lunettes for clerestory lighting, and along the exterior walls slender white columns hold aloft painted I-beams to mark the entrances.

The deep portico framed by slender metal columns at the entry emphasizes the structure's position not dominating but blending in with the landscape, and indeed, with the brick and concrete block of the lighthouse, the aura is that of rural farm buildings such as are found in the Po River valley. The unadorned façade Rossi viewed as related to that of his hotel at Fukuoka, in turn rooted in his appreciation for the Parma baptistery. Each constituted a timeless architecture where materials gained in importance, carefully chosen because they most revealed the passage of time. The connection between the materials and time he believed the Vassivière art center especially exalted, where the woods and the lake sharpened the awareness of the marks of time.[58] In ruminating on these matters, as he often did in his notebooks, he imagined relationships between built and unbuilt projects, but also photographs by Luigi Ghirri of Rossi's Domestic Theater at the Milan Triennale (see fig. 5.17). They emphasized the Domestic Theater as a true Aristotelian theater, an interior reduced to an almost primal essence but which was also a sort of museum, in that it anticipated the arrival of guests who would never appear, or perhaps it recalled long-gone owners. The materials yielding to the marks of time and the interiors of abandoned structures awaiting undefined and impossible arrivals: for Rossi they were of a piece and had long been part of his vision of architecture as evocative of stories awaiting the telling.

The next year, Thomas Krens of the Guggenheim Museum in New York sought to meet with Rossi to discuss the possible completion of the unfinished Guggenheim Museum in Venice.[59] That the project did not survive the discussion phase is not surprising given Rossi's thorough dislike of Frank Lloyd Wright's New York Guggenheim Museum. He found it a complete failure, difficult to visit, and with a form possibly of interest to the architect and of mild interest in the massing but certainly not successful on the level of function.[60]

The commission for a Maritime Museum in Galicia, Spain, in 1990, particularly pleased Rossi. His long history with and many friends in the country made working there appealing, and especially in Galicia, where the cathedral and convents in Santiago de Compostela had long given wing to his imagination. The fishing village of Vigo, on the Atlantic coast about 90 kilometers (56 miles) south of Santiago, offered the perfect setting for a museum dedicated to the region's relationship with the sea. The regional government elected to renovate for a museum and aquarium an abandoned nineteenth-century cannery (later slaughterhouse) hugging the coast. Rossi began work in 1992, but the architect's death came a couple of years prior to completion. If he could have completed the complex and converted the cannery, it probably would have looked much as it does today, unpretentious and clear volumes aligned near the coast (fig. 4.19). The museum consists of the simple, gable-roofed structures of the old cannery that enclose a courtyard, a new structure for the aquarium, and a granite walkway extending out to the lighthouse—an authentic lighthouse, to Rossi's delight. The patio constituted the true image of this architecture, he believed, in part because rendered in the region's typical granite. But the project's heart for Rossi was the pier extending to the sea and the lighthouse. The granite pier revealed the disquieting beauty of the sea, at once a source of life and sustenance and a terrifyingly destructive force of nature. Bound to this unease, in the museum with the sturdy roughened stone of the pavilion on the pier, Rossi hoped to represent and convey this restlessness without resolving it.

Rossi only managed to see through to completion one museum, the Bonnefanten, in Maastricht, Limburg, the southernmost region of the Netherlands, adjacent to the Belgian border (1990–94). Perhaps because of the singular nature of the project within his body of work, for Rossi it abounded with images, features, elements of his architecture, his memories, his reflections: as if it harbored the full range of his intellectual and

FIGURE 4.19
Aldo Rossi and César Portela, Maritime Museum, Vigo, Galicia, Spain, 1992 (Carmen de Sela)

emotional portfolio within. When he received the commission, the museum's collection included historical and archaeological artifacts, subsequently transferred to a different location; the collection now consists only of art, early modern European to contemporary. Founded at the end of the nineteenth century, the museum's name came from its former headquarters in a convent orphanage known as "good children," or *bons enfants*. The current location—along the banks of the Maas River, a deindustrialized part of the city—underwent transformation into a residential and commercial neighborhood in part through the arrival of the museum.

Rossi engaged in a lively and informative dialogue with then museum director Alexander van Grevenstein about what the museum could be. Van Grevenstein selected Rossi for the project without a competition because, remarkably, he grasped the essence of Rossi's architecture. In Rossi he found "great expressive inventiveness with a reserved visual language."[61] Understanding the city and the site, Rossi designed a complex that employed materials traditional to Maastricht—brick, stone, and wood—over a reinforced concrete structure. For the architecture Rossi turned to part of a scheme he had proposed for the Muggiò town hall decades earlier—a building laid out as an E, here with three wings facing the river and a grand domed tower attached to the end of the middle wing (fig. 4.20). He wrote that he had in mind Alessandro Antonelli's domed structures in Turin when he designed the tower, particularly the elegant slim dome of San Gaudenzio, something of a stretch given the sturdy robustness of the Bonnefanten tower. Rossi placed a zinc-clad dome atop the tower, around which a belvedere serves as a platform for enjoying a panoramic vista of the city, especially the historic center directly across the river. As splendid as those views are, the tower itself as a beacon on the riverbank became the most distinctive feature of the project, the only part visible from the river and the historic center. Despite his reference to Antonelli's projects, in his letter to Van Grevenstein Rossi alluded to a quite different source, the beehive tombs of antiquity, such as the tholoi of ancient Myceneae and the nuraghi of Sardinia, for example that of Santa Cristina, where the descent into the sacred well framed by stone walls is precipitous and dangerous (fig. 4.21).[62]

Unusually for a museum, Van Grevenstein wanted daylight for many of the galleries, spectacularly provided in part by the high staircase compressed between soaring brick walls beneath a glazed skylight (fig. 4.22). In the text accompanying the presentation of the project, Rossi described the staircase as a typical Dutch feature, linked to the seafaring world of Holland and its colonies where "the land ends and the sea begins."[63] As we saw in the last chapter, Rossi drew on specific experiences and places in his emphasis on stairs, from the tradition of ascending to sacred spaces to the personal pilgrimages he undertook as a youngster to the statue of San Carlone and to the Sacri Monti (see chapters 5 and 6). Such a staircase, with wooden steps and uninterrupted high, richly textured brick walls, recalls precisely those childhood experiences. Ascending stairs, particularly high, difficult stairs, with all that such movement suggested, reinforced the sacred character of movement through the museum. Just as Schinkel's staircase set the stage for an encounter with treasures of human civilization, so Rossi crafted an experience that, he acknowledged, might leave seniors gasping for breath, but it also prepared the visitor for an encounter different from the quotidian, as one would expect from the experimental contemporary art Van Grevenstein envisioned hosting there.

Describing the stairs in a letter to Van Grevenstein as a *scala santa*, holy stairs, Rossi drew a direct parallel to two of the most important stairs in Catholicism, the holy stairs designed by Bernini at St. Peter's, and the holy stairs at San Giovanni in Laterano, throughout the middle ages the primary seat of the papacy.[64] Identifying the staircase as "a special part of any building," Rossi noted that one both ascends and descends stairs, and one also risks falling. The ascent of a *scala santa*, he reminded Van Grevenstein, is a laborious act. His reference to the beehive temples specifically concerned those where one descended stairs in search of purification, the reverse of those in Christian and Western European sites, where one ascends to purification. In the former case, one descends to seek mercy and compassion, while in ascending, justice. Nothing, he wrote

FIGURE 4.20
Aldo Rossi, Bonnefanten Museum, Maastricht,
Netherlands, 1995

FIGURE 4.21
Sacred Well, Nuraghe of Santa Cristina, Paulilatino, Oristano

FIGURE 4.22
Bonnefanten Museum, stairs

with admirable understatement, "is more moving than falling." Indeed, in his attention to the risk of falling on stairs he drew a parallel to representations of the Deposition and Entombment of Jesus, which he believed were "always dramatically superior to those of the Ascension."[65] His musings continued with reflections on the miserable state of the profession of architect, for in his view architects were either asleep or riding on the cusp of fashion and developing strategies for destroying cities. To all of this he proposed an architectural form, such as the beehive tomb, that marginalized the pomposity of current bourgeois architecture and, as in the case of the Bonnefanten, joined the ancient Roman bridge that still today crosses the Maas River, as a beacon, a marker, on the river.

Rossi entitled his project statement "Verlust der Mitte," the title of Hans Sedlmayr's 1948 book, in English entitled *Art in Crisis: The Lost Center*.[66] Rossi responded to some of Sedlmayr's arguments, particularly his focus on the content, or meaning, of art. Sedlmayr's formation as an art historian took shape under the influence of Alois Riegl, Austrian art historian and supervisor of monuments for the Austro-Hungarian empire at the end of the nineteenth century.[67] With the notion of *Kunstwollen*, will to art, Riegl hypothesized an evolutionary progress in artistic style whose logic could be identified in individual cultures. Art historians explore documents regarding the provenance and history of individual works of art, but in addition to those skills, Sedlmayr chose to pursue that essential core, that *Kunstwollen*, in works of art, which he did with exceptional skill in a study of Francesco Borromini's architecture. In the years immediately following World War II, Sedlmayr lost his academic post because of his staunch membership in the Nazi Party.

Architecture played a large role in Sedlmayr's essay on the lost center, with an entire chapter dedicated to "The Attack on Architecture." Since the end of the eighteenth century, he argued, a relentless attack on the field began with the designs of Claude-Nicholas Ledoux and came up-to-date with those of Le Corbusier. Sedlmayr essentially argued that the process of modernization had in general dragged culture down in a steep decline over the previous 150 years.[68] Other than the relatively benign influence of Riegl, Sedlmayr succumbed to the lure of Oswald Spengler's two-volume lament in *The Decline of the West* (1918, 1922), his well-known organic theory about the rise and fall of cultures that included specific attacks on the breakdown of all the arts, painting, sculpture, and music. For Sedlmayr, all cultures necessarily faced the same decay and destiny, but he especially despaired the loss of religious culture and spirituality in general. He railed against the substitution of the museum for the temple, or church, with the persistent secularization of sacred art that robbed it of its spiritual core. He perceived his task in *Art in Crisis* to consist of identifying both the trend's manifestations and the signals of imminent decline. Rossi found himself in agreement with some of these analyses, recognizing the emptiness of much contemporary architecture. To the first concern, he responded simply through his architectural design, as evident in the monuments, theaters, and cemeteries. To the second, he outlined strategies with which to counter the monotony and fake moralism of the modern movement through his own practice rather than via strident polemics. Like Sedlmayr he believed that no artist or art could claim autonomy; everything we do is rooted in something greater. For Rossi, this recognition brought not despair but a commitment to vanquish the emptiness he found in much contemporary practice, to subvert it by anchoring his approach to a different, rigorous yet liberating practice. Sedlmayr's "loss of center" did not plunge Rossi into a similar pit of despair, for he never stopped distancing himself from the conundrums posed by modernism. One of Rossi's few contemporaries to have grasped the substance of his architecture was Carlo Aymonino. In a 1977 article, Aymonino countered the criticism of Rossi's architectures as being silent or an architecture of crisis by asserting that, instead, Rossi's architecture was one of optimism.[69] Indeed, Rossi maintained a core belief that things could indeed be improved, even transformed.

That he titled his essay on the Bonnefanten Museum "Verlust der Mitte" raises the question of why—why should he reference "the loss of center" in writing about a museum of which he was quite proud? In the essay, he asserted that the museum, and his building, rejected the Enlightenment belief that everything of importance could be measured, but that the building did leave open the question of whether a museum constitutes a collection of mementoes of life, or whether it is, itself, part of our lives. After describing the museum's spaces and their characteristics, he concluded that the museum viewed as a whole is perhaps "a lost whole which we only recognize thanks to those fragments [preserved within], which are also fragments of art and Europe of bygone days." Rossi did not clarify further the "lost whole" to which he referred. From the context, it seems clear he speaks of history, specifically European history, at once inevitably past and present today—the Presence of the Past. He could not locate the present any more than St. Augustine could, but like Augustine he could pose incessant questions about time, loss, and hope, envisioning perhaps the apprehension of loss as the first step toward communication beyond time.[70] He also described Sedlmayr's title as referring to the condition of the survivor, the individual or the city, but not with the implication of lost in the sense of impossible to recover. It is lost, he wrote, "because it is far away, but loss is presented also as a discreet condition of making, . . . and so describing the Venetian theater [Teatro del Mondo, ndr] as a work of joy with childlike components, . . . [it is] a reference to a lost condition and for this reason, poetic."[71]

# 5  Rossi and the Theater

> Memory is not an instrument for surveying the past, but its theater.
> —WALTER BENJAMIN

Though Venice abounds with seductions, nothing drew more bemused and intrigued gazes in La Serenissima in late 1979 than the yellow and blue, zinc-roofed wooden structure set on a barge floating in the San Marco lagoon (fig. 5.1).[1] Initially proposed for the Theater Biennale as an ephemeral structure in the manner of the city's water-borne theaters of the sixteenth century, Aldo Rossi's Teatro del Mondo so delighted Venetians and visitors alike that it lingered on to become the iconic image of the first Architecture Biennale opening in July of the following year.[2] Adjacent to the church of Santa Maria della Salute and the Punto della Dogana (the former customs house), the structure rested near the point where the Grand Canal flows into the lagoon proper, though the barge could be towed to various sites. The metal revetment of the upper section sparkled in the sunlight, picking up the delicate hues of Santa Maria della Salute. The disarmingly simple structure of wood, Unistrut, and gray-green zinc roof seemed too fragile to resist the choppy waters through Venice's famously violent *bòra* winds, driving rain, searing heat, and bone-chilling fog for several months. Yet it did.

Not only did the Teatro withstand a year of Venice's challenging climate, after the Biennale closed in late summer a tugboat towed it across the Adriatic to the bay of Dubrovnik in August 1980, where it overcame equally hazardous seas to serve as a spectacular archetype for the city's theater festival. Although dismantled after its tour on the Croatian coast, the Teatro survived as an iconic image, perhaps among the most beloved of all of Rossi's designs. Though in some respects it appears radically different from other Rossi projects, it is not. Rossi's fascination with the theater extends from his youth—his interest in movies and his youthful desire to be a director, his childhood experiences while in boarding school. Over the course of his career, he not only designed several new or reconstructed full-scale theaters, he also inserted small theaters into projects such as the former GFT in Turin and the Scholastic Building in New York, and he often treated certain parts of his projects as small theaters. In more ways than one,

FIGURE 5.1
Aldo Rossi, Teatro del Mondo, Venice, 1979
(Ben Huser)

the Teatro del Mondo sits at the halfway point between his first and last theater designs: from his university thesis for a theater and cultural center in Milan (1959); to the first competition proposal for a theater, the Paganini Theater in Parma (1964); and finally, the La Fenice Theater in Venice (1997).

This chapter begins with a review of Rossi's major theater designs and proceeds to an exploration of his wide-ranging ideas about theaters and, finally, the resources upon which he drew in writing about and designing theaters.

### ROSSI'S THEATER AS URBAN MONUMENT

During the 1970s, the successes of Rossi's *Architecture of the City* and the Modena cemetery led to more commissions and more competitions. In his office on Via Maddalena in Milan, Rossi designed and constructed what he named "The Little Scientific Theater" (Il Teatrino Scientifico) (fig. 5.2).[3] Fabricated of sheet metal and wood and outfitted with a small stage, the Teatrino's movable architectural elements and different backdrops allowed Rossi to experiment with endless combinations—akin to piano's five-finger exercises—for larger designs, understanding each new configuration not simply as a work of architecture but as itself encapsulating an entire approach to architecture.

Why did Rossi repeatedly turn to the theater as a source of inspiration, as a challenge, as a device for probing ways of thinking about architecture? There are no easy answers. From his first to his last project, the topic intrigued him: to Rossi, theaters were the quintessential places where architecture ends and the world of imagination begins, and in this delicate intersection, architecture remained essential to the conjunction. In 1979 he wrote about three built projects—the school at Fagnona Olona, the Modena cemetery, and the Little Scientific Theater: "life, death, and imagination, the link is direct and ambiguous.... The house of death and the house of childhood are part of the theater... although the school is incomplete, the cemetery a fragment, and the theater a model. But the building's form is perfectly planned, and from thought to physical reality nothing changes."[4] Rossi knew well the history of theaters from ancient Greece forward, not only their physical form but also their origins and roles within their cultures. In the sixth century BCE, religious festivals included theatrical productions of tragedies, and later, comedies supplemented the repertoire.[5] Scholars dispute the precise evolution of Greek drama and theaters, but that sacred rituals figured in the early tragedies seems probable. Greek theaters carved out of landscapes, such as the earliest dedicated to Dionysius Eleuthereus on the flank of the Acropolis in Athens, gave way first to republican Rome's freestanding wooden structures and later to imperial brick and stone monuments, such as the Theater of Marcellus in Rome. For Rossi, Roman theaters formed a bridge between the extraordinary outdoor examples from ancient Greece and those of the early modern period in Europe, and he attended particularly to the more recent examples.[6] Rossi often referred to Andrea Palladio's Teatro Olimpico in Vicenza (1585),

FIGURE 5.2
Aldo Rossi, Little Scientific Theater, 1978

the earliest and most famous theater in Renaissance Italy modeled, according to Palladio, as if it were a contemporary reconstruction of an outdoor Greek theater as described by Vitruvius in *De architectura*.[7] Although compressed into an ellipse because of the site and therefore not precisely embodying Vitruvius's scheme, the theater enjoyed instant success even if it represented the end rather than the beginning of an architectural tradition of theater design in Italy.[8]

In 1964, Rossi entered the competition to restore the Paganini Theater and reorganize Piazza della Pilotta in Parma. On the piazza had once stood the church of St. Peter Martyr, demolished in 1818 and replaced in 1867 by Teatro Reinach, later Teatro Paganini, which in turn was destroyed by Allied bombs in 1944, and this was the building to be replaced. With his competition entry, Rossi necessarily confronted Giovanni Battista Aleotti's extraordinary Farnese Theater (1618) in the adjacent Palazzo della Pilotta, one of only three Renaissance Italian theaters to survive the ravages of time. Aleotti's scheme had entailed a new approach to theater design destined to dominate until the nineteenth century.⁹ The elliptical layout of the Palladio's Teatro Olimpico gave way to a horseshoe-shaped auditorium within a rectangular structure, to which Aleotti also introduced a new element: a grand proscenium arch to frame the stage.

The invited, three-stage competition at Parma included projects by an emerging generation of Italian architects, including Carlo Aymonino, Giancarlo de Carlo, Paolo Portoghesi, Roberto Gabetti and Aimaro Isola, and Rossi; the winning proposal by Luigi Pellegrin remained unbuilt.¹⁰ Designing for this site and reconfiguring the piazza itself were daunting tasks: Palazzo della Pilotta is a mass of diverse structures erected over time, with unfaced brick elevations dominating, while Aleotti's theater tucked inside the palace remains, as Rossi noted, perhaps the most beautiful in Italy. Parma's relatively small historical center includes several independent structures to which Rossi drew attention: the Palazzo della Pilotta, the baptistery, the cathedral, the episcopal palace, the basilica of Santa Maria della Steccata, and the Teatro Regio (Royal Theater), each a freestanding, urban monument.

Immersed in writing *The Architecture of the City* and having recently designed the Monument to the Resistance at Cuneo, Rossi not surprisingly from the outset focused on the theater above all as an urban monument. The ancient Greek theater had been an urban artifact, he argued; within its boundaries it contained the city, and even if it provided the setting for a theatrical spectacle, it also embodied its own architectural reality, one that we too live as we climb up the stone steps of the theaters at Epidaurus or Delphi. For a contemporary theater in the center of an ancient city such as Parma, Rossi took his most direct cues not from the ruins of the Paganini Theater but from the early-thirteenth-century baptistery just a few blocks away, a freestanding structure poised between the eleventh-century cathedral and the episcopal palace. With its alternating bands of white and rose-hued Veronese marble, the octagonal baptistery stands as an urban work of art, of architecture, a collective accomplishment transformed over time by those who erected it and those who modified it—exactly as Rossi described urban architecture in his book published the next year, and much as he had proposed in his thesis project for a theater and cultural center in Milan in 1959.¹¹

His scheme for this complicated site in Parma, a cylindrical theater adjacent to a portico topped by a triangular passageway, precisely embodied his concept of an urban monument (fig. 5.3). The city and its architecture persist through transformations, with each work of architecture a unique component, he argued in *The Architecture of the City*, and they resist being reduced to mere function. The baptistery a few hundred meters away still anchored the piazza framed by the cathedral and the episcopal palace as it did when first erected, and all three serve the same kinds of activities that they did nearly a thousand years ago. So too Rossi's two structures expressed the notion of design by parts, analogous to the construction of the city in time through the persistent insertion of individual pieces into an existing urban fabric. Rossi's attention fell particularly on the many varied types of buildings to be found in different cities, recognizing them

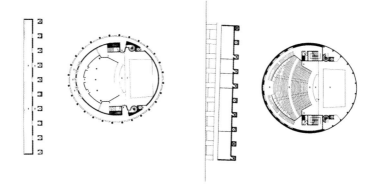

FIGURE 5.3
Aldo Rossi, Paganini Theater and portico, Parma, 1964, plan (redrawn by Marino Bortolotti)

as monuments that persisted over time despite, or even because of, changes in their purposes—the former amphitheaters in Nimes and Lucca, the Palladian Basilica in Vicenza, to name just a few.[12] Though designed to fulfill specific functions, they lent themselves to many other uses over the centuries, or, to use surrealist writer Raymond Roussel's terminology, each was a *locus solus*, a unique site or place in the city, as was Parma's historic center with its monumental urban structures.[13]

Prior to entertaining any architectural intervention, Rossi enjoined the designer to consider many factors, but especially type, which he defined as something "permanent and complex, a logical principle prior to form."[14] No one form embodies a specific type, he continued, "even if all architectural forms are reducible to types."[15] The design for Parma exemplifies how he acknowledged type without succumbing to the temptation to adopt the forms of theaters he particularly appreciated—Aleotti's Farnese, Scamozzi's theater in Sabbioneta, Schinkel's Schauspielhaus in Berlin. When he chose the cylindrical form, he deliberately avoided those earlier models and turned instead to the concept of a central plan, usually associated with sacred structures as for example in the nearby octagonal baptistery and much as he had proposed for the theater in his thesis project. The urban setting of the Paganini Theater, for Rossi, mirrored that of the baptistery—that is, powerful buildings already dominated, so the site called for a unique form, one that would achieve a distinct presence. He described the theater's circular plan as fusing elements that he appreciated in many kinds of theaters, from Mantua's little scientific theater, the anatomical theater in Padua, open-air theaters in Greece, to those of Aleotti, Scamozzi, and Schinkel, plus planetariums and theaters of the cosmos. The portico and the theater stand as independent *fatti urbani* (urban artifacts), each a *locus solus*.[16] Wanting to separate and distinguish formally the two structures to emphasize the uniqueness of each, instead of setting the theater on piers as suggested in the competition brief Rossi also buried the parking, services, and restaurants underground while providing a portico for other shops and eating establishments, separated from but linked underground to the theater-cinema complex. As he had done with the piazza at Segrate, Rossi proposed repaving the entire piazza with small porphyry blocks, subtly unifying the otherwise disparate structures from the different eras.

FIGURE 5.4
Antonio Averlino (Il Filarete), Ca' del Duca, Venice, ca. 1460 (Mindy Curtis)

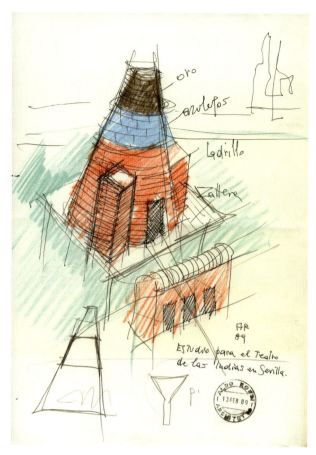

FIGURE 5.5
Aldo Rossi, Theater of the Indies for Expo '92, Seville, Spain, 1992 (Fondazione AR/© Aldo Rossi Heirs)

For the portico, Rossi found ideal inspiration in a fragment of Duke Francesco Sforza's unfinished palace on the Grand Canal in Venice: a thick, unadorned cylindrical column without base or capital. Known as Filarete's column for the architect Antonio Averlino's moniker Filarete (in Greek φιλάρετος, "lover of virtue"), as we have seen, such columns became one of the most distinctive and oft repeated features of Rossi's designs, for example in the monument at Segrate and in the Gallaratese housing project, among many others (fig. 5.4).[17] Filarete's columns (Rossi always referred to the one column at the corner, but in fact there are two) intrigued him as utterly unique fragments among the Grand Canal's otherwise harmonious mosaic of Gothic and Byzantine façades, but they also responded to his growing interest in forms and fragments that, bereft of decoration, facilitated multivalent meanings and relationships. The impression of this left-over fragment, Rossi wrote, "gave birth to my architecture with cylindrical elements, and for me, an entirely new vision of architecture."[18] That vision embraced elements in their most essential state, understood as fragments, as parts to be conceived and accreted in the construction of the city, as parts to be assembled over time.

Rossi's design for Parma did not survive to the final rounds. Despite proposing many theaters in the ensuing years, he returned only occasionally to this type of scheme, although the elements—the portico, the triangle, the cylinder—became staple features to be deployed in other projects, other theaters. They appeared again nearly thirty years later in his 1992 proposal for a Theater of the Indies for Expo '92 in Seville, as part of a truncated, conical structure with flanking wings and a barrel-vaulted portico (fig. 5.5), and in the theater for the Fontevegge project in Perugia (1982). Here he also proposed a conical structure as the entrance to a three-story structure for offices and a grand central space for musical and theatrical spectacles or for union and public meetings.[19] In his Little Scientific Theater, a narrow proscenium arch topped by a pediment with an inset clock frames a stage crowded with porticoes, unadorned columns, and stairs backed by painted scenery. As with his monument designs, Rossi never entirely abandoned a scheme, even an unbuilt one, always restlessly seeking to reconfigure, to revise, to bring one or more parts to life in subsequent architectures and drawings, partly because no single design exhausted all of the possibilities for an architectural element, and partly because of his declared fascination with fragments as expressions of "confidence in a fragment of ourselves."[20]

Following the temporary Teatro del Mondo, Rossi gained his first full-scale theater commission with his victory in the competition to reconstruct the Carlo Felice Theater in Genoa (1983; fig. 5.6). The original theater (1825) designed by Carlo Barabino

FIGURE 5.6
Aldo Rossi, Carlo Felice Theater, Piazza Ferrari, Genoa, 1983

FIGURE 5.7
Carlo Felice Theater, interior from stage (Maurizio Beatrici)

suffered severe damage during World War II, first from bombs and then from looters. Provisionally rebuilt immediately after the war, followed by two failed attempts by architects Paolo Chessa and Carlo Scarpa to reconstruct it, the theater finally became the subject of a two-phase competition in 1981, which Rossi won (with Ignazio Gardella and Fabio Reinhart) in 1984. Remarkably for a public project in Italy, where corruption regularly inflates construction costs, the Carlo Felice Theater came in on time and under budget. Notably, almost all of Rossi's projects did.

Rossi envisioned reconstructing the old theater's exterior, while completely remodeling the interior and adding the technological apparatus and facilities necessary for a contemporary theater. The sight of the ruins also fascinated him for several reasons: "The ruins of a city are the subject of imagination precisely when it is possible to connect them in a scientifically erected pre-established system with clear hypotheses.... In this sense ... I proposed the theory of the analogous city: that is, a compositional procedure that pivots on some fundamental facts of the urban reality around which other facts are constituted within a framework of an analogous system."[21] Rossi explored the concept of analogous architecture as a design method in the urban sphere in writings and urban projects, but he found it particularly relevant for theaters, both for the buildings and for stage sets. Together, his reflection on ruins and his developing notion of the analogical city helped clarify his approach to this design. For Genoa the competition rules defined the aims: maintain the old footprint, replace the exterior configuration of the original theater, especially the pronaos, or portico, but add a large new stage tower, or fly tower, to accommodate new technical demands. Rossi described the royal portico and the fly tower as "almost irreconcilable in their splendid autonomy."[22] In the modern

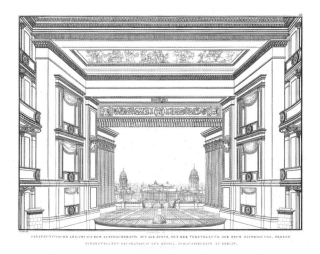

FIGURE 5.8
Karl Friedrich Schinkel, Schauspielhaus, Berlin, opening night curtain, 1821 (from *Sammlung Architektonischer Entwürfe*, issue 2, 1821, pl. 14)

interior he included a conical tower-lighthouse (*torre-faro*) bathing the foyer in a flowing synthesis of external and interior light from above. The tower suffused the atrium with a sense of intimacy, of isolation, despite being set in a grand and bustling public square. Above all, at the Carlo Felice, the Genoese streetscapes recreated on the walls of the auditorium, with windows and balconies on the lateral walls, invade the interior's autonomy, summoning the audience to enter into the story even prior to the spectacle. The inside folds into the outside, which in turn enfolds the interior, an endless process that draws close to what Rossi understood of the architect and the theater (fig. 5.7): "[Architects] are only given [the possibility] to predispose the skeleton of this fixed scene, some element[s] that permit the action to unfold."[23] At the Carlo Felice, the reconstructed historic exterior and the invented Genoese cityscape nested one within the other brilliantly summon parallels to the image on the opening night curtains at Karl Friedrich Schinkel's Schauspielhaus (Berlin, 1821), with a view of the theater itself framed by the colonnades of the two adjacent domed baroque churches and with the city of Berlin sprawling in the background (fig. 5.8).[24] This stratagem appeared repeatedly in Rossi's theater designs, where he placed the exterior elevation on an interior one, as at the GFT Casa Aurora building in Turin (1984), in the interior bar of the Il Palazzo Hotel in Fukuoka (1987), in a lecture space in the Scholastic Building in New York (1997, completed 2001; fig. 5.9). Divided into three roads converging on the stage, the backdrop at Scholastic depicts SoHo neighborhood streets, but it also pays homage to the wonderful steeply foreshortened perspective crafted by Vincenzo Scamozzi for Palladio's Teatro Olimpico. Here as in Schinkel's curtain at the Schauspielhaus, viewers are invited to reflect on their positions in the urban landscape, in the city, to remember how deeply the fantasy staged within lodges in the world without. Such an internal stage "participates in the action and constructs it: it creates further nexuses and reinforces them."[25] Not least, they remind the viewer of the fragile tissue of the theater's public and private dimensions, intimately and silently bound in brick and stone as in tears and laughter. Rossi especially cultivated the joyous, happy aspects of the theater as a site of freedom and imagination.

The cheerfulness Rossi detected, or imagined, in theaters may have been most obvious in a structure such as his Lighthouse Theater (1988) set on the shores of Lake Ontario in Toronto, Canada. He envisioned a theater along the lines of an ancient Roman theater as described by Vitruvius, only here constructed of wood. The stage backdrop for the nearly semicircular auditorium consisted of fragments of Rossi's urban designs, or something that seemed similar to them. Behind the audience rose a brightly painted red and white lighthouse topped by a green lantern and observation platform, linking,

FIGURE 5.9
Aldo Rossi, Scholastic Building, New York, completed 2001, auditorium-theater (Morris Adjmi)

in Rossi's imagination, the site with the enormous lake but also with other lighthouses in analogous maritime ports throughout the world. Rossi drew the complex this way, but he also imagined it in an urban environment, inserted between the brick façades typical of New York and found in many of his drawings. Open to the sky, the Lighthouse Theater seemed to bring together in happy juxtaposition land, water, and sky, an all-encompassing panorama outside of time, rooted in this space but also evoking many other analogous ones.

For this reason he found the baroque retablos (altarpieces) of the Iberian peninsula and the New World enchanting examples of theatrical backdrops.[26] In Seville he marveled at the elaborate and enormous altarpieces that he even found himself repeating in some of his designs, keeping them vividly alive in his memory.[27] In late 1978 he visited Minas Gerais in southeastern Brazil, and the towns of Ouro Preto, Belo Horizonte, and Congonha. Here the retablos in churches such as Our Lady of Carmine, but especially that in the church of Our Lady of the Conception, so overwhelmed Rossi that he wrote how he rediscovered his passion for architecture and artifacts that resisted rational explanations. In the work of eighteenth-century sculptor Aleijadinho he encountered the sacred themes familiar to him in Europe, the Sacri Monti, and the theaters. In these compelling Brazilian baroque churches he found himself lingering in front of the retablos, pausing somewhere between attention and memory and noting how the same themes in a different context produce profound differences. The chapels in the church of Carmine that recorded the phases of the Passion, for example, depicted Christ with long black hair in a sequence culminating with Christ "terribly dead" in front of the jewel and gold encrusted retablo that ascends vertically behind him. The entire church of Our Lady of the Conception he likened to a theater, where lateral passages in the dividing wall between the altarpiece and the nave (corresponding to the choir) opened to boxes similar to those in theaters. The retablos were, he continued, like machines around which the project or building are disposed, an emotional space where the retablo is the theatrical backdrop.[28] Much later, his Domestic Theater for the Milan Triennale appeared to him a fixed stage rather than a temporary backdrop, much like what he recalled of these altarpieces. This in turn reminded him of his passion for these baroque creations and his "absurd hope to be able to construct a *retablo*."[29]

Here again we see Rossi's kaleidoscopic memory drawing him back, with insistent regularity, to things he had seen during his travels or recalled from childhood. Each time recollections surfaced in connection with a new encounter, different emphases and contexts led him to draw new analogies and to discover new elements, which then became part of his drawings and his writings. As in the case of the retablos, where their beauty attracted and at times repelled him, these immersions of memory in new artifacts or events focused his attention more sharply. In the Domestic Theater, the enormous vertical section, with its humble implements and decorations, the retablo seems to have arisen unbidden, tumbling out from the recesses of his memory to be rendered in a radically different language as a newly sacred space. Perhaps the Domestic Theater indeed partially fulfilled his unrequited desire to fashion a retablo of his own.

A theater also came to be Rossi's final project in Italy. In September 1996, the city of Venice announced an invited competition to rebuild the historic eighteenth-century La Fenice Theater after it was gutted in a spectacular blaze on 29 January 1996.[30] The city of Venice, under the direction of Mayor Massimo Cacciari, extended invitations to teams of architects and construction firms. Rumors that the results of the competition were fixed circulated widely at the time.[31] Professor of administrative law Leopoldo Mazzarolli chaired the jury, which included Daniel Commis, Francesco Dal Co, Ernesto Bettanini Fecia di Cossato, and Angelo Di Tommaso.[32] The jury awarded points to each entry in four categories: aesthetics and design, time to complete building, cost, and cost of long-term maintenance. Mayor Cacciari (a professor of philosophy and former student of Manfredo Tafuri) enthusiastically celebrated the decision on 30 May 1997 to award first place to Gae Aulenti's submission, even though she failed to design about one-fifth of the building, therefore receiving the highest points in the categories of time of construction and cost. Rossi's project earned more points on aesthetic grounds and on long-term maintenance costs, arguably far more important than time and cost of construction. And because La Fenice had burned almost to the ground three times in its history, Rossi had also proposed, even though it would delay the start of construction, a large underground vat of water so that there would always be sufficient water in the event of a future fire.

On his own, Rossi would never have filed a lawsuit against his old friend Aulenti, but the German construction firm A.T.I. Holzman, unwilling to tolerate what they saw

FIGURE 5.10
Aldo Rossi, La Fenice
Theater, 1997, model
(Arassociati)

as a scandalous, corruption-plagued competition, suffered no such scruples and filed an administrative lawsuit, losing at the regional level but finally winning when the State Council issued its verdict in February 1998 in favor of Rossi—a decision that Cacciari predictably greeted with dismay.[33] Rossi died in September 1997, but his former staff in Milan brought the project to completion in 2004. While the city's public works chair maintained that Rossi had left only general ideas, in fact the design was as detailed as any competition project, though moving to working drawings is always a daunting task. Although Count Francesco da Mosto collaborated on design development, and Rossi's staff at Arassociati oversaw construction, the design is nevertheless unequivocally his (fig. 5.10).[34]

Venetians wanted their La Fenice back as it had been (*dov'era, com'era*—where it was, how it was), a position with which Rossi agreed to a large degree, although he had doubts about being able to recreate it as it had been). Even though he believed his project adhered faithfully to the competition rules, the "family picture" of La Fenice could only be granted by time and a personal imprint. On the other hand, rebuilt structures, such as Mont-Saint-Michel, acquired their own histories over time.[35] His choices to restore much of the exterior of the Carlo Felice theater had excited polemics in the early 1980s as being "nostalgic," neither "new" nor "modern," and the same responses erupted from the world of architects as the rebuilding process in Venice wore on.[36] Rossi had articulated his views about ruins and the role of the past as entailing the embrace of resources in history in *The Architecture of the City,* long before winning either competition, and distance has only confirmed the soundness of his approach. In the new wing where it would have been possible either to adopt a modern language or even to incorporate some of his own signature details—such as the cylinder, the triangle, the steel I-beam, the narrow, high staircase—Rossi chose instead to turn to history, even in the new section. In the Rossi Room in the new wing added after the fire, along one wall he recreated Palladio's spectacular serliana façade for the Basilica in Vicenza (fig. 5.11). This he did not only for the beauty of Palladio's design but in an effort to restore something of the ancient Venetian world of wooden architecture with the introduction of this fragment.[37] Particularly effective for acoustic issues, the double-height sequence of columns and arches crafted in polished wood paid homage to Palladio as theater designer and as architect of some of Venice's grandest churches, here in a room used for practice, small concerts, and conferences.

Assembling fragments of earlier projects to create something new characterized much of Rossi's architectural design strategy, but this was rarely done with such intriguingly winning aplomb as in the object known as the Macchina Modenese (Modena

FIGURE 5.11
La Fenice Theater, Rossi Room (Arassociati)

FIGURE 5.12
La Fenice Theater, interior from the stage (Arassociati)

Machine) for an exhibition of his architecture in Modena in 1985, a veritable theatrical machine. Rossi crafted a large wooden construction to place beneath the dome of Modena's civic art gallery. Here he set out a sequence of key elements of his best-known theatrical projects: the column and triangular passage as at Segrate, the cubic columbarium of Modena, the stacked red tower. The structure most resembles his drawings in the way it culls elements from a wide range of building types and juxtaposes them to one another. The strategy of designing by parts speaks to Rossi's understanding of the role and character of monumental public buildings in cities. Ideological and formal purity in design destroy rather than enliven cities, and the scourge of modern movement architects was their failure to acknowledge, or even recognize, this. Rossi instead turned to a complex and rich analytical and investigative process to first understand the city and its history, and second, to design with respect, comprehension, and above all imagination. Rather than an impediment to creativity, such a process instead spurs it, as is nowhere more apparent than in Rossi's Teatro del Mondo, Carlo Felice Theater, and the restored La Fenice.

*The Architecture of the City* emphasized the importance of history in thinking about architecture, the life of buildings being indelibly bound with their pasts, so that even a new or remade structure should "breathe the atmosphere of the place and even intensify it."[38] Rossi's ideas about history, the analogous city, and design by parts all figured in his decision to restore the destroyed structures, but so too did his reflections on theater and theatrical productions (fig. 5.12).

FIGURE 5.13
Aldo Rossi, "Il Teatro," sketch, 1983 (Fondazione AR/© Aldo Rossi Heirs)

ROSSI AND THE THEATER OF INCOMPARABLES

In sketches such as "Il Teatro" (1983), a version of the Little Scientific Theater abuts an octagonal, baptistery-type building, while in the background a stacked, pyramidal tower flanks a dome not unlike Filippo Brunelleschi's ogival cupola for Santa Maria del Fiore (Florence, 1418–34; fig. 5.13). Almost a collage of the building types that typically frame Italian piazzas, the sketch inserts structures that are formally remote but here jostle against one another, coherent in their singularity, much as Rossi wrote about the analogous city. For such drawings Rossi drew inspiration less from artists' collages, he wrote, than from the writings of Raymond Roussel, particularly the first version of his *Impressions of Africa* (1910).[39] This weird and amusing text fascinated Rossi to the point that he wished *he* had written it.[40] His "master in architecture," he wrote, "was probably the poet Raymond Roussel."[41]

What was it about Roussel's writings that so captivated him? Roussel was a wealthy eccentric and a passionate, even obsessive writer. His first published novel, a complete failure, headed a long list of equally unsuccessful books. None of the works published during his lifetime brought him the fame and respect that he craved. Despite the support of Surrealists, André Gide, and later writers such as Alain Robbe-Grillet, Michel Butor, Leonardo Sciascia, and Michel Foucault, few readers purchased his self-published books.[42] Roussel later turned his novel *Impressions of Africa* into a play. In the most general terms, the book recounts a strange tale of travelers on a shipwrecked vessel who, to pass the time while awaiting rescue in the form of a ransom, elaborate a grand, Carnivalesque gala to be staged by some of the passengers, an impromptu collaborative known as The Incomparables. Such is the plot, to the degree it has one, but Rossi lingered over the author's minutely detailed descriptions in which Roussel collapsed the distance between the banal and the outlandish, rendering something like a cat playing a zither quite normal indeed, while the deranged and amazing Incomparables embodied the zany unpredictability of life.

In his publications and in his notebooks, Rossi returned repeatedly to Roussel's book, each time reflecting on a slightly different aspect. Although the antic sensibility animating the text certainly appealed to him, Rossi aligned Roussel's use of description as a device for penetrating the mechanisms that triggered his writings with his own aspiration to elucidate the mechanisms that gave rise to his architecture. By mechanisms Rossi meant not something like autonomous techniques but rather something that arises almost unbidden, beyond description, even as he continually sought ways to describe it. However carefully one articulates, describes, or even designs, notions of type, structure, and function in urban architecture, for Rossi they never approached what he called the

FIGURE 5.14
"God as Geometer," ca. 1220–30, frontispiece of a Bible Moralisée, Austrian National Library, Codex Vindobonensis 2554, f. 1v

FIGURE 5.15
Aldo Rossi, Untitled on antique French paper, lithograph, 1989, detail of addition to De Amicis school in Broni (Private collection/Marino Bortolotti © Aldo Rossi Heirs)

city's soul.⁴³ What did he mean, and what did it mean for the design process itself? Far more than typology was at stake; Rossi urged the architect to acknowledge and to plumb *l'âme de la cité*, that which springs from a hazy, layered, and unfathomable depth but is at once radiantly visible, a bifurcated wonder intuited even—or perhaps especially—where words fail. For Rossi, as for most artists, translating the ineffable into form transpires in the making itself, in the act of creation, through the enigma unfolding from within. In this ramified process, specific forms play essential roles. With the cylindrical theater, historic associations about the shape of the cosmos, the planets, infinity—in its essence a geometrical figure, no beginning, no end—enrich the form. As with a centrally planned baptistery, the cylindrical theater denotes the unity of a marvelous created world painfully vulnerable in its enduring repetition of destruction and creation, of which the La Fenice fire was but a microcosm. The circle also intimates an archaic belief in a world organized according to *numerus, pondus, mensura* (number, weight, and measure), the pragmatic, tactile, the real, but more pointedly, as suggested in the Bible, the idea that God engineered our world by taking to hand a compass, thereby affixing the circle upon and within the earth itself—a medieval image of the deity as architect that gained force in architectural practice and theory during the Renaissance (fig. 5.14).⁴⁴ Dante too referred to the Creator as

> He who His compass turned
> around the world's last verge, and in it
> parted its many hidden things
> from those revealed.⁴⁵

So the small figures at the window or emerging from the portico in a drawing of the first school addition at Broni, or in another of the theater project for Parma where the figures raise their arms in exultation before the theater and the portico, signal the joyful flight of imagination, beyond function, beyond type, that Rossi intended to summon to life and reify with the theater and portico (fig. 5.15). In this, the drawings suggest, the school and the theater became centers of civic life, of theatrical spectacles, of performances real and imagined, ever fixed within the impenetrable geometry of the cosmos.

Yet Rossi's ambition went beyond this. For years he struggled with his desire to produce a book to be entitled "Alcuni dei miei progetti" (Some of my projects), a proposal floated repeatedly in his notebooks but that never became what he sought.[46] What was he seeking? His cues came from Adolf Loos, whom he quoted as remarking, "One can describe great architecture," and again, from Roussel the idea of descriptions that reach to the heart of a project, "a search within a mechanical purism that dismantles and reassembles objects."[47] Among other things, Roussel's book fascinated Rossi because the Frenchman described everything twice, in meticulous detail, the first time leaving the reader entirely in the dark about what, if anything, it all meant, while the second time casting some illumination even while remaining ambiguous. Each successive description called for a further version, never to be realized fully, in endless succession. Roussel's cryptic outline and detailed description of the Theater of the Incomparables especially struck Rossi, who wrote, "No theater is more real, by means of rigorous description nothing more is necessary than the portraits of the Electors of Brandenburg on the white rear wall."[48] Roussel's cryptic account of the Incomparables Club and theater on the first page identifies the stage backdrop consisting of paintings of the Electors, with no explanation of why their images should be present.[49] The search for a complete and rigorous description became a mandate, even an obsession, wherein Rossi could essay an analysis of his own designs. He followed Roussel in describing and explaining how he wrote, remote from any pedantic undertones, to "rupture the unknown of imagination, to uncover the rules of the game, in the end to desecrate the gesture of the unconscious down to its roots."[50] Boullée had undertaken precisely this operation when he spoke of buried architecture, of its ineffable origins, according to Rossi a search destined ever only to draw near without fully arriving, at once a horizon and a boundary. Years of writing in notebooks, in published essays, in texts for competition entries, in descriptions for books about his buildings, ultimately yielded prose at times not unlike that of the first half of *Impressions of Africa:* they barely delineated a still enigmatic architecture, one with special relevance for theaters.

As much as Roussel intrigued Rossi, he was unable to follow the French writer in the latter's endless foray into cryptic, if entertaining, incomprehensibility. Rossi reflected, assessed, made judgments and took positions, in ways foreign to Roussel. Rossi encountered a world he understood to be full of meaning, a world with which he was in constant engagement, a world in which in every project he sought to convey the meaning

FIGURE 5.16
Aldo Rossi, Stage setting for *Lucia di Lammermoor*, Rocca Brancaleone, Ravenna, 1986 (Fondazione AR/© Aldo Rossi Heirs)

of his designs. He could never have traveled the world as Roussel did, never leaving his hotel room, for Rossi's curiosity would have given him no peace.

Where freed from the constraints imposed by permanent structures, Rossi's designs for opera and ballet settings crisply evidenced some of these enigmas. *Lucia di Lammermoor* (Gaetano Donizetti, 1835) and *Madama Butterfly* (Giacomo Puccini, 1904) were both staged in a setting that could hardly have been more Rossian: the fifteenth-century Rocca Brancaleone along the northeastern walls of Ravenna, renovated and reused repeatedly over the centuries.[51] Erected by the Venetians over an existing structure as part of a defensive network in the early fifteenth century, the Rocca included the castle proper and a citadel with a large bailey, or open space, within the citadel's walls. For these operatic tales of love and betrayal, Rossi incorporated the Rocca in one stage set, essentially ignoring it in the other. The open-air theater sat adjacent to the castle. For *Lucia*, Rossi partly utilized the existing walls of the Rocca, to which he added a few houses and towers, "an imaginary Gothic city," primarily of towers and high chimneys (fig. 5.16).[52] In theater, almost anything is possible, so Rossi mixed towers and steeply pitched rooflines from Delft and Bruges, with images of houses drawn from Auxerre, Dijon, and other northern European cities—ostensibly for a setting in southern Scotland. Much of the action unfolded outdoors, with a single marble table standing for all of the interior scenes. For *Madama Butterfly*, however, bright and solid colors emphasizing the simplicity of the spare Japanese house sharpened the focus on the plot as it developed indoors. Large curtains rose and fell over a wooden structure with several square openings and connecting stairs, essentially a section of a Japanese house without further architectural definition. Rossi's designs for these two operas, though lean, straightforward backdrops for what would transpire—as he believed to be the role of architecture in the public realm—entailed devising settings by layering and juxtaposing impossible, irreconcilably diverse architectures that nonetheless imaginatively conveyed the sense of the productions.

The scenography for the Zurich Opera House staging of the ballet *Raimondo* in 1993, by contrast presented a remarkably assertive assemblage of typical elements of Rossi's architectural designs, here cast as an insane asylum, a prison, a factory, a temple. A bright red truncated cone, a red cubic structure perforated by square apertures as in the Modena cemetery's ossuary, and a stone pyramid loosely based on the ancient Cestius pyramid in Rome vividly countered the fin de siècle extravagance of the late-nineteenth-century auditorium. For the arrival of the Saracen villain, Rossi designed an exotic, even fantastic backdrop of eastern structures, more imaginary than real. For each of these stage sets, Rossi's theory of accumulated parts, of design via fragments radically different from one another, found ideal expression as a vehicle for positing an urban architecture at once time bound and timeless, an enigmatic foil for a neo-classical opera house interior or an improbable Scottish palace in a medieval Italian castle on the Adriatic coast.

In a body of drawings produced throughout his entire life, a veritable mountain ranging from the smallest tentative sketches to full-scale paintings, Rossi ventured to render that same enigma in ways impossible to accomplish with actual buildings. In one, for example, he positioned the Duomo of Milan adjacent to the Pertini Monument. In another, he depicted an empty can of Coca-Cola and a pack of cigarettes at the same scale as and adjacent to one of his works of architecture, or counterposing two buildings that in reality are quite remote from one another geographically. In certain projects and drawings, such as the student housing at Chieti, the Little Scientific Theater, and the cabins of Elba, Rossi wrote in 1977 that he sought that Rousselian descriptive clarity, positioning his projects "within a theoretical frame of his thoughts on architecture." In reality, he continued, "over time this could be expanded to a general vision of the meaning of life."[53] In some drawings of the San Cataldo cemetery in Modena, Rossi inserted fragments of the Chieti project, in others the ossuary at the Modena cemetery, or he supplemented a fragment of the San Carlone statue: as with Roussel's books, the explanation of the mechanism that produced the architecture explains only *that* mechanism. We can explain how we made something, Rossi finally admitted ruefully, but not why.[54] Instead he strove to design an architecture outside of time, conditions, and emotions, even while acutely aware of their presence behind that mechanism, a full range of intentions, justifications, dreams, and meanings that suffuse every work.[55] Much of the poetry of his architecture hovers around this bifurcated wonder, but its sources go well beyond purely architectural ones.

### THEATER AND SPECTACLE IN THE SACRI MONTI

Forms such as the centrally planned Paganini Theater, Rossi's thesis project, or even the Teatro del Mondo with its octagonal cupola poised over a square theater, only hint at the range of issues that Rossi struggled with in the theaters he designed. What, after all, is a theater? Rossi posed that question in an unpublished public lecture in April 1997, just a few months before his death.[56] Theater is far more than the hallowed structures of yore that one thinks of today, such as La Scala, La Fenice, the Globe Theater, he remarked, giving as an example his stage setting for the Milan Triennale "The Domestic Project" of 1986. Entitled "Domestic Theater," it consisted of a section of a house, not dissimilar to the *Madama Butterfly* stage set, a series of rooms outfitted with table, chairs, windows, doors, and oversized coffeepots—but no people (fig. 5.17). Rossi mused about the intimacy of the scenic backdrop of such a space, like the Domestic Theater a space imbued with a sense of waiting, of silence. Never far from his mind too were his recollections of bombed-out buildings in the center of Milan in the years after World War II (fig. 5.18), or the empty houses left in the *golena* (internal embankments) along the Po River after the devastating flood in the southern Veneto region of the Polesine in November 1951. At the time the worst flooding to have hit Italy since the war, the waters extended out more

FIGURE 5.17
Aldo Rossi, Domestic Theater, Milan Triennale, 1986

than 250 miles, and remained for some eight months before finally slowly drying out. Even years later Rossi encountered rooms with jackets, cups, and other detritus of quotidian life in homes and apartments savaged by allied bombs or as in the Polesine layered with mold, gaping open to curious but quickly averted eyes. He admitted to feeling invisible, of being on the other side of a spectacle.[57] Shortly before he died, Rossi was working on drawings of an abandoned house based on those damaged by the floods that he had studied for the province of Rovigo shortly after receiving his degree. "La casa abbandonata" (The Abandoned House) was erected in the sculpture park in San Donà di Piave in 2001 (fig. 5.19).

Rossi perceived the theatrical spectacle as extending far beyond a question of type or the performances enacted on the stage; it burrows into the very labyrinth of life, deep into its internal, quixotic, unpredictable dimensions. The Domestic Theater's outsized kitchen equipment, the coffee maker, the faded wallpaper, and the blind light fixture paradoxically for Rossi also summoned memories of childhood summers on the lake, sitting in his grandmother's kitchen and sketching the kinds of kitchen tools and implements that he drew repeatedly over the course of his life. Rather than nostalgic forays into his

FIGURE 5.18
Milan after bombing, August 1943

FIGURE 5.19
Aldo Rossi, "The Abandoned House," sculpture park, San Donà di Piave, 2001 (Setteo)

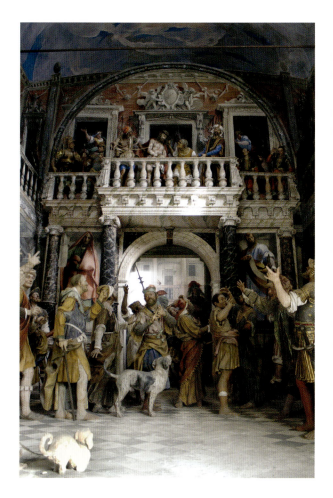

FIGURE 5.20
Giovanni d'Enrico (sculptor) and Pier Francesco Mazzucchelli (painter) "Ecce Homo," Chapel 33, Sacro Monte of Varallo, 1608–16, polychrome statues and frescoes (Marino Bortolotti)

personal past, such images were instead scenes such as those on a stage, or on a street, or in a house, where lives are lived and activities take place. For Rossi those recollections stood suspended in time, not as if they were still-life images but as lyrical pauses prior to events unfolding, that tremulous instant just before action takes place. In that brief moment, he memorably described what he anticipated would occur: "In some of my recent projects, or ideas for projects, I try to stop the event just before it occurs, as if the architect could foresee—does foresee—the unfolding of life in the house."[58]

As his point of reference he recalled one of his most powerful childhood experiences, visits to some of the Sacri Monti pilgrimage sites in the Lombardy and Piedmont regions.[59] Initiated in Varallo, an alpine region near Lecco, in 1486 by Franciscan friar Bernardino Caimi as an effort to recreate an earthly Jerusalem for aspiring pilgrims unable to undertake the journey to the Holy Land, the Sacri Monti (literally, sacred mountains) consist of a series of chapels outfitted with scenes from the life of Christ. At Varallo, a combination of painted and life-sized plaster figures depict biblical scenes, beginning with Adam and Eve and continuing through the Passion, Resurrection, Pentecost, Ascension, and the Assumption of the Virgin Mary. Subsequent Sacri Monti usually celebrated the Passion, but others recounted the life of St. Francis of Assisi (Sacro Monte of Orta), St. Jerome Emiliani (Sacro Monte of Somasca), or the Holy Trinity (Sacro Monte of Ghiffa). The sequence of chapels entails a mini-pilgrimage, with pauses to peer through a grate or enlarged apertures in a wire or metal screen at a succession of scenes, affording an invitation to prayer and reflection. "For one who ascends the Sacro Monte, the repetition of experience is similar to art," Rossi observed.[60] Each such chapel is in effect a mini-theater (fig. 5.20). As a student during the war years at the Somaschi Fathers' Episcopal College Alessandro Volta in Lecco, Rossi visited the Sacro Monte of Somasca recounting the life of St. Jerome Emiliani (1486–1537), founder of the Somasco order.[61] Initiated more than two centuries after the saint's death, on the Via delle Cappelle (Street of Chapels) a series of individual chapels flank a road that winds around Mount Magnodeno and culminates at the cemetery and the saint's hermitage—and at the ruins of the castle famous as that of the Innominato (The Unnamed) from Alessandro Manzoni's classic novel *I promessi sposi* (*The Betrothed*, 1827).[62] The life-sized plaster or Portland cement figures in the chapels glow, brightly painted in natural colors and dressed in fabric garments with expressive

FIGURE 5.21
Giovanni d'Enrico, Chapel 29, "Jesus Appears Before Pontius Pilate the Second Time," Sacro Monte of Varallo, ca. 1639, detail of Roman soldier, polychrome statue

faces as if on the verge of springing to life. Emblematic is the scene at the Sacro Monte of St. Jerome Emiliani where the grieving saint bore the body of a plague victim to be buried, or another where he prepared to distribute bread to famished orphans. Other Sacri Monti included depictions of the guards and gawking crowds who accompanied Christ in the evolution of the Passion (fig. 5.21).

Even as an adult, Rossi undertook pilgrimages to these sanctuaries, accepting fully what he lightly termed "the almost neurotic gesture of the pilgrimage."[63] He wrote to Polesello that he harbored ever more within him a different, perhaps impossible type of research, on a certain type of seventeenth-century Lombard naturalism, where rational architecture halts in a cognitive moment, one in which the plaster cast, or mold, as object, is introduced rather than the statue, or traditional sculpture. He found that the scenes in the chapels of Varallo and similar sanctuaries stimulated endless reflections, where the things in themselves, set within chapels designed by Pellegrino Tibaldi and other Renaissance artists, were transfigured.

The great and enduring impression on Rossi of these scenes and these chapels suffused both his drawings and his architecture and also recurred insistently in his written reflections. He often referred to what he described as an "amore coatto," a compulsive, irresistible love—despite himself—for the Sacri Monti.[64] What did he mean? For one thing, the Sacri Monti constitute among the grandest expressions of popular art and architecture from early modern Italy, part of their appeal but also exactly why they usually do not figure in the grand histories of art and architecture of Renaissance Italy. Individual and architecturally distinct chapels or oratories typify the region's Sacri Monti, where the architecture frames a scene as if on a stage, captured at a key moment

FIGURE 5.22
Chapels 17, 18, and 24, Sacro Monte of Varallo, ca. 1650 (Marino Bortolotti)

of the tale being recounted and made available to the pilgrim. Emblematic of the architecture at Varallo is the first chapel, a cylindrical structure with a four-columned seriliana portico topped by a pediment on the façade, with the scene (Adam, Eve, the serpent, and the tree of knowledge) set within. Some rectangular chapels at Varallo have arcaded porticoes, others are octagonal, while still others align in enclosed and vaulted passageways (fig. 5.22). Not surprisingly, in Venice the octagonal interior of Rossi's Teatro del Mondo replicates that of the adjacent baroque church, Santa Maria della Salute, known as La Salute (1681), another sacred space widely recognized as profoundly theatrical in its interior design. The centrally planned octagon also recalls Italy's medieval baptisteries, the very reason for which the shape often also appeared in the chapels of Sacri Monti. An even more compelling, direct link between Rossi's floating theater and La Salute lies in the unusual decision of the Venetian Republic to name the Somasco Fathers as administrators of La Salute, no doubt in honor of the order's founder, St. Jerome Emiliani, a Venetian nobleman who abandoned title and riches to follow his vocation.[65]

In Sacri Monti chapels, the diverse architectures as frames for elaborate, life-sized tableaus parallel the proscenium arches as configured by Aleotti for the theater in Parma: they frame and contain the sequence of events displayed within. Similar architecturally unique chapels populate the Sacri Monti at Ossuccio, Orta, Crea, and Ghiffa, the latter the town on the shores of Lago Maggiore where Rossi purchased and remodeled a lakeside villa for weekends and holidays. "The Sacri Monti are an architectural construction," Rossi wrote, "the construction of a non-utilitarian world of architecture.... They construct meaning by virtue of sequence and order."[66] Apart from the buildings' sacred purpose, with wonderful inventiveness the designers positioned chapels of diverse architectural styles adjacent to one another in what Rossi later called an architecture of fragments, a composition according to parts, which underlay his own assertions about architecture and cities.

Intriguing as the chapels' architecture is, of equal interest to Rossi were the sacred scenes themselves into which the visitor trespasses, almost as a voyeur, to experience the suffering of Christ during the stages of the Passion, or the joys of motherhood at the Nativity. He wrote of the "chapels with the colored plaster [figures] and the Last Supper with tablecloths, glasses, objects, things [that are] authentic and irreplaceable."[67] Though far removed from the Holy Land and hence lacking the actual sites to trigger memories, the scenes provide an alternative *locus memoriae,* wherein through imagination the past unfolds anew in the present. The fully outfitted figures—complete with hair, helmets, arms, foodstuffs—frozen in expressions of anger, puzzlement, grief, or indifference, all have animated but endlessly varied faces, poised at highly specific, emotional moments and, despite the apparent suspension of time, they are nonetheless destined to succumb to decay.

Just as in traditional theater, the scenes in the Sacri Monti chapels aimed to project the viewer into the scene through the images themselves, in this case to evoke contemplation of the mysteries of faith and the suffering of the Christ. The scenes acted as aids to a process already proposed in the Catholic faith during the fifteenth century in texts on the practice of meditation such as *Zardino de oratione* (*The Garden of Oration,* 1454, printed 1493) and *Considerazioni sulla passione di nostro Signore* (*Considerations on the Passion of our Lord,* before 1488) of St. Camilla Battista da Varano.[68] In a process known as constructing a *memoria locale* (local memory), the texts ask believers to compose a mental image of a city familiar to them, therein to situate the characters and moments of the life and Passion of Christ. To construct a *memoria locale* later, then, one recalls something by imaginatively recreating the space, location, and events at a specific moment so as to summon forth the particular recollection, a process dating back to the story of Simonides and his recollection of the celebrants' seating arrangement at a banquet. In the case of the Sacri Monti, the vivid visualization of the scenes intends to facilitate mental repetition at a later time.

The Sacri Monti for Rossi thus became true *theatrum pietatis,* theaters of piety from Counter Reformation Italy. Rather than being simply static representations, they were also stations along a pilgrimage route, to be viewed sequentially, one by one in the slow and steady ascent toward a sanctuary. What did these experiences, these passages, mean for Rossi's architecture? He wrote about scenes such as these, "I was, as I now am, attracted by stasis and naturalness, by the classicism of architecture and by the naturalism of people and objects. . . . I wanted to pass beyond the window grate, to set out one of my own objects on the tablecloth used at the last meal, to escape the condition of a passerby."[69] Exactly as the theater is meant to draw the viewer into the drama itself, and as the Sacri Monti did for Rossi, so too did his theaters offer the prospect of engagement, enticing one to become a participant rather than a viewer or a mere passerby. Such a profound entry into another's world fulfilled the aspirations of the designers of the Sacri Monti, where the distance between the events depicted and the viewer collapsed in service of the more profound immersion of the viewer in the event. The singular chapels visited equaled in importance the individual moments depicted, as did the pilgrimage practice itself, as each pilgrim slowly moved from structure to structure, scene to scene: "The [Sacri Monti] constitute meaning through their sequence and their order. Independent of the fact that they contain a sacred story ... they constitute a place.... A story is explained by inserting ourselves into the story."[70]

A theater for Rossi, then, struck a fine balance between urban artifact, a *locus solus* among other singular sites, and the setting for the human comedy, the lives lived in the streets and houses of the city just as they do within the theater itself. When Rossi repeatedly juxtaposed quite different structures in his invented urban landscapes and drawings, he in effect recreated the rich and architecturally diverse landscapes of the Sacri Monti, each a *locus solus* in which equally singular events unfold. Rossi wrote of seeking "a unity, or a system, made solely of reassembled fragments," where one could capture the "potential for being lived in."[71] In this sense, the reconstruction of the theater of Carlo Felice in Genoa illustrates how Rossi ushered such reflections into built form, nestling the lively street life into the auditorium through the replication of urban streets on the lateral walls. The scenography for the performance of *Electra* at the Greek Theater in Taormina instead involved a theatrical setting not unlike those of the Sacri Monti, where the architecture speaks the tragic events it has witnessed.

Lanza Tommasi invited Rossi to design the stage sets and costumes for the Richard Strauss opera *Electra* in July 1992.[72] In the play by Sophocles, Electra, her father Agamemnon, and brother Orestes descended from the house of Atreus, the Atreidae, among the most savage families of ancient Greek mythology. Brothers killed brothers, slew their nephews and fed them to their father; wives slaughtered husbands, and sons sought revenge for the deaths of their fathers. In this version, Electra demanded justice for her father Agamemnon, slain by his wife Clytemnestra and her lover on Agamemnon's return from the Trojan War.[73] Rossi proposed as a setting the courtyard of a palace populated by victims and assassins alike, its walls punctured by irregularly placed windows, a palace crumbling into ruin, semi-abandoned, bearing the signs of neglect and the violence enacted therein. Rossi imagined stones with stories to tell, in part through the mask of Electra bearing the pallor of the helpless witness, and the giant reproduction of the gold "mask of Agamemnon," and in part through two other remarkable features.[74] The first consisted of deep red fissures in the palace wall, where blood mars and disfigures the battered stones; in some early drawings blood flowed from a single deep gash onto the stage as visceral testimony of past and present carnage (fig. 5.23). The Lion Gate reproduction over the doorway also tells a story, but a different one. In the original at Mycenae, two headless lions flank a single, tapered column

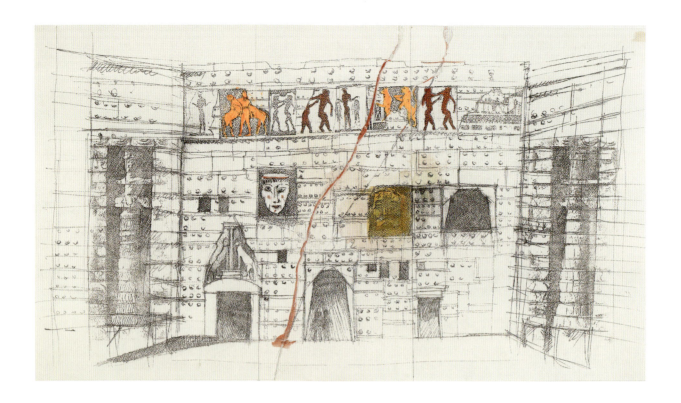

FIGURE 5.23
Aldo Rossi, Stage setting for *Electra*, Taormina, 1992, handcolored lithograph (Private collection/© Aldo Rossi Heirs)

in a triangular block of limestone, known as a relieving triangle, set atop a cyclopean lintel at the main gate to the citadel of Mycenae (fig. 5.24).[75] Although the ancient meaning eludes us, that the lions guarded and protected, as they did in most Mediterranean cultures, is obvious. The column, however, yields to no ready explanation. The lions perch on their rear legs on a plinth-like altar, with the column between them: a symbol of solidity, of strength? Whatever the case, the triangular form and the single column link the ancient citadel's architecture with Rossi's own—the triangle and the column—spanning the millennia and binding the ancient with events he envisioned unfolding in spaces shaped by his architecture. Rossi commented on the "strange serenity" offered to the architect by theaters, where "the interior separates the worlds of reality and fiction," where their "reciprocal exchanges [are] then theater."[76] In this case, the reality of his architecture merged with the ancient city gate, condensed to its essence in the *Electra* stage set.

The Teatro del Mondo, once positioned in the Venetian lagoon enjoyed a special opening, even if the structure could only accommodate an audience of 400 people, 250 seated and 150 in the upper porticoes. To Rossi's delight, the Theater Biennale officials decided to open the Biennale by staging Jorge Luis Borges's short story titled "The Aleph," a word that denotes the first letter of the Hebrew as well as the Phoenician, Aramaic, Arabic, and Persian alphabets, and in the Kabbalah is associated with infinity and the godhead, a point in space that envelops and exposes every other possible point.

FIGURE 5.24
Lion Gate, Mycenae, Greece, ca. 1400 BCE

From this spectacularly unique position, the viewer sees everything in the universe simultaneously, without overlaps, folds, or distortions, with all of the ugliness, beauty, mystery, and madness in which we live.[77] For Borges this Aleph referred to the panorama of the divine, a perspective unavailable to humans. In the brief tale, Rossi appreciated Borges's figure of Daneri, the mad poet driven by a lifelong ambition to write an epic poem in which he would describe every single location on the planet in intimate, fulsome detail—much as Roussel had done. Borges's narrator's brief encounter with the Aleph in the dark cellar of Daneri's house summarizes the terrible beauty and enigma of experience, for though he launches into an exacting description of that vision, his most intimate and essential tool as a writer—words—ultimately fail him, as they indeed fail the mystic, and he is left in a state of "infinite wonder, infinite pity." So too Rossi conceived of the impossibility of translating the ineffable into built form, or even into words, but in some fashion possible to render visible in the theater, where "every theater, as a place of liberation, is a happy theater."[78]

# 6   Cemeteries for Modena and Rozzano

> In God seeing and being seen coincide; and,
> likewise, His seeing Himself is His being seen
> by Himself, and His seeing of all Creatures
> is His being seen by all Creatures.
>
> —NICHOLAS OF CUSA

In 1972, Rossi won the competition for an addition to the nineteenth-century San Cataldo cemetery in Modena (fig. 6.1). Nearly two decades later, in 1989, he received a second cemetery commission, also an addition, this time to a cemetery at Ponte Sesto for the town of Rozzano, a bedroom suburb of Milan (fig. 6.2). In the interval between the two projects, Rossi also designed two private mausolea, both in the Lombard region. The first cemetery gained international recognition, while the others received scarce attention then or later. Yet though expressed quite differently, the four designs spring from the same profound understanding of death and the cemetery in Italian—and arguably even Western—culture, from a Catholic perspective.

Like the other participants in the Modena competition, Rossi submitted three primary views of his first-round proposal along with a project statement entitled "L'azzurro del cielo," (The Blue of the Sky) (fig. 6.3).[1] The first image set the project in the context of Cesare Costa's existing nineteenth-century cemetery, the second rendered the plan in more detail, and the third provided a bird's-eye view. The scheme—a large, enclosed rectangle, high cubic ossuary for veterans, tall, conical structure for communal graves and religious services, and rows of columbaria laid out as a triangle—stood out from the other entries for its monumental and diverse forms expressed with compelling simplicity.[2] In adjudicating the first round, the jury failed to come to an agreement on Rossi's submission, and the minority drafted a stinging rebuttal to the majority decision.[3] They described Rossi's project as indifferent to the individual, directed toward an imprecise collectivity and an equally vague collective memory, therefore essentially ignoring the significance of the mystery, the intimacy, of death.[4] The next round, in which the top three proposals competed, ended with no decisive winner declared, however Rossi

FIGURE 6.1
Aldo Rossi, Modena Cemetery (San Cataldo), 1971, entrance

FIGURE 6.2
Aldo Rossi, Rozzano Cemetery, Ponte Sesto, portico and columns of chapel, 1989

FIGURE 6.3
Modena Cemetery, presentation drawing, 1971 (MAXXI, Rossi/© Aldo Rossi Heirs)

FIGURE 6.4
Modena Cemetery, final project, 1973 (Fondazione/© Aldo Rossi Heirs)

remained in first place, having made some key adjustments between the first and second rounds, and he ultimately received the commission.[5] Time has borne out the wisdom of the majority decision.

    Within the next two years, several magazines published the project and a model, along with the addition of some of Rossi's earliest elaborations on the original proposal.[6] Although the definitive design remained incomplete until 1976, the project and especially Rossi's variations on the initial drawings soon fired imaginations across the globe (fig. 6.4), even though the competition submission itself has rarely been published. Rather, the many versions Rossi produced over the next twenty-six years prompted sustained interest and secured its status as an icon of twentieth-century architecture. As the cemetery structures slowly rose over the decades, photographs by Luigi Ghirri and others captured its haunting beauty and added to its fame. The project's renown was remarkable in part because it overturned many of the basic principles governing late modernist architecture; it constituted a radical challenge to everything that western European and American architects took to be unquestionable in architectural design. Jury member Paolo Portoghesi praised the courage of Modena's officials for choosing Rossi's unfashionable project in an era of consumerism and the rule of technology and especially for challenging Italian architects to confront a problem for which the modern movement lacked answers.[7]

    The questions I pose here are several: in what ways does the cemetery fit with Rossi's theories of architecture? How, if at all, does it express a civic conscience, as Rossi hoped it would? What is it about the cemetery—in its many iterations in multiple drawings and photographs—that exerts such an appeal that it became, and remains, an

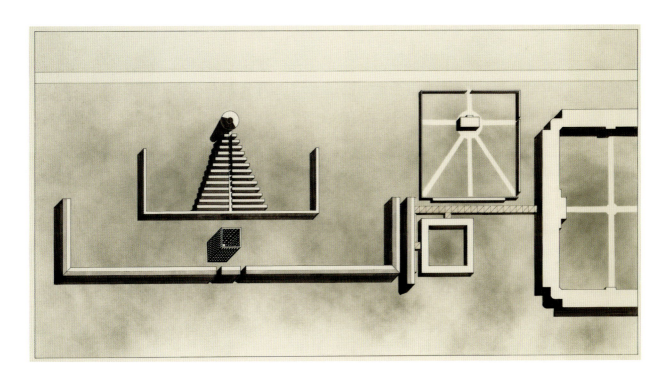

architectural icon? (And this is despite the fact the construction firm that won the later construction competition did so allegedly by seriously underbidding costs and using the cheapest possible materials.) What does the cemetery reveal about Rossi's ideas on time? From the perspective of some forty-five years after the fact, the contours of the historical moment sharpen to yield images of an era rife with ideological battles in which critics summoned the cemetery to illustrate one or another position independent of, and alas with apparent disinterest in, the architect's representations or even the building itself.

How this unfolded in the Modena cemetery project emerges first in a comparison with the proposals of the other contestants who, invariably embracing modernist planning principles, scattered an array of structures across the site. Rossi instead chose to adopt the historic typology of Italian cemeteries and specifically, the adjacent one. Arguing that the first task entailed joining the typical nineteenth-century neo-classical cemetery by Costa and the Jewish cemetery to the new addition, Rossi took his cues from the existing cemetery and enclosed the site as a walled precinct outfitted with structures of simple, almost primitive architectural forms. Indeed, his own final resting place is precisely such a small-scale, nineteenth-century cemetery, overlooking Lago Maggiore. One notable feature distinguished Rossi's perimeter walls from Costa's original: large square windows punctuate them, at once breaking up the severe practice of tough enclosure and emphasizing the parallel between the cemetery and a house. In the final project Rossi inserted a high portico with burial niches between the addition and the Jewish cemetery. Unlike the Costa design and most similar cemeteries, for San Cataldo Rossi did not envision widely spaced individual structures; rather he planned three significant and unique forms (cone, ossuary, and central triangular spine consisting of rows of burial niches) surrounded by the three-story rows of loculi (burial recesses), and the cemetery walls.[8] The rows of burial chambers, a triangle in plan, rose gracefully from the longest and lowest row (70 meters [230 feet] by less than 5 meters [16 feet]) to a peak 11 meters long and 11.5 meters high (36 by almost 37 feet) just before the truncated cone. The perimeter wall tightly frames the open, grassy courtyards; unlike the courtyard house for the living, Rossi observed, this courtyard for the city of the dead should be empty except for these three monumental structures (fig. 6.5).

While he was revising the Modena competition entry, Rossi also was beginning work on the elementary school in Fagnano Olona. Certain parallels between the two began to come to his attention, notably that both articulated "a single architecture of a series of structures united by an axis."[9] As he mused on this, he began to understand both as having forms reminiscent of that of a human figure, indicating the cemetery in particular as being anthropomorphic, but he imagined still more than that. Rossi characterized his vision as being that of an inert body sprawled on the ground, like the Deposition of Christ from the cross (see fig. 4.5).[10] He returned to this image of the Deposition more than once in his writings, at one point in reference to the grave or

FIGURE 6.5
Modena Cemetery, ossuary and columbaria wings

mound in the forest identified as architecture by Adolf Loos. Rossi differentiated the functionalist view of the human body as a "reduction of what is possible and its denial" from the Deposition, where the limp "body of Christ was the simplest and most intense thing in the great baroque churches of the Jesuits, and the white sheet of the *sudarium* their purest ornament." The more it shaped itself to the human corpse, Rossi continued, the more it would be architecture. The Modena cemetery in this way became "a sort of 'deposition,' [a] deposition on a floor, on the earth, etc."[11]

Rossi did not present the two designs and their relation to the Deposition as a metaphor; quite the contrary, his perception expressed that of William Blake's Isaiah in his response to a query about his faith: he had not seen God, but "my senses discovered the infinite in every thing."[12] The retrospective image of the human body in these two designs led Rossi beyond musings about specific architectural features to a confrontation with one of the great mysteries of his faith: the death and resurrection of Christ, and to discovering the infinite in everything. He liked to quote poet Vladimir Mayakovsky's way of distinguishing himself from Boris Pasternak. A lightning bolt prompted Mayakovsky to see electric light; Pasternak, on the other hand, saw God.[13]

Reflections on such matters in Rossi's writings converged with remarkable consistency in his designs. In thinking about the layout of the Fagnano school, for example, he recalled Velazquez's *Crucifixion* (ca. 1632) at the Prado Museum in Spain: "a man nailed to two pieces of wood." But, as he pointed out, the image also embraces the entire history of painting. This in turn prompted him to mull over the idea that one could no more invent architectural elements than one could a language; the way the architect deploys them may be both inventive and autobiographical; "it is [my] history and [my] future."[14] As we have seen, the autobiographical and subjective dimensions of architecture remained stable reference points in all of his work, whether drawings, writings, or buildings.

To be sure, such thoughts also brought him to further meditations on architectural design, where geometric solids, bricks, panels, columns, and pilasters combine geometry and history; elements of progress, though scarce and fragmentary, Rossi held, they could always assume new meanings. Rossi saw both San Cataldo and the Fagnano Olona school enclosed within a single line, as if to isolate them from a continuous or overwhelming plan. This concept of an architecture assembled of parts but bound together emerged both in the cemetery and in the Fagnano school with the axial orientation and other structures aligned along it, an approach remote from modern movement design strategies.

In three key respects, then, Rossi shunned prevailing fashions: first, he departed from the existing Costa wing by reducing its architectonic features to the most elemental and historically consolidated forms; second, he rejected modernist planning and architectural forms; third, he incorporated color—a brilliant blue, a deep red—at a time when his peers rejected any color in favor of white.[15] In an era when flat roofs were de rigueur signs of a "modern" structure, for example, Rossi fashioned the perimeter buildings with gabled blue roofs. If, as he noted in the project statement, the cemetery as a city of the dead also enfolds the space of memory for the living, summoning references to domestic architecture at the urban scale only gives life and body to this underlying principle. For these building blocks, the most direct reference is to his earlier design for the Monument to Partisans at Segrate. He proposed for a city of the dead a radical inversion of city planning and domestic design. Crowds throng the piazzas and public buildings of an Italian city such as Modena most of the day, crisscrossing the city in cars, buses, motorcycles, and bicycles. They are noisy, bustling, chaotic, and full of life. Rossi's Modena cemetery is everything that the city is not: hushed, it has no crowds, there are no vehicles of any sort except those that pull up on the perimeter, and even they linger only for brief periods. The generous open spaces remain just so; they never fill up, they never bustle. The cemetery buildings may resemble others found in the city, but only on the level of form, dignified, even grand. Absence, then, is the most salient characteristic of Rossi's cemetery; it is nothing but bones and buildings.

In the heyday of postmodernism, Rossi excluded that which postmodernist architects and theorists celebrated most—irony, playfulness, brash historical allusions and deformations—and so for critics the cemetery and its representations could only be seen, by contrast, as lugubrious and exuding melancholy.[16] How was this possible?

To begin with, the meanings attached to the cemetery's architectural forms rest on convention as much as do words. As Rossi himself observed, "Hundreds and thousands of people can see the same thing, yet each perceives it in his own unique way."[17] This he grasped as many observers unfortunately have not: architectural forms constitute the language of architecture, their meanings are at once conventional and contingent,

FIGURE 6.6
Aldo Rossi, Borgoricco Town Hall, 1983, chimney

therefore also personal. Above all, this understanding infuses his drawings, the ways he chose to represent his architecture, and also constitutes the core of his notebooks, his *Quaderni Azzurri*.

One example will suffice. To Anglo-American critics such as Ada Louise Huxtable, the brick conical structure Rossi designed for Modena summons references to the chimneys and crematoria of Auschwitz.[18] To historians such as Eugene Johnson, the chimney derives from Rossi's fascination with the theories and designs of Étienne-Louis Boullée. To Italians, on the other hand, it recalls the chimneys of schools, factories, and brickworks typical of the Po Valley and northern Italy more generally; to this end Rossi featured just such a conical chimney in many of his public projects of the 1970s and 1980s, including the school at Fagnano Olona and the town hall at Borgoricco (fig. 6.6). In the competition entry, he described the cone as like "the chimney of a deserted factory," a reference to the process of deindustrialization then underway throughout northern Italy.[19] He made the same references in discussions about the school in Fagnano, so while all such associations are theoretically legitimate, Rossi had in mind these images of deindustrialization so characteristic of the periphery of Milan and its hinterland, therefore clearly more relevant for a formal analysis of the design.

In several writings, including the project description that accompanied the competition entry, Rossi repeatedly referred to "bones" as the structural concept underlying his design—bones being appropriate because they are conserved in the cemetery.[20] Specifically, the block between the cone with the common burial site and the ossuary he considered a spine, or vertebrae, with ribs that rise and slightly tend to enclose as they reach the cone and the common graves. Rossi commented in his project statement that because since antiquity death has become increasingly private, with the associated rituals reduced to keeping alive regrets, or grief, this left to architecture the task of expressing history and the public, or collective, aspects of death. For Rossi, the architectural features of the cemetery and the character of his drawings of it yielded to a simple explanation: "The meaning of every representation is thus fixed in advance: every work or part [of a work] is the repetition of an occurrence, almost a ritual since it is the ritual and not the event that has a precise form."[21] For the revetment, Rossi chose to employ the same stucco plastering technique used for houses and factories *alla maniera antica* (in the ancient way), a lime or stucco base beneath a mix of brick and sand, in this too binding the housing of the living with that of the dead.[22] From the earliest days of design development, Rossi conceived of the cemetery as a city of the dead; in August 1971 he already wrote of the cubic ossuary as being like an abandoned house, the house of the dead.[23] With the concept of abandoned houses, he sought to render evident that which is at once absent and "at the root of every private terror."[24] He imagined resolving technical issues as one does in a house, a school, or a hotel, but unlike the house that life itself modifies over time, in the cemetery what will happen has already been anticipated; "its time has a different dimension."[25] The tempo, the measure, is that of death; its rituals both collective and private and their relationships, though ineffable, are concrete in a way different from that of a church to the eyes of a believer.[26] In this Rossi drew on St. Augustine's *Confessions,* where the saint asked himself about the nature of time but in response could only acknowledge that while he knew what it was, he could not explain it. He continued distinguishing three distinct times: a present of things past, a present of things present, and a present of things future. "For these three do exist in the mind. . . . The present time of things past is memory; the present time of things present is sight; the present time of things future is expectation."[27]

The title of the 1980 Venice Biennale, The Presence of the Past, clearly draws from this well-known passage where the saint reflected on the difficulty of grasping the concept of time. The three times exist in our souls, according to Augustine, for he found them nowhere else. Augustine ultimately acknowledged time as of God, whose temporality consists of eternity, and he described what is termed presentification, wherein even though we recognize that we can neither recover the past nor anticipate the future, we negate neither: rather, the past and the future remain suspended in a fluid state, held together by the present. Presentification, in which we summon the past into the present, renders possible the act of memory, a process prompted by rituals, rites, and the repetition of events. Memory in this sense attaches to the place and to the living, a practice rendered vivid in cemeteries, where the theme ultimately is that of spatial and temporal expansion, between time and eternity.

Rossi therefore advanced the notion of the cemetery as a house of the dead related to the city of the living, a concept to which he returned many times in writing about or drawing San Cataldo. The individual family tombs in the form of small houses that Rossi designed to be of uniform size also triggered a firestorm of protest precisely because prosperous Modenese families wanted to demonstrate their wealth with individualized, showy mausolea. Rossi successfully resisted what appeared to him a profoundly undemocratic notion: why would this be appropriate in a public cemetery, he wondered. Nonetheless, a few years later he received requests to design two private family mortuary chapels elsewhere, both in the region of Lombardy. The earlier of the two, the Marchesi chapel, was not built, but the second, for the Molteni family, was erected in Guissano, north of Milan near Lake Como (fig. 6.7). This chapel consists of a severe brick box set on a *pietra serena* plinth with a deep marble cornice based on one designed by sixteenth-century architect Jacopo Barozzi (also known as Il Vignola) that wraps around the corners but breaks laterally and on the rear elevation. A glazed gabled roof allows light to flood into an interior divided into two sections, the underground level for the burial niches and the upper level where, over a blue background, Rossi placed a beautifully carved wooden reproduction of the Borsari Gate in Verona. He likened the slightly detached wooden wall to a retablo, similar to what he had proposed for the Marchesi chapel, and he placed a metal grid at the entrance in homage to the apertures and grids of the Sacri Monti where the metallic grid "separated the indistinct of the sacred and of death from the surrounding world."[28] Clearly fascinated by the classical orders, he produced dozens of drawings of columns, orders, and capitals as he developed the designs. External stairs led to the underground burial chamber while another staircase led to the upper level with a small walkway around a large aperture for light to penetrate even below ground. Here Rossi specifically appealed to the entrances to prehistoric tombs, where the sense of religion derived from descent into the structure as if linking life with death, precisely what he hoped to convey here.

Some years after winning the Modena competition, Rossi received a letter from an elderly woman who was a regular visitor to San Cataldo. Remarking on the winter cold of an early morning, she wondered if he could open some windows. Rossi exulted because he saw in the desire for a window an affirmation of his scheme to be understood as a house, a house for the dead.[29]

With the title "The Blue of the Sky," Rossi signaled that his San Cataldo addition at Modena embraced a concept of death far richer and more complex than a simplistic reading of melancholic entombment in the earth. That blue sky, viewed from what elsewhere he described as a celestial observatory, embodied all of the hope and optimism he believed infused the cemetery's design. Certainly he also drew on Georges Bataille's description in his book *Le bleu du ciel* of the cemetery in Trier, which his debauched protagonists end up peering down upon while perched perilously on a high cliff. Here it seemed as if the "space below our feet was no less infinite than the starry sky above our heads."[30] For Bataille the blue sky had already been swallowed up by the looming darkness of Fascism and the prospect of an ugly new war, but no such shadow darkened Rossi's San Cataldo, where the blue sky was also the blue of the Madonna—who was

FIGURE 6.7
Aldo Rossi, Molteni Funerary Chapel, Guissano, 1980
(Marco Introini)

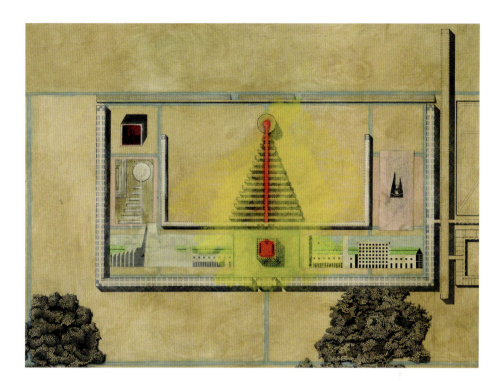

FIGURE 6.8
Modena Cemetery, photocopy plus added drawing (Fondazione AR/© Aldo Rossi Heirs)

often represented in a pale blue mantle—figuratively and protectively cloaking the cemetery. As he remarked in one of his *Quaderni* in 1971, when he was elaborating the San Cataldo addition, "[This] time that consumes and changes everything is as much a sign of death as it is of that which endures, of a sense of death that pertains more to you the more you read it in things."[31]

Rossi produced many drawings of the Modena cemetery over the years, and he incorporated fragments of the cemetery in many other drawings. He utilized photocopies or other reproductions of the original competition plan as a base for a new version, usually colored and with additions or modifications. A good example of this type of drawing is one held by the MAXXI in Rome (fig. 6.8). Where the first competition entry consisted of a straightforward plan, this and subsequent drawings included lush trees and elevations of some of the project's elements. A deep red spine drives through the center from the conical structure through the rows of tombs aligned in plan as a triangle to reach the ossuary, all a striking shade of red. Laterally, in the L-shaped spaces between the two main blocks of tombs Rossi inserted drawings that amount to explications of the project. In contrast to the stark competition entry, Rossi here fleshed out the blocks that compose a pyramid in plan so that the progressive rise in elevation toward the conical chimney became clear. Visible in the fragments of elevations are the blue roofs, part of the porticoes, the ossuary punctured by multiple square windows, and part of the cube and cone sequence again, each rendered in pale pastels. Barely visible to the far right, the adjacent Jewish cemetery separates Rossi's design from Costa's neo-classical one.

FIGURE 6.9
Aldo Rossi, Architectural fantasy drawing with San Carlone statue (MAXXI, Rossi/© Aldo Rossi Heirs)

The contrast between the crisp presentation drawings and those that followed points to Rossi's intertwined, twin souls: on the one hand, the intellectual and professional architect, and on the other, the poet. With the first, as we saw, he spelled out the reality of his architecture with lucid, almost scientific rationality, while as a poet he indeed furnished information, but most of all, in this second group of drawings he transmitted the meanings of things, their past and thereby also the present. In Rossi's case, the poetry inheres in the fragments and pieces of his designs, images drawn from the world around him—past and present—assembled in drawings and collages he often titled "architectural fantasies" (fig. 6.9). It does more than inhere, however, as we have seen, because the former would not be possible without the latter—they are, and must remain—inextricably intertwined. This second type of drawing seeks not to transmit information but rather to convey expressive meanings, precisely for their elusive and enigmatic qualities; they are the product of imagination, not of reason or science, even if the latter remained the necessary foundation. In most cases Rossi emphasized the shadows cast across a structure or extended behind it; in distinguishing dark from

FIGURE 6.10
Aldo Rossi, Il Gioco dell'Oca, drawing, 1972 (MAXXI, Rossi/© Aldo Rossi Heirs)

light, they draw the visitor's attention to time and its passage, but with movement that is slow, stately, measured—and repetitive. In one sketch, Rossi depicted the same urban backdrop three times, from bright daylight to evening shadows, emphasizing how he always understood his architecture not at some single ideal moment but as undergoing constant transformation by light and time. It would be too easy to dismiss Rossi's twin souls as irremediably separate; on the contrary, however, intertwining and nourishing one another they fulfilled Rossi's expectation for any architect. To this point he returned repeatedly; as we have seen, he found inspiration in Boullée's discussion of the same topic, for to neither man could the technical and material be separated from the poetic.

Other than the actual design then, Rossi advanced his vision of a cemetery through drawings, in a concerted effort to clarify, not obscure, the rationale underlying his choices of architectural forms. Far from engaging in a "persistent attempt to expunge meaning from architecture," as one critic asserted,[32] Rossi took pains to generate multiple visual and written accounts of "meaning" in his architecture, and specifically, in the Modena cemetery. "My projects seek the meaning of architecture," Rossi wrote in 1972, "meaning that is stronger than function, use, organization and form, but meaning is expressed through form."[33] Among the early drawings, Rossi labeled one from 1972 "Il Gioco dell'Oca" (fig. 6.10).[34] While developing the second-round project, Rossi realized that the perimeter walls began to remind him of a labyrinth, but especially of the Gioco dell'Oca (Game of the Goose), where the box with skull and sickle suggests a game of death, and the player moves around by steps to arrive at the central, final square.[35] A board game of obscure origins, the Gioco dell'Oca dates at least to the end of the sixteenth century, when the Florentine ambassador Francesco de' Medici presented one to

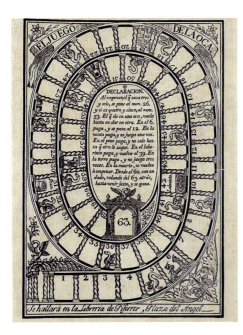

FIGURE 6.11
Il Gioco dell'Oca, Portuguese version of the game, 19th c.

King Philip II of Spain around 1580.[36] Sixty-three numbered spaces, usually organized in a spiral, constitute the main elements; players advance counter-clockwise according to a throw of the dice, with their movement occasionally spurred by a bridge or a goose, or blocked by landing on a well, a maze, a prison, or a skull that symbolizes death (fig. 6.11). The Knights Templar had invented a similar game consisting of steps along a pilgrim's journey to the church of St. James in Santiago de Compostela in northern Spain, the Way of St. James. In private, Rossi often described himself as a pilgrim, a wanderer who travels toward a specific objective but encounters unexpected milestones along the way, some happy, others not. The pilgrimage through life and beyond, with death as represented by the skull simply one moment along an uncertain journey, affixes the trajectory of the goose game to that of the cemetery design.

In the traditional version of the game, Rossi knew, the pieces move counter-clockwise, that is, against our notion of passing time, in effect moving players forward by going backward. In fact movement is not in reverse, but reflects precisely that ambivalent relation of time's forward thrust against the clock and the desire to step backward, which for Rossi emblematically inhered in his design. "Death," he wrote, "expressed a passage of unclear boundaries from one condition to another."[37] The parallels Rossi perceived between his cemetery project and the Gioco dell'Oca tightened in another drawing from 1973 that he entitled "Il Gioco della Morte" (The Game of Death). Journeys and pilgrimages he perceived to be like the Catholic ritual of following the Stations of the Cross in that they anticipate the fullness of the drama of the Passion, the simultaneous "bad and happy endings."[38] For boundaries Rossi used the Italian term *confine,* from the Latin *cum finis,* a line signifying where a given datum is divided from another. The liminal space between life and death may not be specified or known in advance, but the halting journey of rapid progressions and stubborn pauses, even reversals, characteristic of the Gioco dell'Oca, bears no small resemblance to the journey of life whose contours Rossi embodied at San Cataldo, with its blocks of long corridors cast in shadow but at intervals punctuated by light streaming in through single windows. By contrast with T. S. Eliot's recognition of the pastness of the past, for Rossi the past was ever present, just as in the Gioco dell'Oca, where the vagaries of fortune hurtle the pilgrim backward and forward in random but never aimless fashion.

Deep shadows in the "Gioco dell'Oca" and in other drawings mark time's passage, as do the sixty-three squares for the game. Shadows, like clocks, visibly record the flow of the present into the past and anticipate the future, two of Rossi's most persistent images. But shadows also point to the pilgrim's experience of it—that is, not only does time march relentlessly, the pilgrim is also constantly aware of it, engaging it, confronting it, living it. Such reflections in Rossi's notebooks were not casual; journeys and pilgrimages surface insistently in his *Quaderni Azzurri*, as do shadows. Indeed, one of Rossi's earliest sketches of the cube-spine-cone scheme emphasized what he described as the problem of the shadows cast forward on the elevation drawing, clearly a concern from the outset.[39] From such shadows Rossi learned about light—light that, however briefly, periodically dispels the darkness and offers an obstinately bright hope.[40] To realize the shadows, he needed the brilliant light; one is impossible without the other. For reasons still unclear, most critics of Rossi see only the shadows.

### ROZZANO AND THE NEW JERUSALEM

Situated to the southwest of Milan, the community of Rozzano consists of five separate small towns united into one. Over the course of the twentieth century the formerly rural area slowly slid into becoming a bedroom suburb of Milan. The community counts two cemeteries, the earliest in the old town of Rozzano, and the more recent one (1970–77) in the Ponte Sesto area. The addition proposed in 1989 entailed expanding the existing cemetery by inserting two five-story blocks cut away on an angle, with a semicircular raised entryway and three intersecting paved circles. Describing the original cemetery as "horrible," Rossi bemoaned the absence of structures such as Modena's Jewish cemetery and Costa's splendid nineteenth-century monument as foils.[41] Instead he in effect turned away from the existing buildings, placing a block of loculi, burial recesses similar to those at Modena, as a barrier between the two complexes (fig. 6.12). A long, tree-lined passageway flanked by tombs aligned on either side leads to a tall octagonal chapel, its façade defined by three tiers of brick columns with their handsome brick cornices (fig. 6.13). In the block of tombs, the walkway summons references to the external corridors, or *ballatoi*, typical of some traditional Milanese housing, once again drawing a place-specific parallel between the houses of the living and those of the dead. The crematorium in turn separates the new blocks from the walled precinct beyond, which is reserved for interment in the ground and for an ossuary. The Modena cemetery, bereft of any decorative elements other than the architectural forms themselves, differs from the Rozzano cemetery in this respect. So thick have the evergreens at Rozzano become that they almost obscure the corridors and the tombs.

Perhaps as a result of Rossi's growing older, or his near simultaneous work on the Pertini monument, or perhaps simply having had greater experience with building in general and with cemeteries in particular, at Rozzano he directed his attention toward creating an accommodating space that invited one to stay, to meditate. The smaller, more intimate scale at Rozzano

FIGURE 6.12
Aldo Rossi, Rozzano Cemetery, 1989, view of columbaria

FIGURE 6.13
Rozzano Cemetery, chapel

also endows it with a greater sense of privacy, at least partially due to the trees. Some of the features—such as the light standards and benches—replicated those used at the monument to Pertini, but where at Via Croce Rossa he situated the benches to face the open square, at Rozzano they sit beneath the porticos that shelter the burial chambers, facing the tombs and partly hidden by the trees, deliberately minimizing distractions (fig. 6.14). Modena had no benches or light standards. For the chapel interior with its octagonal cupola, Rossi deployed a blue similar to that for the roofing at Modena, a color he described as "il celeste della Madonna" (the blue of the Madonna), often called "baby blue" in English (fig. 6.15). In the tradition of medieval Italian baptisteries such as that in Parma, Rossi designed an octagonal chapel for Rozzano in harmony with the traditional setting for ritual introduction into the Catholic faith via baptism—the new life—and to affix birth and death together in the setting for the ceremonies and rituals marking departure from life at the cemetery. The centrally planned octagon unites both as, again, a symbol of perfection. Just as with the Gioco dell'Oca, the journey between the two points, between life and death, wanders unpredictably, erratically; but once begun, only one end is possible.

❖ ❖ ❖

FIGURE 6.14
Rozzano Cemetery, portico and columbaria

FIGURE 6.15
Rozzano Cemetery, chapel ceiling

A man of deep culture, Rossi read widely in philosophy, literature, theology, art, poetry, and architecture, often inserting citations or reflections drawn from his readings into his writings, and he exhorted all architects to do the same, to become great thinkers again.[42] In his well-known commentary on painting, Leonardo da Vinci had asserted the primacy of painting over poetry, whereas Dante Alighieri, in affirming the power of poetry, revealed the necessity of poetry for all forms of knowledge and the "poetic foundation of both philosophical and theological knowledge."[43] Without denying Dante's fundamental insight, indeed embracing it, Rossi also explicitly rejected a hierarchical ordering of text and art. His passion for technique could only spring from an idea, he argued, and that idea could be expressed in writing, "the most precious, plastic, and powerful means we have," or in a drawing, with "its immediacy, its being without apparent explanations. [My] recent drawings are a kind of handwriting where writing and drawing identify with one another."[44] He envisioned the two as intimately bound and in constant dynamic tension, as indeed they were for him; he addressed the issues that engaged him through both. He could no more stop writing than he could stop drawing.

It will come as no surprise, then, that a large part of Rossi's extensive personal library consisted of books of poetry in Italian, English, and Spanish, among other languages.[45] Not because he wanted to write poetry; no, he read poetry precisely because of its capacity to trigger insight and reflection, not to offer rational answers or explanations which he understood as ultimately only minimally relevant. One of his favorite poets, Delio Tessa, opened a book of poems in Milanese dialect entitled *L'è el dì di Mort, alegher!* (*It's the Day of the Dead, Be Happy!*) with a quote from the Russian novelist Ivan Turgenev: "The most interesting thing about life is death."[46]

A powerful sense of wonder at the world, the beings and things that inhabit it, sparked Rossi's lyrical writings and his poetic images. In the most poignant drawings and paintings of San Cataldo, the representations are personal, interpretive, and evocative, capable of capturing imaginations and displacing and replacing private grief with faith in the continuity of the single life and that of the collectivity. And so too in the cemetery itself. Even nonprofessionals clearly recognized this. A contractor who tendered an unsuccessful bid for the construction contract sensed precisely this quality of joyous hope each time he visited the cemetery as it was under construction and beginning to receive remains; instead of sadness, he found himself overcome with delight, dazzled by the majestic continuity of life nestled in the penumbra of the corridors.[47]

Some critics describe the San Cataldo cemetery as "mute and cold," an amusing notion when placed beside the strident criticism of the design's emphasis on the collectivity by a minority of the competition jury. Even the most superficial of features—the architectural forms and colors—render such a judgment puzzling. The blue roofs and gates, the deep rusty red of the columbarium, the green metal framings of the windows, the warm rosy-orange of the exterior walls, the rich texture of lights, flowers, and colors in the rows of loculi, the shafts of light that punctuate the long rows of tombs, even the individual family tombs modeled on small houses: all of these elements lend the cemetery what I and others find to be an unexpected warmth, something that has grown over the decades since I first saw it in the late 1970s. Rossi did more than speak through color and form. A search for deeper and more complex forces at work in the design compels us to discard the superficial and come to terms with the cemetery as an architecture of desire. Where and how does this become evident?

The intricacy of Rossi's representations of the Modena cemetery mirrors the ramified character of his thought and his artistic processes, apparent with increasing resonance as he returned repeatedly to the image of the cemetery over the years. He rarely depicted the cemetery alone, almost always setting it amid fragments of other designs, or the objects and artifacts of daily life; as with many of his urban projects, here too Rossi pursued an architecture of parts. Observation for Rossi was fundamental; attentive and detailed scrutiny of one's environment united science and imagination, he believed, as in Leonardo da Vinci's fantastic constructions.[48] In every case, the compulsion to look, to draw, to reflect, was bound to an enormous curiosity about everything, which in turn doubled back to a constantly renewed capacity to see, always paired with an almost childlike, unquenchable sense of wonder at the world in a man who found himself unable to determine the boundary between memory and imagination. This in turn led him to return especially to the objects of his childhood: coffeepots, tableware, cigarette packages, bottles, but also to the Duomo in Milan, the Sacri Monti, and the San Carlone at Arona.[49] The copper-clad saint stands with head slightly tilted down and right hand extended in blessing. As a youngster in boarding school, Rossi accompanied his aunt on weekend visits to various sanctuaries, including to this statue. It became a recurrent element of his drawings; at times he depicted only the hand, other times part of the right side almost to the shoulder. The gesture he depicted conveyed benevolence, a gesture of benediction, and its appearance in so many of his drawings testifies not just to his fascination with this monumental structure but specifically with that gentle hand; indeed, he rarely represented the monument's architectural structure—the hand raised in blessing was by far his most persistent representation of San Carlone. Even in the 1991 photograph he snapped from inside the statue, the only feature of the saint visible is the hand (see fig. 3.16). The point I make is not biographical—Rossi's psychological makeup is not the point here—but rather the impact of his spirituality on his drawings, his writings, and his architecture.

Although consistently ignored in discussions of Rossi's architecture and as we have seen in these chapters, San Carlone and other references to Catholic traditions provide clues to his ideas beyond the architectural, and while imperfectly understood, they are gateways into the thoughts of one of the most important architects of the twentieth century. For Rossi, the associations with his religion were not trivial. The very persistence of San Carlone underscores its significance to him—but it is not alone. A month after he submitted the competition entry for the Modena cemetery, he wrote a short autobiographical note concerning his formation through his education: "I have always been grateful," he wrote, "to my Catholic education that enabled me to choose extremely different types of logic and beauty inasmuch as they referred to something beyond themselves."[50] His Catholic upbringing, its beliefs and rituals, his sense of the deity, infused his work to such a degree that one wonders why it has gone unremarked by critics and scholars. In his *Quaderni Azzurri* he often identified time and seasons that marked the Church calendar, such as Lent, saints' feast days, Easter. He even referred to the passage of time by reference to the Divine Office, or Liturgy of the Hours, in an introduction to a book of photographs of Milan by singling out the image of the city at the hour of *vespertina*, a service of the liturgy held at twilight. Vespers prayers welcome the arrival of the night and symbolically, the darkness of death—that is, the passage from life to death. Yet the psalms sung at this worship also anticipate the coming resurrection of Christ and our own triumph over death with the arrival of dawn.[51]

In his published personal writings, such as *A Scientific Autobiography, Il libro azzurro, I Quaderni Azzurri*, as well as other unpublished essays, Rossi repeatedly referred to Catholic saints such as Augustine, Alfonse, and Jerome; to texts by patristic fathers and those of visionaries such as St. John of the Cross; to the calendar of Catholic feasts and saints' days; to his own visits to important Catholic pilgrimage sites; and more generally, to the rituals and practices of the Catholic Church, all of which surface in his private correspondence as well. Similar references appear in his drawings, including San Carlone, and in project descriptions such as for the San Cataldo and Rozzano cemeteries. Nonetheless, the lengths to which scholars are prepared to go to avoid dealing with the substance of Rossi's Catholicism, or his spirituality, as it pertains to his architecture are remarkable. For example, near the end of *A Scientific Autobiography*, Rossi cited a passage from St. Augustine: "Lord God, give us peace—for you have granted us all things—the peace of quiet, the peace of the Sabbath, which has no evening. For indeed this most beautiful order of things that are *very good* will finish its course and pass away, since in it there was morning and evening."[52]

In a text in which he emphasized that one of Rossi's chief objectives was to halt time, from this quote Giovanni Poletti concluded that "the theme seems to be that of an evolving fixity of things."[53] Whatever that means, it cannot be a reasonable interpretation of what Rossi intended in citing St. Augustine, especially when the passage continues: "But the seventh day is without evening. The sun does not set on it because you sanctified it to last forever.... So may the voice of your book tell us in advance that we too, after our works (which are *very good* only for the reason that you have given them to us) may rest in you in the Sabbath of eternal life."[54]

Rossi's hardly appears to be an effort to stop time; on the contrary, with this passage he generously acknowledged quite the reverse, for he anticipated eternity, part of a sequence, a rhythm intrinsic to creation both benevolent and constant. More than one historian insisted that Rossi sought to stop time, but that one could make such a claim hinges on a refusal to *see* what infuses Rossi's writings and drawings, the sources he cited and the texts he read.⁵⁵ In fact, some seem more willing to repeat that Rossi briefly associated with the Communist Party than that he was Catholic.⁵⁶ Renowned Dante scholar Giuseppe Mazzotta, however, realized the enormously rich interiority and religious character of Rossi's architecture at the San Cataldo cemetery:

> The corridor, in reality, is a street, like a path in a park, in contact with the earth or the dry bed of an invisible river, the river of time that enters into the great sea of eternity.... The gaze extends along the horizontal line of the corridor as if it longs to go beyond the vanishing point.... By doing this Aldo Rossi has altered the representation and the sense of death that the philosophers, from Heidegger to Sartre, with their celebrated formulas, have defined as the arrival point for human finitude. The architecture of Aldo Rossi, a non-finite science, meditates in depth the sense of death and brings it to a purer spiritual order, that envisioned by St. Augustine, Dante, Carlo Borromeo and Manzoni.⁵⁷

References to Catholicism filter through Rossi's writings, omnipresent. And yet, that historians and critics quite literally have not seen them is striking—or if they have, they do not want to discuss them. How can we explain that? I can only offer some suggestions. Medieval crusades, Renaissance and baroque convents, nuns, a corrupt papacy, the foundation of missions in California, and other historic problems concerning the Church are sufficiently distant from today that studying them generally seems unproblematic. This may be so in part because in most cases, scholars do not have to take the spiritual and religious elements seriously, or if they do, it is usually with unsympathetic skepticism. While there are exceptions, to be sure, they only prove the rule.⁵⁸ The recent analysis by art historian Willibald Sauerlander of Flemish painter Peter Paul Rubens's Catholicism in early-seventeenth-century Europe is helpful here. Sauerlander criticized the self-proclaimed "enlightened" (secular) historians since the nineteenth century who detached Rubens's altarpieces from churches and from his religion by treating them as "aesthetic trophies" and thereby robbing them of meaning. Saurlander singled out the "cognitive and ethical chasm" that separates historians of today from Rubens's faith and, as a consequence, their inability to understand his painting.⁵⁹

In like manner, critics untether the cemetery and Rossi's representations of it from their moorings in his spirituality and his Catholicism, in effect cutting them loose as free-floating objects potentially to be affixed anywhere. The question here is one of degree: multiple possibilities exist, but to denude the cemeteries of their most salient feature constitutes a deliberate decision to ignore the architect and everything he intended. The situation in Italy is further complicated because for much of the academic world of architecture, people tend to define themselves and others with reference to political affiliations rather than religious belief, even if Rossi and many in his generation considered themselves as Catholics even more than as members of political parties. This tendency emerges with striking clarity in analyses of the Modena cemetery, the design that garnered the most attention over the years. From Eugene Johnson forward, scholars focused on Rossi's Marxism as an explanation for the specific features of the cemetery, particularly the emphasis on the architect's aspirations to give form to the community's collective memory both then and as the complex evolved through daily use.[60] Johnson, for example, conducted an extended and thoughtful aesthetic genealogy of the historical precedents from which Rossi might have drawn for his design, many of which may be quite accurate as instances of Rossi's visual repertoire. Johnson commented on the Communist government of Modena and the political orientation of many other cities in what was known then and later as *Emilia rossa* (red Emilia); the Emilia-Romagna region, from Bologna toward the west, often had city councils dominated by members of the Partito Communista Italiano (PCI). Johnson therefore largely defined the cemetery as secular in orientation, lacking in features having to do with religion. This interpretation also relied on Rossi's youthful engagement with the PCI, something already long abandoned by the late 1960s. His interest in and concern for the collectivity, for groups other than the wealthy bourgeoisie, owe far more to his Catholic formation than to a brief association with the PCI. Indeed, as Pope Francis I remarked in a not entirely lighthearted aside, Catholicism is more radical than communism.[61]

So too for Rossi in his designs, particularly ones as significant as a cemetery, in which the collectivity did not overshadow the individual. In a memorable conversation, he recounted a visit by a group of German architects to the Modena cemetery, still in the early years of construction in 1986 (fig. 6.16).[62] When they then appeared in his office, they extravagantly praised the views of the long rows of still empty columbaria while excoriating those with tombs in place. The messiness of the latter, with multiple types of lights, materials, mountings for photographs, floral arrangements, and other features, distressed them to the point that they argued that Rossi needed to insist on controlling such disorder (fig. 6.17). After they left, Rossi remarked that they had not understood at all; only when the chaos of the individual tombs had obliterated the orderliness of the empty loculi, the bare architecture, only then did the structure become architecture.[63] When Rossi wrote about the need to "forget architecture," he meant precisely this: that life itself overtakes and supersedes architecture, as indeed he anticipated and believed it should.

Quotidian meditations and collective celebrations in song such as in the Divine Office, mentioned from time to time by Rossi, serve as reminders of the core messages of the Church, of sin and salvation, and ultimately, of the triumph over death through the miracle of salvation.[64] Like the sequential spaces in the Gioco dell'Oca, rituals of prayer and song signal the passage of time and the approach of death, whether we attend to it or not. But Rossi did attend to it. On Good Friday in 1989 he wrote about an important ritual for him, one that he regularly enacted, known as the Visit to the Seven Churches (formerly Seven Sepulchers).[65] The popular origins of the Good Friday visits to seven sepulchers are lost in the mists of history sometime in the middle ages, but the popular

FIGURES 6.16 AND 6.17
Modena Cemetery, columbaria

practice converged with one initiated by St. Philip Neri in the sixteenth century which specified visits to seven churches. On Good Friday, a day on which no Mass is celebrated, the faithful undertake a pilgrimage to seven churches, where they view representations of the Passion and the death and resurrection of Christ and venerate the Eucharist. Although the Church formally defined the practice as visits to seven churches, in the popular lexicon—and for Rossi—it remained the seven sepulchers. In Milan this entailed visits to seven churches known for their representations of various moments of the Passion, including the churches of Santa Maria delle Grazie (where Leonardo painted *The Last Supper*), Santa Maria della Passione (St. Mary of the Passion), San Maurizio al Monastero Maggiore, Sant'Eustorgio, San Marco, Santa Maria presso San Satiro, ending up at the church of San Fedele. Rossi described Good Friday as a beautiful day, "beautiful as is everything to which we are bound by love and by a tie."[66] Even if in a state of slow decay (Gaudenzio Ferrari, artist and sculptor of scenes for the Sacro Monte of Varallo, frescoed now deteriorating scenes in some of the churches), for Rossi they retained a reassuring beauty and sweetness in that they foresaw the arrival of Easter. In these images and this pilgrimage, the mystery and marvel of death pervades all, but not as something macabre; death here specifically anticipates resurrection, the joyful promise of life after death.

In Rossi's drawings, such rituals and their meanings loom in the shadows, in the persistent representations of clocks, and at Modena in the settings for private and collective encounters with death. Instead of being morose or lugubrious, as some critics claim, Rossi's images essay the more complex task of revealing at once the bounty of life and its inevitable arrival at death. For this reason, for example, in drawings where figures appear, they often have their arms raised in gestures of cheerful greeting, and they are frequently children and adults together in images of familial closeness. Anyone raised in a Western culture immediately recognizes the cemetery as the quintessential meeting point of life and death endlessly nested in one another, reduced to their primordial essences precisely as are the architectonic elements—again, such as the octagonal chapel at Rozzano and its parallel with the early Christian baptistery. Rossi's designs and especially his drawings place these features in high relief, as for example he wrote of Modena, "This cemetery project does not deviate from the idea of a cemetery that all possess."[67] Viewers recognize this shared idea of the cemetery, with all that it says about belief, death, the journey of life, and the more specific issues concerning houses, public spaces, and cities. In this he believed he fulfilled his aspiration to give expression in his architecture to civic values, values that the collectivity would recognize and share. To understand this, we need to explore another point, concerning Rossi's understanding of the deeper origins of his design.

The genesis of Rossi's San Cataldo cemetery is to be found in sources remote from a purist fascination with architectural forms. The cubic ossuary is an ideal starting point. At Luca Meda's suggestion, Rossi had developed the Cuneo project as a cube, and he returned to it more than twenty years later for the Pertini monument, in both cases adapting it as a frame for stairs to ascend to a point of meditation on the events commemorated, among other things. At San Cataldo this geometric form—a symbol of perfection—traces its origins to the vision of the heavenly Jerusalem as described by John in Revelations 21:15–17.[68] Within the context of this apocalyptic text, John revealed both the suffering of early Christians and the promise of eternal life to the believer. In chapters 1 to 3, John directed messages to seven churches of Asia (within the confines of the Roman empire), which prompts a reminder of the Good Friday visits to seven churches or sepulchers so important to Rossi. In chapter 21, John recounted his vision of the heavenly Jerusalem, the highly specific promise of life after death. The city formed a perfect square, in line with the design of Solomon's Temple as described in 1 Kings 6:19–20, where Solomon fashioned a gilded cube for the inner sanctum, the holy of holies—like other centrally planned structures a symbol of perfection. The Jerusalem John envisioned emerging from the heavens had three gates on each exterior wall, its measurements multiples of the number twelve (for the twelve tribes of Israel and the twelve apostles) as a symbol of the deity's power and authority, and of government on earth.

Drawing on both Solomon's Temple and John's description in Revelations, Rossi proposed an earthly Jerusalem to anticipate the heavenly one (fig. 6.18). By contrast with English and American cemeteries, those in Italy typically repeat the configuration of the medieval walled city, and Rossi too enclosed both cemetery additions within protective walls. In the original design for Modena, Rossi set some of the columbaria below ground, a design choice subsequently altered because of unfavorable hydrologic conditions, but as a proposal it referred to the underground segments of Solomon's Temple. The city John saw in his vision had twelve gates, three per side, while Rossi placed nine openings, or passageways, on the ground level on each side of the ossuary cube.[69] The relevance of numbers at San Cataldo betrays Rossi's attentiveness to them, for such solutions did

FIGURE 6.18
Modena Cemetery, view with ossuary (Massimo Alberici)

not result from random choices. The nine gates on the cube's four sides equal a total of thirty-six entrances, four times nine. Rows of nine and columns of seven window apertures delineate the rhythm of the four elevations: nine times seven equals sixty-three apertures—also the number of spaces in Il Gioco dell'Oca, the board game very much on Rossi's mind as he developed the scheme. The digit sum of six plus three is nine, the number of passageways into the ossuary on each side, and also three plus six equals nine, or sixty-three windows. Three also signifies the Trinity, often represented as an equilateral triangle, a form not commonly used in architectural design but which was one of the most prevalent and distinctive forms in Rossi's repertoire. He often crafted a triangular fountain, with water representing both life and divine grace flowing out of it.

Mathematicians describe nine as a "magic" number, something I discovered as a child when I learned to check my math by "casting out nines" (in Italian, *la prova del nove*).[70] Apart from the marvelous things one can do with nines in mathematics, in religion the number nine also denotes both the hour of prayer and of finality. In Acts 3:1, Peter and John prayed at the temple at the ninth hour, and Christ died at the ninth hour, None in the canonical hours, three o'clock p.m. As noted above, in some of his writings Rossi referred to the Divine Office, which consists of a sequence of prayers throughout

191   CEMETERIES FOR MODENA AND ROZZANO

FIGURE 6.19
Modena Cemetery, ossuary interior (Diego Terna)

the day, part of the public prayer rituals of the Catholic Church. The canonical hours fall on multiples of the number three: Matins at midnight; Lauds at three o'clock a.m.; Prime at six a.m.; Terce at nine a.m.; Sext at noon; None at the ninth hour, or three p.m.; Vespers at six p.m.; and Compline at nine p.m., before retiring.[71] The cubic ossuary at Modena, as the inner sanctum, with its precise numbers and form thus summons references to the earthly Jerusalem and Solomon's Temple, our home that precedes death and the ensuing passage to the heavenly Jerusalem. As Mazzotta described it, the "river of time entering the great sea of eternity."

A further reference helps decipher the complex symbols and meanings with which Rossi invested the Modena cemetery. One enters the cubic ossuary to find an open-air structure lined with small square loculi accessible by metal staircases and open air corridors such as those of external fire escapes.[72] Nine openings on each side allow easy entrance from all sides. Rossi set double columns of loculi between the passageways, and double rows of the burial niches between the window openings (fig. 6.19). Most visible on the lowest level but consistent through the height and breadth of the cube, the columns and rows of niches form a sequence, horizontally and vertically, of Latin crosses—perhaps the most sacred symbol in Roman Catholicism. Visitors pass between the individual crosses at the ground level and can lean out of windows between them on the upper levels. The cross, at once a symbol of death and a promise of resurrection in the Catholic faith, provides yet one more indication of how Rossi intended the cemetery design to be understood. Invisible from outside and secreted within the earthly figuration of John's heavenly Jerusalem, the crosses embody the mysteries of faith, death, and resurrection in Catholicism. More awaits us, however, when we enter more deeply into Rossi's cemetery design.

The spirituality that so evidently informed San Cataldo quietly surfaced in a particular collage from 1978 (fig. 6.20). Rossi represented only the central part of the cemetery, the spine, ossuary, and conical structure, with elevation fragments forming a triangle—a clear reference to the Trinity here as elsewhere in Rossi's designs but also, as we have seen, to the structure of the human body, as at Fagnano Olona. To the right he attached a holy card (*santino*) of St. Rose of Viterbo. This was not a casual choice; Rossi had a large collection of holy cards from which he could have selected any number of saints.[73] Who was St. Rose? A fervent lay woman (ca. 1233–1251) from a poor family who joined the Third Order of St. Francis at the age of ten, St. Rose led a pious life of prayer and solitude at home because a convent refused to admit her without an adequate dowry to support her. She suffered from an extremely rare condition, the absence of a sternum at the front of her rib cage.[74] Rossi described the central section of San Cataldo as a spine with ribs—lacking the sternum precisely as did the young saint. On her deathbed at age eighteen, Rose's final words to her parents, as reported by her hagiographers, were: "I die with joy, for I desire to be united to my God. Live so as not to fear death. For those who live well in the world, death is not frightening, but sweet and precious," thoughts

FIGURE 6.20
Aldo Rossi, Collage with St. Rose of Viterbo
(Fondazione/© Aldo Rossi Heirs)

that beautifully voice the principles of the cemetery, the architecture, and the drawings that Rossi lovingly produced over the years.[75] Rossi chose this holy card precisely for the saint's dying message to her relatives as one that coheres with that of San Cataldo cemetery, where death is not an end but part of a journey whose contours are unclear, to be met not with fear but with joy; grief and remorse are for those who remain behind, just the sensibility that Rossi hoped the architecture of his cemetery would convey.

In the Roman Catholic calendar of saints' days, St. Rose's feast day is 4 September. Aldo Rossi died on 4 September 1997.

# 7   Aldo Rossi and the Spirit of Architecture

> The architect must become once again a great thinker; he designs, studies, and writes to make clear the creative aspect of his thought.
> —ALDO ROSSI

This book set out to explore a diverse range of ideas that informed Aldo Rossi's architecture, design, and drawings. Rather than review the entire corpus of his architecture, I selected certain groups of building types and specific buildings to explore in some depth not only the ideas that informed them but what Rossi himself described as that which lies "beyond architecture." Rossi's writings and buildings served as guides, in addition to the texts and buildings to which he referred and which he understood as pivotal for his development as an architect and theorist. His theories and designs open rather than close ways of thinking about architecture—all architecture, and specifically, his architecture. In this last chapter I want to consider some matters only marginally addressed in the preceding chapters.

## THE CRITICS

Not surprisingly, Rossi's success has triggered a wide array of critical opposition. Some of these opinions have concerned Rossi's designs directly, others emerged from the work of theorists who positioned Rossi's work within a presumably wider critical arena. Let us begin with the first group. Critics normally advance three chief and not unrelated arguments about Rossi: one, that he was a "literary" architect, more important for his writings—and his drawings—than for his architecture; two, that he was indifferent to such matters as construction and materials; and three, that after the early "purist" designs he lapsed into a personal, nostalgic poetics.[1] As to the first point, underlying such criticism is an erroneous assumption that one could not do both. Rossi responded by pointing to Michelangelo—artist, sculptor, architect, and poet as well; Andrea Palladio, architect who also wrote a treatise; Vincenzo Scamozzi, architect and treatise writer; Karl Friedrich Schinkel, an extraordinarily cultured man who also wrote—and if one

Detail, figure 7.6

considers artists in media other than architecture, the list lengthens considerably. Quite the contrary, Rossi believed that the architect needed to be not just a maker but also a thinker, the latter of which almost demanded writing in some form—that is, the capacity to reflect upon the work being produced. The *Quaderni Azzurri* abound with Rossi's reflections on the role of writing, something he took seriously and undertook to do every day.

The second point regarding his presumed indifference to construction and materials could only come from those who neither spent time in his studio nor visited a construction yard with him.[2] He cared as deeply about materials, textures and colors, and the craft of construction as he did about the clarity of his written expression and the art of his drawings. Visits to building sites generally entailed lengthy conversations with workmen who freely offered their perspectives to an unusually attentive architect. Rossi knew how to listen, and he recognized a wise idea for a modification whatever the source—indeed, in many ways, those that came from the building site he found to be among the most precious, coming as they did from those with the most intimate connection to the materials and the site.

Rossi also strove to select materials and technologies appropriate to a project's budget. For this reason, he faced no lawsuits or complaints about over-budget buildings, poorly selected materials, or construction technologies, such as regularly occur with many famous architects today. In addition, many critics do not realize that in Italy an architect has virtually no control over a public building project once the design is complete. A bidding competition to identify the lowest bid ensures that cheap and less durable materials will be used even if the architect specified something more substantial in the working drawings. Public construction costs in Italy regularly vastly exceed those of other countries, leading to an increase of approximately 40 percent in almost every large public works project. Much of this is also due to the close relations between public administration, politicians, and organized crime.[3] The cemetery in Modena suffered from underbidding and excessive costs, as did some of the Rossi's school buildings in Italy. Then, too, the Modena cemetery is incomplete; the large expanses of ill-maintained grass would shrink were the rows of columbaria and the cone to be constructed. Rossi's buildings outside of Italy and a few inside (such as the Carlo Felice Theater, the funerary chapel at Guissano, Borgoricco town hall) instead reveal the attention Rossi dedicated to materials and quality of construction. Despite these systemic difficulties, he sought materials and treatments that would best survive the vagaries of the Italian construction industry. Rossi thoroughly enjoyed visiting the building sites, or *cantieri*, of his projects, affectionately referring to them as *visite pastorali*, after the visits Catholic bishops undertook at regular intervals to evaluate each of the parishes and churches in their dioceses.

Critics such as Diogo Seixas Lopes lament the presumed shift in Rossi's work following the great success of the Modena cemetery, the Gallaratese housing, and the three school projects.[4] Though some critics characterize Rossi's second book, *A Scientific*

*Autobiography,* and his later architecture as signals of a retreat into a personal, erratic poetry, as has been made clear in this book nothing could be farther from the truth.[5] That Rossi did not continue to produce work that mirrored his earliest projects for some could only be the sign of such a retreat—for reasons that elude me—rather than one of continued growth and regeneration. The first and second books are individual parts of a significant whole, as are the early and late designs, flowing inevitably out of one another. Rossi would not have minded a criticism based on his "personal poetry," but he might have been dismayed to think that critics failed to recognize this in all of his architecture, not just that of his last few years.

Outright untruths and misstated hyperbole have also crept into the record. At a conference at Harvard that Rem Koolhaas organized in 1993 to consider issues of international practice, Koolhaas chose to address the topic with quips rather than substantive assessments of the issues.[6] In the book that followed, among other things he claimed that Rossi never visited the site and only drew a brief preliminary sketch of Il Palazzo Hotel in Fukuoka. Both statements are wildly untrue but were used to support Koolhaas's typically ill-informed closing comment: "It is a building that no Japanese could ever have imagined, but that Rossi could never have built."[7]

Rossi's work has also been done a disservice by the theoretical interpretations of the Venice School of architectural theorists. So Manfredo Tafuri, following a model articulated by Michel Foucault, dismissed "La città analoga" as an example of the "negative avant-garde," saying "for what binds the fragments of the collage together is the voluntary act of association, even if that association does not yet come to terms with its own conditionings."[8] Apart from the strange and meaningless concept of an "act of association . . . coming to terms" with something, one strains to find any avant-garde pretensions in the collage. In his apocalyptic text, "L'architecture dans le boudoir," Tafuri spoke of "the desert of history, . . . destruction, . . . dissolving [and] disintegrating" of objects, in which "man . . . is forced to ricochet between architecture as pure object and the redundancy of hermetic messages." Rossi's architecture in particular vexed Tafuri, for in his view it deployed "a syntax of emptied signs, of programmed exclusions, of rigorous limitations, it reveals the inflexibility of the arbitrary—the false dialectic between freedom and norm inherent to the linguistic order." Rossi's work evidenced, according to Tafuri, a decision to "free architectural discourse from all contact with the real, from all incursions by chance."[9] Further, it betrayed a "surly indifference . . . resorting to . . . a geometric elementarism reminiscent of Durand's tables."[10] The reader who has followed Rossi's projects and words in the preceding chapters will find Tafuri's assessments at best puzzling. Either he did not read Rossi's writings or did not understand them, and certainly he never visited Rossi's studio nor a building yard to watch Rossi delight in eruptions of chance occasions in the building process, or engage in stimulating chats with workmen and artisans. Such niceties did not deter Tafuri's acolytes either, for Massimo Cacciari, Francesco Dal Co, and K. Michael Hays, among others, enthusiastically jumped on the nihilist bandwagon. Hays indeed intoned that in the Fagnano Olona school, "to become a library the rotunda must negate its origins as baptistery or theater."[11] Yet the rotunda as a building type did not need to shed or deny anything to become a library, either for Rossi or for earlier architects who adopted the type, as we saw in chapter 4.

Italian critics like Tafuri, Cacciari, and Dal Co and American commentators from Hays to Peter Eisenman have produced analyses of Rossi's work and writings that are permeated with a sense of loss, despair, and decadence, usually in turn based on theories posited by various theorists from other disciplines, in the service precisely of making architecture conform to them. Worse, these theorists often cite one another as proof of their respective arguments.[12] For Dal Co, "La città analoga" is "the very place where monuments express mourning for the lost order to which they allude," more or less paraphrasing Tafuri's analysis of the project.[13] Anthony Vidler elaborated by stating that "for Dal Co, the idea of 'autonomous' architecture which results does not come about through the simple removal of function from form. Like the epistemological void proclaimed by Nietzsche, which allows thought to operate but which does not itself demand to be filled, so the architecture of Rossi tries to refer to itself."[14] Apart from the amusing notion of thought "operating" but generously not asking to be filled, whatever that means, these fanciful abstractions badly mischaracterize Rossi's conception of autonomous architecture. Emblematic too in this respect is Cacciari's tortured account of the crisis in architecture under capitalism, where the philosophy of negative thought focuses on the irresolvable contradictions of capitalism.[15] For him, as for Tafuri, avant-garde architects follow the standard practice of earlier avant-gardes in demolishing values and celebrating the resulting chaos, yet they also seek to innovate. Rossi certainly never considered himself to be part of an avant-garde—quite the contrary. In Tafuri's view the only stark and unforgiving choice for the contemporary architect trapped in the box canyon of capitalist imperatives consists of more or less willing complicity with the capitalist regime. Even Theodor Adorno's suggestion that the avant-garde attempt to develop a critical practice could only result in a practice as marginal as it is useless.[16] Under Hays's labored analyses, the dead end of an Adornian-inspired "criticality" dominated elite discussions of architecture for two decades, followed by post-criticality and ultimately the unapologetic recognition that nearly thirty years of hand-wringing had been wasted on such nonsense.[17]

The twisted if at times earnest logic of these discussions need not trouble us here; we should only note that they all claimed to resist the power of capitalism. Works such as Rossi's "Analogous City" erred for many reasons, according to Tafuri, chiefly because they avoided confronting the reality of the conditions of architecture under capitalism, but equally importantly, Tafuri argued that the "Analogous City" expressed nostalgia, a nasty notion to the nihilists. The irony of criticizing Rossi for creating work that did not confront capitalism by offering a body of theory consisting of nothing more than lamentations on the topic should not escape us. I return to the subjects of the analogous city, nostalgia, and repetition below; here we need only note that while Rossi certainly acknowledged the merits of Tafuri's critique of capitalism as substantially correct, to conclude that architecture under capitalism is impossible to Rossi was a stretch. Indeed, when he dedicated the drawing "L'architettura assassinata" (Architecture Assassinated) to Tafuri, Rossi implicitly identified Tafuri himself as one of the assassins.[18]

For this reason one of Rossi's often quoted remarks is relevant here: "To what, then, could I have aspired in my craft? Certainly to small things, having seen that the possibility of great ones was historically precluded."[19] His tacit acknowledgment of Tafuri's critique of capitalist production as precluding great projects did not negate his belief that small things remained possible and indeed necessary, if one considers the Modena cemetery small. His character alone militated against any such despair, for Rossi was above all an optimist who believed in the possibility of a better world; he could never embrace either the bleak despair or the relentless pursuit of fashionable but unrelated theories characteristic of the critics mentioned above. As Cantàfora put it, "Indeed, Rossi simulated cynicism but he was of a crystalline purity."[20] Similarly, Rossi abandoned communist politics when he realized that they could never become a vehicle for change, that as they then existed in Italy, they foreclosed rather than expanded possibilities. But his faith he never abandoned.

## ROSSI AND THE ANALOGOUS CITY

Virtually from the outset of his studies Rossi reflected on the grand themes that dominated the discipline in the twentieth century, and he did so by reading not only in the architecture field but also broadly across disciplines apparently remote from architecture. To this he appended the study of buildings and cities for what he could learn about how and what we built in the past and continue to do today. As we have seen, he presented his theories and the substance of a methodology in his first book, *The Architecture of the City,* with the second, even more significant aspect of his approach to architectural design largely in his second book, *A Scientific Autobiography,* concerning imagination and analogical architecture. He never ceased his efforts to explain and clarify what he meant when he wrote, for example, about an "analogical architecture" or "the analogous city," or about an architecture of parts. If we look closely, these matters become clear, to the degree that they can be expressed in words, although many critics appear to have found them too elusive to grasp.

We begin with the concept of analogy. Rossi drew his definition from that proposed by Carl Jung: " 'Logical' thought is what is expressed in words directed to the outside world in the form of discourse. 'Analogical' thought is sensed yet unreal, imagined yet silent; it is not a discourse but rather a meditation on themes of the past, an interior monologue. . . . Analogical thought is archaic, unconscious and practically inexpressible in words."[21] To Rossi, this definition of analogical thought offered a "different sense

FIGURE 7.1
Antonio Gilardi, Marco Ruffo, Pietro Antonio Solari, Aliosio de Carcano, Kremlin, Moscow, south wall, 1485–95. From left: Taynitskaya Tower, First Unnamed Tower, Second Unnamed Tower (Dimitry Ivanov)

of history conceived of not simply as fact, but rather as a series of things, of affective objects to be used by the memory or in a design."[22] Canaletto's *Capriccio con edifici Palladiani* (*Caprice with Palladian Buildings,* ca. 1755) ideally illustrated this concept, where the painter transported structures such as Palladio's Basilica and Palazzo Chiericati of Vicenza to the Grand Canal in Venice: they frame Palladio's unbuilt proposal for a new Rialto Bridge, thereby creating a thoroughly unreal setting that nonetheless seemed possible—and Rossi even claimed it to be as real as the actual Ponte del Rialto. The imaginative displacement and idealized composition of a potential scene along the Grand Canal perfectly captured Rossi's understanding of analogy, just like that which he repeatedly configured in his own designs. Following Rossi's ideas, analogical thought, neither reductive nor presenting positive identities or essences, instead offers frameworks for provisional understandings "that speak more of beginnings than of endings."[23] How can we identify this in Rossi's architecture?

Think of the Teatro del Mondo. The obvious reference to floating Venetian theaters of the sixteenth century counts as just one of Rossi's imagined analogies, but even a cursory glance at representations of those theaters reveals no formal or visual affinities beyond the fact that they too float in the Venetian lagoon. He spelled out several compelling possible analogies for this structure but emphasized one in particular, the towers, built by Italians in the fifteenth century, of the Kremlin's walls in Moscow: "The campanile might be a minaret or one of the towers of the Kremlin. . . . I experienced the *frisson* of the Kremlin's towers and . . . of wooden watchtowers set on some boundless plain" (fig. 7.1).[24] These stepped red brick towers with their pointed pinnacles and colorful green trim today seem less like defensive bastions than winsome vantage points, watchtowers over the surrounding countryside. Yet they constituted ideal examples of late-fifteenth-century fortifications typical of Italian architecture, including machicolation and *feritoie*, opening slits for shooting arrows—exactly the type of opening Rossi often inserted into his projects not, of course, for arrows but as vantage points framed by architecture. He commented on having seen these towers during his youthful visit to the Soviet Union. Much has been made of his celebratory references to Soviet architecture but virtually nothing of his fascination with other examples of historic Russian architecture that he encountered. In this case, the towers bore a particular relation to Italy, and especially Lombardy, because designed and erected by Italian architects who had been summoned to Moscow by Ivan III in 1485, probably at the suggestion of his second wife and the last direct descendant of the rulers of Byzantium, Sofia Paleologa, who lived in Rome until her marriage in 1472. Among the architect-engineers invited to Russia, four northern

Italian architects—Antonio Gilardi, Marco Ruffo, Pietro Solari, and Aloisio da Carcano—stood out, and all worked on the Kremlin's new walls and towers.[25]

In appealing to his long-ago memories of this architecture by Italian architects in Russia five hundred years past, Rossi found that the geographic transposition of architectures from Italy to Russia and back, enlivened by personal memories of his encounter with them, ideally expressed what he understood as analogous architecture—even as he cautioned the reader that "the analogies are limitless." Rossi knew Schinkel's architecture very well, for example, so the lighthouse at Kap Arkona designed by Schinkel—a red brick stepped square tower with dentilated cornice and stringcourses and topped by a round observation tower—also figured in Rossi's imaginary.[26] More importantly, Rossi "sensed things in this way far more than as elements reducible to those we call architecture."[27] The Teatro del Mondo, ephemeral, fragile in its structure of tubes and wooden planks, neither directly nor formally "imitates" or "copies" the Kremlin towers or Schinkel's lighthouse. The distance between the Kremlin's solid brick (double weight, thick bricks) and stone outfitted exclusively as robust defensive bulwarks against invading troops could hardly be more remote from the temporary theater facing the Doge's Palace not even planted on solid ground. Yet those fifteenth-century towers whispered softly around the edges of memories embellished and transfigured by time and, mingled with Schinkel's lighthouses, rested lightly on that pinnacle afloat in the lagoon, on the cheerful yellow and blue of the Teatro. Inexpressible in words, they nonetheless emerged here and there in drawings, in buildings, in other juxtapositions.

The same measure of analogic thought underlay Rossi's Domestic Theater at the 1986 Milan Triennale, where the abandoned houses on the *golene* of the Po River after the 1951 floods, the shells of bombed out houses in Milan following World War II, the retablos of churches in Brazil, his grandmother's kitchen, and countless other allusions congealed into the splendid stage-set-like reproduction of a domestic interior. I use the verb "congeal" quite deliberately, to convey Rossi's belief in the open-endedness of such analogical thought, even when the project or drawing assumed an apparently definitive form. More personal analogies such as colors of the *granite,* a refreshing Italian summer dessert of flavored and colored ice chips, related, in Rossi's view, to his Il Palazzo Hotel in Fukuoka. When he recreated a bay of the Palazzo Farnese façade at Schüstzenstraße, Rossi referred less to Michelangelo's design than to the *androni* of the palace and to Berlin's historic *Mietkasernen* tenements, where the one in Rome drew the visitor toward splendor, the other toward squalor. Together in Rossi's design they ventured an optimistic analogy in a city only then undergoing rehabilitation of its earlier ruins.

Rossi here spoke to the designer, not to the historian. The latter investigates genealogies of forms, a history of what the architect may have seen and transported more or less clearly into the work under study so that the historian can order such influences in a clear and definitive narrative. Dubious about the prospects of such a definitive study,

Rossi believed that the analogous architecture he described would spring from an unpredictable but winning combination of technical mastery, historical analysis, and creative imagination. The imaginary need not extend back hundreds of years; in many of his drawings but also in his architecture Rossi offered his own designs as analogous.

How did he explain the relation between imagination and the "real"? Quite early in his long history of ruminations on architecture and design, Rossi reflected on the topic from multiple perspectives, but one of the most succinct dates to 1970, as he was working on the Gallaratese housing estate. "Imagination and fantasy," he wrote, "can only be born from knowledge of the real, and this knowledge demands a notable fixity on the things that we observe, until from within [us] spring other possible directions for development." He flatly rejected the notion that this process could be automatic; on the contrary, when we undertake research we are not venturing on a sudden raid into an unknown world, even if every research project inevitably opens to matters we did not anticipate. In dismissing much contemporary research as gratuitous and stupid, improvised rather than developed, Rossi turned to his evolving notion of the analogous city, a compositional process that pivots around key facts, *fatti urbani,* of urban reality around which to constitute other facts within the frame of an analogical architecture.[28] To this end he frequently inserted figures into drawings of his projects, even as early as his school years at Milan Polytechnic. He found a tender joy in what Walter Benjamin described as the porosity of the city and its architecture, "where building and action interpenetrate in the courtyards, arcades and stairways ... the stamp of the definitive is avoided."[29] Benjamin wrote about Naples, but his insights into the porosity of the architecture and the city nearly perfectly encapsulated the exuberance Rossi too detected in Milan and other cities, where, as Benjamin observed, "Buildings are used as a popular stage, ... innumerable, simultaneously animated theaters."[30]

### AUTONOMOUS ARCHITECTURE

From the era of the Tendenza movement forward, Rossi often wrote about architecture as autonomous, a concept unfortunately often misunderstood as it pertains to his work. From his earliest years as a student, Rossi opposed the injustices of capitalism, expressed in both architecture and urbanism. As we have seen, he argued that the building enterprise could not be separated from the social or the political any more than it could from the subjective and the personal. Speculative building as the primary feature of capitalist intervention in cities, along with large-scale planning, remained constant targets for Rossi, even if over the last two decades of his life he largely withdrew from engaging in polemics through publication. As evidenced at the 1973 Milan Triennale, by autonomous he intended a focus on the tools and methods inherent to the discipline itself and which he stressed as part of the methodologies and analytical approaches he had outlined in *The Architecture of the City.* Pier Vittorio Aureli's detailed explanation of autonomous architecture largely captured the essence of Rossi's arguments, with one important and essential exception. Aureli ignored the subjective aspect of design that Rossi saw as inseparable from the rational social and political approach he supported.[31] The locus, to Aureli, consisted purely of politics, whereas Rossi pointed to an infinitely richer, open-ended concept imbued with history, tradition, analogies, and all of the other ephemeral and not so ephemeral factors he considered essential to any significant architecture. Indeed, Rossi challenged the bourgeois capitalist approach—and the bourgeois left-wing critique of it—through his emphasis on an architecture of parts each unique in its own way, and through the focus on architecture in the city, collective memory, the analogous city, and the actions of individuals across time. An image from one of Rossi's university projects reminds us that individuals, those who populate and animate cities, always took precedence (fig. 7.2). This too is what he meant when he wrote that architecture must be forgotten.

When a critic claims that Rossi's teaching at ETH Zürich in the early 1970s consisted of a "programme for an autonomous architecture, where form and history were the only things worth thinking about ... [and] that architecture was primarily about form, not social action," he clearly missed the point.[32] For Rossi, history was both the grand history of buildings and architects and the personal memory, insistently and inevitably intertwined, interdependent on one another—but both, he believed, grounded in the social and political realities of their times. The 1976 "La città analoga" panel at the Venice Biennale, where Rossi superimposed his built and imagined projects on real urban plans and significant historic buildings, evidenced at once form, history, *and* imagination—that is, analogies underlying the collaged pieces but also among a potentially infinite number of others. As he commented in 1976, "If I must talk about architecture today, be it mine or other people's, I maintain that it is important to illuminate the threads that lead imagination back to reality, and both of these back to freedom."[33] He continued to affirm that he believed in the "capacity of imagination [to be] a concrete thing." The reader who continues following Rossi in *A Scientific Autobiography* will find him describing how he stood at the window of his office at ETH and contemplated the stone pinnacles of the Duomo in Modena and the verdigris stains on the white stone from the metal of the domes; the imagined wooden Venice before the stone Venice of the late middle ages and the architecture of Jacopo Sansovino and others. Obviously he could not see any of these Italian buildings from his obscure vantage point in Zurich. But in imagination and in memory, yes. These images and many others jostled in Rossi's thoughts to emerge, through that stubbornly indefinable mechanism, in his architecture (fig. 7.3). The stains on the Duomo's stones bothered him no more than did other accidents or unexpected events in his own architecture: they brought him joy. He understood that the accidental helped trick out architecture with an otherwise elusive beauty, the beauty of the real. As Giuseppe Mazzotta observed, "So far away is Aldo Rossi from claims of completeness in architecture to allow us to underline the distance

FIGURE 7.2
Aldo Rossi, Project drawing for a building for a class on composition, Milan Polytechnic (Fondazione AR/© Aldo Rossi Heirs)

FIGURE 7.3
Aldo Rossi, "Architecture in the Blue of the Sky," 1973 (Fondazione AR/© Aldo Rossi Heirs)

that separates him from [Max] Planck's scientific spirit." Instead, Rossi's autobiography more closely related to Dante's *Commedia,* where he goes beyond "the crystallizations of memory."[34]

### TRADITION, HISTORY, AND NOSTALGIA

In *A Scientific Autobiography,* Rossi described the things he had observed over the course of his life as if "arrayed like tools" in a catalogue that lay "somewhere between imagination and memory, [but which] is not neutral; it always reappears in several objects and constitutes their deformation and, in some way, their evolution."[35] Not only did they reappear in various designs and architectures, they layered upon one another, superimposing and shifting objects that consist of "relationship[s] of things." Rossi followed Benjamin in affirming, "Therefore I am deformed by connections with everything that surrounds me here."[36] Instead of being dismayed by such deformation, as was Benjamin, Rossi celebrated it in that "the emergence of relations among things, more than the things themselves, always gives rise to new meanings."[37] By this he meant relations not only among the contiguous or contemporaneous but also across time and distance. For Rossi the unpredictable, the idiosyncratic, the inexplicable in many ways drove straight to the heart of any true architectural project, in that a building is "a primary element onto which life is grafted," by its very definition unforeseeable even if anticipated. Memories, forms, imagination: three words that in a nutshell capture Rossi's sense of the world and his architecture. He enjoyed what Giambattista Vico described as poetic wisdom, springing from a metaphysics "not rational and abstract like that of learned men now ... but felt and imagined ... [by men who were] all robust sense and vigorous imagination."[38] Vico turned to the ancient Greek concept of the poet (meaning the creator or the maker) as the fundamental source of wisdom and as the springboard for all of the arts and sciences that followed. In his emphasis on poetic imagination, Rossi sought to explore precisely this poetic wisdom in his designs and to convey it in his writings as well.

Even the casual observer will note that certain themes, forms, and elements persisted in Rossi's built work as in his product designs and drawings. Dal Co assessed this in Rossi as "veer[ing] toward a mannerist practice, apparently replacing stubbornness with repetition."[39] Tafuri identified it as a symptom of Rossi's frustration—whether speaking of forms, domestic artifacts such as coffeepots, the hand of the San Carlone statue, or the insistent re-elaboration of projects such as the San Cataldo cemetery—forcing Rossi therefore to "annul space and time, to collapse into nothingness."[40] Nostalgia, or a return to features of historical architecture, through much of the twentieth century and into the twenty-first, ranked high on architectural theorists' lists of unacceptable approaches in contemporary architecture. The past, repetition, and memory meant something quite different to Rossi; to grasp this we must probe his understandings a bit more fully. One of his favorite painters, Edward Hopper, put his response to similar remarks this way: "In every artist's development the germ of the later work is always found in the earlier. What he was once, he always is, with slight modification. Changing fashions in methods or subject matter alter him little or not at all."[41] The use of repetition and quotations from his own and other works reveal the affinity between Rossi's writings and drawings with the religious literature he cherished, in particular the mystical texts of St. Teresa of Avila and St. John of the Cross, neither of whom elaborated a philosophical system.[42] Rossi's writings proceeded not as a sequence of logical arguments but as extended reflections on multiple subjects. Late in life he wrote that he wished to live a long life so he would have time to redo his projects, not because of a lack or a missing piece, but rather as a way of incorporating that which he had accumulated in the intervening years, as a form of enrichment. In this, his sense of his personal history intertwined with that of the world itself, a concept that we have traced in the preceding chapters but that merits further consideration here.

The design process, Rossi believed, could never be an objective one. He ceaselessly repeated to students and others that design could *only* be a subjective enterprise—and by that he meant that without a profound subjectivity, that deep personal engagement, that passion, there could be no architecture.[43] The poetic wisdom that he elaborated predated his studies in the discipline of architecture, even if the latter were fundamental to the expression of the former. In the same essay on museums, he urged every architect to write a book entitled "How I Made My Architecture"—something he promised to do in his next book. In 1981, with the publication of *A Scientific Autobiography*, Rossi did just that, not by recounting each technical and formal step of a design but rather by opening a window into his imagination, by giving full place to the elusive aspects of his poetic wisdom through reference to the things he drew, observed, and remembered, the things, places, and images that he cherished, those that struck him because of their beauty, the sense of wonder they roused in him. He nourished something on the order of what poet William Wordsworth called "a spot of time," those experiences lived in the past that when recalled in the present restore and replenish imagination and creativity.[44] Unlike Wordsworth, Rossi did not encounter those moments in mystical union with nature, remote from other humans, but from within the dense tapestry of a world crafted of human activity. These treasures re-emerged in drawings and designs where, as he noted, "the concept of repetition in different conditions produces profound changes or subversions of the very order that presides over it."[45] The architectural forms that he identified across time, in Mazzotta's words, "make up a field within which are disseminated the seeds of the search for happiness and a hope in a future that however remains invisible."[46]

In his drawings and projects, then, he did not produce banal repetitions of elements found in other, earlier works, but rather he produced revisions, which he perfectly well understood as steps forward rather than simplistic returns to a lost past. The joy of rediscovering an element to be re-elaborated and lived again in a fresh and different fashion illuminated Rossi's way of creating. He invited the viewer to join him in a narrative not only of personal but also of collective memories precisely through the connections he deliberately sought to recover and deepen, including reflections on his own memories. Understanding, he knew, could never hope to be anything other than fragmentary, but rather than chafe against this or embark on a grand totalizing project in a vain effort to counter it, Rossi lived ambiguity and uncertainty in part through a sunny embrace of the fragment and the fragmentary in the immediacy of their elusive, even aleatory meanings. Rossi's designs and drawings, replete with imperfect fragments, unfold in multiple registers, contrapuntal and polyphonic in their rich complexity. The lucidity of the forms he proposed, although apparently converging at an almost ideal moment in architecture's history, instead draw us to its visible and essential heart. Take, for example, the many drawings of the Modena cemetery, where colors and elaborations carry the viewer from somber reflections to explosions of brilliantly hued delight, as in the drawings deliberately produced in bright, almost fluorescent colors in the late 1970s (fig. 7.4).[47] Or the cemetery itself, where Rossi shrouded an atmosphere seemingly

FIGURE 7.4
Aldo Rossi, Modena Cemetery, with reworking by Jesse Reiser, sepia ink and gouache on paper, 1979 (Drawing Matter/© Jesse Reiser, Aldo Rossi Heirs)

permeated by death's victory with another, quite different one imbued with the promise of faith and redemption. When he affectionately included objects of daily life such as coffeepots, a newspaper, or even the Milan Duomo in his drawings, he did not do so to enclose them in the silence of a painful past; he instead offered them as objects brimming with vitality and possibility, the routines of daily life to which they alluded reconstructing the memories themselves. When he permitted Tiscali telephone company to use his drawing of a design for a carpet produced in Sardinia on a phone card, he not only popularized one of his designs, he also drew on ancient symbols of uncertain meanings into the service of contemporary technology (fig. 7.5). Memory, in these terms, is both a repertory and a generating force of lived experience, of creativity, and therefore quintessentially also of the past brought into the present.

Rossi often commented that he could have pursued other careers, and in a brief presentation in 2014, his collaborator on the design for the La Fenice Theater, Count Francesco da Mosto, observed that "if he had not been a great architect, he could have taken many other paths. Everything sprang from his continuous, personal 360-degree research, his [creative] engine."[48] The year-end evaluations of Rossi's progress as a

FIGURE 7.5
Aldo Rossi, "Studio di Tappetto Nuragico," Tiscali phone card, 1988

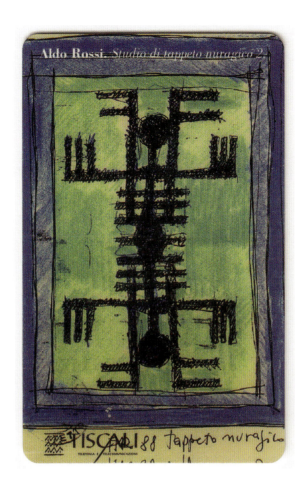

young student at the Episcopal College Alessandro Volta in Lecco demonstrate the accuracy of Da Mosto's observation. The reports consisted of much more than numbers on a report card, for the priests took great care to spell out a detailed narrative evaluation of each of their wards. Two points noted in the end-of-year reports on the young Aldo Rossi merit attention.[49] Observing his particular gift for literary subjects, one of his instructors praised his open mind and his effortless ability to grasp and retain materials. Perhaps more significantly, apart from noting that Rossi was prone to letting his imagination carry him away, the instructor commented on the lad's exceptional sensitivity, leading him to be easily moved by an encounter with beauty.[50] The young Rossi's uncommon joy in beauty, unusually open and supple mind, enormous curiosity, and tendency to let his imagination transport him were childhood characteristics that time only enhanced and refined, enriched by study, experience, setbacks, and successes. The ability of his teachers not only to recognize his particular gifts but also evidently to help him explore and deepen them strikes me as remarkable, and certainly lay behind his lifelong appreciation of his Catholic education in general, and specifically his years with the Somasco priests.

FIGURE 7.6
Aldo Rossi, "Landscape with Basilica," ink and watercolor (MAXXI, Rossi/© Aldo Rossi Heirs)

The years in boarding school complemented the Catholic education he received at home, particularly under the guidance of his deeply religious mother. Then and as an adult, his readings included sacred texts as well as the writings of early Christian figures such as St. Augustine and St. Jerome, and later mystics such as St. John of the Cross and St. Teresa of Avila. He sketched and imagined religious buildings and scenes, such as a basilica or the Deposition of Christ (fig. 7.6). The rituals and practices of Roman Catholicism marked the days and seasons in his agendas and in his notebooks, where he often mentioned the saint of the day, the start of Lent or the celebration of Easter. He also participated in some of the Catholic Church's rituals such as the visits to the seven

FIGURE 7.7
Church of Santa Clara, Santiago de Compostela, façade by Simón Rodriguez, 17th c.

sepulchers. Throughout his journeys around the world, he recorded the most significant events and places he visited, and the vast majority involved some type of shrine or sacred space, whether in Spain, Portugal, Argentina, Japan, or Italy. Not only did he visit them, he reflected on what he observed, often returning repeatedly to certain places. They appealed, such as the convents he visited in Seville and Santiago de Compostela, not only because of their architecture but also because of the emotions burnished into their walls, the lives lived in sadness or joy, even the sense of abandonment common to many of them. In Seville, at the cloistered convent of Santa Paula, Rossi was able to meet with the abbess to discuss the restoration of a painting that was underway. Here as in Santiago de Compostela's cloistered convent Las Pelayas, he found a sense of peace, of human and atmospheric luminosity, an intimate spiritual joy (*letizia*) such as he found in some religious tracts.[51] The convent church of Santa Clara, also in Santiago de Compostela, intrigued him, particularly the façade (fig. 7.7), and he also wrote several times about a retablo that he saw during a visit to Latin America. These were not inanimate objects to him; on the contrary, they were pregnant with meaning, and not only architectural meaning. In Milan, once he had moved his office to a building in front of the church of Santa Maria alla Porta, he commented frequently on the church, its façade and inscriptions. He often fastened holy cards (*santini*) to his drawings, and he marked the start of each new year with a holy card affixed to the first day of the year. Lest these gestures be defined as inconsequential with respect to his architecture, Rossi's own words from the 1971 brief sketch for an autobiography outline his perspective: "The pathway that unites Somasca with the Sacro Monte is for me the basis of all architecture (rectilinear development, etc.). Later I found the same things in the Greek temple."[52]

Other than the two cemeteries with their chapels, Rossi received only one commission for a church, in the Milanese hinterland, the church of San Carlo in Barona in 1990 (fig. 7.8). Certain features responded to traditional Catholic church design, such as the three entrances (the central, ceremonial entrance for the bishop or prince, the right for men, and the left for women) the inclusion of gigantic statues of the two major Milanese saints, St. Ambrose and San Carlo Borromeo, on the façade, the use of a stone base topped by bricks, and the cornices. Other features are less traditional. He deliberately avoided the triangular pediment and the division into high nave and low side aisles, so that in fact the elevation forms a large rectangle. In keeping with his desire for a

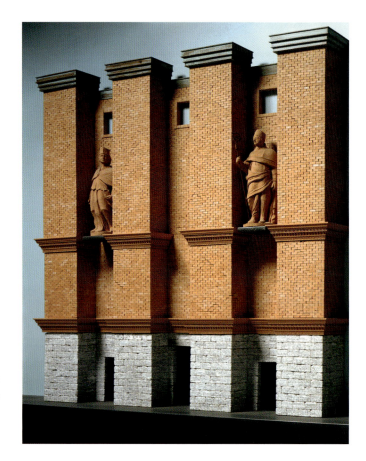

FIGURE 7.8
Aldo Rossi, Church of San Carlo in Barona, Milan, 1990, model of façade: wood, stone, terracotta, and brass (Fondazione AR/© Aldo Rossi Heirs)

simple, severe structure, he planned a gabled copper roof, bell tower, and porticoed cloister, while inside the simple metal truss extended above a single wide nave.

Rossi found it difficult to prepare a project statement, as he noted, for he was unaware of any such architectural project statements for churches. In fact, the patron saint of this church, San Carlo Borromeo, wrote the definitive book on church architecture and decoration in 1577, *Instructionum fabricae et supellectilis ecclesiasticae,* following the end of the Council of Trent in 1564.[53] In these two volumes the Milanese cardinal followed the precepts outlined in the council for the Counter Reformation church wherein the congregation would be reminded of the presence of the divine through the magnificence of the building and its decorations—severe but awe-inspiring, exactly what Rossi imagined for this church. Modernism wrought a dismaying decline in the quality of religious structures, which Rossi also found typical of bourgeois architecture, so he instead opted to seek a design "beyond architecture." In the past, he believed, the relationship between architecture and the church was more natural, the churches so beautiful that even the limited capabilities of one architect or the bizarre solutions of another could not damage them. For the peripheral district of Barona in the southern part of Milan, the façade declared the sacred character of the building while the impoverished and simple interior he meant to be severe in the manner that labor and the sacred are severe, but with the severity of that which is nonetheless alive. Rossi hoped that the lawn extending in front of the church and the façade would also constitute a civic space for the community, and he hoped that it would be big, beautiful, and above all authoritative within the surrounding disorder, as he believed San Carlo Borromeo himself to have been during his lifetime.[54]

The exact character of Rossi's intimate, spiritual life will ever elude us, but as becomes clear in the study of his works, his spirituality specifically as a Roman Catholic infused his writings, his drawings, and above all his architecture. He not only perceived the Deposition of Christ from the cross in analogy to a design such as for the school at Fagnano Olona, for example, he even produced drawings of the Deposition in notebooks along with others of his architectural designs. That it brought him joy and pleasure, that he found beauty both in the images and in his architecture is patently obvious.

Rossi's sense of wonder at the beauty of the world even in simple things infused every one of the designs that he described in his autobiography. As we follow his explorations of these deeply personal experiences in *A Scientific Autobiography*, we can only conclude that this second book, rather than negating the theories outlined in *The Architecture of the City*, fulfilled them. Like Wordsworth, Rossi sought to maintain the delicate equilibrium of the mind and of the flesh, the unity of life with nature, or what we might call reason and sensual life, never conceding the superiority of the one over the other.[55] Not surprisingly, the brilliant vignettes of Wordsworth's spots of time share the heightened sensibility of Rossi's memories as recounted in the *Quaderni Azzurri* and *A Scientific Autobiography*. They are remarkably vivid recollections that Rossi invites the reader to join as he yearns to expose their power and to render them in words, in drawings, and in buildings, retrospectively summoning to the present that which to him was never entirely past, once again bringing to mind the *presentification* of which St. Augustine wrote in his *Confessions* (see chapter 6).

Notably, Rossi did not stand enthralled in some idyllic, static center in his texts and drawings; repetitions themselves imply movement, movement such as with that river of time Mazzotta described as moving toward infinity, toward eternity. Quoting St. Teresa of Avila, Rossi noted that "you already know that he who does not grow shrinks. I hold that it is impossible for love to remain in a static state."[56] In that process of presentification with past, present, and future taut within the fleeting moment, Rossi envisioned constant movement forward, even if the precise character and sequence inevitably eluded him—as it does for us all. Where do the drawings, product designs, and buildings fit in all of this? They are, in key respects, meanderings backward into the throes of those "spots of time," at each turn recalled and enriched as visible testimony to be deployed and renewed again and again, igniting creativity in an ever varying kaleidoscope of impossible beauty, one in which divinity was omnipresent, as Mayakovsky recognized it to be for Pasternak. With no escape from temporality possible, for Rossi the notion that the past projects one forward into the embrace of an ever widening arc containing in one sweep all of the near and remote past—a notion rejected by those who disparage what they call tedious nostalgia—was fundamental, to deny it incomprehensible. Embracing that "river of time" definitively opposes the inherent stagnation of the rush of a self-styled "progressive" modern movement, or its ugly neo-liberal variation today.[57] Untethered from the past and indifferent to the present, a better metaphor would be that of a free fall, without objectives, without horizons, without meaning, without ends. Being a nihilist begs the question of toward what such "progressing" is directed—in a world without meaning, what "progress" is possible? The nihilist claims about architecture and indeed about life in the writings of the critics mentioned above fail to acknowledge an obligation to address this issue. Whatever position one adopts toward such assertions, Rossi's complete detachment from them could not be more profound. And, clearly, the extraordinary appeal of his drawings, products, and architecture suggests a responsive chord in the wider public to his creative work.

Put another way, Rossi found the absence of certainty not a drawback but an acknowledgment of ambiguity as a fundamental verity, one in which his embrace of the fragmentary stood for an acceptance of a search at once unending and untroubling. He never hesitated to densify his drawings and buildings and then to burrow deep within, isolating fragments or shards to spin out in different contexts. His drawings reinforced and countered one another, even as they underwent continuous development and change, even as he maintained a vital tension wherein the clear, limpid, and univocal countered the polyphonic, where he constructed memories and then reconfigured them, where he rediscovered a radiant past while nonetheless experiencing a vague melancholy at having already lived it. As the poet wrote in frank admission of the human condition, "And nothing 'gainst Time's scythe can make defense."[58] That melancholy, neither tragic nor anguished, instead was essential, an acceptance of the rhythm and pattern of life to which Rossi gave voice through his sense of wonder, that state of joy, pleasure, and even playfulness through which to destabilize the power of temporality, or at least hold it at bay. So for him the light that gives shadows also interrupts darkness—as in the cemeteries, relaxing potential stresses and investing us with its vital force.

In the *Quaderni Azzurri* Rossi addressed such matters repeatedly, but perhaps most poignantly in his reflections on a book by the eighteenth-century author St. Alfonso Maria de' Liguori, *Apparecchio alla morte (Preparation for Death).*[59] Rossi delighted in the title of this book, for the verb *apparecchiare* in Italian also means to set or lay the table in preparation for a meal, for Rossi thus linking the quotidian objects he tenderly drew into his designs with the solemn, lifelong preparation for death of which Liguori wrote. There is nothing more sad or more beautiful or more limiting than the knowledge that from dust we came, to dust we return, Rossi wrote in 1991, emphasizing both the beauty and the sadness of this truth. The last words Rossi wrote in his notebooks came from the Italian poet Petrarch, and in many ways they sum up his enduring beliefs about the

FIGURE 7.9
Aldo Rossi in his hotel room in Venice before leaving to receive the Pritzker Prize, 16 June 1990

pain and joy of death: "Vinse molta bellezza acerba morte" (Bitter death conquered great beauty).⁶⁰

The teachings from his youth as explored in Liguori's text sprang to mind on a quiet day, as such thoughts tend to do, but far from being melancholy evocations of the past, he wrote, they constituted "a return to life, a rediscovery of the self and a greater clarity of meaning. I do not mean the meaning of life, but meaning in a [more] general sense, of ourselves, of relationships, of work."⁶¹ Rossi was never disenchanted—on the contrary, anyone who knew him well knew that he never lost his sense of wonder and the sense of an enchanted world—the question for him perhaps remained how to live with the disenchantment of others. As Antonio Monestiroli put it, in perceiving the wonder of the world and seeing it as a grand spectacle, to Rossi the greatest wonder of all was our existence in it (fig. 7.9).⁶²

# NOTES

**ABBREVIATIONS**

ARP — Aldo Rossi Papers at the Getty Research Institute, Los Angeles, Calif.

MAXXI, Rossi — Museo nazionale delle arti del XXI secolo (MAXXI), Collezione MAXXI architettura, Aldo Rossi Archives, Rome.

Rossi, *QA* — Aldo Rossi, *I Quaderni Azzurri.* Ed. Francesco Dal Co. Los Angeles and Milan: J. Paul Getty Museum Publications and Electa, 2000.

### CHAPTER 1. A BRIEF BIOGRAPHY

Epigraph: John Keats, letter to Benjamin Bailey, 22 November 1817, in *The Complete Poetical Works and Letters of John Keats* (Boston: Houghton Mifflin, 1910), 274.

1. Ghirardo, *Italy: Modern Architectures.*
2. Personal communication, Fall 1983.
3. He took many Polaroid photos but invariably gave away those with friends in them, while retaining a drawer full of undated Polariods of the Torre Velasca and the kitchen fireplace mantle.
4. Personal communication, Spring 1984.
5. Aldo Rossi and Vittorio Gregotti, "L'influenza del romanticismo europeo nell'architettura di Alessandro Antonelli," *Casabella-continuità* 214 (February–March 1957): 68–70; now in Rossi, *Scritti scelti*, 25–44; Rossi, "Il concetto di tradizione nell'architettura neoclassica milanese," *Società* 12, no. 3 (1956): 474–93; Rossi, "A proposito di un recent studio sull'Art Nouveau," *Casabella-continuità* 215 (April–May 1957): 45–46; Rossi, "Aspetti dell'architettura tedesca contemporanea," *Casabella-continuità* 235 (January 1960): 27–32.
6. Ernesto Nathan Rogers, "Continuity or Crisis?" *Royal Architectural Institute of Canada*, 393rd series, 35.5 (1958): 188–89; originally published as "Continuità o crisi?" *Casabella-continuità* 215 (April–May 1957): 3–4.
7. Rossi, *Architecture of the City*, 21.
8. Ghirardo, *Italy: Modern Architectures*, 255–57.
9. Reyner Banham, "Neo-Liberty: The Italian Retreat from Modern Architecture," *Architectural Review* (April 1959): 231–35. Rogers's tart response appeared shortly thereafter: "L'evoluzione dell'architettura: Risposta al custode dei frigidaires," *Casabella-continuità* 228 (June 1959): 2–4.
10. Bernard Huet, "Interview with Aldo Rossi, 1992," in *Aldo Rossi, Architect* (London: Academy, 1994), 26–27.
11. Among those who railed against the tower, Reyner Bahnam and Peter Smithson stood out: Banham, "Neo-Liberty: The Italian Retreat from Modern Architecture," *Architectural Review* 125 (April 1959): 230–35; Banham, "Neo-Liberty: The Debate," *Architectural Review* 133 (December 1959): 343.
12. "Come molti ragazzi della sua generazione, era stato allevato tra la mamma, la parrocchia dove faceva da chierichetto, l'educazione cattolica. Quasi tutti quelli della sua generazione hanno avuto questa storia di cattolicesimo spinto alle estreme conseguenze e poi fatalmente l'ingresso nel partito comunista." Arduino Cantàfora, interviewed by Nicolò Ornaghi and Francesco Zorzi, in "Milano 1979–1997: La progettazione negli anni della merce," PhD diss., Milan Polytechnic, 2015, 237.

Detail, figure 1.6

13. Rossi, *Scientific Autobiography*, 40.
14. See, for example, Gianugo Polesello's essay "*Ab initio, indagatio initiorum:* Ricordi e confessioni," in Posocco et al., *"Care Architetture": Scritti su Aldo Rossi*, 17–41, where he discusses their common roots in Catholicism and their common early adhesion to communist ideals.
15. Personal communication, Winter 1983.
16. There are many unnumbered and undated pages of notes among the Rossi papers at the Fondazione Aldo Rossi in Milan, most of which are not linked to any specific publication or study. The comments in this section are drawn from some of these notes.
17. Vasumi Roveri, *Aldo Rossi e "L'architettura della città."*
18. Rossi, *Architecture of the City*, 41.
19. As quoted in ibid., 33.
20. See Giuseppe Di Benedetto, "L'idea di architettura: Da Boullée e Ledoux ad Aldo Rossi," in Rosa Bellanca and Emanuele Palazzotto, *Percorsi didattici di progettazione architettonica* (Palermo: L'Epos Società, 1999), 117–24.
21. See Barry Bergdoll, *Karl Friedrich Schinkel: An Architecture for Prussia* (New York: Rizzoli, 1994).
22. Rossi, "Introduzione a Boullée."
23. Étienne-Louis Boullée, Helen Rosenau, ed., *Boullée's Treatise on Architecture: A Complete Presentation of the Architecture, Essai sur l'art, which Forms Part of the Boullée Papers (MS 9153) in the Bibliothéque Nationale, Paris* (London: Alec Tiranti, 1953).
24. Rossi, "Introduzione a Boullée," 11–12.
25. Rossi, "Preface," in Gravagnuolo.
26. Rossi, *QA*, Book 18, 26 May 1975.
27. See, e.g., Rossi, "Preface," in Gravagnuolo, 12.
28. Ibid.
29. A marvelous recent study of how time figures in the history of architecture is Marvin Trachtenberg's *Building in Time: From Giotto to Alberti and Modern Oblivion* (New Haven: Yale University Press, 2010).
30. Rossi, *QA*, Book 30, 14 March 1981.
31. Ibid., Book 18, 27 May 1975.
32. Ernesto Nathan Rogers, "The Phenomenology of European Architecture," *Daedalus* 93, no. 1, *A New Europe?* (Winter 1964): 358–72.
33. Rogers, "Elogio della tendenza/In Praise of Tendencies," *Domus* 216 (December 1946): 2.
34. The catalogue, *Architettura razionale: XV Triennale di Milano*, was prepared by Rossi and Ezio Bonfanti. For a discussion of the Tendenza, and with it the project for architectural autonomy, see Marco De Michelis, "Aldo Rossi and Autonomous Architecture," in Terence Riley, ed., *The Changing of the Avant-Garde: Visionary Architectural Drawings from the Howard Gilman Collection* (New York: Museum of Modern Art, 2002), 89–98.
35. Projects by this group, with texts by Kenneth Frampton and Colin Rowe, appeared in Rossi and Bonfanti, *Architettura razionale*, 92–111.
36. Massimo Scolari, "Avanguardia e nuova architettura," in ibid., 153–87.
37. De Michelis, "Aldo Rossi," 93ff.
38. Rossi, *QA*, Book 25, 18 June 1979, interview with Ezio Bonicalzi.
39. Among the most vocal critics of the Triennale exhibit were Zevi, Glauco Gresleri, and Andrea Branzi, in an Italy where political loyalties entailed marking rigid lines among different groups, making it impossible either to dialogue or to criticize with any degree of impartiality. The lines had nothing to do with the quality of buildings but everything to do with political affiliations.
40. Guido Canella and Aldo Rossi, "Architettura e realismo" (Winter 1955), ARP, Box 9, folder 151.
41. Rossi, *QA*, Book 38, 20 October 1989.
42. See chapter 4 on theaters for a discussion of Roussel's writings.
43. Rossi, "Une éducation realiste," *Archithese* 19 (1977): 25–28, subsequently in Italian, "Una educazione realista," in Alberto Ferlenga, ed., *Aldo Rossi: Architetture 1959–1987* (Milan: Electa, 1989), 71.
44. Documents regarding the suspension and the legal appeal filed by Rossi and the others can be found in the MAXXI, Rossi, collection. The archive inventories have undergone two major changes and will soon undergo a third, therefore scholars are advised to avoid specific collocations other than titles where appropriate.
45. Léa-Catherine Szacka and Thomas Weaver, "Massimo Scolari in Conversation," *AA Files*, 65 (2012): 36.
46. The Eidgenössische Technische Hochschule Zürich, now known as ETH Zürich.
47. Giovanni Fasanella, *Il puzzle Moro* (Rome: Chiarelettere, 2018), covers many of these events.

48. Rossi, "Architettura per i musei," in Guido Canella et al., eds., *Teoria della progettazione architettonica* (Bari: Dedalo Libri, 1968), 122–37; now in Rossi, *Scritti scelti*, 299–313.
49. Rossi, "Che fare delle vecchie città?" *Il Confronto* 4, no. 2 (February 1968): 41–43, now in Rossi, *Scritti scelti*, 139–43.
50. One of his assistants in Milan, Giovanni da Pozzo, also noted that Rossi had withdrawn from theoretical debates in his later years to focus on his architecture. Da Pozzo, "A Happy City," in Portoghesi et al., *Aldo Rossi: The Sketchbooks 1990–1997*, 179.
51. Cantàfora worked in Rossi's office between 1973 and 1977.
52. The oil painting, by Giovanni Antonio Canal, known as Canaletto, is conserved at the National Gallery of Parma.
53. Recently, Dario Rodighiero produced a full-scale replica of the collage with a guide to the architecture represented printed on the reverse, *The Analogous City: The Map* (Lausanne: École Politechnique Federale de Lausanne, 2015).
54. Aldo Rossi, "La città analoga: Tavola/The Analogous City: Panel," in *Lotus* 13 (December 1976): 5.
55. Aldo Rossi, "An Analogical Architecture," trans. David Stewart, in Kate Nesbitt, ed., *Theorizing a New Agenda for Architecture: An Anthology of Architectural Theory 1965–1995* (New York: Princeton Architectural Press, 1996), 345–52; originally in *Architecture and Urbanism* 56 (May 1976): 74–76.
56. The idea originated with architect Sartogo, who also participated along with the other eleven invitees: James Stirling, Paolo Portoghesi, Romaldo Giurgola, Robert Venturi, Costantino Dardi, Antoine Grumbach, Leon Krier, Robert Krier, Aldo Rossi, Michael Graves, and Colin Rowe. The exhibition took place in Trajan's Markets in 1978; 118 original drawings and panels are conserved in MAXXI, Rossi, Attività professionale.
57. Rossi, *QA*, Book 22, 28 September 1977.
58. Rossi, "Frammenti: Un'architettura per frammenti ovvero un'architettura del possibile," July 1988. MAXXI, Rossi, Didattica e scritti.
59. "Il significato che scaturisce al termine dell'operazione è il senso autentico, imprevisto, originale della ricerca. Esso è un progetto." Rossi, "Introduzione all'edizione portoghese de *L'architettura della città*," now in Rossi, *Scritti scelti*, 419.
60. See, e.g., his "Introduzione a Boullée," now in Rossi, *Scritti scelti*, 321–37.
61. Peter M. Lukehart, ed., *The Accademia Seminars: The Accademia di San Luca in Rome, c. 1590–1635* (Washington, D.C.: National Gallery of Art, 2010).
62. The literature on these three publications is extensive; see my *Architecture after Modernism* (London: Thames and Hudson, 1996) for a brief summary, 13–23.
63. The so-called Whites, or the New York Five, mounted an exhibition of their work in 1969 at the Museum of Modern Art (MoMA) in New York, followed by a 1972 critique of the first group in an article entitled "Five on Five" published in *Architectural Forum*.
64. Graves had an ally on the competition's jury: Philip Johnson, the powerful MoMA curator and a firm supporter of the young Princeton faculty member. See Meredith Clausen, "Michael Graves's Portland Building. Power, Politics, and Postmodernism," *Journal of the Society of Architectural Historians* 73, no. 2 (June 2014): 248–69.
65. "Non sono post-moderno; piuttosto sono post-antico." Aldo Rossi, lecture at the University of Southern California, Spring 1985.
66. Rossi, "Premessa: Un'educazione palladiana," *Quaderno*, August 1996–May 1997, 3. MAXXI, Rossi, Quaderni.
67. Rossi, *QA*, Book 19, 28 October 1976.
68. With considerable amusement I sat in on various reviews in the United States and in Italy with Rossi, which were entertaining because of Rossi's unpretentious directness and the puzzled responses of architecture faculty.
69. Aldo Rossi et al., *Aldo Rossi in America*.
70. Rossi despaired of the design and format of both books, especially *A Scientific Autobiography*, which he described as "horrible." Rossi, *QA*, Book 34, 10 July 1988.
71. For example, a thirteen-page, handwritten document entitled "Note autobiografiche sulla formazione, ecc., 1971" constituted one attempt to write an autobiography. The original is held at ARP and is reproduced in Ferlenga, *Aldo Rossi: Tutte le opere* (1999), 8–25.

72. Rossi explained his perceptions of the various associations to me in 1983 and 1987.
73. Da Mosto worked on part of the design with Rossi, and Rossi wanted to include him as a partner. Da Mosto gracefully declined because he believed Rossi was responsible for the competition proposal. Personal communication with Rossi, April 1997.
74. Most of the notebooks were published as *I Quaderni Azzurri,* under the direction of Franceso Dal Co, in 2000. Apparently he kept notebooks earlier in his career as well, but at some point destroyed them. Others that he started but did not complete are held in MAXXI, Rossi, and in the Fondazione Aldo Rossi in Milan.
75. The last of the notebooks, dated 1996–97, was not published with the others; it is conserved at MAXXI, Rossi.
76. The Biennale opened on 20 July and closed on 29 September 1985.
77. Rossi, "I caratteri urbani delle città venete," in Carlo Aymonino, Manlio Brusantin, Gianni Fabbri, Mauro Lena, Pasquale Lovero, Sergio Lucianetti, and Aldo Rossi, *La città di Padova: Saggio di analisi urbana* (Rome: Officina, 1970), 419–90; also in Rossi, *Scritti scelti,* 353–401.
78. Deconstructivist architecture received its name by the following year, when Philip Johnson and Mark Wigley began to plan the *Deconstructivist Architecture* exhibit held at MoMA in 1988. Its practitioners prominently included Eisenman, Libeskind, Frank Gehry, Rem Koolhaas, Zaha Hadid, and others; perhaps the most distinctive feature of this style are maintenance problems, since among other flaws most of the buildings designed in this fashion began to leak significantly not long after opening.
79. Neither Rossi nor Portoghesi participated in the jury, and Moneo was not present for the final meeting. As a jury member myself, I protestedthe award selections, which I found to be politically motivated as well as effectively ignoring genuinely interesting proposals submitted by then unknown architects and students. Only Gino Valle openly agreed, but the awards went ahead anyway. Other international members of the jury included Robert Krier, Rafael Moneo, Bernard Huet, Werner Oechslin, along with Italians Sandro Benedetti, Gianfranco Caniggia, and Guglielmo De Angelis D'Ossat.
80. Carter Brown, speech at the award ceremony and introduction in the program distributed at the ceremony. The jury included J. Carter Brown, Giovanni Agnelli, Ada Louise Huxtable, Ricardo Legorreta, Kevin Roche, Jacob Rothschild, and Bill Lacy.
81. Cantàfora, interview in Nicolò Ornaghi and Francesco Zorzi, "Milano, 1979–1997: La progettazione negli anni della merce," PhD diss., Milan Polytechnic, 2015, 239.
82. The event took place in Venice, California, in February 1985; I was present with Rossi.
83. Rossi, *QA*, Book 29, 25 December 1980. He had given his son Fausto an edition of Quintilian for Christmas and was delighted to find the citation from Quintilian on hyperbole with which he hoped to begin or end *A Scientific Autobiography.*
84. The one exception that I recall was his fury at Daniel Libeskind in the late 1980s.
85. Both Eisenman and Libeskind assert that they had close friendships with Rossi, but at best, these were short-lived. Libeskind, for example, claimed to have spent entire afternoons discussing architecture with Rossi, describing him as his "soul mate." That may have been the case at an early encounter at Cranbrook, but Rossi was well known to strenuously avoid discussing architecture, much preferring any other topic, even banal ones. Of Libeskind's architectural drawings, in 1984 Rossi wrote: "Credo che a dispetto delle sue belle immagini persegua per vie diverse un disastro formale" (I believe that regardless of his pretty images, in diverse ways he is pursuing a formal disaster). Aldo Rossi, "La stagione perduta," in *Arduino Cantàfora* (Milan: Mondadori Electa, 1984), 7.
86. Communication to students of the University of Southern California in July 1986 during the course of a studio review with Rossi and Aymonino and discussion with students, where I was present in Rome.
87. According to Rossi, the list also included Giorgio Ciucci, Francesco Dal Co, and many others, although it is not possible to verify this today.
88. Rossi, "Adolf Loos, 1870–1933," *Casabella-continuità* 233 (November 1959): 9.
89. "Sono tali i frequenti cambiamenti che spesso

non distinguo NY da Milano, cioè dai due quartieri dove vivo. Dove vivo? Penso a Ghiffa e al Lago ma anche perché questi luoghi sono oramai un'astrazione. O forse tutti i luoghi sono astrazioni." Plus: "L'affermazione che ho sentito ieri notte mi sembra bella, come una legge 'Capisci che hai bisogno di una cosa, quando non ne hai più bisogno.'" Rossi, *QA*, Book 44, 20 January 1991.

90. Hugh of Saint Victor, *The Didascalicon of Hugh of Saint Victor: A Medieval Guide to the Arts*, trans. Jerome Taylor (New York: Columbia University Press, 1991 [1171]), 101. I am grateful to Giuseppe Mazzotta for pointing me toward this great medieval teacher and this specific passage (June 2016).

91. Rossi, "La conica," July 1984. MAXXI, Rossi.

92. Rossi, "Quando Alberto Alessi . . . ," 28 September 1989. MAXXI, Rossi.

93. Rossi, *QA*, Book 31, 16–18 January 1985.

94. Seixas Lopes, *Melancholy and Architecture*, 207–18.

95. Ibid., 209.

96. Rossi, *QA*, Book 31, December 1985.

CHAPTER 2. ARCHITECTURE AND THE CITY

Epigraph: So Virgil described the building under way in Carthage that so impressed Aeneas in the first book of *The Aeneid:* "Pars imperabant, pars architectabantur, pars muros moliebantur, pars amussibus regulabant, pars trullis lienbant, pars scindere rupes, pars mari, pars terra vehere intendebant, partesque diverse diversis aliis operibus indulgebant" (I, II, 423ff).

1. Rossi's Studio di Architettura developed the Scholastic design, with partner Morris Adjmi, who saw the project through to completion following Rossi's death.

2. A recent survey of the postmodern movement is Charles Jencks, *The Story of Post-Modernism: Five Decades of the Ironic, Iconic and Critical in Architecture*, 2nd ed. (Hoboken, N.J.: Wiley, 2011); see also Jencks and George Baird, *Meaning in Architecture* (New York: Braziller, 1970); Jencks, *The Language of Post-Modern Architecture*, 2nd ed. (New York: Rizzoli, 1977); K. Michael Hays, ed., *Architecture Theory since 1968* (Cambridge, Mass.: MIT Press, 2000); Jencks, *The New Paradigm in Architecture: The Language of Postmodernism* (New Haven: Yale University Press, 2002). For a more critical view, see George Baird, *The Space of Appearance* (Cambridge, Mass.: MIT Press, 2003); Diane Ghirardo, *Architecture after Modernism* (London: Thames and Hudson, 1996).

3. The bibliography on this topic is too extensive to include here; one of the best, most crisp and critical outlines of the issues is that by Robin Middleton, "The Use and Abuse of Tradition in Architecture," *Journal of the Royal Society of Arts* 131, no. 5328 (November 1983): 729–39.

4. Aldo Rossi, "La costruzione della città," *Milano 70/70* (Milan: Edi Stampa, 1972), 3: 77–83, now in Rossi, *Scritti scelti*, 447–53.

5. Most historians acknowledge that Rossi drew his understanding of type from Quatremère de Quincy, in part as filtered through Giulio Carlo Argan's essay, "Sul concetto di tipologia architettonica," in Karl Oettinger and Mohammed Rassem, eds., *Festschrift fur Hans Sedlmayr* (Munich: Beck, 1962), 96–101; in English, "On the Typology of Architecture," trans. Joseph Rykwert, *Architectural Design* 33, no. 12 (December 1963).

6. Rossi, *Architecture of the City*, 41.

7. Ibid.

8. A misreading of the book as advancing a doctrine is dismayingly all too common, e.g., as in Seixas Lopes, *Melancholy and Architecture*, 108.

9. Middleton, "The Use and Abuse of Tradition," 737.

10. Rossi, "Introduzione," in Rossi and Bonfanti, *Architettura razionale:* 13–22; 1.

11. Ibid., 17.

12. Ibid., 14.

13. After years of battles to prevent the area from being replaced by a freeway, the Cast Iron District finally received landmark status in 1973: Landmarks Preservation Commission, "SoHo-Cast Iron Historic District Designation Report," City of New York, 1973; Donald G. Presa, "SoHo-Cast Iron Historic District Extension Designation Report," City of New York, 2010.

14. In a day of tributes to Rossi a year after his death, Antonio Monestiroli focused on just this compelling aspect of Rossi's convictions as an architect.

15. Philip Broadbent and Sabine Hake, eds., *Berlin Divided City, 1945–1989* (New York: Berghahn, 2008); Andreas Huyssen, *Present Pasts: Urban*

*Palimpsests and the Politics of Meaning* (Stanford, Calif.: Stanford University Press, 2003); Bernhard Fulda, *Press and Politics in the Weimar Republic* (Oxford: Oxford University Press, 2009).

16. Daniela Sandler, *Counterpreservation: Architectural Decay in Berlin since 1989* (Ithaca, N.Y.: Cornell University Press, 2016).
17. Florian Urban, *Neo-Historical East Berlin: Architecture and Urban Design in the German Democratic Republic, 1970–1990* (Burlington, Vt.: Ashgate, 2009).
18. Ibid., 41.
19. Ibid., 42–43. The irony of gentrification, noted by most students of the process, is the desire of upwardly mobile urban professionals to capture the very alternative qualities their presence ensures will disappear.
20. Rossi, "Che fare delle vecchie città?" *Il Confronto* 4, no. 2 (February 1968): 41–43, now in Rossi, *Scritti scelti*, 139–43; "Nuovi problemi," *Casabella-continuità* 264 (June 1962): 3–6, now in *Scritti scelti*, 165–80; later translated as "New Problems," *Ekistics* 15, no. 87 (February 1963): 101–3.
21. Rossi, "Che fare delle vecchie città," *Scritti scelti*, 139–40.
22. Sandler, *Counterpreservation*, 111–17; Karen E. Till, *The New Berlin: Memory, Politics, Place* (Minneapolis: University of Minnesota Press, 2005), 90–97; Karen E. Till, "Reimagining National Identity: 'Chapters of Life' at the German Historical Museum," in Paul C. Adams, Steven D. Hoelscher, and Karen E. Till, eds., *Textures of Place: Exploring Humanist Geographies* (Minneapolis: University of Minnesota Press, 2001), 273–99.
23. Rossi, "Berlino," 12 December 1995, 7. MAXXI, Rossi.
24. Rossi, "I caratteri urbani delle città venete," in Carlo Aymonino, Manlio Brusatin, Gianni Fabbri, Mauro Lena, Pasquale Lovero, Sergio Lucianetti, and Aldo Rossi *La città di Padova: Saggio di analisi urbana* (Rome: Officina, 1970), 419–90, now in Rossi, *Scritti scelti*, 353–401.
25. Benedetto Gravagnuolo, *Adolf Loos* (London: Art Data 1995 [1982]), 125–33. The original name of the building was Goldman and Salatsch, A Men's Haberdashery.
26. Rossi, *QA*, Book 18, 27 May 1975.
27. Richard Bösel and Christian Benedik, *The Michaelerplatz in Vienna: Its Urban Development and Architectural Development* (Vienna: Culture District Looshaus, 1991); Bernhard A. Macek and Renate Holzschuh-Hofer, *The Viennese Hofburg: The Unknown Pages of the Imperial Residence* (Erfurt: Sutton Verlag, 2014).
28. Rossi, "The Stones of London, Milan, January 7, 1991," *Zodiac* 5 (1991), 142–47.
29. For a summary and deeply partisan analysis of the six competition entries, see Herbert Muschamp, "6 Visions of a New Ferry Terminal," *New York Times,* 5 November 1992.
30. For an astute history of waterfront development in general, and New York's in particular, still unbeatable is Ann L. Buttenwieser, *Manhattan Waterbound: Manhattan's Waterfront from the Seventeenth Century to the Present* (Syracuse, N.Y.: Syracuse University Press, 1999).
31. Ibid., 11–14. The Embarcadero Freeway, ugly but effective, triggered heated debates when city officials began to propose demolition; the 1989 earthquake caused enough damage to settle the debate.
32. Clifford J. Levy, "Not Just a New Ferry Terminal, but a Fanciful One," *New York Times,* 25 February 1997; Herbert Muschamp, "On Staten Island, the New Media Are the Message," *New York Times,* 27 February 2000. Eisenman did not keep the commission; the design of the new St. George Terminal on Staten Island ended up in the hands of Hellmuth Obata + Kassabaum, opening in 2005.
33. John Ochsendorf, *Guastavino Vaulting: The Art of Structural Tile* (New York: Princeton Architectural Press, 2010).
34. Otto Riewoldt, *New Hotel Design* (London: Lawrence King Publishing Company, 2002), 48–51. The hotel changed its name recently to Premier Mojiko Hotel.
35. During the Fascist era, the local government maintained a strict rule that no building should exceed in height the top of the statue of the Madonnina on the cathedral; once the war ended, such constraints disappeared in the rush to build.
36. Carlo Ferrari da Passano, *Storia della veneranda fabbrica del Duomo* (Milan: Cassa di Risparmio delle Province Lombarde, 1973).
37. The construction of the Galleria, initiated

after northern Italians vanquished Austrian dominion, raised polemics in its own day because of the destruction of an existing and historically dense urban fabric. Giuseppe De Finetti, *Milano: Costruzione di una città*, ed. Giovanni Cislaghi, Mara de Benedetti, and Piergiorgio Marabelli (Milan: Hoepli, 2002), 107–10; Danilo Zardin, ed., *Il cuore di Milano: Identità e storia di una "capitale morale"* (Milan: BUR Saggi, 2012).

38. Stephanie Zeier Pilat, *Reconstructing Italy: The Ina-Casa Neighborhoods of the Postwar Era* (Burlington, Vt.: Ashgate, 2016); Jeffrey Hou, Benjamin Spencer, Thaisa Way, and Ken Yocom, eds., *Now Urbanism: The Future City Is Here* (London: Routledge, 2015); Jennifer Scappettone, *Killing the Moonlight: Modernism in Venice* (New York: Columbia University Press, 2014).

39. Carlo Quintelli, *Cosa intendiamo per Food Valley? Atti del Convegno Parma Food Valley Symposium, forum Città Emilia 2* (Parma: FAEdizioni, 2011); Thomas Heckelei and Wolfgang Britz, "Models Based on Positive Mathematical Programming: State of the Art and Further Extensions," in Filippo Arfini, ed., *Modeling Agricultural State of the Art and New Challenges: Proceedings of the 89th European Seminar of the European Association of Agricultural Economists,* Parma, 2005 (Parma: University of Parma, 2005), 48–73.

40. David Philip Waley and Trevor Dean, *The Italian City-Republics* (Abingdon, U.K.: Routledge, 2009); Philip Jones, *The Italian City-State: From Commune to Signoria* (Oxford: Oxford University Press, 1997).

41. Rossi, "Architettura per i musei," in Guido Canella et al., eds., *Teoria della progettazione architettonica* (Bari: Dedalo Libri, 1968), 122–37, now in Rossi, *Scritti scelti,* 306.

42. While Rossi returned to this argument throughout his career, he began discussing it early on in several different texts, such as "Il concetto di tradizione nell'architettura neoclassica milanese," *Società* 12, no. 3 (1956): 474–93, now in Rossi, *Scritti scelti,* 3–23.

CHAPTER 3. MEMORY AND MONUMENT

Epigraph: "De multis grandis acervus erit." The original quote comes from Ovid, *Remedia Amoris,* 424; it has also been rendered as "De parvis grandis acervus erit." Gabriel Rollenhagen's early-seventeenth-century emblem book included this phrase, later translated and published by George Wither, *A Collection of Emblemes Ancient and Moderne* (London: Robert Milbourne, 1635), see Book I, n. 50.

1. "Il monumento di piazza o largo Montenapoleone è terminato. Mi sembra molto bello anche se suscita le solite reazioni, ma io penso che in poco tempo sarà parte della città. E' strano che io non riesca a comunicare la gioia del suo significato e sia invece quasi inteso come opera fredda ecc. per non dire il peggio." Rossi, *QA,* Book 42, 29 May 1990.

2. The sculptor Umberto Mastroianni won the 1966 competition for the Monument to Partisans at Cuneo. The competition in Segrate, entailing the design of the entire piazza, occurred in 1965, and Rossi won in collaboration with Luca Meda, who remained his closest friend until Rossi's death.

3. Rossi, *Architecture of the City,* 57–62, 95–98, 130–33.

4. Rossi, "Introduzione a Boullée."

5. Serviliano Latuada, *Descrizione di Milano,* vol. 5 (Milan: Cisalpina-Goliardica, 1972 [1738]); Carlo Buzzi and Vittorio Buzzi, *Le vie di Milano: Dizionario della toponomastica milanese* (Milan, 2005), vi, 53.

6. Buzzi and Buzzi, *Le vie di Milano,* 239–40.

7. Enrico Griffini, *Progetti e realizzazioni MCMXX–MCML* (Milan: Hoepli, 1952); Federico Bucci and Claudio Camonogara, "Griffini a Milano," *Domus* 819, no. 15 (October 1999): 119–26.

8. Buzzi and Buzzi, *Le vie di Milano,* 182–83.

9. Ibid., 121.

10. Gian Antonio Stella, "'Via il monumento a Pertini': La provocazione di Armani che fa discutere il Quadrilatero," *Corriere della Sera,* 10 April 2009, 6. See also Giovanni Maria Pace, "Rossi premiato Rossi contestato," *La Repubblica,* 22 April 1990, http://ricerca.repubblica.it/repubblica/archivio/repubblica/1990/04/22/rossi-premiato-rossi-contestato.html, accessed 13 July 2018.

11. "I socialisti difendono 'il cubo' di Pertini," *Corriere della Sera,* 30 November 2011, http://milano.corriere.it/notizie/cronaca/11_novembre_30/socialisti-presidio-monumento-

pertini-1902371405662.shtml, accessed 13 July 2018.
12. Eric Sylvers, "McDonald's Sues over Milan Eviction," *Financial Times International*, 16 October 2012, 11.
13. In Rossi's version, the women were prostitutes, while the evidence from the biography of San Carlo suggests that the prelate referred to concubines; calling them prostitutes made for a more effective argument. Giovanni Pietro Giussano, *Vita di S. Carlo Borromeo* (Naples: Stamperia Arcivescovile, 1855), 1: 71–75.
14. Rossi, *Architecture of the City*, 161–62; italics original.
15. Rossi submitted the competition entry with Gian Ugo Polesello and Luca Meda, both classmates from his university years; both his partners and others have always attributed the main design to Rossi. Meda, Rossi's long-time close friend, proposed the cube as a starting point.
16. Personal communication, June 1984.
17. Margarita Sarfatti commissioned the monument on the Col d'Echele in memory of her brother, Roberto, who died there during World War I. The monument has been published in Giorgio Ciucci, ed., *Giuseppe Terragni: Opera completa* (Milan: Electa, 1996), 445.
18. Rossi, QA, Book 10, 22 January 1972.
19. Presumably the ancient Greek poet Simonides of Ceos invented the art of memory; in the famous tale, he was invited to a banquet to recite his verses, and as he left to see someone who came calling for him, the building collapsed. In the aftermath and the attempt to identify the badly mangled bodies, Simonides did so by remembering the order in which the men were seated around the table. Both Cicero and Quintilian recounted the story; Cicero, *De Oratore*, II, lxxxvi; Quintilian, *Institutio Oratorio*, XI, ll.
20. Mieke Bal, *Acts of Memory: Cultural Recall in the Present* (Hanover, N.H.: University Press of New England, 1999); Simon Schama, *Landscape and Memory* (New York: Alfred A. Knopf, 1995); Frances Amelia Yates, *The Art of Memory* (Chicago: University of Chicago Press, 1974).
21. The jury awarded first place to a project by Aldo Calò and Mario Manieri Elia, but the city decided to forgo the emphasis on architecture as spelled out in the competition rules and shift toward a more sculptural monument, hence the selection of Mastroianni's design in 1964.
22. Shortly before the competition results were announced in 1989, Kurt Forster told me he had proposed the broken Star of David motif to Libeskind for the scheme, which Libeskind promptly and enthusiastically adopted; to my knowledge, Libeskind has never mentioned Forster's role.
23. Peter Chametzky, "Not What We Expected: The Jewish Museum Berlin in Practice," *Museum and Society* 6, no. 3 (November 2008): 216–45; James E. Young, *The Texture of Memory: Holocaust Memorials and Meaning* (New Haven: Yale University Press, 1993); Young, "Daniel Libeskind's Jewish Museum in Berlin: The Uncanny Arts of Memorial Architecture," *At Memory's Edge: After-Images of the Holocaust in Contemporary Art and Architecture* (New Haven: Yale University Press, 2000), 152–83.
24. Jason Surrell, *Pirates of the Caribbean: From the Magic Kingdom to the Movies* (New York: Disney, 2005).
25. As it happens, the Pirates of the Caribbean ride was Rossi's favorite; for him, it was impossible to go to Disneyland without completing at least two circuits.
26. Aldo Rossi and Luca Meda, "Fontana monumentale nel centro direzionale di Milano," *Casabella-continuità* 276 (June 1963): 43–45. The same issue sported the Cuneo project on the cover, and included an article about it.
27. Rossi, "Il concetto di tradizione nell'architettura neoclassica milanese," *Società* 12, no. 3 (1956): 486.
28. On his analysis of Halbwachs's theories of collective memory, see Rossi, *Architecture of the City*, 130–56. Maurice Halbwachs, *On Collective Memory*, ed. and trans. Lewis A. Coser (Chicago: University of Chicago Press, 1992); Halbwachs, *La mémoire collective*, ed. Gérard Namer (Paris: Albin Michel, 1994).
29. Barbara A. Misztal, "Durkheim on Collective Memory," *Journal of Classical Sociology* 3, no. 2 (July 2003): 123–43; Emile Durkheim, *The Elementary Forms of the Religious Life*, ed. Mark S. Cladis, trans. Carol Cosman (Oxford: Oxford University Press, 2008 [1912]). Henri Bergson, *Matter and Memory*, trans. N. M. Paul and W. S. Palmer (New York: Zone, 1991 [1896]).

30. Halbwachs, *On Collective Memory*, ch. 4, 130.
31. Rossi, *Architecture of the City*, 130.
32. "Penso allo spazio della chiesa Cattolica. Lo spazio universale è definito come la comunione dei Santi; esso è del tutto indifferenziato. Ma i santuari, i luoghi di pellegrinaggio sono delle eccezioni particolari dello spazio, riconoscibili anche se non hanno nulla a che vedere con lo spazio della chiesa." Rossi, draft of letter to Paolo Ceccarelli, 2 January 1965. ARP, Box 6/68, 58.
33. Ibid., 57–61.
34. Rossi, "Il concetto di tradizione nell'architettura neoclassica milanese," 486.
35. Rossi, presentation of a monument by Franco Buzzi, typescript, January 1955, 1. ARP, Box 6/64.
36. Vera Zamagni, *The Economic History of Italy, 1860–1990* (Oxford: Clarendon, 1993); Jon Cohen and Giovanni Federico, *The Growth of the Italian Economy, 1820–1960* (Cambridge: Cambridge University Press, 2001); John Foot, *Modern Italy* (New York: Palgrave Macmillan, 2003), esp. ch. 3.
37. The library is located on Via XXV Aprile, Segrate; a team headed by Guido Canella with Michele Achilli, Daniele Brigidini, and Laura Lazzari designed the building (1963–66). Canella and Achilli undertook the renovation from 2003 to 2009, although the subsequent and final remodeling did not follow their plans, giving rise to protests from other architects who believed that there should be no changes to the building as designed by the Canella.
38. Following exile in the United States during World War II, Bruno Zevi returned to Italy excited about a tradition of organic architecture that dated back to Louis Sullivan and Frank Lloyd Wright, emphatically proposed anew by Wright in 1939 and celebrated by Zevi, who published a book in favor of this approach. Bruno Zevi, *Towards an Organic Architecture* (London: Faber, 1950); the citation of Wright is on p. 66.
39. Pliny the Elder, *Natural History* (Cambridge, Mass.: Harvard University Press, Loeb Classical Library, 1938), Book XXXVI, 44–45. Pliny observed that entire statues of porphyry were not welcome, but in later years garments and bases were often made of porphyry.
40. "…triangolo elemento permanente come forma e nella composizione sostanzialmente un canale, passaggio coperto, collegamento a sbalzo, valo di timpano." Rossi, QA, Book 7, 30 May 1971.
41. Ibid.
42. See, e.g., the article published with Polesello and Francesco Tentori, "Il problema della periferia nella città moderna," *Casabella-continuità* 244 (July 1960): 39–55.
43. Other than the one dedicated to Giovan Paolo Osio, the murderer in the case of the nun of Monza, columns of infamy can still be found in many Italian cities, including Vicenza, Bari, Milan, and Genoa.
44. Jas Elsner, "Iconoclasm and the Preservation of Memory," in Robert S. Nelson and Margaret Olin, eds., *Monuments and Memory, Made and Unmade* (Chicago: University of Chicago Press, 2004), 209–32; Pierre Nora, *Realms of Memory: Rethinking the French Past*, vol. 1, ed. Lawrence D. Kritzman, trans. Arthur Goldhammer (New York: Columbia University Press, 1996).
45. Rossi, QA, Book 2, 26 November 1968.
46. Ibid., Book 6, 19 March 1971.
47. Alberto Ferlenga, ed., *Aldo Rossi: Architetture 1959–1987* (Milan: Electa, 1989), 33.
48. Rossi, QA, Book 6, 7 February 1971. He had already traveled to Spain by the time his book appeared, but whether he had visited Santiago then is uncertain.
49. "All'origine del progetto vi è un punto di riferimento emozionale e che sfugge all'analisi; esso si associa al tema fin dall'inizio e crescerà con esso lungo tutta la progettazione." Rossi, "Introduzione a Boullée," now in *Scritti scelti*, 329.
50. "Non esiste arte che non sia autobiografica," ibid., 331–32.
51. Rossi, "Il concetto di tradizione nell'architettura neoclassica milanese."
52. "Tutte le ombre disegnate alterano il rapporto con la realtà." Rossi, QA, Book 6, 7 February 1971.
53. "Per questo non credo di essere interessato al silenzio, all'architettura del silenzio, come spesso si dice. In queste pareti, nei ballatoi del Gallaratese, nei cortili in tutto sono attento a questo tumulto che è nella vita: mi sembra di prepararlo, di osservare perplesso tutto quello che accadrà." Rossi, QA, Book 15, 3 October 1973.

54. Rossi could recite Pòrta's poems with gusto at opportune moments, poems of which he was especially fond precisely because written in Milanese dialect.
55. Rossi, *Scientific Autobiography*, 3.
56. The fissure, or opening, through which one gazed from the open platform appears in all three monuments discussed here: all are open-air, and both the Cuneo and Pertini monuments provided a horizontal opening, while the triangular unit at Segrate served the same function. At the same time that he was developing the Cuneo project, Rossi was designing the exhibit at the Museum of Contemporary History in Milan (with Luca Meda, Matilde Baffa, and Ugo Rivolta), where they also introduced a viewing fissure in the interior courtyard.
57. Serviliano Latuada, *Descrizione di Milano ornata con molti disegni in rame delle fabbriche più cospicue, che si trovano in questa metropoli* (Milan: Giuseppe Cairoli 1737), 2: 28.
58. Rossi, *QA*, Book 47, 18 December 1991; the thoughts were triggered by the inscription, but they returned later, when he wrote of the stairs for the Bonnefanten Museum.
59. The notebook detailing this trip is in ARP, Box 20/189; the trip took place between 29 October and 14 November 1961, and Schinkel was one of the architects to whom Rossi devoted particular attention.
60. For his extraordinary analyses of Schinkel, I am indebted to Kurt W. Forster, "Only Things That Stir the Imagination: Schinkel as Scenographer," in John Zukowsky, ed., *Karl Friedrich Schinkel 1781–1841: The Drama of Architecture* (Chicago: Art Institute of Chicago and Axel Menges, 1995), 18–35. At the time of this writing, Forster's new book, *Schinkel: A Meander through His Life and Work* (Basel: Birkhauser, 2018) has not yet appeared.
61. Aldo Rossi and Alexander van Grevenstein, *Brieven/Letters* (Maastricht: Bonnefanten Museum, 1995), 24.
62. Alberto Moravetti, *Il Santuario Nuragico di Santa Cristina* (Sassari: Carlo Delfino, 2003).
63. James I. Porter, "Ideals and Ruins: Pausanias, Longinus, and the Second Sophistic," in Susan E. Alcock, John F. Cherry, and Jas Elsner, eds., *Pausanias: Travel and Memory in Roman Greece.* (Oxford: Oxford University Press, 2001), 74; italics original.
64. "La forma più precisa è anche quella più assente e forse nella volontà imitativa a cui sono sottoposti i miei progetti, vi è espresso qualcosa di questo." Rossi, *QA*, Book 23, 7/8 August 1978.
65. Bonna Wescoat, "Wining and Dining on the Temple of Athena at Assos," in Susan Scott, ed., *The Art of Interpreting: Papers in the History of Art from the Pennsylvania State University* (University Park: Pennsylvania State University Press, 1995), 9: 293–320; John Feely, *Classical Turkey* (San Francisco: Chronicle, 1990), 21–27. Of all the wonders of my visit to Assos in 1988, the empty sarcophagi remain the most compelling.
66. Alison E. Cooley, ed., *A Companion Guide to Roman Italy* (New York: Wiley, 2016), 138–43. The term sarcophagus came from Assos, and meant flesh-eating, in that the caustic volcanic stone sarcophagi consumed bodies within a matter of weeks.
67. "… legata alla luce e alla nebbia. Il Sant'Andrea è foro e piazza coperta, ancora interno/esterno, città/campagna; quasi indefinito nel suo preciso disegno." Rossi, "Architetture padane," in Rossi, *Architetture padane*, 30.
68. "Caratteri tipologici di un edificio pubblico / possibilità di riunione di molte persone. Vedi la chiesa come piazza coperta, spazio unico dove si svolgono funzioni diverse." Rossi, *QA*, Book 16, Easter, 1974.
69. Rossi produced several versions of this drawing, originally prepared as a gift and response to Manfredo Tafuri for the text that became *Architecture and Utopia* (Cambridge, Mass.: MIT Press, 1979).
70. "Io sono deformato dai nessi con le cose che mi circondano." Rossi, *QA*, Book 18, 1975, 3/4 February 1975.

CHAPTER 4. BUILDING FOR CULTURE

1. "Io amo questo progetto—forse la costruzione che in qualche modo ho seguito maggiormente." Rossi, *QA*, Book 34, 24 December 1986.
2. "Mi sembra quest'opera quasi emblematica della mia architettura. O della architettura / o tutto il contrario. Quasi una costruzione archeologica ed un restauro." Ibid., Book 44, 5 February 1991. Complete but unopened in 1985, the building sat another ten years while the town raised sufficient funds to purchase furniture, and when it did, Rossi received the commission for the interiors.

3. Hugh of Saint Victor, *The Didascalicon of Hugh of Saint Victor: A Medieval Guide to the Arts*, trans. Jerome Taylor (New York: Columbia University Press, 1991 [1171]), 137.
4. "Sono poi sempre stato grato alla mia educazione cattolica di poter scegliere tipi estremamente diversi di logica e di bellezza in quanto riferiti a qualche elemento che li supera." Rossi, "Note autobiografiche sulla formazione, ecc., 1971," in ARP; see *Aldo Rossi: Tutte le opere* (2003), 21.
5. "Alla sera malinconia di lasciare le colline ricordi di Somasca, del paese, ecc.... regioni ormai autobiografiche senza scoperte ma confermate nella vita, ecc." Rossi, *QA*, Book 8, 22 July 1971.
6. Ibid., Book 33, 15 December 1986.
7. Andrea Gamberoni, *A Companion to Late Medieval and Early Modern Milan: The Distinctive Features of an Italian State* (Leiden: Brill, 2015).
8. Between 1961 and 1971, Fagnano's population jumped by more than 2,000 people. http://daticensimentopopolazione.istat.it/, accessed 12 August 2017.
9. Étienne-Louis Boullée, Helen Rosenau, ed., *Boullée's Treatise on Architecture: A Complete Presentation of the Architecture, Essai sur l'art, which Forms Part of the Boullée Papers (MS 9153) in the Bibliothéque Nationale, Paris* (London: Alec Tiranti, 1953), 104.
10. Rossi, *QA*, Book 24, 18 June 1979.
11. Ibid., Book 14, 31 December 1972.
12. St. John of the Cross, *Ascent of Mount Carmel*, ed. P. Silverio de Santa Teresa, C.D., trans. E. Allison Peers, 3rd rev. ed. (Garden City, N.Y.: Doubleday Image, 1962).
13. Rossi, *QA*, Book 25, 18 July 1979.
14. Ibid., Book 24, 19 March 1979, and Book 33, 18 December 1986.
15. "Partita dallo sviluppo dell'elemento centrale di Fagnano è diventata una grande corte e giardino interno." Ibid., Book 24, 19 March 1979.
16. Ibid., Book 5, 15 May 1970.
17. Ibid., Book 5, November 1970; *The Rule of St. Benedict*, trans. D. Oswald Hunter Blair, M.A., 2nd ed. (London: Sands, 1906).
18. "Pianta con la fontana al centro del Patio contrapposta alla facciata verticale della chiesa e del palazzo. Rapporto con Fagnano tensione dell'elemento compresso nella piazza e elevazione della facciata sull'interno." Ibid., Book 17, 22/29 November 1974.
19. "Hanno scritto di questi orologi e in effetti essi segnano il tempo della scuola, ogni ora." Ibid., Book 33, 15 December 1986.
20. "Amo la cupola dove si trova il planetario e l'edificio della scuola in genere perché mi sembra che nelle mie scuole si riscatti tutto ciò che nella scuola non ho mai amato." Ibid., Book 33, 15 December 1986.
21. "... mette in crisi la presunta opacità del suo essere continuo." Rossi, "L'orologio o il momento," June 1987. MAXXI, Rossi.
22. "Nell'ora meridiana le aule e i corridoi, scale e spazi e tutto mi sembrava meravigliosa e perduta." Rossi, *QA*, Book 23, 30 July 1978.
23. Tim Rollins to Aldo Rossi, 10 May 1990, reprinted in *Aldo Rossi, Tim Rollins and K.O.S.* (Chicago: Rhona Hoffman Gallery, 1991), 3.
24. Ibid., 12.
25. Ibid., 16.
26. Rossi, *Scientific Autobiography*, 3. See also Eleanor Heartney, "Schools for Thought," in *Aldo Rossi, Tim Rollins and K.O.S.*, 17–40.
27. Still the best study of the origins and development of the medieval Italian town hall is Jürgen Paul, *Der Palazzo Vecchio in Florenz: Ursprung und Bedeutung seiner Form* (Florence: Olschki, 1969). For a recent discussion of town hall symbolism, see Carroll William Westfall, *Architecture, Liberty and Civic Order: Architectural Theories from Vitruvius to Jefferson and Beyond* (London and New York: Taylor and Francis, 2015).
28. The early modern Italian city consisted of gendered spaces, and the public loggia was not open to women.
29. Amedeo Belluzzi and Gianluca Belli, *La Villa dei Collazzi: L'architettura del tardo rinascimento a Firenze* (Florence: Olschki, 2016).
30. Two young architects worked with Rossi: Massimo Fortis and Massimo Scolari. Like the other projects I discuss, the designs are appropriately credited to Rossi.
31. Rossi, *QA*, Book 16, 22 January 1974.
32. Ferlenga, *Rossi: Life and Work*, 42–43.
33. Filarete's fifteenth-century tower collapsed in the early sixteenth century from the weight of gunpowder stored in it. Luca Beltrami conducted research on the history and appearance of the tower, and led a campaign to rebuild it, concluded in 1905. Evelyn Welch's

recent synthesis of the rebuilding is useful for the history of the castle: "Patrons, Artists and Audiences in Renaissance Milan," in Charles M. Rosenberg, ed., *The Court Cities of Northern Italy: Milan, Parma, Piacenza, Mantua, Ferrara, Bologna, Urbino, Pesaro and Rimini* (Cambridge: Cambridge University Press, 2010), 24–26.

34. The *barchessa* of the early modern rural estate consisted of a building to store equipment, seeds, animals, and other agricultural necessities and was usually positioned as wings or adjacent, long buildings.
35. Personal communication, April 1985.
36. Rossi, *QA*, Book 24, 24 December 1986.
37. Ibid., Book 6, 19 March 1971.
38. Ibid., 7 April 1971.
39. Rossi to Ezio Bonfanti, 3 January 1971. AR-Correspondence/18, MAXXI, Rossi.
40. Rossi, *QA*, Book 6, 6 May 1971.
41. Ibid., 13 May 1971; Helen Rosenau, *The Ideal City in Its Architectural Evolution* (London: Routledge and Paul, 1959).
42. Rossi, *QA*, Book 28, 28–29 May 1971.
43. Aldo Rossi, "Prefazione," in Ferlenga, *Deutsches Historisches Museum*, 7.
44. Hans Gerhard Hannesen, "Il museo: Luogo d'incontro democratico nel centro di Berlino," in Ferlenga, *Deutsches Historisches Museum*, 19–36.
45. "Non vorrei sembrare un turista ma sempre meno riesco a discernere le differenze di vita, di costume, persino di lingua." Rossi, *QA*, Book 34, June 1988.
46. Ibid.
47. To be sure, Schinkel's rotunda also gave off to the museum's wings, so it too addressed functional issues.
48. Rossi, "Il progetto di concorso," in Ferlenga, *Deutsches Historisches Museum*, 39.
49. Rossi, *QA*, Book 34, 8 May 1987.
50. Herman G. Pundt, "Karl Friedrich Schinkel's Environmental Planning of Central Berlin," *Journal of the Society of Architectural Historians* 26, no. 2 (May 1967): 114–30; see also Maria Shéhérazade Giudici, "The Last Great Street of Europe: The Rise and Fall of Stalinallee," *AA Files*, 65 (2012): 130–31.
51. Karl Marx, *The Eighteenth Brumaire of Louis Bonaparte*, trans. Daniel de Leon (New York: New York Labor News, 1951), 12.
52. Rossi, *QA*, Book 27, 27 March 1980, citation from Savi, *L'architettura di Aldo Rossi*, 127.
53. "Vivendo fuori dal tempo essa impersonifica l'architettura come i teatri vuoti rappresentano il teatro." Rossi, *QA*, Book 27, 27 March 1980.
54. Rossi, "Il progetto di concorso," 40.
55. Rossi, *QA*, Book 34, 8 May 1987.
56. Rossi, "Il progetto definitivo," in Ferlenga, *Deutsches Historisches Museum*, 72.
57. Rossi, *QA*, Book 46, June 1991.
58. Ibid., Book 39, 12 April 1989.
59. Letter to Aldo Rossi from Michael Govan, assistant director of the Guggenheim, 14 June 1989, inviting him to meet in Venice later in the month. MAXXI, Rossi, Correspondence, 1989.
60. Rossi, "Lezione sui musei," Venice IUAV, updated version October 1994, 17. MAXXI, Rossi.
61. "The Building," Bonnefantenmuseum, Maastricht. http://www.bonnefanten.nl/en/about_us/building_en_architect, accessed 21 August 2017.
62. Aldo Rossi and Alexander van Grevenstein, *Brieven/Letters* (Maastricht: Bonnefanten Museum, 1995), 24.
63. Rossi, "Verlust der Mitte," Bonnefantenmuseum, Building and Architect, http://www.bonnefanten.nl/en/about_us/building_en_architect/verlust_der_mitte, accessed 21 August 2017.
64. Rossi and Van Grevenstein, *Brieven/Lettere*, 22–24.
65. Ibid., 24.
66. Hans Sedlmayr, *Art in Crisis: The Lost Center* (New York: Routledge, 2017 [1948]).
67. Alois Riegl, "The Modern Cult of Monuments," trans. Kurt Forster and Diane Ghirardo, *Oppositions* 25 (1982): 21–51.
68. Ibid., 141–44.
69. Carlo Aymonino, "Une architecture de l'optimisme," *L'Architecture d'Aujourd'hui*, 190 (1977): 46; also cited in Seixas Lopes, *Melancholy and Architecture*, 196.
70. *The Confessions of St. Augustine*, trans. Rex Warner (New York: New American Library, 1963), Book XI, §10–24, 264–77.
71. "È perduto perché è lontano ma la perdita si presenta anche come una discreta condizione del fare, ... per questo posso riprendere la descrizione del teatro veneziano come un'opera di gioia o anche con componenti infantili ... infantile come riferimento ad una condizione perduta e per questo poetica." Rossi, *QA*, Book 26, 3 November 1979.

CHAPTER 5. ROSSI AND THE THEATER

Epigraph: Walter Benjamin, "A Berlin Chronicle," in Michael William Jennings, Howard Eiland, Gary Smith, eds., *Walter Benjamin: Selected Writings*, vol. 2, part 2, 1931–1934 (Cambridge, Mass.: Belknap, 2005), 611.

1. The Venetian Republic has borne the nickname "La Serenissima," meaning "most serene," since the middle ages, an honorific title signaling high status that was also applied to individuals, including the doge or other members of the high aristocracy.
2. Originally erected for the Theater Biennale in November 1979 and retained for Carnevale celebrations in early 1980, the Teatro del Mondo then traveled to the bay of Dubrovnik as its final stop, because no funds were available to absorb the maintenance costs, especially of the rented barge, to preserve it. In 2004, the Teatro del Mondo was reconstructed for an exhibit in Genoa, a project complicated by the fact that not only had all of the original measured drawings disappeared but also Rossi had made revisions during the construction process. The second version thus could only be an incomplete approximation of the original.
3. In an unpublished lecture on his theaters, "I miei teatri," delivered in Venice at the Università Iuav on 24 April 1997, Rossi commented that some cultural body had commissioned the theater, but he could no longer remember which one.
4. "La vita, la morte e l'immaginazione il legame è diretto e ambiguo.... La casa della morte e la casa dell'infanzia sono parte del teatro ... la scuola non è completa, il cimitero è un frammento, il teatro è un modello. Ma la forma della costruzione è perfettamente prevista e nulla cambia dal pensiero alla realtà fisica delle cose." Rossi, *QA*, Book 24, 6 June 1979.
5. For a general history of ancient theater, see Ruth Scodel, ed., *Theatre and Society in the Classical World* (Ann Arbor: University of Michigan Press, 1993); for Greek theater, Graham Ley, *A Short Introduction to the Ancient Greek Theatre* (Chicago: University of Chicago Press, 1991); Jennifer Wise, *Dionysus Writes: The Invention of Theatre in Ancient Greece* (Ithaca, N.Y.: Cornell University Press, 1998).
6. See, for example, his project statement for the Teatro-Faro on Lake Ontario, near Toronto, Canada, where he makes that point. Ferlenga, *Aldo Rossi: Tutte le opere* (1999), 188.
7. Marcus Vitruvius Pollio, *Vitruvius: Ten Books on Architecture*, ed. and trans. Ingrid D. Rowland (Cambridge: Cambridge University Press, 1999), Book 5.iii.1–8.
8. Still useful on this topic is Donald C. Mullin, "The Influence of Vitruvius on Theatre Architecture," *Educational Theatre Journal* 18, no. 1 (March 1966): 27–33; see also Vera Mowry Roberts, *On Stage: A History of Theater* (New York: Harper and Row, 1962); Margarete Bieber, *The History of the Greek and Roman Theater*, 2nd ed., rev. and enl. (Princeton: Princeton University Press, 1961); Hugh Hardy, *The Theater of Architecture* (New York: Princeton Architectural Press, 2013).
9. The earliest example of this scheme is Vincenzo Scamozzi's theater in Sabbioneta (1588–90). Tomaso Buzzi, *Il "Teatro all'Antico" di Vincenzo Scamozzi in Sabbioneta* (Rome: Bestetti and Tuminelli, 1928); Kurt Forster, "Stagecraft as Statecraft: The Architectural Integration of Public Life and Theatrical Spectacle in Scamozzi's Theater at Sabbioneta," *Oppositions* 9 (1977): 63–87.
10. Gianugo Polesello, *Concorso per la ricostruzione del Teatro Paganini a Parma: Progetti di Aldo Rossi e Carlo Aymonino* (Venice: Cluva, 1966). In 1999, Renzo Piano transformed a building from Parma's old Eridania sugar plant into the Paganini Auditorium in a nearby park.
11. Rossi, *Architecture of the City*, 34.
12. Ibid., 47–48.
13. Roussel's *Locus solus* (1914) appealed to Rossi in part because of the strange theater unveiled by the protagonist wherein the dead were brought to life to reenact, in a theatrical setting, the most important moments of their lives. The term *locus solus* became a hallmark for Rossi.
14. Rossi, *Architecture of the City*, 40.
15. Ibid., 41.
16. *Fatti urbani* is a complex term difficult to translate into English; Rossi adopted it in *The Architecture of the City* to signify not just urban artifacts such as buildings but also street networks, events, memories, and more.
17. Filarete received the duke's commission for the palace in 1461, but Venice's leaders, who had granted Sforza the site in gratitude for his military accomplishments on behalf of the Serenissima, soon became wary of a military

man known for his tendency to change sides at will and halted the construction. For an account of Sforza's life, William Pollard Urquhart, *The Life and Times of Francesco Sforza* (Charleston, S.C.: Nabu Press, 2011).

18. "Da questa impressione nascono le mie architetture con elementi cilindrici e per me una visione completamente nuova dell'architettura." Rossi, "Note autobiografiche sulla formazione ecc., 1971," in ARP; see Ferlenga, *Aldo Rossi: Tutte le opere* (2003), 8–25.

19. Aldo Rossi, "Edifici pubblici, teatro e fontana, zona Fontivegge, Perugia," in Celant, *Aldo Rossi: Teatri*, 72–83.

20. Rossi, *Scientific Autobiography*, 8.

21. "Le rovine di una città sono oggetto di fantasia proprio nel momento che è possibile collegarle in un sistema previsto costruito scientificamente per ipotesi chiare.... In questo senso... ho avanzato la teoria della città analoga: cioè di un procedimento compositivo ne è imperniato su alcuni fatti fondamentali della realtà urbana e intorno a cui costituisce altri fatti nel quadro di un sistema analogico." Rossi, *QA*, Book 3, 11 January 1970.

22. From a typescript among the papers at the Fondazione Aldo Rossi; now in Rossi, "Il Teatro di Carlo Felice," in Celant, *Aldo Rossi: Teatri*, 96.

23. Rossi rued the fact that the windows could not be opened nor the balconies occupied, for safety reasons.

24. Karl Friedrich Schinkel, *Sammlung Architektonischer Entwürfe* (Chicago: Exedra, 1981), the folio is a limited edition collection of his architectural drawings based on the 1866 version. The drawings originally appeared over several years in seventeen folio editions; the drawing here first appeared in the second folio, 1821.

25. "Questa scena fissa è partecipe all'azione e la costruisce: essa crea dei nessi ulteriori e li rafforza." *QA*, Book 15, 3 October 1973.

26. Alicia R. Zuese, *Baroque Spain and the Writing of Visual and Material Culture* (Cardiff: University of Wales Press, 2015); Gloria Fraser Giffords, *Sanctuaries of Earth, Stone and Light: The Churches of Northern New Spain, 1530–1821* (Tucson: University of Arizona Press, 2007); Damián Bayón and Murillo Marx, *A History of South American Colonial Art and Architecture: Spanish South America and Brazil* (New York: Rizzoli, 1992).

27. Rossi, *QA*, Book 31, 2–5 December 1985.

28. Ibid., Book 23, 27 November–15 December 1978.

29. "Mi ricordo, guardandolo, la mia passione per il retablo e la speranza assurda di poter costruire un retablo." Ibid., Book 31, 16–18 January 1986.

30. The original La Fenice was erected in 1792 after a predecessor theater of San Benedetto burned, and it also suffered a fire in 1836 prior to the disastrous 1996 fire. See Ghirardo, *Italy: Modern Architectures,* 200–207; Gianluca Amadori, *Per quattro soldi: Il giallo della Fenice dal rogo alla ricostruzione* (Rome: Editori Riuniti, 2003); Maura Manzelle, *Il Teatro La Fenice a Venezia: Studi per la ricostruzione dov'era ma non necessariamente com'era* (Venice: Quaderni IUAV, 1999). Government decree 44/96 converted into law number 401 of 29 July 1996 granted twenty million lire for the reconstruction and designated Venice's prefect to preside over the reconstruction.

31. The official La Fenice website describes the events as follows: "On 7th September 96 the call for bids is published in which ten Italian and foreign firms participate, judged on 30th May 1997. Following a number of appeals, A. T. I. Holzmann wins the contract with the project of architect Aldo Rossi." http://www.teatrolafenice.it/site/index.php?pag=73&blocco=176&lingua=ENG, accessed 30 June 2017. See also "L'incendio alla Fenice di Venezia, vent'anni fa," *Il Post*, 29 January 1996; "Il ritorno della Fenice: Mostra sulla ricostruzione artistica del Teatro La Fenice," interview with Public Works Chair Marco Corsini, one of the reconstruction architects, in connection with the exhibit, published online by the University of Genoa, https://architettura.unige.it/did/12/architettura, accessed 25 June 2017.

32. All jury members were university professors: Mazzarolli of business administration, University of Padua; Commis of acoustics, University of Paris-Belleville and Nancy; Dal Co at the Institute of Architecture, University of Venice; Fecia di Cossato, building systems at Padua; di Tommaso, building science, University of Bologna, all selected by Mayor Cacciari.

33. Holzman filed an administrative appeal on 30 June 1997. The regional administrative body rejected the appeal in court decision number 1497/97. The Consiglio di Stato decision 300/98, issued on 10 February 1998, specifically rejected the jury's decision on the grounds that during the design phase the prefect had clarified to all of the contestants that the property the city of Venice was then acquiring through eminent domain proceedings should be included in the design, approximately 20 percent of the whole. Aulenti's work on the reconstruction was halted three days later, and the decision forced Cacciari to recall the jury to recalculate the points, a task not completed until 19 March 1998. The Agnelli firm appealed this decision, but the Consiglio di Stato rejected the appeal on 1 July 1998. Cacciari, exasperated by these decisions, complained that the right to enter administrative appeals should be canceled to enable projects to be built. Had that been the case, Aulenti's inferior design would have been erected. Alessandra Carini, "Guerra degli appalti a Venezia e la Fenice ancora non risorge," *La Repubblica*, 22 November 1998.

34. Da Mosto was the person who first realized Aulenti's project was incomplete, enabling the construction company to file its administrative lawsuit. Da Mosto was central to persuading the city of Venice that the new and untried partnership, Arassociati, would be able to bring the project to completion. Nonetheless, Rossi's former employees chose not to include him once the original award was overturned and they had signed the contract to complete Rossi's design.

35. Rossi, "La Fenice," MAXXI, Rossi, *Quaderno*, August 1996 to May 1997.

36. See, e.g., Manzelle, *Il Teatro La Fenice*. For the polemics surrounding the reconstruction of the Carlo Felice, see Daniela Pasti, "Che pasticcio quel teatro: Genova proprio non lo merita," *La Repubblica*, 29/30 April 1984; Franco Vernice, "La maledizione del Carlo Felice," *La Repubblica*, 12 May 1984; other newspaper articles highlighted polemics between Bruno Zevi and Paolo Portoghesi.

37. Rossi, "La Fenice," 2.

38. Ernesto Nathan Rogers, quoted in Oscar Newman, ed., *New Frontiers in Architecture: CIAM '59 in Otterlo* (New York: Universe, 1961), 93.

39. Raymond Roussel, *Impressions of Africa*, trans. Mark Polizzotti (McLean, Ill.: Dalkey Archive, 2011); for a biography of Roussel, Mark Ford, *Raymond Roussel and the Republic of Dreams* (Ithaca, N.Y.: Cornell University Press, 2000).

40. Rossi, QA, Book 2, Architettura, 4 December 1968.

41. Ibid., Book 29, Architettura–Grecia, March 1981.

42. Michel Foucault, *Death and the Labyrinth: The World of Raymond Roussel*, trans. Charles Ruas (London and New York: Continuum, 2004 [1963]); Leonardo Sciascia, *Atti relative alla morte di Raymond Roussel* (Palermo: Esse Sellerio, 1971). Roussel committed suicide in Palermo on 14 July 1933 (Bastille Day), when Rossi was two years old.

43. Rossi, *Architecture of the City*, 32. In the original Italian text, Rossi used the French term *l'âme de la cité* without translation: the soul of the city.

44. Wisdom of Solomon 11:20: "But thou hast arranged all things by measure and number and weight"; Proverbs 8:27: Wisdom put forth her voice; "When he established the heavens I was there: when he set a compass upon the face of the deep." See also Maria Grazia Lopardi, *Architettura sacra medievale: Mito e geometria degli archetipi* (Rome: Mediterranea, 2009).

45. "Colui che volse il sesto allo stremo del mondo, e dentro ad esso distinse tanto occulto e manifesto." *Paradiso* XIX, 40–42. Dante Alighieri, *The Divine Comedy of Dante Alighieri: The Italian Text with a Translation in English Blank Verse and a Commentary by Courtney Langdon*, vol. 3: *Paradiso* (Cambridge, Mass.: Harvard University Press, 1921).

46. The unpublished manuscript of the first part of the planned book is preserved at MAXXI, Rossi: "Alcuni miei progetti: Avvertenza"; some shorter typescripts in the same archive carry a similar title.

47. "...una ricerca all'interno di un purismo meccanico che smontava e rimontava gli oggetti." Rossi, QA, Book 22, Architettura e Ospedale di Bergamo, 15 May 1977–21 July 1978.

48. "Nessun teatro è più reale, niente, attraverso una rigorosa descrizione è più necessario per noi della applicazioni dei ritratti degli elettori

del Brandeburgo sopra la bianca parete di fondo." Ibid.
49. Roussel, *Impressions of Africa*, 3.
50. "Spezzare l'ignoto della fantasia, scoprire le regole del gioco, infine dissacrare il gesto dell'inconscio fino alle sue radici." Rossi, QA, Book 23, 30 July 1978–1 January 1979.
51. Giampaolo Bolzani and Paolo Bolzani, *La rocca Brancaleone a Ravenna: Conoscenza e progetto* (Fusignano: Essegi, 1995).
52. Aldo Rossi, "Scenografia di *Lucia di Lammermoor*, Rocca Brancaleone, Ravenna," in Celant, *Aldo Rossi: Teatri*, 122.
53. "...all'interno di un quadro teorico del mio pensiero in architettura. In realtà con il passare degli anni questo quadro della architettura mi sembra si possa ampliare a una visione generale del significato della vita." Rossi, QA, Book 22, 17 July 1978.
54. Ibid., Book 14, 16/17/18 November 1972.
55. "Ho cercato così di costruire una architettura libera dal tempo, dalle condizioni, dai sentimenti. Io mi limito a spiegare questo meccanismo anche se dietro ad esso si erge il campo della motivazioni di ogni tipo che circondano ogni opera." Ibid., Book 13, 1972.
56. Rossi, "I miei teatri," lecture in Venice at the Università Iuav, 24 April 1997; unpublished transcript.
57. Rossi, *Scientific Autobiograpy*, 12.
58. Ibid., 6.
59. On the Sacri Monti: Rudolf Wittkower, "Montagnes sacrées," *L'Oeil* 59 (November 1959): 54–61; William Hood, "The Sacro Monte of Varallo: Renaissance Art and Popular Religion," in Timothy Verdon, ed., *Monasticism and the Arts* (Syracuse, N.Y.: Syracuse University Press, 1984), 291–311; *Atti del I Convegno Internazionale sui Sacri Monti* (Varallo: Centro di Documentazione dei Sacri Monti, Calvari e Complessi Devozionali Europei, 1980); Sergio Gensini, ed., *La "Gerusalemme" di San Vivaldo e i sacri monti in Europa* (Ospedaletto: Pacini, 1989).
60. "La ripetizione dell'esperienza per chi percorre il Sacro Monte è simile all'arte." Rossi, QA, Book 6, 21 March 1971.
61. While the pilgrimage route originated in the sixteenth century, the eleven chapels date from the nineteenth century, each enveloped within its own architectural configuration.
62. Alessandro Manzoni (1785–1873), also Milanese, like Rossi loved the lakes of Lombardy and the Piedmont; he too studied in Somasca with the Somaschi fathers. Every Italian child who attends high school reads *The Betrothed;* mention The Unnamed and every Italian knows of whom you speak.
63. "Visto in questi tempi (e accetto il gesto quasi nevrotico del pellegrinaggio) i santuari della Lombardia," Aldo Rossi to Gianugo Polesello, fragment of a draft of a letter, 20 March 1966. MAXXI, Rossi.
64. Personal communication, February 1985; see also Aldo Rossi, "Villa sul lago Maggiore," in Margherita Petranzan, ed., *Aldo Rossi: Villa sul Lago Maggiore: Progetto di villa con interno* (Venezia: Il Cardo, 1996), 7.
65. Santino Langé and Mario Piana, *Santa Maria della Salute a Venezia* (Milan: Touring Club Italiano, 2006), 59–70.
66. "I Sacri Monti sono una costruzione della architettura: la costruzione di un mondo non utilitaristico dell'architettura. Essi costruiscono un significato dalla loro sequenza e dal loro ordine." Rossi, QA, Book 6, 21 March 1971.
67. "...le cappelle dei gessi colorati e l'ultima cena con tovaglie, bicchieri, oggetti, cose autentiche e insostituibili." Rossi to Polesella, 20 March 1966. MAXXI, Rossi.
68. This process was ably outlined by Eugenio Battisti, "I presupposti culturali," in Attilio Agnoletto, Eugenio Battisti, and Franco Cardini, eds., *Gli abitanti immobili di San Vivaldo il Monte Sacro della Toscana* (Florence: Morgana, 1987), 15–18.
69. Rossi, *Scientific Autobiography*, 5.
70. "[I Sacri Monti] costruiscono un significato dalla loro sequenza e dal loro ordine... Indipendentemente dal fatto che contengono una storia sacra... il loro carattere principale è quello di costuire un luogo.... Una storia viene spiegata immettendoci nella storia." Rossi, QA, Book 6, 19 March 1971.
71. Rossi, *Scientific Autobiography*, 8, 11.
72. Strauss's opera (1909) is based on Hugo von Hofmannsthal's tragedy, which in turn is based on that of Sophocles; the libretto for this opera is also by Von Hofmannsthal. The performances were set for September 1992.
73. Clytemnestra's rage sprang from Agamemnon's decision to slay their daughter Iphigenia so

that the winds would allow the Achaean ships to proceed to Troy and victory.

74. Some scholars question the mask's authenticity; I direct the reader to the following group of articles by John G. Younger, Spencer P. M. Harrington, William M. Calder III, Katie Demakapoulou, David Traill, Kenneth D. S. Lapatin, Oliver Dickinson, "Behind the Mask of Agamemnon," *Archaeology Archive* 52, no. 4 (July/August 1999): 51–59.

75. The lions' heads originally were part of the sculpture, but evidently disappeared over time. An intriguing recent treatment of the city of Mycenae and its Lion Gate is Athina Cacouri, *Mycenae: From Myth to History* (New York: Abbeville, 2016).

76. Rossi, "Il Teatro di Carlo Felice," in Celant, *Aldo Rossi: Teatri*, 96.

77. Jorge Luis Borges, "The Aleph," trans. Norman Thomas Di Giovanni, in *The Aleph and Other Stories* (London: Penguin Classics, 2004); Edna Aizenberg, *The Aleph Weaver: Biblical, Kabbalistic and Judaic Elements in Borges* (Potomac, Md.: Scripta Humanistica, 1984).

78. Rossi, "Il Teatro di Carlo Felice," in Celant, *Aldo Rossi: Teatri*, 96.

CHAPTER 6. CEMETERIES FOR MODENA AND ROZZANO

Epigraph: Nicholas of Cusa, *De theologicis complementis*, n. 14, 21–22, trans. Johannes Hoff, *The Analogical Turn: Rethinking Modernity with Nicholas of Cusa* (Grand Rapids, Mich.: Eerdmans, 2013), 136.

1. Aldo Rossi, "L'azzurro del cielo," *Controspazio*, no. 10 (1972): 4–9; republished in Comune di Modena, *Aldo Rossi: Opere recenti* (Modena: Panini, 1983), 87–90; revised for English as "The Blue of the Sky," trans. M. Barsoum and Livio Dimitriu, *Oppositions* 5 (1976): 31–34. The title was based on an erotic-political novel by Georges Bataille, *Le bleu du ciel*, written 1935–37 but not published for another twenty years (Paris: J. Pauvert, 1957), translated into English as *Blue of Noon* (London: Penguin, 2001). The competition was announced 6 May 1971, with projects due 2 November of the same year. Rossi proceeded to the second round with two other finalists, having placed first in the first round on 8 April 1972. He was awarded first place in the final round on 23 September 1972. In his submission Rossi included the name of his assistant, Gianni Braghieri, who was not responsible for the design. It is a sign of Rossi's generosity that he included Braghieri's name here as he did on other occasions. For convenience, and indeed accuracy, with regard to projects discussed here I most often refer only to Rossi.

2. Eugene J. Johnson published a detailed discussion of the project's various phases to 1982, and an architectural genealogy of the forms, "What Remains of Man: Aldo Rossi's Modena Cemetery."

3. The complete jury consisted of Carlo Aymonino, Athos Baccarini, Umberto Bisi, Ermete Bortolotti, Ugo Cavazzuti, Pier Luigi Cervellati, Mario Ghio, Teodosio Greco, Glauco Gresleri, Pietro Guerzoni, Alessandro Magni, Alfredo Mango, Carlo Melograni, Emilio Montesori, Paolo Portoghesi, Paolo Sorzia, and Rubes Triva. The jury handed down its decision for the first round on 8 April 1972. Minutes of the meetings and other documents regarding the jury deliberations can be found in ARP, Box 12.

4. "Traccia per la mozione di minoranza circa il giudizio di maggioranza della commissione," (anon., n.d.), ibid.

5. The jury report on the final round, "Concorso di secondo grado per la progettazione del cimitero di San Cataldo. Verbale delle riunioni della commissione giudicatrice," was issued 20 April 1974; Aldo Rossi Papers, Centre Canadien d'Architecture, Montreal. Because the first project included subterranean chambers, some jurors appropriately objected because the site's water table did not permit such a solution. In the revised, second-round project, Rossi eliminated the underground chambers, widened the perimeter structures, and added another floor and a new wing of tombs linked the addition to the Jewish cemetery.

6. Rossi, "L'azzurro del cielo," in *Opere recenti*; "Poesia contro retorica: Il concorso per il nuovo cimitero di Modena," *Casabella* 36, no. 372 (1972): 20–26; José Rafael Moneo, "New Trends in Contemporary Architecture: Formalism, Realism, Contextualism," *Space Design* (March 1978): 3–86; "Aldo Rossi with Gianni Braghieri: Cemetery in Modena,"

*Lotus International* 25 (1979): 62–65. Rossi received the monetary award for first place after the first round. In early, contemporary publications such as the *Lotus International* article, the architects were listed as "Aldo Rossi with Gianni Braghieri." Unfortunately, some recent authors, such as Beatrice Lampariello, use "and" instead of the correct "with"; there should be no question about which man was the designer.

7. Paolo Portoghesi, "Concorso per il cimitero San Cataldo di Modena," *Controspazio* 10 (1972): 3.
8. The competition entry proposed two stories above ground and one below; revisions in the final scheme presented in 1976 removed the underground portion and raised the complex to three stories.
9. "… una singola architettura degli edifici seriali uniti da un'asse." Rossi, *QA*, Book 14, 31 December 1972.
10. Ibid., Book 17, 21 May 1974.
11. Rossi, "Preface," in Gravagnuolo, 14.
12. William Blake, *The Marriage of Heaven and Hell* (1790), 12.
13. Rossi, "Preface," in Gravagnuolo, 12. I found the original Italian among Rossi's papers in the MAXXI archives in Rome.
14. "E quando guardo al Prado il Cristo di Velazquez ci penso sempre: è proprio solo il corpo di un uomo inchiodato a due assi con un fondo scuro … è la tua storia e il tuo futuro." Rossi, *QA*, Book 25, 18 June 1979.
15. While the earliest modernists such as Le Corbusier did occasionally employ color, since modern movement architecture was studied and presented in black and white photographs, for most architects then and later, the banishment of history from contemporary architecture cohered with a rejection of color.
16. Ada Louise Huxtable, "Aldo Rossi: Memory and Metaphor," in *Architecture Anyone?* (New York: Random House, 1986), 44; Mary Louise Lobsinger, "Antinomies of Realism in Postwar Italian Architecture," PhD diss., Harvard University, 2003; Seixas Lopes, *Melancholy and Architecture*.
17. "A Conversation: Aldo Rossi and Bernard Huet," *Perspecta* 28 (1997): 108. The passage continues: "It is a little bit like love: One meets many people and nothing happens, and then falls in love with one destined person."
18. Huxtable, "Aldo Rossi," 108; see also Charles Jencks, *The New Moderns* (New York: Rizzoli, 1990), 119–20.
19. Rossi, "L'azzurro del cielo," in *Opere recenti*, 87.
20. Ibid., 90.
21. "Il senso di ogni rappresentazione è così prefissato: ogni opera o parte è il ripetersi di un avvenimento, quasi un rito poiché è il rito e non l'evento che ha una forma precisa." *QA*, Book 4, 30 December 1970.
22. Ibid., Book 9, 2 November 1971; Book 23, 7–8 August 1979.
23. Ibid., Book 9, 5 August 1971.
24. Ibid., Book 13, 19–22 October 1972.
25. Rossi, "L'azzurro del cielo," in *Opere recenti*, 89.
26. Rossi, *QA*, Book 9, 5 August 1971.
27. *The Confessions of St. Augustine*, trans. Rex Warner (New York: New American Library, 1963), Book XI, §14, 20.
28. "[La rete metallica] separava l'indistinto del sacro e della morte dal mondo circostante." Rossi, "Cappella funeraria a Guissano," in Ferlenga, *Rossi: Life and Works*, 94.
29. See the interview with Gianni Braghieri: https://www.youtube.com/watch?v=zWrJXY_x0WQ, accessed 15 July 2017.
30. "Ce vide n'était pas moins illimité, à nos pieds, qu'un ciel étoilé sur nos têtes." Georges Bataille, *Le bleu du ciel* (1957, repr. Paris: Flammarion, 2004), 174.
31. "Anche se questo tempo che consuma e cambia è tanto segno di morte quanto le cose che permangono; di un senso della morte che sempre più ti appartiene quanto più la leggi nelle cose." Rossi, *QA*, Book 8, 22 July 1971.
32. Lobsinger, "Antinomies of Realism," 299.
33. "Le mie opere cercano il significato dell'architettura. Il significato di un'architettura è più forte della sua funzione, della sua tecnica, della sua stessa forma. Ma l'architettura si esprime attraverso il mondo delle forme." Rossi, *QA*, Book 10, 17 January 1972.
34. MAXXI, Rossi, File immagini 00213, 2/134.
35. Rossi, *QA*, Book 14, 31 December 1972.
36. Nerino Valentini, *Il molto dilettevole giuoco dell'oca: Storia, simbolismo e tradizione di un celebre gioco* (Mantua: Sometti, 2006).
37. "La morte esprimeva uno stato di passaggio fra due condizioni i cui confini non si erano precisati." Rossi, "L'azzurro del cielo," in *Opere recenti*, 87.
38. "I Wanderjahre sono forse l'inizio e la fine di

ogni educazione / essi contengono il racconto del Pellegrino e la stessa Via Crucis. La Via Crucis, come in architettura il Sacro Monte, è un percorso che prevede il dramma, il cattivo fine e il lieto fine contemporaneamente." Rossi, QA, Book 23, 30 July 1978. In this passage Rossi referred to the theater and to the dramas that unfold there; Aristotle's *Poetics* identifies the tragedy with a happy ending as one type of tragedy to be staged in ancient Greece, such as Euripides's *Iphigenia among the Taurians*. See Christopher S. Morrisey, "Oedipus the Cliché: Aristotle on Tragic Form and Content," *Anthropoetics* 9, no. 1 (Spring/Summer 2003).

39. Rossi, QA, Book 9, 30 August 1971.
40. Rossi asserted that he learned about shadows from his study of Boullée; he treated them like a material, a solid substance, and from that he also learned about light. Rossi, "Introduzione a Boullée," now in *Scritti scelti*, 321–38.
41. Rossi, QA, Book 38, 18 February 1989.
42. Rossi, "Nuovi problemi," *Casabella-continuità* 264 (June 1962): 6; now in *Scritti Scelti*, 165–80.
43. Leonardo da Vinci, "The Works of the Eye and Ear Compared," in Martin Kemp, ed., *Leonardo on Painting*, trans. Kemp and Margaret Walker (New Haven: Yale University Press, 1989), 20–34; Giuseppe Mazzotta, *Dante's Vision and the Circle of Knowledge* (Princeton: Princeton University Press, 1993), 13, and esp. 96–134; see also Mazzotta, *Reading Dante* (New Haven: Yale University Press, 2014). I do not pretend to be a Dantista, so I rely on the compelling insights of Mazzotta, today's most important Dante scholar, who has also recognized Rossi's genius.
44. "…lo scrivere—la lingua—il mezzo più prezioso plastico potente che possediamo…così gli ultimi disegni, gran parte di questi sono una sorta di grafia dove scrittura e disegno si identificano." Rossi, QA, Book 23, 1 January 79.
45. Other than poetry, Rossi's personal home library consisted mainly of literature, philosophy, and theology; books on architecture remained in his studio.
46. Delio Tessa (1886–1939) was one of the most talented of Italian poets who wrote in dialect. His collection of poems *L'è el dì di Mort, alegher!* appeared in a new edition edited by Claudia Beretta (Milan: Libreria Milanese, 1993). Turgenev's comment appeared translated in Italian as: "La cosa più interessante nella vita, è la morte."
47. Private communication with one of the contractors who bid for the project, July 1987.
48. Rossi, QA, Book 16, 22 January 1974. Rossi was a deeply cultured man, widely read, and thoughtful about the texts he perused; in this book I mention Dante and Leonardo because they figure repeatedly in Rossi's writings, but they are only two among many significant cultural figures that he followed.
49. The artist Giovan Battista Crespi designed the San Carlone statue in 1614, shortly after St. Charles was canonized; it was built by Siro Zanella of Pavia and Bernardo Falconi of Lugano over the course of the seventeenth century and completed in 1698.
50. Aldo Rossi, "Note autobiografiche sulla formazione, ecc., 1971," in ARP; see Ferlenga, *Aldo Rossi: Tutte le opere* (2003), 8–25; quote on 8–9.
51. Aldo Rossi, "Introduction," in *In treno verso l'Europa* (Rome: Peliti Associati, 1993), a book of Gabriele Basilico's photographs. The Divine Office consists of Matins, Lauds, and/or Terce, Sext, None in the afternoon, followed by Vespers in the evening, and Compline, or the night prayers. The primary song of vespers is the Magnificat, a celebration of Mary's faith and wonder drawn from the gospel of Luke (1:46–55). Fernand Cabrol, "Vespers," *The Catholic Encyclopedia*, vol. 13 (New York: Appleton, 1912). http://newadvent.org/cathen/15381a.htm, accessed 13 July 2018.
52. Augustine of Hippo, *The Confessions of St. Augustine*, Book XIII, §35, 349, trans. Rex Warner (New York: New American Library, 1963); fully cited in the Italian edition of Rossi's *L'autobiografia scientifica*, 113; the English edition included only the last two sentences, 77. Italics original.
53. Poletti, *L'autobiografia scientifica di Aldo Rossi*, 91.
54. Augustine, *Confessions*, Book XIII, §35, 349. Italics original.
55. "Arrested like the hands of a clock—his buildings often carry clocks or other markings of time—Rossi's buildings increasingly sought refuge from time." Kurt W. Forster, "Thoughts on the Metamorphoses of Architecture," *Log*, no. 3 (Fall 2004): 23.
56. Lobsinger, "Antinomies of Realism," 194–96;

Pier Vittorio Aureli, *The Project of Autonomy: Politics and Architecture Within and Against Capitalism* (New York: Princeton Architectural Press, 2008). The person closest to Rossi in the 1950s and 1960s, his wife Sonia Gessner, affirms what his closest friends then and later knew: that he briefly joined a group associated with the Italian Communist Party (PCI) when he was about 17, and only at the urgent pleading of friends did he briefly join the party again in 1958. Indeed, he had to initiate an administrative lawsuit in the United States, which he won, to be removed from a terrorist watch list.

57. Mazzotta, "L'autobiografia scientifica di Aldo Rossi," in Ghirardo, *Borgoricco: Il municipio e il centro civico*, 40.
58. Among the exceptions, Gabriella Zarri studied Lucrezia Borgia's religion with a sympathetic ear: *La religione di Lucrezia Borgia: Le lettere inedite del confessore* (Rome: Roma nel Rinascimento, 2006).
59. Willibald Sauerlander, *The Catholic Rubens: Saints and Martyrs*, trans. David Dollenmayer (Los Angeles: Getty Research Institute, 2014). Sauerlander is an agnostic former Protestant and an art historian who remarkably lacked blinders when he studied Rubens.
60. Johnson, "What Remains of Man."
61. In January 2015, Pope Francis I noted that concern for the poor had not been discovered by Communism; it is a fundamental message of the gospel. Orlando Sacchelli, "Papa Francesco: 'Occuparsi dei poveri non è comunismo, è Vangelo,'" *Il Giornale* (11 January 2015). Johnson also erroneously described Rossi as a European Jew.
62. Personal communication, Summer 1986.
63. Personal communication, Spring 1986.
64. Roy A. Rappaport offered a useful definition of ritual: "The performance of more or less invariant sequences of formal acts and utterances not entirely encoded by the performers." Rappaport, *Ritual and Religion in the Making of Humanity* (Cambridge: Cambridge University Press, 1999), 24. Among the numerous studies on rituals, those most influential regarding religious rituals include Branislaw Malinowsky, *Magic, Science and Religion, and Other Essays* (Glencoe, 1948); Clifford Geertz, *The Interpretation of Cultures* (New York: Basic Books, 1973).
65. Rossi, *QA*, Book 39, 24 March 1989.
66. "È bello tutto ciò in cui siamo costretti dall'amore e dal legame." Ibid. The church of Santa Maria delle Grazie also once held Titian's painting of the crowning with thorns; when Napoleon's troops arrived at the end of the eighteenth century, they spirited it away to the Louvre, never to be returned.
67. "Questo progetto di cimitero non si discosta dall'idea di cimitero che ognuno possiede." Rossi, "L'azzurro del cielo," in *Opere recenti*, 87.
68. My thanks go to theologian Dr. Antonella Meriggi for having drawn my attention to this passage during a conversation about the cemetery in the summer of 2017.
69. In the first round of the competition, Rossi left one of the four sides of the cube blank, with no apertures. As he worked on revised versions, ultimately he treated all four sides the same, with the regular square apertures.
70. I attended Catholic schools and learned how to cast out nines along with my first math problems; my sister, who attended public schools, did not, for reasons we have never understood, because it is a sure-fire method for checking sums.
71. Although the practice dates to the earliest days of the Christian Church, St. Benedict articulated the practice and the appropriate prayers in his book on monastic life; seasonal adjustments related to weather changed some of the hours, but the canonical ones were three hours apart. There are many editions of Benedict's book; see *The Rule of St. Benedict*, ed. and trans. Timothy Fry, O.S.B. (New York: Vintage, 1998).
72. There is also a glazed elevator inside.
73. Rossi opened his *Quaderno Azzurro 39* (28 February–30 April 1989) with a small *santino*, noting that he affixed one to the first page of his datebook each year and that he conserved his collection with great care. "Come nelle mie agende pongo ogni anno una di queste immagini, mi piace iniziare questo quaderno di cui non so il contenuto con questa bella figura. Ne ho una collezione che conservo con molta cura." (Just as each year I place one of these images in my datebook, so I like to start this notebook—whose content I do not know—with this beautiful image. I have a collection that I conserve with great care.)
74. Two recent articles address St. Rose's

condition: L. Capasso, S. Caramiello, and R. D'Anastasio, "The Anomaly of Santa Rosa," *Lancet* 353 (February 6, 1999): 504; F. Turturro, C. Calderaro, A. Montanaro, L. Labianca, G. Argento, and A. Ferretti, "Case Report: Isolated Asymptomatic Short Sternum in a Healthy Young Girl," *Case Reports in Radiology* 20 (July 2014): Article ID 761582.

75. Leonard Foley, O.F.M., *Saint of the Day: Lives, Lessons and Feast*, revised by Pat McCloskey, O.F.M., 5th ed. (Cincinnati: Saint Anthony Messenger, 2003), entry for 4 September. St. Rose's body was disinterred after her death and found to be intact even though she had been interred in a simple shroud. It was later damaged by a fire in the convent church to which the body had been moved.

## CHAPTER 7. ALDO ROSSI AND THE SPIRIT OF ARCHITECTURE

Aldo Rossi, "Nuovi problemi," *Casabella-continuità* 264 (June 1962): 6; now in *Scritti Scelti*, 165–80.

1. The list of critics along the lines noted here is a long one; some of the most recent or the most significant include: Charles Holland, "It Works—On Paper," *RIBA Journal* 116, no. 5 (May 2009): 28; Joseph Rykwert, review of *L'architettura di Aldo Rossi*, by Vittorio Savi, *Journal of the Society of Architectural Historians* (*JSAH*) 38, no. 3 (October 1979): 304; Juan José Lahuerta, review of Aldo Rossi exhibit, *JSAH* 59, no. 3 (September 2000): 378–79; Pier Vittorio Aureli, *The Project of Autonomy: Politics and Architecture Within and Against Capitalism* (New York: Temple Buell Center and Princeton Architectural Press, 2008); Val K. Warke, "Type-Silence-Genre," *Log* 5 (Spring/Summer 2005): 122–29; Mary Louise Lobsinger, "That Obscure Object of Desire: Autobiography and Repetition in the Work of Aldo Rossi," *Grey Room* 8 (Summer 2002): 38–61; below are additional citations from writings of Manfredo Tafuri, Francesco Dal Co, Massimo Cacciari, and others.

2. The small book of Rossi drawings edited by Paolo Portoghesi, Michele Tadini, and Massimo Scheurer, *Aldo Rossi: The Sketchbooks 1990–1997*, includes short essays by some of the men who worked in his office in which they describe his attention to materials and details, his visits to construction sites, his concern for staying on budget, and most of the issues raised by critics unaware of how the office operated.

3. European Commission, *Report from the Commission to the Council and the European Parliament: EU Anti-Corruption Report*, 3 February 2014, Com (2014) 38 Final, Annex 112, Allegato sull'Italia, 4–5.

4. Seixas Lopes, *Melancholy and Architecture*, 182ff.

5. Lampariello, *Aldo Rossi e le forme del razionalismo esaltato*; Mary Louise Lobsinger, "Antinomies of Realism in Postwar Italian Architecture," PhD diss., Harvard University, 2003.

6. Michael Graves and I shared a session at the conference on a range of issues surrounding international practice in architecture.

7. Rem Koolhaas, "Architecture and globalization," in William S. Saunders, ed., *Reflections on Architectural Practice in the Nineties* (New York: Princeton Architectural Press, 1996), 235–36.

8. Manfredo Tafuri, "Ceci n'est pas une ville," *Lotus International* 13 (December 1976): 10–13.

9. Manfredo Tafuri, "L'architecture dans le boudoir," in Manfredo Tafuri, *The Sphere and the Labyrinth: Avant-Gardes and Architecture from Piranesi to the 1970s*, trans. Pellegrino d'Acierno and Robert Connolly (Cambridge, Mass.: MIT Press, 1987), 280.

10. Manfredo Tafuri, *History of Italian Architecture, 1944–1985*, trans. Jessica Levine (Cambridge, Mass.: MIT Press, 1989), 135.

11. K. Michael Hays, *Architecture's Desire: Reading the Late Avant-Garde* (Cambridge, Mass.: MIT Press, 2009), 43.

12. Among the many publications by this group along the same lines, Peter Eisenman, "The House of the Dead as the City of Survival," in Rossi et al., *Aldo Rossi in America*, 4–9; Francesco Dal Co, "Ora questo è perduto: Il Teatro del Mondo di Aldo Rossi alla Biennale di Venezia," *Lotus* 25 (1979): 66–74; Manfredo Tafuri, "L'Éphémère est éternel: Aldo Rossi a Venezia," *Domus* 602 (1980): 7–11. For a recent study of Tafuri, see Marco Biraghi, *Project of Crisis: Manfredo Tafuri and Contemporary Architecture* (Cambridge, Mass.: MIT Press, 2013), originally published in Italian as *Progetto di crisi: Manfredo Tafuri e l'architettura*

13. Francesco Dal Co, "Criticism and Design," *Oppositions* 13 (Summer 1978): 10.
14. Anthony Vidler, "Commentary," *Oppositions* 13 (Summer 1978): 171–75.
15. Massimo Cacciari, "The Dialectics of the Negative and the Metropolis," in Cacciari, *Architecture and Nihilism: On the Philosophy of Modern Architecture* (New Haven: Yale University Press, 1993), 1–96.
16. Manfredo Tafuri, *Architecture and Utopia: Design and Capitalist Development*, trans. Barbara La Penta (Cambridge, Mass.: MIT Press, 1976); Tafuri, *The Sphere and the Labyrinth*.
17. K. Michael Hays, "Critical Architecture: Between Culture and Form," *Perspecta* 21 (1984): 14–29; see also his lecture at Rice University, "Toward an Ontology of the Post-Contemporary, or, Ruminations on Autonomy, Criticality, and What Do We Do Now?" 23 August 2012, https://www.youtube.com/watch?v=hrse2s-2jNw, accessed 13 July 2018. George Baird recounted the story of criticality and post-criticality in "Criticality and Its Discontents," *Harvard Design Magazine* (Fall 2004/Winter 2005), 16–21.
18. Rossi sent the drawing to Tafuri following the latter's publication of his essay "Progetto e utopia," not to concur with Tafuri's conclusions but as a graphic image of what Tafuri's implacable conclusions meant for architecture.
19. Rossi, *Scientific Autobiography*, 23.
20. "Rossi simulava cinismo ma di suo era di una purezza cristallina." Cantàfora, interviewed by Nicolò Ornaghi and Francesco Zorzi, in "Milano 1979–1997: La progettazione negli anni della merce," PhD diss., Milan Polytechnic, 2015, 237.
21. Carl G. Jung to Sigmund Freud, 2 March 1910, in *The Freud/Jung Letters: The Correspondence Between Sigmund Freud and C. G. Jung*, ed. William McGuire, trans. Ralph Manheim and R. F. C. Hull (London: Penguin Twentieth Century Classics, 1991), 160.
22. Aldo Rossi, "An Analogical Architecture," in Kate Nesbitt, ed., *Theorizing a New Agenda for Architecture* (New York: Princeton Architectural Press, 1996), 345–54, 349; English trans. David Stewart in *Architecture and Urbanism* 56 (May 1976): 74–76.
23. Ronald Schleifer, *Analogical Thinking: Post-Enlightenment Understanding in Language, Collaboration and Interpretation* (Ann Arbor: University of Michigan Press, 2000), 15–25; Barbara Maria Stafford, *Visual Analogy: Consciousness as the Art of Connecting* (Cambridge, Mass.: MIT Press, 1999).
24. Rossi, *Scientific Autobiography*, 67.
25. Ekaterina Karpova Fasce, "Gli architetti italiani a Mosca nei secoli XV–XVI," *Quaderni di Scienza della Conservazione* 4 (2004): 157–81. These and other architects arrived in Russia with experience as architects and engineers in Italy. The Milanese architect Solari, for example, had long experience with the Duomo and the Ospedale Maggiore in Milan and the Certosa in Pavia, among many other projects.
26. Horst Auerbach, *The Lighthouses at Cape Arkona* (Berlin: Kai Homilius Verlag, 2002). There is some dispute about Schinkel's authorship of the design, but the smaller of the two lighthouses dating to 1828 is usually attributed to him.
27. Rossi, *Scientific Autobiography*, 67.
28. "L'immaginazione e la fantasia non possono nascere che dalla conoscenza del reale e questa conoscenza richiede una notevole fissità sulle cose che osserviamo finché dallo interno nascono altre direzioni di sviluppo." Rossi, *QA*, Book 3, 11 January 1970.
29. Walter Benjamin with Asja Lacis, "Naples," in Walter Benjamin, *Reflections: Essays, Aphorisms, Autobiographical Writings*, trans. Edmund Jephcott (New York: Harcourt Brace Jovanovich, 1978), 165–66.
30. Ibid., 167.
31. Pier Vittorio Aureli, *The Project of Autonomy. Politics and Architecture Within and Against Capitalism* (New York: Princeton Architectural Press, 2008), 53–69.
32. Adam Caruso, "Whatever Happened to Analogue Architecture?" *AA Files* 59 (2009): 74–75.
33. Aldo Rossi, "La città analoga: Tavola/The Analogous City: Table," *Lotus International* 13 (December 1976): 4–7.
34. Mazzotta, "L'autobiografia scientifica di Aldo Rossi," 38–39.
35. Rossi, *Scientific Autobiography*, 23.
36. Rossi quoted this passage probably from Benjamin's *A Berlin Childhood*, although he did not so specify.

37. Rossi, *Scientific Autobiography*, 19.
38. Giambattista Vico, *The New Science of Giambattista Vico: Unabridged Translation of the Third Edition (1744) with the Addition of "Practice of the New Science,"* trans. Thomas Goddard Bergin and Max Harold Fisch (Ithaca, N.Y.: Cornell University Press, 1984), Book II, sec. I, ch. 1, 116. Vico's works have been published in Italian as *Opere di Giambattista Vico*, ed. Fausto Nicolini (Bari: Laterza, 1911–41). The best study of Vico's thought is Giuseppe Mazzotta, *The New Map of the World: The Poetic Philosophy of Giambattista Vico* (Princeton: Princeton University Press, 1999).
39. Francesco Dal Co, "1945–1985: Italian Architecture Between Innovation and Tradition," *A+U: Italian Architecture, 1945–1985* (March 1988, special ed.), 21.
40. Manfredo Tafuri, *Architettura italiana, 1944–1981* (Turin: Einaudi, 1982), on Rossi 148–53; 151.
41. Gail Levin, *Edward Hopper: An Intimate Biography* (Berkeley: University of California Press, 1998), 266.
42. St. Teresa of Avila, *The Interior Castle, or The Mansions*, trans. Kieran Kavanaugh, O.C.D., and Otilio Rodriguez, O.C.D. (Mahwah, N.J.: Paulist, 1979); St. Teresa of Avila, *The Way of Perfection*, ed. and trans. E. Allison Peers (New York: Image, 1964); St. John of the Cross, *The Collected Works of Saint John of the Cross*, trans. Kieran Kavanaugh, O.C.D., and Otilio Rodriguez, O.C.D. (Washington, D.C.: ICS, 1991).
43. Rossi, "Architettura per i musei," in *Scritti scelti*, 308.
44. I am deeply grateful to Herbert Lindenberger for introducing me to Wordsworth's spots of time as a graduate student. Lindenberger, *On Wordsworth's Prelude* (Princeton: Princeton University Press, 1963).
45. "Ma il concetto della ripetizione in condizioni differenti produce profondi cambiamenti o sovvertimenti dell'ordine stesso che lo presiede." Rossi, *QA*, Book 23, 27 November–15 December 1978; Rossi here specifically mentioned church interiors in Brazil.
46. Mazzotta, "L'autobiografia scientifica di Aldo Rossi," 39.
47. Jesse Reiser spent the summer of 1979 in Rossi's Milan studio producing just such drawings of the Modena cemetery, starting with a previous drawing provided by Rossi and applying the bright, glowing colors. "Jesse Reiser on Aldo Rossi," *Drawing Matter—Sets—Drawings of the Week*, 30 September 2017, https://www.drawingmatter.org/sets/drawing-week/jesse-reiser-aldo-rossi/, accessed 10 October 2017; thanks to Jacopo Costanzo for drawing my attention to this essay and to Reiser for discussing it with me.
48. Francesco da Mosto, "Aldo Rossi," unpublished presentation, Borgoricco, conference titled *Borgoricco: Il municipio e il centro civico*, 6 December 2014.
49. Ministero dell'Educazione Nazionale, Pagella Scholastica, Collegio Alessandro Volta, Anno Scolastico 1943–44 (Fondazione Aldo Rossi, Milan); also in Lampariello, *Aldo Rossi e le forme del razionalismo esaltato*, 15–16.
50. "Allo studio porta una mente aperta che facilmente assimila e conserva … per la sua squisita sensibilità si commuove facilmente dinnanzi alle cose belle … qualche volta si lascia portare lontano dalla fantasia e questo nuoce un po' alla sua riflessività" (24 May 1944), ibid.
51. Rossi, *QA*, Book 22, 17 July 1977; Book 31, 2–5 December 1985.
52. "Il percorso che univa Somasca al Sacro Monte è per me la base di ogni architettura (sviluppo rettilineo, ecc.). Più tardi ho constatato questi elementi nel tempio Greco." Rossi, "Note autobiografiche sulla formazione, ecc., 1971," in ARP; see Ferlenga, *Rossi: Life and Works*, 9.
53. Carlo Borromeo, *Instructionum fabricae et supellectilis ecclesiasticae, 1577*, trans. Evelyn Carol Voelker, Book I, 1981; Book II, 2008; http://evelynvoelker.com, accessed 13 August 2017. For a combined Latin/Italian edition, see *Instructionum fabricae et supellectilis ecclesiasticae: Libri II. Caroli Borromei (1577)*, ed. Stefano della Torre and Massimo Marinelli, trans. Massimo Marinelli (Vatican City: Libreria Editrice Vaticana/Axios Group, 2000).
54. Rossi, *QA*, Book 42, 22 September 1990.
55. Jonathan Roberts, "Wordsworth on Religious Experience," in Richard Gravil and Daniel Robinson, eds., *The Oxford Handbook of William Wordsworth* (Oxford: Oxford University Press, 2015); see also Patrick Hutton, *History as an Art of Memory* (Hanover, N.H.: University of Vermont Press, 1993); Philip Fisher, *Wonder, the Rainbow, and the Aesthetics of Rare Experiences* (Cambridge, Mass.: Harvard University Press, 1998), 40–42.

56. "Sapete già che chi non cresce decresce. Ritengo impossibile che l'amore si contenti di rimanere in uno stato." Rossi, *QA*, Book 44, 7 January 1991.
57. Douglas Spencer, *The Architecture of Neoliberalism: How Contemporary Architecture Became an Instrument of Control and Compliance* (London: Bloomsbury, 2016).
58. William Shakespeare, Sonnet 12, in *Shakespeare's Sonnets: Never Before Imprinted* (London: Thomas Thorpe, 1609), 10.
59. Alfonso Maria de' Liguori, *Apparecchio alla morte: Cioè considerazioni sulle massime eterne. Utili a tutti per meditare, ed a' sacerdoti per predicare* (Milan: San Paolo, 2011).
60. Francesco Petrarca, Canzone XLII, *Le rime di M. Francesco Petrarca: Canzoniere (Rerum vulgarium fragmenta), Trionfi e Altre composizioni* (Venice: Presso Giuseppe Bortoli, 1739), 226. The last, unpublished notebook ended in May 1997 with reflections on the phrase "la morte è contagioso" (death is contagious), which Rossi could not remember whether he had heard elsewhere or thought of himself. He ended his brief reflections with two juxtaposed quotes: "But how can death be contagious?" and "The best lack all conviction, while the worst are full of passionate intensity." August 1996–December 1997, MAXXI, Rossi.
61. "È strano ma giusto come in un giorno quieto ci tornano alla mente i primi insegnamenti / eppure questo non appartiene alla malinconia, direi anzi che è un ritorno alla vita, un ritrovare sé stessi e una maggiore chiarezza del significato. Non dico il significato della vita, ma il significato in senso generale / di noi stessi, delle relazioni, dello stesso lavoro." Rossi, *QA*, Book 44, 13 March 1991.
62. Antonio Monestiroli, "Forme realiste e popolari," in Posocco et al., *"Care architetture,"* 63–67; Monestiroli, *Il mondo di Aldo Rossi*, 15.

# CHRONOLOGY OF WORK BY ROSSI

1959
Project for a cultural center and theater in Milan (thesis project, Milan Polytechnic)

1960
Competition for the reorganization of the Via Farini area in Milan, with Gian Ugo Polesello and Francesco Tentori

Villa ai Ronchi, Versilia, with Leonardo Ferrari

1961
Competition for the Peugeot skyscraper in Buenos Aires, Argentina, with Vico Magistretti and Gian Ugo Polesello

1962
Competition for the Monument to the Resistance in Cuneo, with Luca Meda and Gian Ugo Polesello

Project for a country club in Fagagna, with Gian Ugo Polesello

Exhibition design for the Museum of Contemporary History, Milan, with Matilde Baffa, Luca Meda, and Ugo Rivolta

Project for the Directional Center of Turin, with Gian Ugo Polesello and Luca Meda

Project for the Peter Pan School in Monza, with Luca Meda

Project for a monumental fountain in Milan, with Luca Meda

Project for a school in the area of the Villa Reale Park in Monza, with Giampietro Gavazzeni and Giorgio Grassi

Project for housing and a school in Caleppio

1964
Bridge and organization of the park for the XII Milan Triennale, with Luca Meda

Competition for a sports and recreation complex in Abbiategrasso

Competition for the new Paganini Theater and reorganization of Piazza della Pilotta, Parma, with Luca Meda

1965
Project for a monumental fountain in Feltre, Belluno

Project for piazza and Monument to Partisans, Segrate

Master Plan for Broni

Project for a residential quarter in Naples, with Giorgio Grassi

1966
Regional plan for the Veneto, under the direction of Giuseppe Samonà

Master Plan for the Certosa of Pavia

Competition for the residential quarter of San Rocco, Monza, with Giorgio Grassi

1967
Competition for the organization of the central area of San Nazzaro de'Bergundi

1968
Competition for the town hall of Scandicci, with Massimo Fortis and Massimo Scolari

San Sabba Middle School, Trieste, with Renzo Agosto, Giorgio Grassi, and Francesco Tentori

1969
Restoration and addition to the De Amicis School in Broni

Monte Amiato housing complex, Gallaratese, Milan

1971
Modena Cemetery (San Cataldo Cemetery), Modena, with Gianni Braghieri

Salvatore Orrú Elementary School, Fagnano Olona

1972
Competition for the town hall of Muggiò, with Gianni Braghieri

1973
Housing in Broni, with Gianni Braghieri

Exhibition design for the international architecture section for the XV Triennale of Milan, with Gianni Braghieri and Franco Raggi

Project for a villa with a pavilion in the woods, Borgo Ticino, with Gianni Braghieri

Master Plan for the town of Fagnano Olona

1974
Project for a bridge and restoration of the castle in Bellinzona, Switzerland, with Gianni Braghieri, Bruno Reichlin, and Fabio Reinhart

Competition for a regional administration building in Trieste, with Max Brosshard, Gianni Braghieri

Competition for student housing in Trieste, with Max Brosshard, Gianni Braghieri, and Arduino Cantàfora

Project for single family housing in Robbiate, with Gianni Braghieri

1975
Project for the restoration of the Corral de Conde area in Seville, Spain

Competition for housing in Setúbal, Portugal, with Gianni Braghieri, Max Bosshard, Arduino Cantàfora, Jose Charters, and Jose Da Nobrega

1976
Competition entry for student housing, Chieti, with Gianni Braghieri and Arduino Cantàfora

Project for a single-family house in Bracchio, with Gianni Braghieri

Project for housing on the Verbindungskanal in Berlin, with Eraldo Consolascio, Bruno Reichlin, and Fabio Reinhart

"La città analoga" (The Analogous City), collage for the Venice Biennale, with Eraldo Consolascio, Bruno Reichlin, and Fabio Reinhart

Project for "Roma interrotta," Rome, with Max Bosshard, Gianni Braghieri, Arduino Cantàfora, and Paul Katzberger

1977
Competition for the Directional Center of Florence, with Carlo Aymonino and Gianni Braghieri

Housing in Mozzo, with Attilio Pizzigoni

1978
Little Scientific Theater, with Gianni Braghieri and Roberto Freno

1979
Project for single-family houses at Zandobbio, with Attilio Pizzigoni

Competition for the Landesbibliothek in Karlsruhe, Germany, with Gianni Braghieri, C. Herdel, and Christopher Stead

Single-family houses in Goito, with Gianni Braghieri

Single-family houses in Pegognaga, with Gianni Braghieri

Project for a tower in Pesaro's new civic center

Sofa design for Capitolo, with Luca Meda

Teatro del Mondo, Venice Architecture Biennale

Broni Middle School, with Gianni Braghieri

1980
Project for Cannaregio west, Venice, with Giulio Dubbini, Aldo De Poli, and Marino Narpozzi

Entrance Gate for the Venice Architecture Biennale

Project for an area in the ghetto of Pesaro, with Gianni Braghieri

Tea service design for Alessi

Molteni funerary chapel in Guissano, with Christopher Stead

1981
Competition for the Klösterliareal in Bern, Switzerland, with Gianni Braghieri and Christopher Stead

Project for a villa in the country near Rome, with Christopher Stead

Exhibition design for the Architettura—Idea exhibit, XVI Milan Triennale, with Luca Meda

Residential complex for the Southern Friedrichstadt in Berlin, with Gianni Braghieri, Jay Johnson, and Christopher Stead; final project with Reinhold Ehlers, Dietmar Grötzebach, Gunter Plessow, and Massimo Scheurer

1982
Competition for the port district Kop van Zuid in Rotterdam, Netherlands, with Gianni Braghieri and Fabio Reinhart

Project for a tower in Melbourne, Australia, with Gianni Braghieri

"Interior with theater," Alcantara, with Luca Meda

Project for the Fiera-Catena area, Mantua, with Gianni Braghieri

Santini and Dominici Store in Latina, with Gianni Braghieri

Exhibition design for the Santini and Dominici booth at the Bologna Fair, with Gianni Braghieri

Project for the restoration of the Zitelle complex in Venice, with Gabriele Geronzi

Project for the new Congress Hall (Varesino area), Milan, with Morris Adjmi and Gabriele Geronzi

Teatro chair and sofa design for Molteni

Cabins of Elba design for Bruno Longoni

Regional offices and Centro Direzionale, theater, and fountain, Fontivegge, Perugia, with Gianni Braghieri, Gabriele Geronzi, Massimo Scheurer, and Giovanni da Pozzo

1983
Project for house and shop in Viadana, with Gianni Braghieri

"Macchina Modenese" exhibit, Modena

Credenza design for Bruno Longoni

AR2 chair and table design for Bruno Longoni

Project for new terminal at San Cristoforo Station, Milan, with Gianni Braghieri, Miguel Oks, and Massimo Scheurer

Project for residential complex for the Forellenweg area, Salzburg, Austria, with Gianni Braghieri and Massimo Scheurer

House in Rauchstrasse, Berlin Tiergarten, with Gianni Braghieri and Christopher Stead

Town Hall, Borgoricco, with Massimo Scheurer and Marino Zancanella

Reconstruction of the Carlo Felice Theater, Genoa, with Ignazio Gardella, Fabio Reinhart, and Angelo Sibilla

1984
Competition for an office building, Buenos Aires, Argentina, with Gianni Braghieri, Gianmarco Miguel Oks, and Massimo Scheurer

Coffeepot design La Conica for Alessi

Exhibition design for "Pitti-uomo," Florence

Project for a civic center at Pep Farnesina in Piacenza, with Gianni Braghieri and Massimo Scheurer

Office building for GFT, Casa Aurora, in Turin, with Gianni Braghieri, Gianmarco Ciocca, Franco Marchesotti, Massimo Scheurer, Miguel Oks, and Luigi Uva

1985
Project for Piazza Santa Giustina in Affori, with Gianni Braghieri, Massimo Scheurer, Gianmarco Ciocca, and Giovanni da Pozzo

Competition for the restruction of Campo di Marte, Giudecca, Venice, with Gianni Braghieri, Gianmarco Ciocca, Massimo Scheurer, and Giovanni da Pozzo

Exhibition design for the Venice Architecture Biennale, The Venice Project, with Mauro Lena and Luca Meda

Project for hotel and congress hall, Nîmes, France, with Christian Züber

Rilievo table design for Up & Up

Papyro desk design for Molteni

Restoration project for the Villa Cusani-Confalonieri in Carate Brianza, with Gianni Braghieri, Massimo Scheurer, and Giovanni da Pozzo

Design for an exhibition booth, GFT in Florence, with Gianni Braghieri

Centro Torri shopping mall, Parma, with Gianni Braghieri, Marco Baracco, Paolo Digiuni, and Massimo Scheurer

Residential complex, Vialba zone, Milan, with Gianni Braghieri and Gianmarco Ciocca

1986
Domestic Theater, for The Domestic Project, XVII Milan Triennale, with Massimo Scheurer

Competition for the Bicocca area, Milan, with Andrea Balzani, Carlo Bono, COPRAT, Stefano Fera, Francesco Gatti, Gianni Braghieri, Luca Meda, Massimo Scheurer, Giovanni da Pozzo, Donatella Muraglia, and Christian Züber

Stage set designs for *Madama Butterfly* and *Lucia di Lammermoor,* Rocca Brancoleone, Ravenna, Christian Züber

Project for a tower in the garden of Villa Alessi, Lago d'Orta, with Giovanni da Pozzo

Project for the School of Architecture at the University of Miami, Florida, with Morris Adjmi

Project for the Port in Naples, with Stefano Fera

Teapot, sugar, and creamer Il Conico design for Alessi

Coffeepot Pressofiltro design for Alessi

Carteggio furniture design for Molteni

Exhibition design for Hendrik Petrus Berlage at the Venice Biennale, Villa Farsetti, Santa Maria di Sala

Project for a shopping and residential center, Noale, Venice, with Marino Zancanella

Project for reconstruction and new buildings for the convent of Santa Maria de los Reyes in Seville, Spain, with Giovanni da Pozzo, Stefano Fera, Massimo Scheurer, and Fernando Villanueva

La Villette Housing, Paris, with Christian Züber and Bernard Huet

Tibaldi School in Cantù, with Giovanni da Pozzo

Project for remodeling buildings in Este, Venice, with Morris Adjmi, Massimo Scheurer, and Vincenzo Rizzo

1987
Project for museum in Marburg, Germany, with Massimo Scheurer

Prototype for an IP gas station on the Autostrada dei Fiori, with Francesco Saverio Fera and Elena Cattaneo

Project for a gymnasium in Olginate, Como, with Giovanni da Pozzo

Competition for Piazza Üsküdar, Istanbul, Turkey, with Giovanni da Pozzo, Francesco Saverio Fera, Ivana Invernizzi, Daniele Nava, and Massimo Scheurer

Competition for the former high school, piazza, and Valle della Pietrosa in Lanciano, with Camillo Di Carlo, Rosaldo Bonicalzi, Gianni Braghieri, Concetta Di Virgilio, Matteo Ricci, Massimo Scheurer, and Filippo Spaini

Project for a sports and recreation complex in the Zen Quarter and Fondo Patti, Palermo, with Salvatore Tringali, Rossana La Rosa, Giuseppe Terrana, and Massimo Scheurer

Project for a pedestrian bridge, Dolo, with Marino Zancanella

Il Palazzo Hotel and restaurant, Fukuoka, Japan, with Morris Adjmi, Toyota Horiguchi, and Shigeru Uchida

Triumphal Arch for Galveston, Texas, with Morris Adjmi

1988
Competition project for the German Historical Museum, Berlin, with Giovanni da Pozzo, Francesco Saverio Fera, Ivana Invernizzi, Daniele Nava, and Massimo Scheurer

Reorganization project for the area belonging to the Italian State Railroad, Udine, with Marco Brandolisio and Stefano Fera

Reorganization project for the area belonging to the Italian State Railroad, Trieste, with Marco Brandolisio and Stefano Fera

Project for a tower on the lake, Breda, with Umberto Barbieri

Lighthouses in the port for a temporary exhibition in Rotterdam, Netherlands, with Umberto Barbieri

Project for a residential and office complex in the Slachthuis area, The Hague, Netherlands, with Umberto Barbieri, Massimo Scheurer, and Robbert Schütte

Project for a residence, Campo di Marte, Giudecca, Venice, with Giovanni da Pozzo and Francesco Saverio Fera

Competition for the international laboratory "Subterranean Naples," with Stefano Fera

Project for a Walt Disney Hotel, Paris, with Morris Adjmi

Project for a residential, commercial, and administration complex in Lecco, with Stefano Fera, Giovanni Bertolotto, and Barbara Gambarotta

Office Complex for GFT, Settimo Torinese, with Luca Trazzi

Project for a hospital supply company, Sysran, Russia, with Marco Brandolisio, Giovanni da Pozzo, and Francesco Saverio Fera

Project for Sports Palace, Milan, with Barbara Agostini, Giovanni da Pozzo, Francesco Gatti, and Luca Imberti

Project for a Beer Hall, The Hague, Netherlands, with Umberto Barbieri

Project for the area of Monte Echia, Naples, with Francesco Saverio Fera

Project for the Fair of the Sensa, Venice, in Piazza San Marco, with Massimo Scheurer

Design of the Momento clock for Alessi

Design of the Cupola coffeepot for Alessi

Design of carpets for Sardinia

Lighthouse Theater, Toronto, Canada, with Morris Adjmi

Single-family house in the Poconos, Pennsylvania, with Morris Adjmi

Monument to Sandro Pertini, Via Croce Rossa, Milan, with Francesco Saverio Fera and Morris Adjmi, completed 1990

Centre international d'art et du paysage, CIAP, contemporary art center in Vassivière, Clermont Ferrand, France, with Stefano Fera and Xavier Fabre

Urban monument in Zaandal, Netherlands, with Umberto Barbieri

Reorganization of and addition to the Hotel Duca di Milano, Milan, with Giovanni da Pozzo and Massimo Scheurer

Project for Centro Città commercial center (also known as Uny-Gifu Mall and now as Apita Shopping Center), Nagoya, Japan, with Morris Adjmi, Toyota Horiguchi, and Matteo Remonti

1989
Restaurant and beer hall, Sapporo, Japan, with Morris Adjmi

Project for an art gallery, Fukuoka, Japan, with Morris Adjmi

Pinocchio Yatai, mobile architecture for Japan Design Expo '89 at Nagoya, Japan, with Morris Adjmi

Project for an office building, Linate Montecity, Milan, with Andrea Balzani, Gabriella Saini, Giovanni da Pozzo, Francesco Gatti, and Francesco Saverio Fera

Project for a new public library, Seregno, with Giovanni da Pozzo and Luca Vacchelli

Project for an addition to the cemetery of Rozzano at Ponte Sesto, with Giovanni da Pozzo and Francesco Saverio Fera

Project for the valley of the Isle d'Abeau, with Cecilia Bolognese and Stefano Fera

Project for an office building at airport, Frankfurt, Germany, with Stefano Fera and Luca Trazzi

Parigi chair design for Unifor

Exhibition design for the booth of the Berlin Museums, Sime '90, Grand Palais, Paris, with Massimo Scheurer

Ambiente Showroom, Tokyo, Japan, with Morris Adjmi

Urban plan for the development of the area Cosmopolitan Pisorno at the Marina of Pisa (Tirrenia), with Marco Brandolisio, Massimo Scheurer, and Stefano Fera

University of Castellanza Cesare Cattaneo, with Andrea Balzani, Marco Brandolisio, Luca Imberti, and Francesco Gatti

Project for a Tochi shopping center (now Port Walk Minato), Nagoya, Japan, with Morris Adjmi and Toyota Horiguchi

Remodeling of the Villa Alessi at Suna di Verbania, with Cecilia Bolognesi, Stefano Fera, and Massimo Scheurer; executive project and supervision, Massimo Scheurer and Filippo Piattelli

1990
Project for office buildings, Canary Wharf, Docklands, London, with Cecilia Bolognesi, Ivana Invernizzi, Stefano Fera, and Sofia Meda

Project for a new church at Cascina Bianca, Milan, with Giovanni da Pozzo and Francesco Saverio Fera

Project for a new Congress Hall, Milan (area Portello), with Massimo Scheurer and Luca Trazzi

Project for new residences and administrative offices in the Ex-Sogema area, Città di Castello, with Giovanni da Pozzo, C. Dante, and Daniele Nava

Project for the Ocean Hotel in Chikura, Japan, with Morris Adjmi and Jan Greben

Competition for a UBS administrative building, Lugano, Switzerland, with Massimo Scheurer

Competition for the Palace of Cinema, Lido of Venice, with Giovanni da Pozzo, Francesco Saverio Fera, Luca Meda, and Massimo Scheurer

Project for a GFT office building in Corso Giulio Cesare, Turin, with Marco Brandolisio and Luigi Uva

Competition for Potsdamerplatz and Leipzigerplatz, Berlin, with Massimo Scheurer

Competition for the office building "Le Campanile," Bordeaux, France, with Giovanni da Pozzo, Marc Kocher, and Andrea Leonardi

Residential complex in Via Lorenteggio, Milan, with Daniele Nava and Giovanni da Pozzo

Residential complex in the Cavaliera quarter, Turin (first project) with Cecilia Bolognesi, Stefano Fera, and Luca Vacchelli

Project for a social and health complex in Via Canova, Florence, with Giovanna Galfione and Stefano Fera

Project for the organization of the center of Nantes, France, with Thierry Roze, Aldo de Poli, Marino Narpozzi, and Andrea Leonardi

Studio for the designer Katsumi Asaba in Tokyo, Japan, with Morris Adjmi, Toyota Horiguchi, and Erin Shilliday

Project for the reorganization of public space in the Fiera di Lanciano district, with Camillo di Carlo, S. Di Giuseppe, Stefano Fera, Matteo Ricci, Francesco Saini, Marco Brandolisio, and Carlo Ghezzi

Club House, Cosmopolitan Golf Club, Marina di Pisa (Tirrenia), with Marco Brandolisio and Massimo Scheurer

Bonnefanten Museum, Maastricht, Netherlands, with Umberto Barbieri, Giovanni da Pozzo, and Marc Kocher

1991
Project for the entrance to the Venice Biennale, with Luigi Trazzi

Project for the Sacca della Misericordia, Venice, with Marino Zancanella

Project for the Tower of the Sun, at Chiba City, Tokyo, Japan, with Giovanni da Pozzo, Toyota Horiguchi, Yashimi Kato, and Sofia Meda

Competition for the new Directional Center, Kuala Lumpur, Malaysia, with Morris Adjmi, Luigi Trazzi, and Christopher Stead

Project for low-cost housing, Villa Marchi at Marano di Mira, Venice, with Luigi Trazzi

Competition for the Scottish National Museum, Edinburgh, Scotland, with Christopher Stread

Competition for building in Friedrichstrasse, Berlin, with Marc Kocher

Housing and commercial buildings in Cassano Magnago, with Marco Brandolisio and Michele Tadini

Office building, new headquarters for Eurodisney, Paris, with Morris Adjmi and Christopher Stead

Project for the South Bronx Academy of Art, New York, with Morris Adjmi

Project for reorganizing the Garibaldi-Repubblica area in Milan, with Andrea Balzani, Carlo Bono, Giovanni da Pozzo, Luca Imberti, Giuseppe Longhi, Sofia Meda, Gabriella Saini, Massimo Scheurer, and Virgilio Vercelloni

Project for the new Polytechnic of Bari, with Massimo Scheurer

Organization of the station and plaza in Gifu, Japan, with Toyota Horiguchi and Marc Kocher

Project for a hotel in Nara, Japan, with Marco Brandolisio and Toyota Horiguchi

Housing project in Corso Vercelli in Turin, with Luigi Trazzi

La Cubica pan design for Alessi

Consiglio table design for Unifor

Providence sofa design for Molteni

Normandie credenza design for Molteni

Exhibition design for the XVIII Milan Triennale, with Luca Meda and Massimo Scheurer

Addition to Linate International Airport, Milan, with Marco Brandolisio, Giovanni da Pozzo, Marc Kocher, and Virgilio Vercelloni

Project for the residential center Barialto in Bari, with Marco Brandolisio and Michele Tadini

Office complex for Walt Disney in Orlando, Florida, with Morris Adjmi

1992
Residential and commercial project in Terni, with Marco Brandolisio

Project for an administrative complex in Rome, with Giovanni da Pozzo and Michele Tadini

Stage and costume design for *Electra* in Taormina, with Marc Kocher

Service center and offices in the techno-industrial park in Genova Campi, with Massimo Scheurer, Stefano Sibilla, and Marco Broglia

Administration complex and organization of old hospital in Hasselt, Belgium, with A. De Gregorio, A. Leonardi, and Sergio Gianoli

Competition for the new Italian embassy in Washington, D.C., with Giovanni da Pozzo, Marco Brandolisio, Michele Tadini, and Sofia Meda

Project for Whitehall Ferry Terminal, New York, with Morris Adjmi, Michele Tadini, and Wes Wolfe

Hotel complex in Teramo, Pescara, with Luigi Trazzi

Office and residential complex in Corso Garibaldi, with Studio tecnico Bianchi, Giovanni Da Pozzo, Michele Tadini, and Sofia Meda

Metrica chair design for Arte, with Giovanni Da Pozzo

Lux Lamp design for Alessi

Project for an office building in Landsberger Allee, Berlin, with Giovanni Da Pozzo, Marc Kocher, Filippo Piattelli, and Michele Tadini

Maritime Museum in Vigo, Galicia, Spain, with César Portela and Marco Brandolisio

Residence and office complex, Schützenstraße Quarter, Berlin, with Massimo Scheurer, Marc Kocher, Marco Broglia, Sergio Gianoli, and Elisabetta Pincherle

1993
Competition for Olimpia, structures for Mediterranean games, Bari, with Marco Brandolisio and Michele Tadini

Office building, Baricentro, Bari, with Marco Brandolisio

Tourist village, Castellaneta Mare, Taranto, with Giovanni Da Pozzo, Marco Brandolisio, and Michele Tadini

Exhibition design, Asso ceramics, Miami, Florida, with Morris Adjmi, Lisa Mahar, and Joshua Davis

Il Faro dining set for Rosenthal

Project for plazas in Barialto, Bari, with Carlo Aymonino, Guido Canella, and Marco Brandolisio

Office building, Coca-Cola Company, Mexico City, with Morris Adjmi, Michele Tadini, Wes Wolfe, and Joshua Davis

Transformation of the former tobacco manufacturing plant into exhibition and office space, Bologna, with Giovanni da Pozzo, Sofia Meda, and Michele Tadini

Stage sets for *Raimonda*, at the Zurich Opera House, with Marc Kocher

Project for a tourist complex in Kyongju, Korea, with Morris Adjmi, Michele Tadini, David Kang, and Joshua Davis

Terraced housing, Barialto, Bari, with Marco Brandolisio

Project for Club House, Golf Club, Barialto, Bari, with Marco Brandolisio

Proposal for the port of Marseilles, France, with Xavier Fabre, Giovanni Da Pozzo, Massimo Scheurer, Akim Bara, and Sergio Gianoli

Competition for the Landesberger Allee in Berlin, with Marc Kocher and Giovanni Da Pozzo

Mojiko Hotel and commercial complex in the port of Moji, Japan, with Morris Adjmi, Toyota Horiguchi, Wes Wolfe, Joshua Davis, Filippo Piattelli, and Michele Tadini

Project for the market square, Pallanza, Verbania, with Giovanni Da Pozzo and Michele Tadini

Mobile Fiorentino closet design for Bruno Longoni

Technological Park, Lago Maggiore, Fondo Toce, with Giovanni Da Pozzo and Michele Tadini; project supervisor, Edoardo Guenzani

1994
Competition for the Frankfurt Theater on the Oder, Germany, with Giovanni Da Pozzo, M. Pisano, Michele Tadini, Marc Kocher, and M. Valle Engineering

Competition for the reorganization of the Beirut Souk, Lebanon, with Marco Brandolisio, Massimo Scheurer, and Linea 3 Engineering

Competition for a mediatech in Strasbourg, France, with Marco Brandolisio and Stefano Sibilla

Residential complex, Gerona, Spain, with Marco Brandolisio, Giovanni Da Pozzo, and Joana Bover

Walt Disney offices, Los Angeles, California, with Morris Adjmi

Competition for the Belgacom Offices in Hasselt, Belgium, with Giovanni Da Pozzo, Marco Brandolisio, and A. De Gregorio

Office tower for Mexico City, with Morris Adjmi, Michele Tadini, and Joshua Davis

Octagonal coffeepot design

Scholastic Office Building on Broadway, New York, with Morris Adjmi, Wes Wolf, and Patrick Han

Newport Coast Resort, Newport Beach, California, with Morris Adjmi, Wes Wolfe, and Joshua Davis

1995
Control Tower, Stockholm airport, Sweden, with Giovanni Da Pozzo and Michele Tadini

Project for the new town hall of San Giovanni Valdarno, with Massimo Scheurer and Filippo Piattelli

Commercial offices on Leipzigerplatz and Leipzigerstrasse, Berlin, with Giovanni Da Pozzo, Massimo Scheurer, Michele Tadini, Marc Kocher, and Marco Brandolisio

Project for the "Corte del Chiodo" in Garbagnate Milanese (second phase), Milan, with Marco Brandolisio and Giovanni Da Pozzo

Project for a hospital in La Spezia, with Massimo Scheurer and Filippo Piattelli

Project for the new Milan Polytechnic, Bovisa, Milan, with Marco Brandolisio, Giovanni Da Pozzo, and Michele Tadini

Project for the reuse of the Italtel buildings at San Siro, Milan, with Marco Brandolisio, Giovanni Da Pozzo, and Michele Tadini

Project for a hotel, school and theater at Poggio Rusco, with Marco Brandolisio and Michele Tadini

Project for the reuse of the ex-Kursaal, Montecatini, with Luigi Trazzi and Marco Brandolisio

Project for the Leitzipolis shopping center, Zurich, with Giovanni Da Pozzo, Marc Kocher, and Michele Tadini

Cartesio furniture design for Unifor

Project for the IACP district in Mira, with Luigi Trazzi and Giovanni Da Pozzo

Kolonihavehus in Copenhagen, Denmark, with Michele Tadini

Competition for Pariserplatz, Berlin, with Massimo Scheurer, Elisabetta Pincherle, Marco Broglia, and Patrizia Ronchi

Single-family house, Seaside, Florida, with Morris Adjmi, Keith Scott, and Harry Gutfreund

1996
Project for the Kaliningrad airport, Russia, with Michele Tadini and Edoardo Guenzani

Project for a residential complex in Urgnano, with Michele Tadini

Project for a residential district, Ca' di Cozzi complex, Ponte Crencano, Verona, with Luigi Trazzi

Verona Fair, new exhibition pavilion and reorganization of the piazza, Verona, with Giovanni Da Pozzo, Marco Brandolisio, and Michele Tadini

Lario double bed design for Bruno Longoni, with Michele Tadini

Prometheus Lamp design for Artemide, with Michele Tadini

Segreto closet design for Molteni, with Michele Tadini

Passo Groste refuge at Madonna di Campiglio, with Michele Tadini and Edoardo Guenzani

Neuruppin Tourist forum masterplan, Neuruppin, Germany, with Fabio Reinhart, Marc Kocher, and Massimo Scheurer

Competition for an office building in Hauptbahnhof Spree Ufer, Berlin, with Massimo Scheurer, Marc Kocher, and Filippo Piattelli

Competition for "A Piazza for Foro Italico," Rome, with Giovanni Da Pozzo, Michele Tadini, and Marc Kocher

Terranova Shopping Center, in Olbia, with Michele Tadini and ARP Studio-Oristano

1997
Competition for the rebuilding of La Fenice Theater, Venice, with Giovanni Da Pozzo, Massimo Scheurer, Edoardo Guenzani, Francesco Da Mosto, and Marco Brandolisio

Library and new civic center in Castiglione Olona, with Marco Brandolisio and Giovanni Da Pozzo

Third section of the Technopark, Fondo Toce, with Giovanni Da Pozzo and Michele Tadini

Competition for the Cathedral of Santa Maria del Fiore, Florence, with Marc Kocher, Filippo Piattelli, and sculptor B. Fresu

Competition for the expansion of the National History and Art Museum, Luxembourg, with J. Herr, Massimo Scheurer, and Filippo Piattelli

Kleines Haus, prefabricated house, Düsseldorf, Germany, with Massimo Scheurer and Christian Urban

Executive project for the interiors of a boarding house, Numbers 3 to 8, Schützenstraße, Berlin, with Massimo Scheurer, Cecilia Anselmi, and Elisabetta Pincherle

Competition for the Museum of the City of Leipzig, Germany, with Marco Brandolisio, Giovanni Da Pozzo, and Michele Tadini

# BIBLIOGRAPHY

SELECTED WRITINGS BY ALDO ROSSI

*The Architecture of the City.* Trans. Diane Ghirardo and Joan Ockman. Cambridge, Mass.: MIT Press, 1982.

*L'architettura della città.* Padua: Marsilio, 1966.

*Architetture padane.* Modena: Panini, 1984.

"Introduzione a Boullée." In Étienne-Louis Boullée, *Architettura: Saggio sull'arte*, trans. Aldo Rossi. Padua: Marsilio, 1967; Turin: Einaudi, 2005, 321–37, 7–24.

"Invisible Distances." Trans. Diane Ghirardo. *Via* (1990): 84–89.

*Il libro azzurro i miei progetti—My Projects—Meine Entwurfe—Mes Projets.* Zurich: Jamileh Weber Galerie, 1983.

"Preface: The Architecture of Adolf Loos." In Benedetto Gravagnuolo, *Adolf Loos.* London: Art Data, 1995 [1982], 11–15.

*I Quaderni Azzurri.* Ed. Francesco Dal Co. Los Angeles and Milan: J. Paul Getty Museum and Electa, 2000.

*A Scientific Autobiography.* Trans. Lawrence Venuti. Cambridge, Mass.: MIT Press, 1981.

*Scritti scelti sull'architettura e la città, 1956–1972.* Ed. Rosaldo Bonicalzi. Milan: CLUP, 1975; Macerata: Quodlibet, 2012.

*Tre città / Three Cities: Perugia, Milano, Mantova.* With texts by Bernard Huet and Patrizia Lombardi. Quaderni di Lotus. Milan: Electa, 1984.

With Francesco Moschini. *Aldo Rossi, progetti e disegni, 1962–1979 / Aldo Rossi, Projects and Drawings, 1962–1979.* Milan: Rizzoli, 1979.

With Peter Eisenman and Kenneth Frampton. *Aldo Rossi in America, 1976–1979: March 25 to April 14, 1976, September 10 to October 30, 1979.* Trans. Diane Ghirardo. New York: Institute for Architecture and Urban Studies, 1979.

With Ezio Bonfanti. *Architettura razionale: XV Triennale di Milano.* Milan: Franco Angeli and Triennale di Milano, 1973.

SELECTED BIBLIOGRAPHY

Adjmi, Morris, ed. *Aldo Rossi: Architecture, 1981–1991.* New York: Princeton Architectural Press, 1992.

Adjmi, Morris. *Aldo Rossi: Autobiografia poetica.* Milan: Antonia Jannone, 2014.

Adjmi, Morris, ed. *Aldo Rossi: Drawings and Paintings.* New York: Princeton Architectural Press, 1993.

*Aldo Rossi par Aldo Rossi, architecte: 26 juin–30 septembre 1991. Centre de création industrielle, Centre Georges Pompidou.* Paris: Editions du Centre Pompidou, 1991.

Arnell, Peter, and Ted Bickford, eds. *Aldo Rossi: Buildings and Projects.* New York: Rizzoli, 1991.

Aymonino, Carlo, and Aldo Rossi. *1977: Un progetto per Firenze.* Rome: Officina, 1978.

Bandini, Micha. "Aldo Rossi." *AA Files* 1 (December 1981): 105–11.

Belloni, Francesco, and Rosaldo Bonicalzi, eds. *Aldo Rossi: La scuola di Fagnano Olona e altre storie. Atti della Giornata di Studi* (Fagnano Olona, 28 November 2015). Turin: Accademia University Press, 2017.

Bolognesi, Cecilia. *Aldo Rossi: Luoghi urbani.* Milan: Unicopli, 1999.

Celant, Germano, ed. *Aldo Rossi: Teatri.* Milan: Skira, 2012.

Celant, Germano, and Diane Ghirardo, eds. *Aldo Rossi: Drawings.* Milan: Skira, 2008.

Colonna-Preti, Stefania. *Aldo Rossi*. I protagonisti del design 11. Milan: Hachette, 2011.

Conforti, Claudia. *Il Gallaratese di Aymonino e Rossi, 1969–1972*. Rome: Officina, 1981.

Costantini, Paolo. *Luigi Ghirri—Aldo Rossi: Cose che sono solo se stesse*. Milan: Mondadori Electa, 1996.

De Maio, Fernanda, Alberto Ferlenga, and Patrizia Montini Zimolo, eds. *Aldo Rossi, La storia di un libro: "L'architettura della città" dal 1966 ad oggi*. Padua: Il Poligrafo, 2014.

Dotti, Fernando, ed. *Aldo Rossi: Il municipio di Borgoricco*. Padua: Cleup, 2006.

Ferlenga, Alberto, ed. *Aldo Rossi: Deutsches Historisches Museum, Berlino*. Milan: Mondadori Electa, 1990.

Ferlenga, Alberto, ed. *Aldo Rossi, Opera completa (1959-1987)*. Milan: Electa, 1989.

Ferlenga, Alberto, ed. *Aldo Rossi: Opera completa (1988–1992)*. Milan: Electa, 1997

Ferlenga, Alberto, ed. *Aldo Rossi: Opera completa III, 1993–1996*. Milan: Mondadori Electa, 1997.

Ferlenga, Alberto, ed. *Aldo Rossi: The Life and Works of an Architect*. Trans. Laura Davey. Cologne: Konemann, 2001. Original ed.: Ferlenga, ed., *Aldo Rossi. Tutte le opere*. Milan: Electa, 1999.

Ferlenga, Alberto, Massimo Ferrari, and Claudia Tinazzi, eds. *Aldo Rossi e Milano*. Milan: Solferino, 2013.

Ghirardo, Diane. "The Blue of Aldo Rossi's Sky." *AA Files*, 70 (May 2015): 159–72.

Ghirardo, Diane, ed. *Borgoricco: Il municipio e il centro civico. Aldo Rossi*. Borgoricco: Comune di Borgoricco, 2014.

Ghirardo, Diane. *Italy: Modern Architectures in History*. London: Reaktion, 2013.

Giora, Marilena, and Loris Tasso, eds. *Dal municipio di Aldo Rossi a città rifondata: Borgoricco Analoga*. Borgoricco: Comune di Borgoricco, 2009.

Grasso, Maddalena. "Definizione di 'Autentico Razionalismo' in Aldo Rossi: Dal dibattito sulla tradizione al confronto con Étienne-Louis Boullée." Laurea thesis, Turin Polytechnic, 2012.

Huijts, Stijn, and Germano Celant, eds. *Aldo Rossi: Opera grafica. Incisioni, litografie, serigrafie*. Milan: Silvana, 2015.

Johnson, Eugene J. "What Remains of Man: Aldo Rossi's Modena Cemetery." *Journal of the Society of Architectural Historians* 41, no. 1 (March 1982): 38–54.

La Marche, Jean. *The Familiar and Unfamiliar in Twentieth-Century Architecture*. Urbana: University of Illinois Press, 2003.

Lampariello, Beatrice. *Aldo Rossi e le forme del razionalismo esaltato: Dai progetti scolastici alla "città analoga," 1950–1973*. Macerata: Quodlibet, 2017.

Malacarne, Gino, and Patrizia Montini Zimolo, eds. *Aldo Rossi e Venezia: Il teatro e la città*. Milan: Unicopli, 2002.

Mazzotta, Giuseppe. "L'autobiografia scientifica di Aldo Rossi/The Scientific Autobiography of Aldo Rossi." In Ghirardo, *Borgoricco: Il municipio e il centro civico*, 29–41.

Moneo, Rafael. "Aldo Rossi: The Idea of Architecture and the Modena Cemetery." *Oppositions* 5 (Summer 1976) [*Oppositions Reader*, K. M. Hays, ed., 105–34].

Moneo, Rafael. *Theoretical Anxiety and Design Strategies in the Work of Eight Contemporary Architects*. Cambridge, Mass.: MIT Press, 2004.

Monestiroli, Antonio. *Ernesto Nathan Rogers: L'architettura come esperienza*. Bologna: Ogni uomo è tutti gli uomini, 2009.

Monestiroli, Antonio. *Il mondo di Aldo Rossi*. Bologna: Ogni uomo è tutti gli uomini, 2015.

Monestiroli, Antonio. *Il razionalismo esaltato di Aldo Rossi*. Bologna: Ogni uomo è tutti gli uomini, 2012.

Poletti, Giovanni. *L'autobiografia scientifica di Aldo Rossi: Un'indagine tra scrittura e progetto di architettura*. Milan: Mondadori, 2011.

Portoghesi, Paolo, Michele Tadini, and Massimo Scheurer, eds. *Aldo Rossi: The Sketchbooks 1990–1997*. London: Thames and Hudson, 2000. Originally published as *Aldo Rossi Disegni, 1990–1997*. Milan: Federico Motta, 1999.

Posocco, Pisana, Gemma Radicchio, and Gundula Rakowitz, eds. *"Care Architetture": Scritti su Aldo Rossi*. Turin: Umberto Allemandi, 1999.

Savi, Vittorio. *L'architettura di Aldo Rossi*. Milan: Franco Angeli, 1977.

Savi, Vittorio, ed. *Casa Aurora: Un'opera di Aldo Rossi*. Turin: Gruppo GFT, 1987.

Schmidt, Hans. *Contributi all'architettura, 1924–1964*. Milan: Franco Angeli, 1974.

Sedlmayr, Hans. *Art in Crisis: The Lost Center*. Trans. Brian Battershaw. Abingdon, U.K.: Routledge, 2017. Originally published as *Verlust der Mitte*. Salzburg: O. Miller, 1951.

Seixas Lopes, Diego. *Melancholy and Architecture: On Aldo Rossi*. Zurich: Park, 2015.

Tinazzi, Claudia, ed. *Aldo Rossi e l'idea di abitare.* Novate Milanese: Casa Testori, 2013.

Trentin, Annaluisa, ed. *La lezione di Aldo Rossi.* Bologna: Bononia University Press, 2008.

Vasumi Roveri, Elisabetta. *Aldo Rossi e "L'architettura della città": Genesi e fortuna di un testo.* Turin: Umberto Allemandi, 2010.

Vleck, Treena Marie. "Aldo Rossi: From Modern to Post-Modern Architecture, 1960–1990." PhD diss., University of North Texas, 1990.

Zimolo, Patrizia Montini. *L'architettura del museo: Con scritti di Aldo Rossi.* Turin: CittàStudi, 1995.

# ILLUSTRATION CREDITS

The photographers and the sources of visual material other than the owners indicated in the captions are as follows. Every effort has been made to supply complete and correct credits; if there are errors or omissions, please contact Yale University Press so that corrections can be made in any subsequent edition.

Morris Adjmi: 1.17, 2.1–2.3, 2.13, 2.14, 2.16–2.18, 4.10–4.12, 5.9
Massimo Alberici: 6.18
Arassociati: 5.10–5.12
Archivio Storico della Biennale di Venezia, Giovanni Zucchiati: 1.14
Author: 1.2, 1.3, 1.6, 1.7, 1.13, 2.4, 2.8–2.10, 2.23, 3.2, 3.4, 3.6, 3.7, 3.10–3.12, 3.14, 3.15, 3.18, 4.1, 4.2, 4.7, 4.15–4.17, 4.20–4.22, 5.2, 5.6, 5.17, 5.21, 5.24, 6.1, 6.2, 6.5, 6.6, 6.11–6.17, 7.7, 7.9
Maurizio Beatrici: 5.7
Marino Bortolotti: 1.18–1.20, 3.5, 3.19, 5.3, 5.15, 5.20, 5.22, 7.5
Comune di Borgoricco: 4.14
Mindy Curtis: 5.4
Carmen de Sela: 4.19
Claudio Divizia: 2.4, 3.1
Drawing Matter: 4.4, 7.4
ETH: 1.9
Laura Fantacuzzi: 1.15
Martin Feiersinger: 1.5
Fondazione/Eredi: 1.1, 1.4, 1.11, 2.14, 2.20, 3.9, 3.11, 3.13, 3.17, 3.20, 4.4, 4.6, 4.9, 4.10, 4.13, 5.5, 5.13, 5.15, 5.16, 5.23, 6.3, 6.4, 6.8, 6.9, 6.11, 6.20, 7.3, 7.6, 7.8
Maxime Galati Fourcade: 1.16
Gugerell: 2.10
Heinrich Helfenstein: 1.9
Scott Hortop Travel/Alamy: 4.18
Ben Huser: 5.1

Marco Introini: 2.12, 2.15, 2.19, 6.7
Dimitry Ivanov: 7.1
Ned Matura: 2.13
MAXXI Museo Nazionale delle Arti del XXI Secolo. Collezione MAXXI, Architettura, Aldo Rossi Archive: 1.10, 1.11, 3.3, 3.16, 4.5, 6.3, 6.8–6.10, 7.6
Nacasa & Partners: 2.15
Palladium: 1.15, 2.11, 3.1, 4.8
Private collection: 1.4, 1.18–1.20, 2.19, 2.21, 3.13, 3.15, 3.20, 5.8, 5.15, 5.18, 5.23, 7.5
Jesse Reiser: 7.4
Ruhrputtler: 2.4
Setteo: 5.19
Diego Terna: 6.19
Nina Aldin Thune: 2.6
Federico Torra: 3.8, 3.21, 4.3, 4.9
Paul Warchol: 2.1–2.3
Julie G. Woodhouse/Alamy: 2.7

# INDEX

Illustrations are indicated by page numbers in *italics*. Architectural works by Rossi are found under their geographic location, unless cross-references indicate otherwise.

Aalto, Alvar, 29
Abraham, Raymond, 28, 32
Accademia di San Luca, 21
Acme jewelry, 35, *35*
Adjmi, Morris, 26, *38*, 61, 62
Adorno, Theodor, 200
Agnelli, Gianni, 33
airports, railways, and port facilities, 56–61, *57–60*
   *See also* specific facilities
Alberti, Leon Battista, 96
Albini, Franco, 13
Aleijadinho (sculptor), 146
Aleotti, Giovanni Battista, 139–41, 161
Alessandro Volta College (Lecco), 1, 159, 211
Alessi, 26, 29, *34*, 35, 112
Alfonse, Saint (of Liguori), 186
Ambrose, Saint, 213
ancient Greeks, 35, 49, 81, 92, 95, 131, 138–39, 140, 163–64, 208, 213, 226
ancient Romans, 5, 19, 51, 54, 66, 75, 94, 119, 134, 145
Antonelli, Alessandro, 2, 131
Antonelliana, Mole di, 2
*Architecture: Essai sur l'art* (Boullée), 7–10, 19, 74
   Rossi's translation as *Architettura: Saggio sull'arte*, 7–8, 89–90

*The Architecture of the City*, 3, 5, 7–12, 19, 21, 22, 24, 28, 40–41, 48, 60, 66, 69, 70, 79, 89, 138, 140, 148, 150, 201, 204–5, 215
"Architettura e realismo" (article), 13
"Architettura per i musei" (Architecture for Museums, Rossi essay), 69
*Architettura razionale* (Rational Architecture), 12
Archizoom, 12
Argan, Giulio Carlo, 19
Aristotle, 95
Armani, Giorgio, 77, 78
Arona. *See* San Carlone statue
Art Nouveau, 2
artwork, drawings, sketches, models
   architectural fantasy drawing with San Carlone statue, *178*
   "Architecture in the Blue of the Sky" (1973), *207*
   Bible frontispiece (ca. 1220–30), *152*
   Il Bollitore tea kettle (sketches 1985), *36*
   Borgoricco Town Hall (section, 1983), *120*
   C. Ferrini Middle School, Broni (pen and marker on paper, 1979), *111*
   "La città analoga (collage, mixed media, 1976, with Consolascio, Reichlin, and Reinhart), *18*
   "Ecce Homo," Sacro Monte of Varallo (Enrico polychrome statues and Mazzucchelli frescoes, 1608–16), *159*

*Electra* opera stage setting (lithograph, 1992), *164*
Feltre fountain (sketch, 1965), *76*
La Fenice Theater (model, 1997), *148*
German Historical Museum, Berlin (model, 1988), *124*
Il Gioco dell'Oca (drawing, 1972), *179*
"Jesus Appears Before Pontius Pilate the Second Time," Sacro Monte of Varallo (Enrico polychrome statues, ca. 1639), *160*
"Landscape with Basilica" (ink and watercolor), *196*, *212*
"L'architettura assassinata" (Architecture Assassinated) (lithograph, 1974), *100*
"Milanese Interior with Person Observing the Duomo. With Fog" (lithograph, 1989), *65*
Modena Cemetery (final project drawing, 1973), *169*
Modena Cemetery (photocopy plus added drawing), *177*
Modena Cemetery (presentation drawing, 1971), *169*
Modena Cemetery with reworking by Reiser (sepia ink and gouache, 1979), *210*
Monument to Partisans, Segrate (ink drawing, 1970), *87*
Monument to Pertini with Milan Duomo (photocopy plus ink and felt tip pens), *97*
Monument to the Resistance, Cuneo (Bortolotti project drawing, 1962), *80*

artwork, drawings, sketches, models (continued)
  Paganini Theater and portico, Parma (Bortolotti redrawn plan, 1964), *141*
  Pietà or Deposition (pen and watercolor study), *110*
  project drawing for a building for a class on composition, *206*
  "Roma interrotta" (collage, mixed media), *20*
  St. Rose of Viterbo collage (1978), *194*
  Salvatore Orrù Elementary School, plan, site and massing studies (pen and maker), *109*
  San Carlone (mixed media), *93*
  Scandicci Town Hall competition entry (photocopy plus watercolor, 1968), *118*
  School of Architecture, University of Miami, Florida (pen and ink, 1986), *116*
  South Bronx Academy of Art (1991), 115–16
  South Bronx Academy of Art, New York (ink sketch on mylar), *116*
  South Bronx Academy of Art, New York (section, 1991), *115*
  "Studio di Tappetto Nuragico" (phone card, 1988), 210, *211*
  "Il Teatro" (sketch, 1983) for Little Scientific Theater, *151*
  Theater of the Indies for Expo '92, Seville, Spain (proposal design, 1992), *142*
  Untitled (lithograph, 1989), *7*
  Untitled . . . detail of addition to De Amicis school in Broni (lithograph, 1989), *152*
  Untitled . . . with coffeepot and San Carlone (lithograph, 1989), *2*
  Whitehall Ferry Terminal (watercolor and markers), *59*
  Whitehall Ferry Terminal model (painted plexiglas, wood, brass, 1992), *58*
Ascension, 134
Aschieri, Pietro, 21

Asiago: Sarfatti Monument, 81, *81*, 91
Assumption, 94
Athens
  Acropolis, 92, 138
  Parthenon, 92
A.T.I. Holzman (construction firm), 147–48
Augustine, Saint, 135, 186, 212
  *Confessions*, 174, 215
Aulenti, Gae, 3, 32–33, 147
Aureli, Pier Vittorio, 204–5
avant-gardes, 12, 22–23, 199–200
Averlino, Antonio. *See* Filarete
Aymonino, Carlo, 3, 10, 32, 135, 140

ballet set designs. *See* opera, ballet and theater set designs
baptisteries, 105, 152
  *See also* Parma
Barabino, Carlo, 143
Barbieri, Umberto, 26
baroque, 24, 27, 89, 92, 126, 145–47, 161, 171, 187
Barozzi, Jacopo, 175
Bataille, Georges: *Le bleu du ciel*, 175
Battista da Varano, Saint Camilla, 162
BBPR (Banfi Belgioioso Peresutti and Rogers), *3*, 3–4, 13, 22
Beaux Arts, 8, 59
Behrens, Peter, 16
Benjamin, Walter, 137, 204, 207
Bergson, Henri, 84
Berlage, Hendrik Petrus, 28
Berlin
  AEG building, 16
  Altes Museum, 49, 94, *95*, 125, 127
  German Historical Museum, 46, 123–25, *124*, 127
  IBA residential complex, 26, 46, 48
  Jewish Museum, 82–83
  Landesberger Allee office building, 51
  *Mietkasernen* tenements, 48, 203
  Rauchstraße housing, 46
  Schauspielhaus, 141, 145, *145*
  Schützenstraße Quarter, 35, *46*, 46–50, *48*, *50*, 51, 55, 71, 203
  Verbindungskanal, 46

Bernini, Gianlorenzo, 21, 131
Bevagna town hall, 117
Bible and scriptural citation, 152, *152*
  Acts 3:1, 191
  1 Kings 6:19–20, 190
  Proverbs, 103
  Revelations 21:15–17, 190
Blake, William, 171
"blue of the Madonna," 29, 175, 182
Il Bollitore tea kettle (1985), 35, *36*
Bologna, 12
Bolognini, Mauro, 14
Bonicalzi, Rosaldo, 11
Bonnefanten Museum (Maastricht, Netherlands), 35, 89, *102*, 129–35, *132–33*
Borges, Jorge Luis: "The Aleph," 164–65
Borgoricco
  Museum of the Roman Centuriation, 122
  town hall, 27, 35, 103, 117, 119–22, *120–21*, 173, *173*, 198
Borromeo, Saint Carlo, 78, 91–92, *91–93*, 213–15
Borromini, Francesco, 134
Bortolotti, M., *80*, 141
Bottoni, Piero, 12
Boullée, Étienne-Louis, 42, 107, 111, 153, 173, 179
  *See also* Architecture: Essai sur l'art
Braghieri, Gianni, 26
Breton, André, 88
Broni schools, 11, 89
  De Amicis elementary school, 104, 105, *152*, 153, 198
  C. Ferrini Middle School, 105, 109–14, *111–13*, 198
Brunelleschi, Filippo, 151
Byzantine, 142

Cacciari, Massimo, 147–48, 199–200
Caimi, Bernardino, 159
Calamai, Clara, *15*
Calatrava, Santiago, 56
Canaletto
  *Capriccio: A Palladian Design for the Rialto Bridge with Buildings at Vicenza*, 16, *19*

*Capriccio con edifici Palladiani (Caprice with Palladian Buildings)*, 202
Canella, Guido, 3, 13, 28, 32, 85
Cantàfora, Arduino, 4, 201
  "La città analoga" (The Analogous City), 16–17, *17*, 31–32
Cantù: Tibaldi Middle School, 111–12, 126
de Carlo, Giancarlo, 3, 140
Carteggio desk, *34*
Casa Aurora (GFT building). *See* Turin
*Casabella*, 16
*Casabella-continuità* (periodical), 2–3
Catholicism, Roman, 4, 27, 81, 84, 103–4, 131, 134, 162, 180, 182, 185–95, 198, 211–15
  *See also* Sacri Monti chapels
Ceccarelli, Paolo, 5, 84
Centre international d'art et du paysage (CIAP, Vassivière, France), 127–28, *128*
Chessa, Paolo, 144
Chicago, 8
Chieti student housing, 11, 156
Cistercian Royal Abbey of Santa Maria de Poblet, 111
"La città analoga" (The Analogous City)
  by Cantàfora, 16–17, *17*, 31–32
  by Rossi with Consolascio, Reichlin, and Reinhart, 17–19, *18*, 69–70, 199–201, 205
classicism, 10, 162
coffeepot, 1–2, *2*, 26, 29, 35, *35*, 36, 37, 69, 100, 112, 123, 156, 185, 208, 210
Communism, 4, 9, 25, 32, 187, 188, 201
Como, Lake, 1, 103, 104, 175
La Conica coffeepot, 35, 36–37
Consolascio, Eraldo, 17–19, *18*
consumerism, 35
*Contropiano* (periodical), 16
*Controspazio* (periodical), 16
Cooper Union, 24
Cornell University, 24
Cortona, Pietro da, 21
Costa, Cesare, 167, 170, 172, 177, 181

Council of Trent (1564), 214
Counter Reformation Italy, 162, 214
Crespi, Giovanni Battista, 91, *91*
Cuneo Monument to the Resistance, 9, 73, 76, 79–84, *80*, 89–92, 95, 98, 140

Da Carcano, Aloisio, *202, 203*
Dal Co, Francesco, 199–200, 208
D'Amato, Claudio, 28
da Mosto, Count Francesco, 26, 148, 210–11
Dante Alighieri, 152, 184, 187
  *Commedia*, 25, 207
de Chirico, Giorgio: *Piazze d'Italia* paintings, 88, 89, 90
deconstructivism, 28
*Dedalo* (periodical), 16
d'Enrico, Giovanni, *159–60*
Deposition and Entombment of Jesus, 109, *110*, 134, 170–71, 212, 215
Diocletian, 66
Dionysius Eleuthereus, 138
Directional Centers, 23–24
Disneyland, 82–83
Divine Office, 191–93
*Domus* (periodical), 16
Doric, 69, 92
drawings. *See* artwork, drawings, sketches, models
Dubrovnik bay, 137
Duomo. *See specific cities*
Durkheim, Emile, 84
Dutert, Ferdinand, 45

8 1/2 (film), 14
Einaudi (publisher), 16
Eisenman, Peter, 12, 24, 28, 32, 58, 200
Elba cabins, 17, 35, 36, 69
Eliot, T. S., 180
Engels, Friedrich: *The Condition of the Working Class in England in 1844*, 8
Enlightenment, 135
Essen, Germany
  Krupp Colliery, 45, *45*
ETH Zürich, 15, 17, 205

Fagnano Olona, 104, 117
  Salvatore Orrù Elementary School, 11, 104–11, *105–6, 108–9*, 113, 138, 170–73, 193, 198, 200, 215
Falconi, Bernardo, 91, *91*
fantasy, 14, 145, 178, 204
Il Faro China, 35, *35*
Fascism and Fascist Party (PNF, Partito Nazionale Fascista), 1, 3–4, 13, 74, 79, 81, 85, 87, 118–19
Felice Theater. *See* Genoa
Fellini, Federico, 14
Feltre fountain, 76, *76*
La Fenice Theater. *See* Venice
Ferrari, Gaudenzio, 189
Ferrari, Leonardo, *9*
Filarete (Antonio Averlino)
  Filarete's columns, 25, 45–46, 142, *142*
  Grand Canal palazzo (Venice), 122
  Sforza Castle (Milan), 119
Fiorentino, Mario, 10
Fischer von Erlach, Joseph, 54
Flagg, Ernest, 43, *43*, 45
Florence
  Palazzo Vecchio, 117
  San Giovanni, 105
  Santa Maria del Fiore, 151
Fondotoce Techno Park, 29
Fontana, Carlo, 21
Fontivegge government complex. *See* Perugia
formalism, 13–14, 23
Forster, Kurt W., 82
Fortis, M., *118*
Foucault, Michel, 199
Francis I, 188
Franco Angeli (publisher), 16
Frankfurt Kitchen, 23, 48
Frederick II, 124
Fukuoka, Japan: Il Palazzo Hotel, 35, 55, 60–62, *61*, 128, 145, 199, 203
functionalism, 12, 21

Gabetti, Roberto, 140
Galicia, Spain: Maritime Museum, 129, *130*
Gallaratese housing. *See* Milan
Gangemi (publisher), 16
Gardella, Ignazio, 13, 144
Gehry, Frank, 32

Genoa: Carlo Felice Theater, *143–44*, 143–45, 148, 150, 163, 198
Getty Research Institute, 27
GFT building. *See* Turin
Ghiffa, 29–30, *30–31*, 33
  Sacro Monte of, 159, 161
  Villa Rossi, 29–30, *30–31*
Ghirri, Luigi, 96, 129, 168
Gilardi, Antonio, *202, 203*
Il Gioco dell'Oca, *179*, 179–80, 182, 188, 191
  Portuguese game, *180*
Giordani, Gianluigi, 56
Giuliani, Rudy, 58
Good Friday, 188–89
Gothic, 142, 155
Granada, Spain: Alhambra, 6
Grassi, Giorgio, 26
Grassi, Pietro, 117
Graves, Michael, 12, 23
Grays (avant-garde group), 22–23
Gregory XIII, 21
Gregotti, Vittorio, 3
Grenada: Alhambra, 6
Greppi, Giovanni, *80*, 81, *83*, 91
Griffini, Enrico, 75
Gropius, Walter, 3
Gruppo Finanziario Tessile (GFT) office building. *See* Turin
Guastavino, Rafael, 59
Gucci Communists, 4
Guggenheim Museums (New York and Venice), 129
Guissano funerary chapel, 175, *176*, 198

Hadid, Zaha, 23, 56
Halbwachs, Maurice, 6
  *On Collective Memory* (book), 84, 94–95
Harvard University, 3, 24, 199
Hasselt, Belgium, hospital, 51
Hays, K. Michael, 199–200
Hejduk, John, 12, 24, 32
Hopper, Dennis, 32
Hopper, Edward, 208
Horiguchi, Toyota, 26
hotels, 60–65, *61, 63–65*
  *See also specific hotels*
Houston Galleria, 65
Huxtable, Ada Louise, 173

Impregilo (construction firm), 33
Institute for Architecture and Urban Studies (IAUS), 24
International Style, 3, 13
Ionic, 92, 94
Isola, Aimaro, 140
Italian State Railway, 60
Itard, Jean, 123
Ivan III, 202

Jacobs, Jane: *The Death and Life of Great American Cities*, 22
Japan, 33, 63
  shopping malls, 66, *66*
  *See also* Fukuoka; Moji
Jeanneret, Charles-Édouard. *See* Le Corbusier
Jerome, Saint, 186, 212
Jerome Emiliani, Saint, 92, *94*, 159–61
Jerusalem, 159, 190, 193
Jews and Jewish cemeteries, 82, 170, 177, 181
John, Saint, 190, 191, 193
John of the Cross, Saint, 186, 208, 212
  *The Ascent of Mount Carmel*, 25, 109
Johnson, Eugene, 173, 188
Johnson-Reed Act (1924), 1
Jung, Carl, 19, 201

Kap Arkona lighthouse, 203
Keats, John, 1
Knights Templar, 180
Knossos, Palace of, 17
Koolhaas, Rem, 199
Krens, Thomas, 129
Krier, Leon, 116
Krier, Rob, 12, 13
*Kunstwollen*, 134

Last Supper, 162
Lateran Accord (1929), 1
Laterza (publisher), 16
Lavedan, Pierre, 6
Lecco. *See* Alessandro Volta College; Somasca
Le Corbusier (Charles-Édouard Jeanneret), 12, 13, 23, 27, 40, 134
Ledoux, Claude-Nicholas, 134
Leonardo da Vinci, 184, 185, 189

Libeskind, Daniel, 28, 32, 82–83
libraries, 29, *31*, 105–7, 200
*Il libro azzurro* (book), 27, 186
Lichthof, University of Zurich, 25, *25*
lighthouses, *35*, 35–36, 145–46, 203
Liguori, Alfonso Maria de' (saint): *Apparecchio alla morte (Preparation for Death)*, 216–17
The Little Scientific Theater. *See* Mantua
*locus solus*, 141
London, 26
  Docklands, 55
Longoni, Bruno, 26, 35
Loos, Adolf, 7–9, 12, 16, 33, *54*, 54–55, 153, 171
  *Ornament and Crime*, 8, 54
*Lotus* (periodical), 16
*Lotus International* (periodical), 16
Lucca: Roman amphitheater, 5, 141
Luccichenti, Ugo, 21
Lynch, Keven, 123

Maastricht, Netherlands. *See* Bonnefanten Museum
Macchina Modenese (Modena Machine), 148–50
Maggiore, Lago, 29, 91, 161, 170
  *See also* Villa Rossi (Ghiffa)
Mantua
  The Little Scientific Theater, 20, 138, *139*, 143, 151, *151*
  Sant'Andrea church, 96
Manzoni, Alessandro: *The Betrothed (I promessi sposi)*, 88, 159
Marchesi chapel (unbuilt), 175
Marseilles, 60
Marsilio (publisher), 16
Martelli, Francesco, 117
Marx, Karl, 126
Marxism, 188
Mastroianni, Umberto, 82
Mayakovsky, Vladimir, 171, 215
Mazzarolli, Leopoldo, 147
Mazzotta, Giuseppe, 187, 193, 205–7, 209, 215
Mazzucchelli, Pier Francesco, *159*
McDonald's, 78
Meda, Luca, 26, 32, 73, 79, *80*, 83, 190

Medici, Francesco de', 179
medieval, 24, 68, 105, 117, 119, 125, 152, 155, 161, 182, 187, 190
Michelangelo, 49, 117, 197, 203
Middleton, Robin, 41
Mies van der Rohe, Ludwig, 4, 23, 27, 29
Milan, 1–2, 3, 9, 40, 67, 156, *158*, 203
  Armani Hotel, 75
  Bescapé palace, 75
  Church of San Carlo (Barona), 213–15, *214*
  Duomo, 63–65, 76, 96, *97*, 185, 210
  Gallaratese housing, 10–11, *11*, 16, 20, 48, 73, 89, 90, 98, 118, 198, 204
  Galleria Vittorio Emanuele II, 65, 78
  Giuseppe Verdi Civic Center, 85
  Hotel Duca di Milano, 63–64, *64*
  Linate Airport, 56, *57*, 71
  Orsini palace, 75
  Perego palace, 75
  San Cristoforo Rail Station, 60, *60*
  San Fedele church, 189
  San Marco church, 189
  San Maurizio al Monastero Maggiore church, 189
  Santa Maria alla Porta church, 92, 94, 213
  Santa Maria della Passione church, 189
  Santa Maria delle Grazie church, 189
  Santa Maria presso San Satiro church, 189
  Sant'Eustorgio church, 189
  Sforza Castle, 119
  Taverna palace, 75
  Torre Velasca, 2, *3*, 3–4, 22
  Via Croce Rossa piazza, 73–78, *74*, 90, 96, 182
  Via Tibaldi public housing, 15
  *See also* Monument to Partisans at Segrate; Monument to Sandro Pertini; Rozzano Cemetery
Milano chairs, *34*
Milan Polytechnic. *See* Polytechnic University of Milan

Milan Triennale XV (1973), 12, 13, 14, 16, *17*, 129, 204
Milan Triennale "Domestic Theater" (1986), 129, 147, 156–57, *157*, 203
Minas Gerais, Brazil
  Our Lady of Carmine church, 146
  Our Lady of the Conception church, 146–47
Misasi, Riccardo, 14
models. *See* artwork, drawings, sketches, models
Modena cemetery (San Cataldo), 10, 11, 17, 25, 29, 37, 41, 73, 98, 104, 109, 118, 138, 150, 156, *166*, 167–81, *169*, *177*, 184–95, 198, 201, 208–10
  collage with St. Rose of Viterbo, 193–95, *194*
  columbaria and ossuary, 150, 170, *171*, 189, 190–93, *191–92*
  drawing with reworking by Jesse Reiser (sepia ink and gouache on paper), 209–10, *210*
  "Il Gioco dell'Oca" drawing (1972), *179*, 179–80, 191
Modena Duomo, 205
modernism, 4, 9, 11–12, 14, 20–23, 40, 168, 172, 214
*Modo* (periodical), 16
Moji: Mojiko Hotel, 62–63, *63*
Molinari, Guy, 58
Molteni family, Funerary Chapel for (Guissano), 175, *176*, 198
Molteni furniture, 26, *30*, *34*, 35
Momento, *34*, 36
Monestiroli, Antonio, 217
Monte Amiata public housing. *See* Gallaratese housing
Monument to Partisans at Segrate (Milan), 16, 20, 69, 73, 76, 79, 83, 85–91, *86–87*, 95, 98, 100, *101*, 118, 122, 142, 150, 172
Monument to Sandro Pertini (Milan), 35, *72*, 73–79, *77*, 83, 89–91, 95–98, *97–98*, 100, 181–82, 190
Monument to the Resistance at Cuneo. *See* Cuneo
Moore, Charles, 23

moralism, 8
Muggiò
  town hall, 9, 117, 119, 131
  Villa Casati Stampa, 119
Muzio, Giovanni, 63
Mycenae, Greece, 131
  Lion Gate, 163–64, *165*

Nagoya, Japan
  Tochi shopping center (now Port Walk Minato), 66
  Uny-Gifu Mall, 66, *66*
Naples, 12, 60, 67, 204
Nativity, 162
Nazism, 79, 81, 85, 87, 134
neo-classicism, 60, 68, 177
neo-Fascism, 15
neo-realism, 13, 14
Netherlands, 26, 33
Neuruppin, Germany, 60
New York
  Battery Maritime Building, 59
  Cast Iron District, 39, 42–43
  Guggenheim Museum, 129
  Little Singer building, 43, *43*, 45
  Rouss Dry Goods building, 42, 43, 45
  Scholastic Building, *38*, 39–40, 42–46, *43–44*, 48, 50, 51, 55, 58, 66, 71, 137, 145, *146*
  South Bronx Academy of Art, 114–15, *115–16*
  Whitehall Ferry Terminal, 57–59, *58–59*
Nicholas of Cusa, 167
Nietzsche, Friedrich, 200
nihilism, 216
Nimes: Roman amphitheater, 5, 141
999 (studio), 12
Nolli, Giovanni Battista, 19–20
*La nuova abitazione* (film), 14

Olympia and York, 55
opera, ballet, and theater set designs, *154*, 155, 163–65, *164*
*Ornamento e delitto* (Ornament and Crime, film), 14
Osaka: Il Monte, 63
*Ossessione* (film), 14, *15*
Otto, Frei, 29
Ovid, 73

Padua, 5–6, *6*, 70, 119
　Palazzo della Ragione, 5–6, *6*, 70, 119
Paganini Theater. *See* Parma
Il Palazzo Hotel. *See* Fukuoka, Japan
Palermo, 67
Palladio, Andrea, 16, 29, 138–40, 145, 148, 197, 202
　*See also* Vicenza
*Parametro* (periodical), 16
Paris
　Centre Pompidou (Place Beauborg museum), 23, 123
　National Library (Boullée's proposal), 107
　Park de la Villette, 26, 125–26
　Tristan Tzara house, 8
Paris Exposition (1889), 45
Parma
　baptistery, 128, 140, 141
　Casa Gasparoll, 119
　Centro Torri shopping mall, *67*, 67–68, 71
　Farnese Theater, 139–41, 161
　Paganini Theater, 9, 105, 119, 138–42, *141*, 156
　Palazzo della Pilotta, 139–40
　Piazza della Pilotta, 139
　Santa Maria della Steccata, 140
　Teatro Regio (Royal Theater), 140
The Passion, 159, 162, 180, 189
Pasternak, Boris, 171, 215
Paul, Saint, 95
PCI (Partito Communista Italiano), 188
Pei, I. M., 124
Pellegrin, Luigi, 140
Pertini, Sandro, 73–74
　*See also* Monument to Sandro Pertini
Perugia
　Bevagna town hall, 117
　Fontivegge government complex, 23–24, 89, 98, *99*, 143
Peter, Saint, 191
Petrarch, 216–17
Philip Neri, Saint, 189
phone card ("Studio di Tappetto Nuragico," 1988), 210, *210*

Piano, Renzo, 23, 123
Piccinato, Luigi, 13
Pilliteri, Paolo, 74
Piranesi, Giovanni Battista, 69
Pius XI, 1
Planck, Max: *Scientific Autobiography*, 25, 207
Pliny the Elder, 87
PNF (Partito Nazionale Fascista), 118–19
Poète, Marcel, 6
Polesello, Gianugo, 26, 73, *80*, 160
Poletti, Giovanni, 186
Polytechnic University of Milan (Politecnico di Milano), 2, 13, 14–15, 25, 204
Pòrta, Carlo, 91
Porter, James, 95
port facilities. *See* airports, railways, and port facilities
The Portland Building, 23
Portoghesi, Paolo, 15, 27, 28, 32, 140, 168
postmodernism, 22–23, 172
Prague: Villa Müller, 9
Pritzker Prize, 28–29, 33, 56, 70
Progetto Venezia (The Venice Project), 27–28

*Quaderni Azzurri* (notebooks), 14, 26–27, 30–31, 92, 103, 111, 123, 124–25, 173, 177, 180–81, 186, 198, 215, 216–17
Quaroni, Ludovico, 3, 13
Quintilian, 32

railways. *See* airports, railways, and port facilities
Raphael: *School of Athens*, 90
*Rassegna* (periodical), 16
Rational Architecture, 12
rationalism, 8
*Raumplan*, 9
Ravenna: Rocca Brancaleone, *154*, 155–56
realism, 13–14, 178, 204
Red Brigades, 15
Redipuglia: Sacrario Militare, *80*, 81, 83, 91
Reichlin, Bruno, 17–19, *18*
Reinhart, Fabio, 15, 17–19, *18*, 144

Reiser, Jesse, *210*
Renaissance, 39, 49, 117, 139, 152, 160, 187
Ridolfi, Mario, 21
Riegl, Alois, 134
*Rinascita* (periodical), 16
Rizzoli (publisher), 16
Robinson, Maurice, 42
Robinson, Richard, 42, 43
Rogers, Ernesto Nathan, 2–3, 10, 11, 12
Rogers, Richard, 23, 123
Rollins, Tim, 114
*Roma* (film), 14
Romanesque, 62, 96
Rome, 67
　Cestia Pyramid, 16
　Corviale housing, 10
　MAXXI, 23, 177
　Palazzo Farnese, 49, 203
　Pantheon, 16
　St. Peters, 131
　San Giovanni in Laterano, 105, 131
　Theater of Marcellus, 138
Rose of Viterbo, Saint, 193–95, *194*
Rosenau, Helen, 123
Rosenthal, 26, 35, *35*
Rossi, Aldo, photographs of, *17*, 217
Rotterdam, 60
Roussel, Raymond, 14, 141, 151, 165
　*Impressions of Africa*, 151, 153–56
Rozzano Cemetery, Ponte Sesto, 167–68, *168*, 170–91, *181–83*. *See* Milan
Rubens, Peter Paul, 187
Ruffo, Marco, *202*, 203
Rule of St. Benedict, 111
Ruskin, John, 125
Russia. *See* Soviet Russia

Saarinen, Eero, 56
Sabbioneta theater, 141
Sacri Monti sites of Lombardy and Piedmont regions, 25, 131, 146, *159–61*, 159–63, 175, 185, 213
Saint Victor, Hugh of, 35, 103
Salvatore Orrù Elementary School. *See* Fagnano Olona
San Carlone at Arona (statue), *2*, 20, 25, 91–92, *91–93*, 94, 96, 98, 131, 156, 185, 208
　architectural fantasy drawing with statue, 178, *178*
　Rossi photograph from inside, 94, *95*, 185
San Cataldo cemetery. *See* Modena cemetery
San Dona di Piave: "The Abandoned House" sculpture park, 156, *158*
Sangallo the Younger, Antonio, 49
San Giovanni Valdarno town hall, 119
San Rocco Directional Center, 69
Sansovino, Jacopo, 205
Santa Clara convent. *See* Santiago de Compostela
Santa Cristina archaeological site. *See* Sardinia
Santiago de Compostela, 213
　Church of Santa Clara, 24, 25, 89, *89*, 213, *213*
　Las Pelayas convents, 25, 213
　St. Jane's church, 180
Sardinia: Santa Cristina archaeological site, 94, 131, *133*
Sardinian tapestries, 35
Sarfatti, Roberto, monument to (Asiago), 81, *81*, 91
Sartogo, Pietro, 19
Sauerlander, Willibald, 187
Savi, Vittorio, 32, 126
Scamozzi, Vincenzo, 141, 145, 197
Scandicci town hall, 9, 89, 117–18, *118*, 123
Scarpa, Carlo, 144
Schinkel, Karl Friedrich, 7, 27, 49, 60, 94, *95*, 118, 119, 125–27, 131, 141, 145, *145*, 197, 203
Schmidt, Hans, 12, 41
Scholastic Building. *See* New York
Schwartz, Frederick, 58
*A Scientific Autobiography* (Rossi), 24–25, 30, 41, 186, 198–99, 201, 205–10, 215
Scolari, Massimo, 11, 12, 15
　Scandicci town hall (Florence), *118*
Secession movement, 8, 62

Sedlmayr, Hans: *Art in Crisis: The Lost Center* (Verlust der Mitte), 134–35
Segrate monument. *See* Monument to Partisans at Segrate
Seixas Lopes, Diogo, 198
*Selected Writings on Architecture and the City, 1956–1972*, 21
*Senilità* (film), 14
*Senso* (film), 14
Seregno library, 107
Seville, Spain, 24, 146, 213
  Santa Paula convent, 213
  Theater of the Indies for Expo '92, *142*, 143
Sforza, Francesco, 142
shopping centers, 64–67, *66–67*
Simonides, 162
Sironi, Mario, 2, 88
sketches. *See* artwork, drawings, sketches, models
Smith, Thomas Gordon, 23
Sofia Paleologa, 202
Solari, Pietro, *202*, 203
Solomon's Temple, 190, 193
Somasca (Lecco), 1
  Sacri Monti of, 159–60
  Sanctuary of St. Jerome Emiliani in, 92, *94*
Somasco Order, 1, 103, 159, 161, 211
Song of Songs, 92
South Bronx Academy of Art. *See* New York
Soviet Russia, 4, 12, 26, 33
  Kremlin towers, *202*, 202–3
Spengler, Oswald: *The Decline of the West*, 134
Stations of the Cross, 180
Stern, Robert A. M., 23
Studio di Architettura, 26
Sullivan, Louis, 8
Superstudio, 12

Tafuri, Manfredo, 3, 32, 147, 199–201, 208

Tanzio da Varallo: *David and Goliath*, 17
*Tendenza* movement, 11–13, 204
Teresa of Avila, Saint, 208, 212, 215
Terragni, Giuseppe, 12, 81, *81*, 91
Tessa, Delio: *L'e el di di Mort, alegher!* (*It's the Day of the Dead, Be Happy!*), 184
theaters. *See* opera, ballet and theater set designs; *specific theaters by locations*
Thomas Jefferson Medal, 29
Tibaldi, Pellegrino, 160
Tibaldi Middle School. *See* Cantù
Tiscali telephone card, 210, *211*
Tommasi, Lanza, 163
Toronto: Lighthouse Theater, 145–46
Torre Velasca. *See* Milan
Trieste, 12, 67
Turgenev, Ivan, 184
Turin, 2, 9, 67
  Basilica of San Gaudenzio, 131
  Casa Aurora (GFT building), 51–55, *53*, 126, 137, 145
Turkey, 26, 95

Uchida, Shigeru, 62
Ungers, Matthias, 12
Unifor, 26, 35
Uniplan, 56
United States, 16, 24, 26, 30–32
University of California, Los Angeles, 24
University of Castellanza Carlo Cattaneo, 115
University of Miami School of Architecture, 105, 115–16, *116*
University of Zurich, 25, *25*, 69
urbanism, 16, 126, 140–41, 144–45, 204
*Urbanistica* (magazine), 40
urban renewal, 66–67

Van Grevenstein, Alexander, 94, 130–31

Varallo. *See* Sacri Monti
Velazquez, Diego: *Crucifixion*, 171
Venice, 16
  Doge's Palace, 203
  Duke Francesco Sforza's unfinished palace, 142
  La Fenice Theater, 26, 32–33, 138, 147–50, *148–50*, 152, 210
  Grand Canal, 202
  Grand Canal palazzo, 122
  Palazzo Grassi, 33
  Ponte del Rialto, 202
  Santa Maria della Salute, 137
  Santa Maria della Salute church "La Salute," 161
  Teatro del Mondo, 21–23, *22*, 27, 29, *35*, 116, 135, *136*, 137–38, 143, 150, 156, 161, 164, 202–3
  Villa Farsetti, 27, 28
Venice Architecture Biennale (1976), 17, 205
Venice Architecture Biennale (1980), 126, 137, 174
Venice Architecture Biennale (1985), 27–28, *29*
Venice Biennale Theater (1979–80), 21, 27, 137, 164–65
Venice School of architectural theorists, 199
Venturi, Robert, 28
  *Complexity and Contradiction in Architecture*, 22
Venturi, Scott Brown, 58
Verbania: Pallanza (proposed), 68
Vercellina Gate, 92
"Verlust der Mitte" (Bonnefanten project statement), 134, 135
Verona
  Borsari Gate, 175
  Ca' di Cozzi Complex, 50–51, *51*, *52*
Versilia: Villa ai Ronchi, 8–9, *9*
Via Maddalena office, 26, 138
Via Santa Maria alla Porta office, 26

Vicenza
  Palazzo Chiericati, 202
  Palladian Basilica, 51, 55, 141, 148, 202
  public buildings, 119
  Teatro Olimpico, 138–40, 145
Vico, Giambattista, 208
Vidler, Anthony, 200
Vienna
  Looshaus, *54*, 54–55
  Michaelerkirke, 16, 54
  Villa Savoye, 13
Virgil, 39
Virgin Mary at the Gate, 92–94
Visconti, Luchino, 14
Visconti family, 51, 104, 117
Visit to the Seven Churches, 188–89, 212–13
Vitale, Daniele, 11
Vitruvius, 7, 145
  *De architectura*, 139
Voids, 82
Vottoni, Piero, 12

Walt Disney Company, 35
Washington, D.C.: Vietnam Veterans Memorial, 82, 88
"What to Do with Old Cities?" (Rossi essay), 47–48
Whitehall Ferry Terminal. *See* New York
Whites (modernists), 22–23
Wordsworth, William, 209, 215
Wright, Frank Lloyd, 129

Yale University, 24

Zanella, Siro, 91, *91*
Zeebrugge, Belgium, 60
Zevi, Bruno, 12, 86
*Zodiac* (periodical), 16
Zucker, Alfred, 42, 43, 45
Zurich, 15, 17, 25, *25*, 69, 205
  *See also* ETH Zürich; University of Zurich
Zurich Opera House, 155